HISTORY OF AMERICAN THOUGHT AND CULTURE

Paul S. Boyer, *General Editor*

ON WISCONSIN WOMEN

Working for Their Rights
from Settlement to Suffrage

Genevieve G. McBride

The University of Wisconsin Press

The University of Wisconsin Press
114 North Murray Street
Madison, Wisconsin 53715

3 Henrietta Street
London WC2E 8LU, England

Printed in the United States of America

Library of Congress Cataloging-in-Publication Data
McBride, Genevieve G.
    On Wisconsin women: working for their rights from settlement to suffrage /
Genevieve G. McBride.
        376 p.   cm. — (History of American thought and culture)
    Includes bibliographical references and index.
    ISBN 0-299-14000-8   ISBN 0-299-14004-0 (pbk.)
    1. Women — Suffrage — Wisconsin — History.   2. Women's rights —
Wisconsin — History.   I. Title.   II. Series.
JK1911.W6M38   1994
324.6'23'09775 — dc20   93-846

Negative numbers for the illustrations provided by the State Historical Society of Wisconsin are as follows: cover, WHi(X313)2816E; p. 17, WHi(X3)36475; p. 20, WHi(X3)2101; p. 29, WHi(X3)19844; p. 49, WHi(X3)46671; p. 82, WHi(X313)2819E; p. 95, WHi(X3)46421; p. 104, WHi(X3)25872; p. 111, WHi(X3)48224; p. 128, WHi(X3)22944; p. 129, WHi(X3)44302; p. 155, WHi(X3)45950; p. 164, WHi(X3)37030; p. 182, WHi(L61)43; p. 205, WHi(X3)65; p. 211, WHi(X18)22777; p. 230, WHi(X3)48222; p. 268, WHi(X3)44301; p. 287, WHi(X3)15265; p. 292, WHi(X3)2903.

Cover illustration: Photograph of Theodora Winton Youmans of Waukesha, Wisconsin. Youmans, the last president of the Wisconsin Woman Suffrage Association, is in "suffrage regalia" and holds the "On Wisconsin" banner which she carried for the state's contingent in the National American Woman Suffrage Association parade, called to protest the refusal by the national convention of the Republican Party to endorse a federal woman suffrage amendment. Photograph courtesy of the State Historical Society of Wisconsin, negative WHi(x313)2816E.
Cover design: Susan Gutnik

For
John McBride Caspari
and
Catherine Southmayd Caspari

THE WISCONSIN SLOGAN

On Wisconsin, On Wisconsin,
Grand Old Badger State,
We shall surely win the ballot,
Be it soon or late.
On Wisconsin, On Wisconsin,
"Forward" be the cry,
Slow but surely, late but coming,
Bound for Victory.

On Wisconsin, On Wisconsin,
We thy daughters true,
Bound to make a land of Freedom
We are, out of you.
On Wisconsin, On Wisconsin,
Cannot stop or stay
'Til thy children all are equal.
Hail the mighty day!

—Lyrics by Theodora Winton Youmans
for the 1914 convention of the
Wisconsin Woman Suffrage Association

CONTENTS

ILLUSTRATIONS

FOREWORD

Genevieve McBride's engaging monograph sustains the intellectual distinction of the University of Wisconsin Press's History of American Thought and Culture Series. Professor McBride's study of the women's movement in Wisconsin possesses a strong regional flavor, yet for precisely this reason it also makes a substantial contribution to the larger world of scholarship. While several studies of the American women's movement have appeared in recent years, including monographs on such specific facets as temperance, moral reform, and suffrage, the story has rarely been told from the perspective of a specific state, and even more rarely with the interpretive breadth and stylistic flair that distinguish Professor McBride's work. This book thus represents the finest kind of regional history: that which retains the feel and texture of the particular, while maintaining a broad focus and never succumbing to merely antiquarian or parochial concerns.

The eight decades spanned by this study saw several critical transitions in the history of organized effort by American women, from the broad-gauge antebellum "woman's rights" movement to a diversity of Gilded Age reform campaigns to the highly targeted suffrage drive that culminated in the ratification of the Nineteenth Amendment in 1920. Led by the two-million-strong National American Woman Suffrage Association, the final successful campaign for the vote relied heavily on well-organized state suffrage organizations and on dedicated regional leaders, so that close attention to a key state like Wisconsin, and to women like the redoubtable Theodora Winton Youmans, fleshes out our understanding of the national movement in critical ways.

In terms of Wisconsin history, these years encompass the period from the earliest settlements by Euro-Americans in the remote reaches of the old Northwest Territory through the period when Wisconsin boasted major cities like Milwaukee; a thriving agricultural and industrial economy; and a volatile mix of Native Americans, Yankees, and immigrants from Germany, Scandinavia, and elsewhere. By the turn of the century, Wisconsin citizens ranging from conservative Republicans to Socialists sustained a vigorous and sometimes raucous political culture. The work culminates in the era when Wisconsin led the nation in a variety of reforms that collectively made "the Wisconsin idea" a hallmark of the Progressive movement.

On Wisconsin Women unfolds against this background of social and political change. Treating feminist reform as a conceptual whole, Professor McBride insightfully traces the subtle interactions of successive women's movements in the state, including temperance, women's clubs, kindergarten reform, and so forth, culminating in the battle for the vote. Another of the book's valuable features is its focus on the *tactics* that woman reformers utilized to publicize and promote their diverse causes. Brilliantly improvising new techniques of publicity, they pioneered what in the twentieth century would emerge as the field of public relations. Genevieve McBride brings to the study of the American women's movement a distinctive perspective as a professor of journalism and mass communications, and in the process sheds light on the ways this movement both exploited and contributed to the evolving techniques of mass persuasion.

The story Professor McBride tells with such insight anticipates in fascinating ways the ideological differences, organizational diversity, and publicity strategies of the modern women's movement that arose in the United States in the 1970s. *On Wisconsin Women* thus fits very neatly into a series whose dual objective is to enhance our understanding of American intellectual and cultural history on its own terms while at the same time illuminating contemporary social issues and cultural trends by placing them in historical perspective.

PAUL S. BOYER

PREFACE

There are many stories that need to be written on Wisconsin women and this is only one, the one I could write. This story is a case study of the campaign for woman's rights in Wisconsin, the first state to ratify the Nineteenth Amendment—although long the last state expected to do so. If only for the historic ratification, this study is overdue because Wisconsin is one of the few states for which there has been no book-length history of "the struggle," as women called their campaign in the hundreds of contemporary accounts that proudly recounted how woman suffrage was won—and won by women. Yet as the last leader of the Wisconsin campaign wrote in her account, they feared all too correctly that the "careless world will probably continue to think that woman suffrage just happened," and that historians would judge their story only by its happy ending.[1]

This study suggests that the end of the "Votes for Women" campaign was a bittersweet victory, in Wisconsin and elsewhere, and the end of the story of only one struggle waged over a century by women because suffrage was only one of the rights of citizenship that they sought. This is the story of their tragedies as well as triumphs, a story of their heroism and hard-won wisdom—and a story that they told with the wit and humor that women so needed in Wisconsin, for nowhere was "the struggle" fought so hard and so long. But this study, like its subjects, seeks to accomplish more than simply a retelling of the stories that women told.

First, this study places the Wisconsin campaign in the context of the far longer struggle for full participation in the "public sphere" by women who worked not only for woman's rights but also in many other movements in a state renowned for reform. Their part in Wisconsin's past is missing from many otherwise excellent histories that support its reputation for progressivism; none, for example, quotes the Wisconsin suffragist who wrote as late as 1912 that "the last thing a man becomes progressive about is the activities of his own wife."[2] Inclusion of women's work may require revision of Wisconsin history as we know it, but so be it. That Wisconsin was not the one that women knew, nor the one that many know even now. That Wisconsin will not be realized unless we know that history, like justice, never "just happens"—especially in a democracy that requires a consensus of so many constituencies for the least empowered of them to win their Constitutional rights. However, that women's quest for justice was a "pursuit of happiness" in itself is another and more welcome lesson of history, and this story.

This study also provides a starting point for the construction of the other half of Wisconsin history—a "usable past" on Wisconsin women, for Wisconsin women—but it too is only a start, and hardly a history of all Wisconsin women. Only those who were privileged by birth or race and class could even attempt to claim the birthrights of citizenship for all women. Neither Native American descendants of Wisconsin's first settlers nor the daughters of African-American freedwomen from the South—nor even the "daughters' daughters" of many other migrant groups that became dominant in the state only early in this century, late in this story—will find more than hints of their history here. However, they also will find inspiration and instruction in the stories of the "century of struggle," of others who won access to the education that equipped them with the expertise to escape "women's place" for a place in the "public sphere." Even the most fortunate of women at first were denied their fundamental rights to politics and the podium, the pulpit and the press—the primary means of empowerment that proved crucial in the woman's rights campaign, as in any public opinion campaign.

This study may prove usable even for the many women whose past is not in these pages because it examines the means by which some women empowered themselves by becoming wise in the ways of power, especially the power of the press. It is significant that, although historians examine the motivation of reformers more than their means, the last leader of the state suffrage campaign called her account "How Wisconsin Women Won the Ballot." But her approach to the strategies and tactics of making women's history happen was hardly unique. Indeed, hers was only one of hundreds of submissions from women in every state to the six-volume *History of Woman Suffrage,* started by Elizabeth Cady Stanton and Susan B. Anthony to serve not only as a historical record of women's heritage of reform—and a "major propaganda effort," as a historian of women suggests[3]—but also as a "how-to" book to be handed down to the successors of the women who won once before, and well.

Finally, finding the sources for this study is a story in itself, a lesson for other historians in how to tell other stories as yet untold if their historical subjects also told them in nontraditional ways, in letters to the editor and newspaper columns rather than in lengthy correspondence and leatherbound volumes. That this story of Wisconsin women has not been told is not for lack of effort by historians. But they have been hampered by lack of primary sources, particularly the early organizational records of the Wisconsin Woman Suffrage Association that apparently were lost to a fire in the state Capitol. Historians also have been stymied by a dearth of diaries, letters, and other private papers by women who apparently were too busy reforming Wisconsin to leave a more revealing record of their work, at least in traditional ways.

Yet the leaders of women's movements, and many a follower, did bequeath a wonderful legacy of women's work, in women's words. A record of their reform activities is readily accessible to those who recognize that the "public sphere" is the province of the press, and that the press provided many leaders of women's movements in Wisconsin and nationwide. In the Wisconsin press, from settlement forward, women wrote a contemporary record that was rich in detail of their day-to-day work, week by week, decade after decade. Although women wrote primarily for readers in the past, they also wrote for posterity consciously, and conscientiously. Historians have only to read women's news as women did — beyond the bylines, between the lines — to be rewarded with abundant sources for research far beyond this book.

But this is the book I could write, because so many leaders of the woman's rights movement were writers by trade — my trade. The professions of journalism and public relations were long the province of women, from the first "female correspondents" in letters-to-the-editor columns to the pioneering woman editors and publishers in the Wisconsin press, to the last leader of Wisconsin woman suffragists — a woman journalist as well. Yet few of those who wrote for a living also wrote about their work for woman's rights in the form of diaries or histories. However, as well I knew, newswomen are likely to write the stories of their lives as news stories, if only between the lines, because women who made history — or, at least, make it into history books — needed first to make news. Because they needed to win headlines as well as bylines, women also became expert in publicity, press agentry, and other practices of public relations.

I knew how to read the stories written by Wisconsin women who made the news because I was born to one, and raised to write this book. My mother was a pioneering woman practitioner in public relations in Milwaukee before I was born, and later was one of the first women to rise to leadership of a political party in Wisconsin and one of the first women on the political beat for the *Milwaukee Sentinel*. By her example, she taught me much about politics and the press—and about working women—because she exemplified the best of both professions, and was a better mother than she knew. More important, she taught me how to read between the lines of women's stories, even those that bore her byline, to seek the subtle lessons in stories of women's lives. The legacy of Marian Dunne McBride is in every line of this book, and remains with me every day—and every long working night, like hers—of my life.

However, it was one of Wisconsin's finest newsmen and wisest storytellers who first taught me the joy of writing with a sense of journalism as history—and a sense of humor—as he did for almost half a century at the *Milwaukee Journal*. More important, my father's example also educated me to seek the men in this book who could not be called feminists by their principles or politics but became suffragists for the most personal of reasons. Because their daughters wanted the ballot, many a man helped to make women's history happen. Because I wanted to write this book—and because it would make me happy, which is all he ever wanted for me—Raymond E. McBride helped to make it happen, and bequeathed to me the happiest of endings for any story and storyteller.

Many other women and men have contributed to my education in the newsroom and other classrooms of life, and thus to this book. Leonard L. Wilson, then of Carroll College, was a born teacher who provided on-the-job training in public relations as a practice that may require compromises with political realities, but ought never to result in a compromise of professional integrity. Henry A. Youmans, Jr., who was born into a family tradition of ethical practice at his "school of journalism," the *Waukesha Freeman*, first hired me and later helped me again with research on the historic work of his *Freeman* and his family in Wisconsin reform. Family genealogists Miriam Youmans Wellford, Juanita Williams Youmans, and Anne Youmans Liban also gave invaluable assistance, and Gilbert H. Koenig, John Engelbert, and Tom Rickert of the *Waukesha Freeman* gave invaluable insights into the newspaper and the city that they have served so well. Robert M. Witas of the *Milwaukee Sentinel* willingly shared his research on his historic paper for this work in progress, and Patrick Graham of the *Milwaukee Journal* gave an expert and exhaustive reading to this work in its final form.

No one read more of this work in progress, more often, than James L. Baughman, who believed in this book and in me from the beginning. Also at the University of Wisconsin–Madison, Stephen L. Vaughn guided my readings on propaganda and gave an expert reading to early versions of this work, and Paul S. Boyer provided readings on reform and expert readings of early and final versions of this result, and the Foreword that honors this work as well as his former student. John M. Buenker of the University of Wisconsin–Parkside provided a reading of the final version that especially benefited from his expertise on progressivism. Walter B. Weare, J. David Hoeveler, and Frederick L. Olson of the University of Wisconsin–Milwaukee and two former colleagues, Dwight L. Teeter, Jr., and Gail Radford, gave of their expertise whenever asked. All, and my once-and-future colleague Ceil Moran Pillsbury, also offered encouragement whether asked for or not, for which I am even more grateful.

My most generous mentor at the University of Wisconsin–Milwaukee was Margo Anderson, who provided experience and expertise in editing portions of this work and encouragement throughout. Other historians of women—including many whom I have yet to meet—also responded to my calls, letters, and personal pleas for help in finding research and resources. Linda Gordon and Ellen C. DuBois gave this work its impetus, and its most important criticism, in a course at the University of Wisconsin–Madison. Anne Firor Scott and Gerda Lerner guided me to unpublished studies by other students of women's history that proved almost as useful as their own, and works in progress were shared willingly by Elizabeth Burt, Ann Colbert, Gail E. Mason, and Barbara Ulichny. None was more helpful than Catherine B. Cleary, who repeatedly set aside her own research questions to answer mine—including some I had not anticipated, lacking her unparalleled expertise and experience in the law.

Other historians and women who have heard me tell portions of this story on podiums across the state of Wisconsin also have offered support, financial and otherwise. The Waukesha County Historical Society provided my first and most memorable forum, before the descendants of my historical subjects. The Waukesha Altrusa Club, the Waukesha Women's Center, the University of Wisconsin–Milwaukee Center for Women's Studies, the Milwaukee chapter of Women in Communications, Inc., PRO/Public Relations Organization of Central Wisconsin, and the Wisconsin Council for Social Studies also have provided friendly audiences. The Association for Education in Journalism and Mass Communication, especially the Divisions of History, Public Relations, News-papers, and Mass Communication and Society, provided opportunities for presentations of portions of this research as well as remuneration and research awards. Major funding for research was provided by Jour-nal/Sentinel, Inc. through a Donald Abert Fellowship, and by the Foun-dation for Public Relations Research and Education of the Public Re-lations Society of America through a Rea W. Smith Fellowship, and funding for iconographic services was provided by the Department of Mass Communication of the University of Wisconsin–Milwaukee.

No audience has been more supportive than my students at the Uni-versity of Wisconsin-Milwaukee in public relations, in media history, and in women's studies. Many contributed their own research on women and media, and some returned even after grading or graduation to hear me tell this story again, and to give their own insights into the practice of public relations, among them Ann Dekorsi, Lisa Anderson, Sandra Spann, Tina DePrez, Sandra May and Anne Martino.

My work relied most on the work of well over a century at the State Historical Society of Wisconsin. Many a staff member provided assis-tance that was invaluable to a novice in interlibrary loans, microforms, and the remarkable Newspaper Collections upon which this study most relies. Paul H. Hass of the *Wisconsin Magazine of History* was a pa-tient teacher of historical writing; James P. Danky, Maureen E. Hady, Cynthia Knight, Harry Miller, Thomas McKay, and John O. Holzhueter were helpful instructors in historical research; and Andy Kraushaar of the Iconographic Collections provided most of the portraits of the women that illustrate their stories as words cannot.

Many local historians, librarians, curators, and archivists also helped immeasurably with their research on Wisconsin towns, large and small. Among them were Judith A. Simonsen of the Milwaukee County His-torical Society, Jean Penn Loerke of the Waukesha County Historical Society, Maurice Montgomery of the Rock County Historical Society, Jean E. Smith of the Sauk County Historical Society, and Jerry Bower and Twylah Kepler of the Richland County Historical Society. Helmut Knies of the Fort Atkinson Historical Society was especially helpful in accommodating the interruption of my unscheduled visit amid the hi-larity of high school fiftieth-year reunion festivities at his facility, the W. D. Hoard Historical Museum and Dairy Shrine.

Similarly harried historians, archivists, and librarians at educational institutions across Wisconsin also invited my intrusions on their work, including Paul Starr and James Van Ness of Carroll College, Carol Butts of Lawrence University, Charlotte Sherman and Louise Schang of Ripon College, and the staff of the Golda Meir Library at the University of Wisconsin–Milwaukee. Also at UWM, Donna Genzmer Schenstrom of Cartographic Services supervised production of the map of the state's "suffrage strongholds," including some that no longer exist but live on in this book because of the heroic efforts of local historians.

The efforts of so many in the research for this book, as well as mine, have been rewarded by the imprimatur of the University of Wisconsin Press. I am grateful to Allen H. Fitchen for his immediate interest in a history of Wisconsin women, to Colleen Heinkel for expediting editorial approvals, to Raphael Kadushin for editorial supervision, to Carol Olsen for production supervision, and to Sheila Leary and Melissa Hill for marketing of this work which the women in it would applaud. Susan Tarcov provided a careful copyediting for which the readers will be as grateful as is the author.

However, if even the efforts of so many gentle readers and researchers have not prevented errors in this work, may they reap only the rewards of these acknowledgments and take credit for all that is correct. The responsibility for the rest is mine.

The burden of responsibility for my brief respites from research has been borne by family and friends, who have taken me into their hearts and even into their homes for rest and recovery. Sharon Murphy, Phyllis and Ness Flores, and Jeri and Charlie Phillips have been sources of solace and inspiration many a time, Foyne Mahaffey and Connie Blomberg have given me musical inspiration and the best of times, and Bill Holahan has been the best of friends in the worst of times.

I have been most blessed by the friendship of one of the best historians of women and Wisconsin of our time. As another Wisconsin woman wrote in her history of the suffrage movement, "how much of time and patience, how much work, energy and aspiration, how much faith, how much hope, how much despair went into it. It leaves its mark on one, such a struggle." Mine has been a far lesser struggle, but writing a book also "fills the days and rides the nights," and, like woman suffragists' work, "it was there" always.[4] But no matter the time of day or night — as her husband Ross can attest — Ellen D. Langill was always there as well, and is the sister I never had.

I am more blessed with brothers than any sister deserves to be, but that they have chosen wisely in their wives has given me a belated education in the significance of sisterhood in women's history. That my sisters-in-law legally retained their names is another lesson in history that I have attempted to follow faithfully in this book, not only because so many of the women of a century ago did so as well but also because it helps immeasurably in reconstructing the past. For all their past and future lessons in brotherly love and sisterly support, I will ever be indebted to Joseph P. McBride and Ruth O'Hara, Michael F. and Kerin O'Brien McBride, Patrick E. and Kimberly Schappe McBride, Dennis R. McBride and Melanie Aska, Mark B. and Kimberlee Stanton McBride, and Timothy D. McBride and Shirley Porterfield. I am also grateful for a reading of this work in progress by my niece Jessica, the first of the next generation of the clan to carry the family tradition into the newsroom, first at the *Milwaukee Journal* and then at the *Waukesha Freeman*. She bears the proud burden of the McBride byline well, and always will.

I am most indebted to my son and daughter, to whom this book is dedicated because I promised it would be. They are deserving of far more for all the times when they let me get to my work, but even more for the times when they would not and gave me no rest until I read them other stories. By their example and love, they reminded me that this story, like those of the women who wrote it first, was written about the past but for the sake of the future—a future far better for our sons as well as our daughters because of the promises that women made and meant, and meant for us to remember.

I hope that other "daughters' daughters" and sons of Wisconsin will read this story for the reason that it first was written by their foremothers: as a "how-to" book for making history happen. That they succeeded is their story, but it was only a start. This story will have succeeded as well if it serves as a model for making history—and more history books—because there are many that need to be written on Wisconsin women, and this is only one.

GENEVIEVE G. MCBRIDE

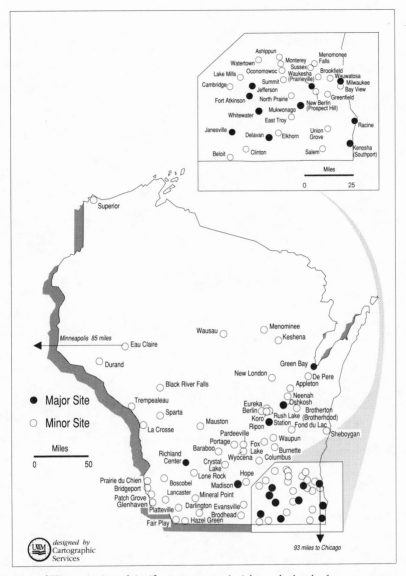

Map of Wisconsin sites of significance to woman's rights and related reform movements.

On Wisconsin Women

1

Women's Place, Men's Press
Moral Reform, Abolition, and Temperance, to 1866

THE year 1848 was pivotal in the histories of Wisconsin, and of women. Wisconsin celebrated statehood at the end of May, at last. Two years before, the men of Wisconsin—the voters—had rejected a constitution and deferred statehood after divisive debate on reforms including woman's rights. In 1846, at the first constitutional caucus, transplanted easterners pored over a copy of proposed revisions to New York State's constitution—including a provision for married women's property rights—which was rushed to the West. Debate "raged for several days" among "the ablest men of the territory," according to historian Louise Phelps Kellogg, "many of whom were advanced thinkers on social questions." However, the question of universal suffrage—for freedmen, not women—reportedly led a less advanced speaker to suggest the ultimate result of such foolishness as enfranchising former slaves. The "Irishman from Milwaukee who had the reputation of being a 'wag'" raised the specter of female suffrage, for comic relief. "There was no serious consideration of women's right to suffrage" at Wisconsin's inception, as Kellogg writes, but "only an attempt to ridicule and embarrass the favorers of [freedmen's] suffrage and to show how preposterous it was."

Some more reform-minded men at the first constitutional caucus seized the moment to propose property rights for married women, enraging men of the "propertied class." The "ablest member" to argue against

3

the clause, according to Madison's *Wisconsin Argus,* was Edward G. Ryan of Milwaukee. Women's property rights, Ryan declaimed, would destroy "the character of a wife" and were "contrary to the usages and customs of society" and "the express commands of the Bible." The *Sentinel and Gazette* echoed Ryan's argument, calling the clause "a violation of the laws of God—an outrage upon the moral sense of the community" and "a disgrace to our territory." Ryan also won the agreement of another "able member," Marshall Strong of Racine. If women's property rights "become a part of the constitution," he said, "a sense of duty will compel me to oppose the whole instrument with my utmost zeal." Strong did "resign his seat and went home to do all he could to defeat the adoption of the constitution," according to a historian.

Although women could not speak for themselves in Wisconsin's constitutional debates, a Rock County Democrat named David Noggle spoke for every woman on the frontier who had left home, family, and "friends that were near and dear to her" in the East "to embark with her barehanded husband for the far West." Opponents of woman's rights, he said, were "all humbug." A Fond du Lac County delegate, Warren Chase, was one of the few who supported women's property rights and even woman suffrage. He later wrote that "the men would sooner let the negroes have their rights than the women" and "that the slavery of women was deeper and more lasting, than that of negroes in the hearts and prejudices of the people." Worse, it was "often approved and sustained by woman herself."

The reform clauses doomed Wisconsin's first constitution. As Ryan recalled, delegates who had "convened in disorder and ill humor" and "sat in confusion" now "adjourned in disgrace." The clause for freedmen's suffrage, relegated to a separate referendum, was defeated two to one when put to the voters of the territory. The provision on married women's property rights caused the rejection of the constitution in its entirety at the polls.

Two years later, when a second constitutional convention was called, reform did not stall statehood again. Delegates did again model the new constitution on that of New York State, which also had rejected the clause for married women's property rights in 1846 but now was reconsidering the question. When the men of Wisconsin did the same, Marshall Strong—a delegate again, despite his precipitous departure from the previous caucus—pronounced that the clause would leave a woman's "every trait of loveliness blotted out." More important, a husband would be left with a propertied wife whose "welfare, and feelings, and thoughts" would not "be all wrapped up in his happiness." Strong cited incontrovertible proof of the effect of married women's property rights: "It now exists in France, and I will merely say that more than one-fourth of the children annually born in Paris are illegitimate."

The speech was widely publicized in the press and printed in pamphlet form for distribution across Wisconsin while Strong and other opponents of woman's rights took to the circuit. One, E. V. Whiton of Janesville, asserted that "a woman immersed in business" would neglect "her family . . . and the home as we know it." The defenders of the home and husbands defeated the provision, fifty-six to five. With a constitution otherwise modeled on New York's, Wisconsin voters approved statehood in April 1848. At the same time, New York became the nineteenth state—of thirty—to provide for married women's property rights.[1]

Less than six weeks after Wisconsin statehood, in July 1848, another convention was called in upstate New York which would have immeasurable impact on the new state to the West—a convention called by women, for woman's rights, for the first time. In Seneca Falls, five women—Elizabeth Cady Stanton, Lucretia Coffin Mott, Mary Anne McClintock, Jane Hunt, and Martha Wright—met for tea at a kitchen table to issue the call. All were reformers with experience in the abolition movement and expertise in the strategies and tactics of public opinion campaigns. Their first step was publicity, writing a call to be placed in the local paper for the convention only ten days away. At a second planning meeting, the women set an agenda and speakers, and drafted a document drawn from research into other organizational mission statements. The women "felt helpless and hopeless" in recording the "humiliating fact" of "their faithful perusal of various masculine productions" as a model for their own—"although all seemed too tame and pacific for the inauguration of a rebellion such as the world had never before seen."

In a decision inspired for its impact and imagery, the women drew primarily from the Declaration of Independence. Imitating "the historic document, with some slight changes," their Declaration of Sentiments and Resolutions at Seneca Falls stated the revolutionary principle "that all men and women are created equal."

The Declaration of Sentiments was both a statement of principles and an action plan for a public opinion campaign. "To promote every righteous cause by every righteous means" and "every instrumentality within our power," the women listed the tactics of the time: "We shall employ agents, circulate tracts, petition the State and National legislatures, and endeavor to enlist the pulpit and the press in our behalf," which would be accomplished "by a series of Conventions embracing every part of the country" and "by writing and by speaking . . . in any assemblies proper to be held."

Their planning was rewarded with a turnout of three hundred, primarily women, for the first woman's rights convention in the country. On July 19 and 20 in Seneca Falls, the convention endorsed the Declaration of Sentiments and a dozen resolutions by acclamation, except for one: ominously, Stanton's resolution for woman suffrage went through by only a narrow margin and only with the support of a former slave, Frederick Douglass. Still, some organizers were optimistic; Lucretia Coffin Mott wrote that "the press universal will echo the glad sound." Others were less sanguine, and they were correct. The women's publicity won extensive coverage of the convention, which caused them to be "unsparingly ridiculed by the press," "denounced by the pulpit," and made "the target for the jibes and jeers of a nation," especially for the resolution on woman suffrage. As the Declaration of Sentiments warned, women could "anticipate no small amount of misconception, misrepresentation and ridicule" for decades to come.[2]

In 1848 at Seneca Falls, the woman's rights movement was born. Women had waited seventy-two years since the first Declaration of Independence to write their own. Seventy-two years after their Declaration of Sentiments, women would win woman suffrage with the Nineteenth Amendment to the Constitution.

The first state to ratify the Nineteenth Amendment would be Wisconsin. That woman's rights, temperance, and freedmen's suffrage were on the political agenda even before statehood was promising. That none was adopted suggests the magnitude of reform campaigns to follow for the Thirteenth, Fourteenth, Fifteenth, Eighteenth, and Nineteenth Amendments. The last to succeed, for woman suffrage, would be the hardest fought and subject to the most ridicule in Wisconsin.

That the Nineteenth Amendment was ratified first in Wisconsin was no coup for the state famed for progressive reform. The struggle for suffrage would be so long in the state that women still were organized in Wisconsin well after women elsewhere had won. The struggle was so long because, from the beginning, opponents of woman's rights dominated the political scene and the legal system. For example, of the "able members" in statehood debates, Marshall Strong would be an influential early legislator, while E. V. Whiton and Edward G. Ryan both would be chief justices of the Wisconsin Supreme Court.

With little hope of reform through the legislature or the courts, the only recourse for women would be a campaign in the "court of public opinion," in the words of a public relations practitioner in the next century. In the nineteenth century, the profession did not exist. Nor did textbooks for campaigns, theories for strategies, or even terminology for many of the tactics—press agentry and publicity, lobbying and fundraising, opinion research and issues management—which women would have to learn on their own to win woman suffrage.

The strategies and tactics of public opinion campaigns were not easily learned by women restricted from the "public sphere," even women in the well-settled East who founded the first "female reform societies" and their own newspapers at a time when the Wisconsin territory was only just opening. For women isolated on the frontier, organization was far more difficult because newspapers were few and of notable instability. Even fewer were favorable to reform—and none favored woman suffrage in Wisconsin, at first. Even after a reform press endured in Wisconsin, woman suffrage rarely won editorial support until women endured in newspapers of their own, after 1866. But from settlement forward, women wrote in Wisconsin's reform press, if at the whim of men, and left a record of organizing for woman's rights, again and again—and on their own.

In its politics and press, the Wisconsin territory was but an outpost of the "burned-over district" of upstate New York, the birthplace in the 1820s of the reform fervor which soon swept the East. In the 1830s, the opening of the Erie Canal in the East and the end of the Black Hawk Wars in the West sent a flood of so-called Yankees to the then Michigan Territory. Settling along Lake Michigan's shore in the southeastern sector of what would be Wisconsin, the easterners brought with them their moral baggage of abolition, temperance, and—to an extent—woman's rights. But the southwestern sector, bordered by the Mississippi River, became the province of southerners who brought north their way of life and their slaves despite the illegality of the "peculiar institution" in the territory. The battle lines of the war to come in Wisconsin over abolition were set early on.

Abolition would dominate antebellum politics, but another cause led the reform agenda in the 1830s in Wisconsin, where it would be a lost cause before long. The first temperance society in the territory was founded in 1832 in Green Bay, followed in 1833 by another in nearby Fort Howard, both by and for men only. In 1836 in Walworth County, admirers of a New York reformer named Delavan founded a temperance colony which included women, but membership in its temperance society apparently was restricted to men.[3]

In Wisconsin as in the East, women unwelcome in reform organizations soon formed their own, although the first espoused neither abolition nor temperance. The first national women's organization was the Female Moral Reform Society, founded in 1833 for the purpose of eradicating prostitution and saving fallen women for the sake of all women, in an era when venereal disease was an epidemic unchecked and a subject unspoken. By 1834, the society had purchased its own national newspaper, renamed *The Advocate of Moral Reform,* and put in place an all-woman staff. By 1837, their 16,500 subscribers made it one of the nation's leading religious papers. By 1840, the society had almost 450 local auxiliaries across the country.[4]

Within a year of the founding of the first Female Moral Reform Society in the East, Wisconsin had a counterpart in Waukesha. Then called Prairie Village, later Prairieville, the town of two hundred residents was the largest inland settlement in the eastern sector of the Wisconsin territory. The 130 charter members of the Female Moral Reform Society of Prairie Village included "most of the prominent ladies of the vicinity," mainly "educated, cultured" exiles from New York; many were mothers, sisters, or wives of men who would be prominent in politics, including a United States ambassador, a Wisconsin governor, and a Chicago editor. One member, Peggy More, was a former slave. She and her husband had been manumitted in the East through the intervention of Lucy Ordway, a founder of the society, and her husband. The Reverend Moses Ordway was Prairie Village's first Presbyterian minister, and, as a local historian later wrote, "abolitionists of that time practiced what they preached. . . . Peggy had good standing in society and was on terms of apparently perfect equality with her white neighbors" in the town known as an "abolition hole."

The society became increasingly formalized, and prospered. At first, members met in homes, rotated leadership, and raised funds to free slaves as well as fallen women through sale of stitchery and dues of a shilling. By 1839, women had moved to a Congregational meetinghouse and then a schoolhouse, adopted a constitution and bylaws, and elected officers including a directress — the first was Lucy Ordway — and vice-directresses, a secretary, and a treasurer. Minutes in 1840 recorded expenditures of fifty cents for postage for correspondence and a "circular" sent "to the parent society," several dollars for circulars "for distribution among the sinful," and $1.57 for a buckskin. The last "was rather mystifying to the people of a later generation," according to a later account, but they surmised that "the skin was doubtless purchased to be converted into gloves or mittens, or possibly shoe-laces, to be sold for the benefit of the treasury" and the women's causes.[5]

Women's contributions to abolitionism rarely were recorded, but a charter member of the society won fame in the first instance of the Underground Railroad in the Wisconsin Territory. In 1843 in Pewaukee, near Prairieville, a farm wife hid fugitive slave Caroline Quarrels in cornfields and faced down armed slave catchers alone. Her identity is recorded, in accounts of the rescue and of the society, only as "Mrs. Brown." Known only by a surname, and not even the one she was born with, she is at least recognized as a hero in Wisconsin histories.

More often, nameless women did only thankless drudgery for the cause. When the abolitionist *American Freeman* was founded in Prairieville, women provided free room and board for printers who nobly found "living upon the charity of the people of little consequence," according to a historian. He did not mention the burden of boarders on women already overworked on the Wisconsin frontier.[6]

The difficulty of communication also deterred organization on the frontier. A stepson of Lucy Ordway recalled "carrying notices from one end of that town to the other, of the proposed meetings, month after month, which relieved the society entirely from the want of and at the same time the expense" of more sophisticated methods.

Prairieville did not have a newspaper until 1844; by then, the society was nearly defunct because internal communication was more easily resolved than the increasing internal dissension within the moral reform movement. The Prairieville society's minutes recorded "reproach brought upon some of the members for having attended balls, which is contrary to the principles of the Moral Reform Society." A resolution to boycott "balls or parties for sinful amusement" caused some members to resign. Soon, the society could muster only quarterly meetings, "irregularly attended," and by 1844 the minutes recorded that "the cause seems to languish." A final rift apparently resulted from a fund-raising proposal to sponsor "sinful amusement"—card parties—although an unofficial account implies that women found little adultery worth eradicating on the banks of the Fox River. By 1850, when a former editor of *The Advocate of Moral Reform* moved to town, she found few remnants of the Female Moral Reform Society.[7]

Other early movements also faced the problem of communication on the Wisconsin frontier, where fiscal instability was the bane of the press, but especially for reform papers. In the antebellum era alone, more than four hundred newspapers would be founded in Wisconsin, but few survived, and even fewer were for reform. The first abolitionist agent in Wisconsin, the Reverend Edward Mathews, had found "a great work to be done by exceedingly feeble means" in 1838, because "no newspaper would advocate emancipation" and "the presses were all under the influence of the two parties" and both waved the "slave-party banner." For the next decade, no reform paper would prosper in Wisconsin. Antislavery men organized a society in 1842 at Delavan and met again in 1843 at Prairieville but could not muster support sufficient for a press: the *Wisconsin Aegis* was founded and failed in Racine in 1843, followed by futile attempts at antislavery papers in Platteville and Madison.

The first reform paper in Wisconsin was a "temperance sheet" which also was short-lived, and without a successor for most of the antebellum era. The *Wisconsin Temperance Journal* rose and fell within a few months in 1841 in Milwaukee, although the monthly paper's impressive masthead included Asahel Finch, a prominent lawyer; the Reverend Stephen Peet, pastor of the Presbyterian church; and Harrison Reed, editor of the *Milwaukee Sentinel.* Reed provided free printing and distribution, but fiscal support was precarious. The *Journal* folded after only three issues.[8]

However, the temperance movement was increasingly well publicized in the general press owing to new strategies and tactics which revolutionized reform in the 1840s. Earlier elitist appeals, sedate campaigns, and scattered "local option" efforts were rarely seen after 1842, upon the introduction into the territory of the first of several temperance organizations to invade Wisconsin from the East: the Washingtonian Society. "A spontaneous and spectacular eruption," according to historian Jed Dannenbaum, Washingtonianism was reliant on revivalist "appeal to the emotional sensitivities of mass response," according to historian Joseph R. Gusfield.

Washingtonians' colorful and crowd-pleasing events won a wider public, and publicity, for temperance in Wisconsin. Societies sent advances to the press, staged parades, and sought coverage for nonalcoholic picnics and meetings which featured confessions by reformed drunkards. The first Washingtonian lecturer in Milwaukee, a recently sobered Chicagoan, won more than five hundred converts in a two-day tour, to the despair of an editor whose denunciation of the tactic only gave the movement more publicity. There was adverse publicity, as well; as historian

Robert C. Nesbit writes, "on occasion, a travelling performer on the Washingtonian temperance circuit would backslide spectacularly, bringing joy to the skeptics and civil libertarians," including the city's few editorial advocates of free speech. Touring troupes performed "The Reformed Drunkard or the Lost One Reclaimed" and "The Drama of the Brothers," a temperance men's glee club entertained Kenosha, and alcohol-free men's reading rooms opened in Milwaukee. Both cities also boasted auxiliaries of the Children's Cold Water Army, comprising boys marching in matching badges.

Little was written of women's participation in Wisconsin in Washingtonian societies and in the next organization imported from the East, the Order of the Sons of Temperance. The refusal of male reformers to enlist "the sisters" into regular ranks relegated women, like children, to auxiliary status. The work of Martha Washington Societies and Daughters of Temperance in Wisconsin can be surmised from accounts in the East, where women went door-to-door to redeem families ruined by drunkenness while men managed the movement.

The Sons of Temperance were better managed than their anarchistic predecessors, with a more hierarchical structure, and would eclipse Washingtonianism by the end of the decade. The instability of Washingtonianism is evident in an account of an *American Freeman* editor's first sojourn to southeastern Wisconsin, which at one time supported as many as six nonalcoholic "temperance houses." But, as Nesbit notes, "temperance taverns . . . found it difficult to compete with the genuine article," especially in Milwaukee where a saloon on every streetcorner was a matter of civic pride. Upon making port in Milwaukee, the editor secured safe lodging for his family in a "well-regulated Temperance House . . . uninfested with the spirit of drunkenness"—until, within a week, the owner introduced the "evil spirit of Rum" into the only dry haven in the city. Not for the last time, an editor despaired of a Milwaukee overrun by "pest houses," "Bowling Saloons and Billiard Tables," and "grog shops as thick as the frogs of Egypt."[9]

The remarkable *American Freeman* was the first reform paper of longevity in Wisconsin. Originally a Democratic party organ in Milwaukee, the paper turned antislavery in 1844 when editor and publisher Charles C. Sholes covered a series of lectures by the Reverend Ichabod Codding, a Connecticut agent sent on the circuit by the Illinois Anti-Slavery Society. Codding was a charismatic speaker. The plain and portly Mathews described him as a "man of mark" and "rather tall," with "eyes of extraordinary mesmeric power" which left "on the mind an impression not to be removed." Another admirer wrote that "friend Codding" caused "considerable fervor" in Southport, later called Kenosha, where Sholes's brother also would publish an abolitionist paper. In Milwaukee, Codding's editorial convert promptly adopted abolition, renamed his paper, and moved it from Milwaukee to Prairieville, center of the antislavery Liberty party. Its leaders promised financial support and formed a stock company to purchase the paper—for a dollar—in July 1844.

Until 1846, the *Freeman* survived only precariously, with the assistance of a series of itinerant antislavery ministers who were notable for enthusiasm but not for journalistic expertise. The Reverend A. L. Barber of Milwaukee was a regular assistant, and the Reverend Mathews signed on as an apprentice when in town; on the circuit, he sold subscriptions and served as a correspondent. Other ministers also sent correspondence, Mathews recalled, "so that the paper had a high literary standing." Despite their earnest and erudite contributions, the paper "soon passed through some vicissitudes." However, status as the "official organ" of the newly founded Liberty party meant little in monetary terms for the *Freeman,* with minimal funding and few subscriptions.

The low subscription rate suggests that the *Freeman*'s fiscal instability was primarily due to lack of news content. Historian Kate Everest Levi finds that Sholes was "unable to give character" to the paper, while William J. Maher faults Sholes for filling the *Freeman* with "relatively unimportant" news, religious tracts, and editorials which "denounced slavery with regular monotony." Sholes's mentor, Codding, was more kind. Sholes "labored under all sorts of embarrassments and never had an opportunity of really impressing himself upon the paper." In sum, the paper was preachy and dull, in part a result of Sholes's reliance on evangelical correspondents—except for the effervescent Reverend Mathews. His anecdotes of antislavery "agitation" provided the paper's rare readable copy.[10]

News of and by women, if anonymous, increasingly found its way into the *Freeman* once they organized for abolition. Denied equal status in antislavery societies, women were slower in forming their own on the Wisconsin frontier than in the East, where the first women's antislavery societies had organized in 1833, held a national convention in New York in 1837, and conducted a massive petition campaign by 1843.[11] In "Milwaukie" in 1844, a Ladies' Anti-Slavery Society formed to raise funds for freed slaves and sent publicity and a constitution to the

Freeman. Within a week, the paper reported, men belatedly but "unanimously resolved to invite the Ladies of Milwaukie who feel friendly to, or interested in, the Anti-Slavery cause" to their next meeting—but not into their society. The women declined, courteously, continuing to meet on their own and contributing a "Ladies Department"—decorously unsigned or under pseudonyms, of course—to the *Freeman.*

Women's news continued to be welcome in the *Freeman* under the next editor, the Reverend Codding, who returned to Wisconsin. Codding had previous experience in the reform press in Connecticut, where he also withstood criticism to publicly debate strategies and tactics of abolitionism with one of the first women to brave a podium, Abby Kelley. In 1846, Codding was lured to Prairieville by Liberty men who offered a paper as well as a pulpit. His return rescued the *Freeman* from fiscal instability; the paper achieved regular publication and even became interesting. Turgid tracts, moralistic homilies, and familiar fiction and poetry remained, but Codding also ran cutting commentary with reprinted articles and speeches, chatty fillers on farming, home production tips, and tightly edited correspondence.

Women had a place in the press under Codding, who also provided women with a place to meet. An organizer of a Female Anti-Slavery Society in Prairieville in 1846 sent notices, signed only "E——," which reported that the society had convened at Codding's Congregational church to approve a constitution and elect officers, and achieved membership of twenty-nine within two months. Not all women sought out the press, but many sought a place in reform, as other records indicate. In 1847 in Milwaukee, for example, a "female prayer meeting" in the Presbyterian church led to the founding of a Women's Anti-Slavery Society. In the same year in Mukwonago, to the west of Milwaukee, an Anti-Slavery Society formed with women a full third of founding members. Several of the founders, women and men, were surnamed Youmans—a name of significance to the woman suffrage campaign in the next century. [12]

However, among all contributors to the *Freeman,* women were comparatively few; women worth courting as readers would not count at the polls, and politics was all the news as Wisconsin neared statehood. A rare editor who raised the subject of woman suffrage was James Densmore of the Oshkosh *True Democrat.* For his stand, according to a historian, "Densmore said he expected to be called a 'visionary fanatic,'" but he "challenged the editor of the Milwaukee *Sentinel* to say why women should not have a voice in making laws." The *Sentinel* responded with ridicule, replying "in a tone of levity, 'Women are confessedly angels, and angels do not vote.'"[13]

The *Freeman*'s minister-editor might have offered theological insight to the *Sentinel,* but in 1848 Codding was near the end of his tenure. His congregation complained that the paper curtailed time for preaching, and he had "no old barrels of sermons to go to," wrote Codding. He did not reveal that he was resigning his pulpit as well as the press to attempt a political career. Codding handpicked his successor, Sherman Miller Booth, a colleague from the Connecticut reform press. "A correct and strong writer," "a fine speaker, powerful debater, and accomplished statistician," he would "devote his whole time to the editorial character of the *Freeman.*"

The new *Freeman* editor arrived in 1848, on the eve of statehood, fortuitous timing for the paper and Wisconsin politics: neither would ever be the same. Booth cultivated an arresting presence, with shoulder-length hair and a dark, bushy beard which accentuated his black, piercing eyes. A political maverick and unabashed propagandist, Booth would bring fame to the *Freeman* but more to himself, because he combined an evangelical style with secular business sense. Even before his arrival, Booth had the *Freeman* moved back to the boomtown of Milwaukee to increase circulation and reduce postal costs. His first issue proclaimed a wide-ranging reform agenda for Wisconsin, with something for every reader: abolition, temperance, free public lands and free trade, direct taxation, agricultural dominance over industry, and even woman's rights, although not woman suffrage.

Booth also affiliated with a series of coalitions—Liberty men, Free Soilers, Free Democrats—as fast as they formed in an era of chaotic politics across the country, but especially in Wisconsin. The *Freeman* soon topped two thousand subscribers, more than the total of the state's five other antislavery papers. In 1850, Booth bought the paper from the remnants of the Liberty party, renamed it the *Free Democrat,* and went daily.[14]

Even better evidence of the popularity of reform, or the chaos in Wisconsin politics, was the stunning news of statewide prohibition in 1850. The law won headlines nationwide when the three thousand Wisconsin men in the Sons of Temperance won the campaign with pressure tactics from petition drives to boycotts of legislative candidates. The order was so powerful in state politics, according to historian Joseph Schafer, that editors "treated it with diplomatic caution, if they did not openly sympathize with it."

The order's astute use of the press included sponsoring its own paper, elegantly named *The Old Oaken Bucket and Organ of the Sons.* Under the Reverend A. Constantine Barry of Racine, the sixteen-page monthly promoted the Sons primarily through poetry and fiction, the "temperance tales" typical of reform-press fare which, according to historian Joseph R. Gusfield, were "probably the most effective media of mass persuasion in the cause." One tale in the *Oaken Bucket* told "how a social drinker steadily marched down the road to alcoholic ruin until his beautiful young wife rescued him by venturing into the dread confines of the alehouse."

However, the 1850 prohibition law was the last gasp of "Yankee" hegemony. Enforcement was weak even in the strongest of temperance towns such as Waukesha and Whitewater. Officials openly defied the law in Milwaukee; as a newcomer reported to a Michigan paper, "the Christian finds enough to grieve him, especially in larger towns upon the lake." The *Oaken Bucket* editor, also aggrieved that the law led only to a "glorious revival in intemperance," actually endorsed repeal. The pride of the temperance movement only a year before, "Wisconsin had forfeited the good name she had everywhere," Barry wrote. "Unless enlightened public opinion and sentiment go along with a law and sustain it, it is good for nothing," he mourned, against "the mightier law— Public Opinion."[15]

Prohibition was repealed within a year, in the first of many ignominious losses for temperance forces in Wisconsin. The only advantage for women was a press distracted from "stormy debate" on another bill passed in the same biennium, establishing property rights for married women. But the prohibition law's primary legacy was the first organized opposition to reform in Milwaukee, where Germans turned to violence in the streets and then turned out to vote out "Yankees" at the polls. A convention was called to found "a German state" for "German customs" in Watertown, which proved unnecessary.[16] With repeal, Germans won the state of Wisconsin.

Not all Germans were opposed to all reforms, and the massive influx into Milwaukee of German freethinkers after 1848 included the first woman to breach the male bastion of the Fourth Estate in the state. The magnificent Mathilde Franziska Anneke had been a successful lecturer, author, publisher, and leader of reform in her German homeland, where her work helped to alter marital law before she was exiled for her role in the 1848 revolution. Anneke's work was widely known even before her emigration; decades later, at an International Council of

Women in Berlin, Susan B. Anthony credited "Madam Anneke" as the inspiration for her first stand for suffrage. Anneke conducted a long correspondence with Anthony and Stanton and, years later, would send funds east for Anthony's legal fees.[17]

In her new country, Anneke attempted to continue her career as a lecturer, with limited success. She later related the story of her "strangely varied life," "struggle for independence," and survival "through the terrors of bloody revolution," which "brought her to this effulgent shore" and, in 1852, to her first major address in America. The eastern audience was not receptive, at first.

> I stood before a large assembly . . . to utter, in the name of suffering and struggling womanhood, the cry of my old Fatherland for freedom and justice. At that time my voice was overwhelmed by the sound of sneers, scoffs, and hisses—the eloquence of tyranny, by which every outcry of the human heart is stifled. Then . . . I was allowed, in my native tongue, to echo faintly the cry for justice and freedom. What a change has been wrought since then! . . . Such a gigantic revolution in public opinion![18]

Anneke attributed the rude reception to her topic, but admitted difficulty with "a strange idiom." Decades later, she still would be "constrained" by the language of her "beloved adopted land."

But in bilingual Milwaukee, nativism was not the cause for persecution of Anneke and her paper. The *Deutsche Frauen-Zeitung,* a "radical, free-thinker's journal dedicated to the complete emancipation of women," debuted in March 1852 to immediate opposition, apparently less on account of Anneke's prosuffrage philosophy than of her policy of hiring and training women to work in the composing room. Irate male typesetters enlisted Milwaukee printers who, to a man, boycotted her paper and shut down her business after six issues, in September 1852. The Annekes left Milwaukee soon after.

With the rise of the first "women's papers" in the 1850s in the East, the failure of Anneke's paper in Wisconsin was not typical. In Chicago and Springfield, Illinois, editors not only employed women typesetters but also recommended them to their brethren of the press. Similar attempts in the East met some resistance from male printers, but none was closed down; in New Jersey, Anneke would revive her *Frauen-Zeitung* yet again, this time with success, before returning to Milwaukee. However, in the "German Athens," Anneke would not again attempt to publish a paper.[19]

"I stood . . . to utter, in the name of suffering and struggling womanhood, the cry of my old Fatherland for freedom and justice."—Mathilde
Fransziska Anneke, an internationally known suffragist and author, and
the first woman publisher and editor in Wisconsin until male printers
in Milwaukee closed down her *Deutsche Frauen-Zeitung*. Photo courtesy of the State Historical Society of Wisconsin.

Germans' otherwise successful invasion of Wisconsin caused another repercussion of prohibition's brief reign with the failure of another reform paper in 1852. The Sons and their *Oaken Bucket* never recovered from repeal; the Reverend Barry left the news business for the pulpit, and the feisty "temperance sheet" folded soon after. Indeed, repeal "completely undid" the movement in Wisconsin, where temperance peaked too soon. Elsewhere, the movement gained momentum owing to the Maine Law, so called for a statute first won in that state which soon crossed the country.

The Maine Law campaign marked the emergence of women as a significant and recognized source of support for reform, in Wisconsin and elsewhere—although women everywhere met resistance. At a World's Temperance Convention in New York City in 1853, Susan B. Anthony was denied the right to speak owing solely to her gender. As Anthony and other women left the hall to hold their own Whole World's Temperance Convention, a Wisconsin delegate—none other than the *Freeman*'s Sherman Miller Booth—won national notoriety for defending Anthony against the "Woman Gag Act," and for defying New York's finest. Police tossed Booth into the street and onto the front page; back home, he publicized his exploit in his paper.

In Wisconsin, women and the ubiquitous Booth scored the publicity coup of the local Maine Law campaign. The men of the Wisconsin Temperance League planned the usual tactics—lecture tours, torchlight parades, a newspaper named the *Wisconsin Temperance League*—which inspired wives of Temperance League men to take to the podium as well, a courageous act. Coverage in eastern papers led two well-known lecturers, Lydia Fowler and Clarina Howard Nichols, to volunteer their services to the league, but the men refused to "sanction their labors" only to see their spouses found a Woman's State Temperance Society and call a convention for Lake Mills, where women voted to sponsor the tour. As the *Free Democrat* reported, the men decided instead "to employ a Rev. Mr. Crampton, well known for his violent opposition to Woman's public efforts in this cause. They have not contented themselves with neutrality in this matter, but have taken ground openly against the action of the Woman's State Temperance Society and their agents."

At the women's convention, the *Free Democrat* editor and champion of their right to speak in the "public sphere" volunteered to chaperone the easterners around the state. The trio's novelty guaranteed notice in the press and in pulpits; one minister publicly accused the women of obvious infidelity—perhaps, as a later suffragist wrote, because they were "incidentally scattering suffrage seed" as well.

The Maine Law won at the polls but was lost in Madison, among corrupt politicians newly attentive to German newcomers. They overturned the voters' verdict and required that the measure be resubmitted to a referendum in 1854. The Maine Law drive died and with it the *League,* railing to its end at a "rising tide of intemperance and political treachery" by reformers wooing the "Teutonic vote."[20]

From 1854 on, abolitionism would overshadow all other causes in Wisconsin owing to the exploits of Sherman Miller Booth. The *Free Democrat* reflected his frustration over public apathy to the cause even after passage of the Kansas-Nebraska Act allowed expansion of slavery. A week later, Booth capitalized on the capture of a fugitive slave named Joshua Glover. Booth's call for action brought forth a mob of five thousand, some of whom freed Glover from Milwaukee's jail and helped him flee to Canada by way of Waukesha. Booth apparently did not engineer the escape—that was the work of a Dr. Erastus B. Wolcott—but Booth became a scapegoat because of his ill-timed and ill-tempered editorial commentary about the local judiciary, which bordered on the libelous.

The *Free Democrat* editor's flair for publicity and press agentry made "the Booth case" a cause célèbre across the country. His first conviction in Milwaukee was overturned by the Wisconsin Supreme Court which, in effect, nullified the federal fugitive slave law, to nationwide praise from abolitionists and their papers. In the next thirteen years, Booth would be tried nineteen times, including two futile appeals to the United States Supreme Court, but his letters from jail to the *Free Democrat* had their intended effect. "Booth clubs" arose in Ripon and spread across the state to raise funds for his defense, and began a bandwagon effect in the press among Booth's more cautious colleagues. The "avowed abolitionist" editor of the *Lancaster Herald,* for example, admitted, "I did not say much in the paper on the slavery subject until after 1854, when . . . I felt fully warranted by public opinion in taking a bold, even an antislavery stand." Booth's stand cost him his paper before a presidential pardon finally freed him from jail, if not the judicial process, just before the inauguration of Abraham Lincoln. But Booth was a jubilant martyr: he and his "Booth clubs" had helped a local rebellion become the Republican party.[21]

Between the prohibition battle and the "Booth case," woman suffragists could not compete for a place on the public agenda until Mathilde Fransziska Anneke returned to Milwaukee. In 1855, Anneke arranged

"[The men] have not contented themselves with neutrality . . . but have taken ground openly against the action of the [women] and their agents."— Sherman Miller Booth, publisher and editor of the *American Freeman* in Milwaukee and a proponent of women's right to speak in public. Photo courtesy of the State Historical Society of Wisconsin.

a tour of the state by eastern suffragist Lucy Stone, who lectured in at least Madison, Kenosha, and Shullsburg, and possibly elsewhere; as a historian wrote, "it is not possible to reconstruct her itinerary as only progressive papers noticed her visit." However, Stone's tour had a noticeable impact. Women organized a petition drive for a suffrage amendment to the state constitution and enlisted the support of two leading legislators, both editors. In the state senate, Christopher L. Sholes of the Southport *Telegraph* submitted three petitions for woman suffrage led by the names of Annea Lewis, Janet Bone, R. H. Deming, and E. M.

Brande. In the assembly, Hamilton H. Gray of the Shullsburg *Pick and Gad* submitted a partial suffrage bill, for *"feme covert* and *feme sole"*— married and propertied single women—"in certain cases."

Not for the first time, Wisconsin's reputation for reform raised the hopes of eastern suffragists. "God bless these young states," exclaimed Stone in an address at the seventh National Women's Rights Convention in New York City. "Wisconsin . . . has granted almost all that has been asked except the right of suffrage. And even this, Senator Sholes . . . said, 'is only a question of time, and as sure to triumph as God is just.'"

In Wisconsin in 1856, the time had not come. "To counteract the influence of the women's rights society," editors sought out women who were against woman's rights—the first "traitors to their gender," according to a later suffragist, but there would be more. The *Janesville Gazette* advertised a lecture entitled "The Social and Domestic Influence of Women" by a Delphia P. Baker who was "opposed to the strong-minded feminines"—an epithet for suffragists—"of these latter days." The suffrage bill was tabled, "never to be heard from again." The campaign did result in a related bill to strengthen the 1850 statute on married women's property rights against misreading by "conservative judges," according to a contemporary account. Historian Louise Phelps Kellogg calls it "the first serious effort to interest Wisconsin lawmakers in the movement," because they did not laugh the bill down. But they did vote it down. Two years later, the law was amended—although married women still could not conduct business, make contracts, retain their own earnings, or sue and be sued in their own names.[22]

In 1856, more than two decades since the founding of the first formal women's organization in Wisconsin, the prospects for progress in politics or the press seemed abysmal. However, from the farm wife who faced down slave catchers to anonymous contributors in the *Freeman* "Ladies Department," from temperance men's wives who stumped the state for the Maine Law to Mathilde Fransziska Anneke, women had made their potential evident to the men running reform.

The next organization to invade Wisconsin from the East actively, astutely enlisted women and accorded them equality, which would swell membership to record numbers for reform. The Order of the Knights of Good Templar, introduced in Wisconsin in the mid-1850s, inducted women into regular ranks and officially allotted them half of lodge offices—although in practice, at least in Wisconsin, women usually won election only to lesser posts.

The new trend in temperance was typified by the unusual press partnership of siblings Emma and Thurlow Weed Brown. The masthead of their *Cayuga Chief* listed both as co-publishers and co-editors from the beginning in 1849, in upstate New York, where temperance and the Templars began. At thirty, Thurlow invested his life savings of seven dollars in a list of 170 subscribers, while his twenty-two-year-old sister trained as a typesetter and compositor. The paper soon soared to a prosperous circulation of three thousand, while Thurlow also became a sought-after author, organizer, and lecturer. Once described as "timid and delicate" with a "bashful look—a mere farmer boy," Thurlow added a beard and became a commanding presence on the podium. One reporter wrote of Brown as "tall and a little angular, large boned and muscular, equally at ease in driving home a philippic against the rum-seller or a spoke in a carriage." Another found his only flaw to be "a nose too fleshy for beauty." Thurlow replied with a delightful defense of his too-prominent feature, asserting that he would "follow it to the end of life, and the very grave."

But Thurlow Weed Brown was the beauty of the family. His sister was heavyset and heavy-browed, resembling him only in having the same unfortunate nose. In her favor, she had large, heavy-lidded, and riveting eyes and a far more determined jaw than her brother. It was the plain and reticent Emma who ran the office and put out the paper to free the frenetic Thurlow for "the circuit."

In 1856, for the good of the order and Thurlow's health, the Browns uprooted their paper—printing press, subscription list, and even name-plate intact—to come to Wisconsin. He had become enamored of the West on a lecture tour, returned to visit relatives and purchase assets of the defunct *Jefferson Republican,* and went to Fort Atkinson first, in 1854, the same year as the founding of the first Templar lodge in Wisconsin. However, he left the *Chief* and his sister in the East for two years. In 1856, at the same time that state Templars achieved grand lodge status, she brought by boat the paper and Wisconsin's first power press, which would keep the *Chief* financially afloat with a prolific printing business. But she never shared Thurlow's enthusiasm for the West, followed only reluctantly, and resisted changing the logo to the *Wisconsin Chief* until 1857. Years later, Emma would write that the "paper saw its best days" in New York, while the "pull was always against the tide" in Wisconsin, which she still referred to as her "new home" even after three decades in the state—when the *Chief* became the nation's longest-lasting "temperance sheet."[23]

At first, Wisconsin was not the "genial climate" for which Thurlow

"The highest privilege of journalists [is] to conduct an independent press, and make the world the better for its living."—Thurlow Weed Brown, a nationally known temperance lecturer and author, and a co-publisher and co-editor of the *Wisconsin Chief*. Photo courtesy of the Fort Atkinson Historical Society.

"In crystallizing and combining public sentiment, the more we simplify our work, the more we commend it to the masses."—Emma Brown, a co-founder of the *Wisconsin Chief* and the first woman publisher and editor in Wisconsin to last. Photo courtesy of the Fort Atkinson Historical Society.

had hoped, for his consumption or the temperance cause. He called Fort Atkinson a "constellation of accursed grog hells" for good reason—and got as good back, according to author Alexis Crane Hart, whose boyhood home was near the *Chief* office. Hart recalled "a saloon keeper and his following who were greatly angered by attacks in the *Chief.* Once, when Miss Emma was passing the saloon on her way to the office, she was grossly insulted" and informed her brother, who "immediately went to the saloon intending to horsewhip the offender." However, "in the melee, the saloon keeper had the best of it and Brown himself was badly beaten up."[24]

But Thurlow recovered better than did the relocated *Chief;* the paper went up and down with the family's fortunes, ranging from four to twelve pages and varying in page size as well as circulation. The Browns claimed a readership of fifteen thousand, but circulation rarely topped two thousand in the West, and long relied on a faithful following in New York for half of the subscribers and advertisers.

Like their counterparts in the partisan press, the Browns made a living only in part from their paper. Emma ran the *Chief* and printing shop, while Thurlow augmented their income with lecture fees as state agent for the Templars and as president of a State Temperance Convention. Apparently, neither position was salaried. Templars did designate the *Chief* as official "Paper of the Order" and subscribed for state and local officers, a clever combination of patronage and sales incentive which encouraged their agent to organize new lodges. Thurlow also was part owner of a sawmill, a land speculator, and a farmer. None was enough to live on, for the family homestead, The Oaks, housed his wife, children, father, and the occasional field hand or printer's apprentice, as well as his self-supporting sister.

The Browns were comparable to self-employed consultants and considered their *Chief* editorially independent because they relied on no single source of income, including Templar patronage. Accused of "neglecting the field" and "sharp practice" for raising lecture fees, Thurlow haughtily replied that he did not "depend on such labor for a livelihood" but relied "on his hands for his bread, thank heaven," and would not "submit to, or be humiliated by—the 'tender mercies' of the hat." But, "as to being an 'organ,'" he wrote that "the *Chief* has ever been one; so it will be always. If to be controlled by any individual, clique, party, or organization, is to be an 'organ,' the *Chief* is not; never will be." However, his claim to "the highest privilege of journalists, to conduct an independent press, and make the world the better for its living," most often came in defense of near-libelous name-calling.

The *Chief* was written primarily by Thurlow, the paper's traveling correspondent and best copy. Posting his speeches and press reviews to Emma, he "spent his time mostly in the field," where "few men could equal his moving eloquence," according to a Fort Atkinson admirer. Another saw "strong men weep like children" as Brown "held his audience as if by magic," with "no manuscript, not even notes . . . for two and a half hours," and an Ohio reporter described Brown as the "Mad Anthony of the Reform."

Thurlow's rantings on the road matched those on the "rum traffic" at home, where he did not spare colleagues in the press. The *Chief* was "the most vitriolic temperance paper published in Wisconsin," according to historian Frank L. Byrne.[25] Even a Templar admirer found Brown overly "bitter in his feelings and his language. . . . None knew better than he how to rain hot shot, and shell, and Greek fire upon the enemy," especially the enemy within; Thurlow "claimed extra privilege . . . to criticize anything among his fellow partizans [*sic*] which he disapproved." He blamed "moral pestilence" on Republicans who only masqueraded as reformers and "should be perpetuated in a monument of toddy sticks." Brown found the press equally at fault and initiated lively editorial debates in attacks on the "inky swill" of the *Wisconsin State Journal* and *Milwaukee Sentinel* for favorable coverage of German saloon life.

The *Chief* and the prolific Thurlow also provided readers with lighter fare. He even penned sheet music for temperance tunes which ran on the back page of the *Chief,* at least relieving an uninspired layout. A press critic considered his lurid temperance tales and poetry "very commonplace" as the result of Thurlow's "lack of school refining, and native antipathy to all manner of rigid rules any way." A kinder press peer praised the *Chief* 's "versatility of talent" as unmatched in the state.

> There are the light gossipy sketches; the dashed off snatches of seasonable sentimentalism; the sharp, clashing caustic retort upon some doughty opponent; the labored and stately leading editorial. . . . the etchings of burlesque, broadest humor and pungent wit, to mock parade, and then lance through some vainglorious foe. . . . the squibs and brevities of local, transitory interest . . . the measured cadences of verse . . . the columns of storytelling . . . the puns and witticisms, the quips and cranks of thought. All . . . found an inky bridge of passage to his weekly columns.[26]

There was no mention of Emma. She rarely signed her wry, spare commentary on "exchanges" culled from papers and periodicals, or her replies to letters to "T. W. & E." from fellow reformers such as Neal Dow of Maine Law fame, temperance lecturer and press agent Phineas T. Barnum, or the Reverend Edward Mathews, long gone from Wisconsin but still a loyal and loquacious correspondent under the pseudonym "Father Dred," an allusion to the character modeled upon him in the antislavery novel *Dred* by Harriet Beecher Stowe.

The Browns' grab bag of a paper became "must reading" among foes as well as friends of reform, and revived the moribund state temperance movement. In "organ-grinding," as Emma Brown called her brand of journalism, success was measured less by circulation than by organization. From few more than one thousand members in 1856, when Emma Brown brought the *Chief* to Wisconsin, the order grew to more than eight thousand by 1860, when temperance men marched off to war. In a desperate attempt to forestall the loss of Templars, and subscribers — and despite his declining health—Thurlow undertook a hectic itinerary to dozens of towns in and out of the state.

Toiling alone in the *Chief* office in Fort Atkinson, Emma Brown could not see strides made by women in the Civil War, except in "exchanges" and Thurlow's eyewitness accounts. Only two weeks into the war, women in the North and South formed twenty thousand aid societies to provide supplies for wounded soldiers and support for war widows, and to found orphanages and soldiers' hospitals. While southerners' work stayed localized, women in the North centralized work in their Sanitary Commission and raised $15 million, a level of fund-raising never before seen. Their Sanitary Fairs "set the pattern for effective money raising events held by women across the nation" for years to come, according to historian Ruth Bordin.[27]

Wisconsin women's work in the Sanitary Commission provided organizational models and established networks—state, regional, and national—which would continue well after the Civil War. The evolution of organization can be seen in the example of Waukesha, where women organized upon outbreak of war in 1861. Within a few weeks, they sewed 231 shirts for soldiers from flannel furnished by the state and rolled hundreds of yards of bandages. Within months, Waukesha women formally founded a Soldiers' Aid Society with two directors, a secretary, a treasurer, and a "soliciting committee" of six. In 1862, when a statewide Ladies' Aid Society formed to coordinate activity with the national Sanitary Commission, the board of managers sent a solicitor to Waukesha. Harriette T. Olin, a new member from Racine, was a novice but "not at all daunted" by the mission, because she expected only to "meet with a few ladies in their homes." Instead, she "nearly fainted away" when escorted to a church where bells were ringing in midweek and hundreds of women were awaiting an address from the representative of the state society. "I think I must have experienced something of the tremor that a soldier felt in storming a fort of the enemy, or in advancing upon the ranks of an undaunted foe," Olin recalled. "I found only Waukesha's best and noblest women, and was made welcome."

Statewide organization was a logical step but a logistical task of considerable significance for women unaccustomed to collective effort beyond town boundaries, yet Waukesha women enlisted with enthusiasm. By 1865, Olin recalled, they "added $1,000 or more to proceeds" of the Milwaukee Sanitary Fair, "the first important step toward the establishing of the Soldiers' Home in Milwaukee."

The massive Milwaukee Sanitary Fair alone raised $116,000 for one of the first veterans' homes and hospitals in the country, built by Wisconsin women. As early as 1864, Milwaukee women had founded temporary shelters at several sites in the city for housing and nursing wounded Wisconsin soldiers. But the need for more permanent facilities was evident to many women. One was Cordelia A. Perrine Harvey, widow of a Wisconsin governor and war hero, and a hero in her own right as a war nurse. Appointed state sanitary agent by her husband's successor, Harvey went to Washington to petition President Lincoln for support, and persuaded him. However, Congress had no funds—and no intention to find any—for veterans and other victims of the war.

Women promised proceeds of fund-raising efforts to the federal government, staged a series of Sanitary Fairs, and won passage of a bill for institutions in Madison, Prairie du Chien, and Milwaukee. In Madison, in a home built by former governor Leonard J. Farwell but renamed for the state sanitary agent's late husband, the Harvey U. S. Army General Hospital opened in 1863. In 1865, Cordelia Harvey came home with several war orphans from the South. Her return coincided with estimates that as many as eight thousand Wisconsin children also were orphaned by the war, and she launched a lobbying and fund-raising campaign to provide for their care. But the state proved as incapable of swift action as had the federal government. Harvey enlisted "the soldier's friend," war hero and governor Lucius Fairchild, and a board comprising prominent businessmen from Milwaukee as well as Madison. The campaign raised more than $20,000—more than twice the amount allotted by the legislature, at last, more than two months after the Soldiers' Orphans' Home had opened its doors in the former Harvey Hospital. In 1866, the facility housed more than two hundred children and a staff of twenty-six under the first superintendent, Cordelia Harvey.

In Milwaukee in 1866 and for the first two years following the war, women funded the care of 31,650 veterans. By 1869, women also had built the National Asylum for Disabled Volunteer Soldiers, under reform leader and slave rescuer Dr. E. B. Wolcott. Known as the "Veterans' Hos-

"All over this region, the women seem to be waiting, longing for some soul to animate the body of work with which we have been so long and lovingly busying ourselves."– Maria Preston Codding, a press correspondent for the Baraboo Ladies' Loyal League, writing on the work of women including Cordelia Perrine Harvey (pictured) of Madison, a Civil War nurse and a pioneer in establishment of veterans' hospitals in Wisconsin and nationwide. Photo courtesy of the State Historical Society of Wisconsin.

pital" and now the oldest in the country, the Victorian Gothic steeple of the "Domiciliary" still dominates the Milwaukee site, surrounded by acres of regimented rows of white military grave markers.[28]

As early as 1863, through the Sanitary Commission, Wisconsin women established regional connections with counterparts elsewhere, especially in Illinois. Chicago's first North-Western Sanitary Fair, in 1863, drew sixty thousand spectators including the *Chief*'s Thurlow Brown, who could only comment charitably on the Wisconsin booth despite its "German department." A favorite of the fair, the ethnic crafts made by Wisconsin women raised $6,000 toward a total net of $80,000. Brown returned to Chicago in 1865 for the famed North-West Sanitary Fair, the most successful fund-raiser of the war. Recounting the fair booth by booth, Brown let readers linger with him at the sight of picturesque spoils of war, the "torn, rent, soiled and shattered symbols" of the Confederacy: captured flags and standards, a slave auction block. A northern symbol, one of the most popular features in the fair, was "Old Abe," the famed bald-eagle mascot of Wisconsin's fighting Eighth Regiment.

In 1863, in addition to Soldiers' Aid Societies and the Sanitary Commission, women founded Ladies' Loyal Leagues across the North and in Wisconsin. Madison was the site of the first such organization in the state—and, so members claimed, in the country—by mid-February 1863. First named the Ladies' Union League, its founders wrote to Susan B. Anthony that "without delay we issued our preamble and constitution in the form of a circular-letter" and "organized visiting committees [to] examine into and report upon all cases of want in soldiers' families," in part to prevent the destitute, "discouraged wife" from writing "appeals to her soldier in the field," which was "one of the most productive causes of discontent in the army," they opined. But women's primary project was a massive letter-writing campaign to soldiers, "the most direct and practical means which were in our power . . . reaching nearly every private in the army to encourage and stimulate him in the way that ladies know how to do."

Madison women boosted military morale by an innovative use of the press as a clipping service for soldiers whose "personal bravery" earned a line in local papers. "We save the newspaper notices, cut these out, and inclose them, with a few hearty, earnest words, to some member of the army of the Potomac," they wrote. Women "thus become a medium for the diffusion of all that can stimulate and inspire courage and loyalty."

Women also used the press to bolster their own courage by communicating organizational strategies and tactics. "We must not forget that knowledge is power," wrote a Cassville woman, Ursula Larned, to Anthony. "The minds of this country are molded and governed by the press; let us therefore, in whatever sphere we move, aid and encourage the reading and circulation of loyal newspapers." As Larned wrote, "the papers of the Revolution did almost, if not quite as much, for us as for our soldiery." As another of Anthony's correspondents wrote from Baraboo, "I cannot tell you with what joy I received through the *Anti-Slavery Standard* the account of the formation of the 'Loyal Women's League of Hartford, Ct.' I forthwith communicated with the women met for sanitary purposes and we organized a 'Loyal Women's League' here. Forty women signed at once, and others now are constantly added," she wrote. "All over this region, the women seem to be waiting, longing for some soul to animate the body of work with which we have been so long and lovingly busying ourselves." The writer was Maria Preston Codding, long time co-worker in reform with her husband, the former editor of the *Freeman*. She correctly deduced, and endorsed, Anthony's intent to turn women's wartime fervor to woman suffrage.

Most women could not so readily read between the lines of a call to a Women's National Loyal League convention by Anthony and Elizabeth Cady Stanton for "anniversary week" in New York, an annual and simultaneous onslaught of reform conventions in the city. Larned had "lately noticed in the *New York Tribune* a call for a meeting of the loyal women of this nation" to "act in concert in our country's cause." Another correspondent who misread the call was Emily Hoyt of Madison, who wrote to Anthony that she wanted war work "kept sacred from Anti-Slavery, Woman's Rights, Temperance, and everything else, good though they may be." It would not be the last time suffragists used a war as well as the press to press their cause. But the first time, the blatant attempt to enlist the homefront army would backfire.

Of the thousand women at the convention, none was more enraged to discover its agenda, or more articulate, than Hoyt of the Madison Loyal League. She had "never before spoken except in private meetings" but was eloquent in debate with Anthony and other easterners. Hoyt denounced the deception of "earnest women of the country" who "came hundreds of miles to attend a business meeting of the Loyal Women of the North . . . not to hold a Woman's Rights Convention." Her cohort did not "object to the philosophy—we believe in the philosophy." However, said Hoyt, "in the West which I represent, there is a very strong objection to Woman's Rights; in fact, this Woman's Rights matter is odious to some of us from the *manner* in which it has been conducted." Hoyt called for recognition that "Woman's Rights as an *ism* has not been received with entire favor by the women of the country," and that promoting "any *ism* obnoxious to the people" was "prejudicing public sentiment."

Hoyt identified a source of discord on strategy and tactics in the woman's rights movement for decades to come. That she spoke for a significant number of women was evident; they applauded Hoyt almost as often as easterners interrupted her. Ridiculing Hoyt's midwestern "manner" as "exceedingly amusing," Ernestine Rose noted that "if it had not been for Woman's Rights, that lady would not have had the courage to stand here and say what she did. . . . Some women out in the West are opposed to the Woman's Rights movement—though at the same time they take advantage of it."

Anthony's resolution for woman suffrage failed, and with it the reason for the meeting in the minds of organizers. The only moment of unity—and levity—occurred when a man in the hall attempted to speak. Anonymous "cries of 'Question, question,'" "Men have no right to speak here," and "You are not a woman, sit down" were quelled by Anthony, who won laughter with a lighthearted reminder of the many times when women who "burned for utterance" had been shouted down and ruled out of order. However, she overruled "the gentleman" when he requested the right to vote.

The Loyal League went forward for abolition, not suffrage, but gave women organizational skills on a larger scale. With Stanton as president and Anthony as secretary, at twelve dollars a week, the league led a petition drive for emancipation. "The Prayer of One Hundred Thousand" required a year of work by women who counted and packaged rolls "in yellow paper, and tied with the regulation red tape" for presentation to Congress. In 1864, women had amassed almost four hundred thousand signatures including four thousand from Wisconsin, the ninth highest of twenty-three states. Senator Charles Sumner hailed women's work as "a stage of public opinion in the history of slavery" which sped passage of the Thirteenth Amendment.

The campaign also was significant in the history of suffrage, in training women to win their own amendment to the Constitution. As historian Sara M. Evans writes, the "mammoth effort brought thousands of women into public and political action, giving them organizational experience and new skills." However, as historian Anne Firor Scott suggests, there was a "bitter irony" in the extraordinary efficiency of the Loyal League, the Sanitary Commission, and their counterparts in the Confederacy. Union generals blamed women of the South—but not the North—for prolonging the war with their "assiduous labor." As Scott writes, "if women on both sides had kept closer to their assigned sphere and let the two governments muddle on without their labor, the short war which so many had predicted might indeed have occurred, and nearly everybody would have been better off."[29]

While national organizations educated Wisconsin women, at least one national leader's tour of the state taught her a sad lesson on those left worse off by the war. Mary A. Livermore, head of the Sanitary Commission and a Chicago urbanite, "turned away in aversion" at her first sight of women harvesting farm fields. However, upon learning that their men were gone to battlefields, Livermore wrote that her "eyes were unsealed" regarding women's sacrifice for the war.

The war sent thousands of Wisconsin women into the workforce for the first time, on farms and in cities. Teaching and other professions opened to women, as did colleges forced to admit women students to stay open during the war. In Wisconsin, women were admitted to the state's first college, Carroll, in 1863—when regents of the University of Wisconsin were still "contemplating the admission of women," as they had been since 1851.

Far more filled vacancies in offices, and wartime shortages of workers even forced a few trades to admit women, if reluctantly. The Milwaukee printers' union—the same one which, a decade before, had forced Mathilde Fransziska Anneke's paper to fold—protested when a *Sentinel* printer hired a dozen "female compositors" in 1863. The *Sentinel* felt constrained to explain, apologetically, that the paper had received "hundreds of letters from young ladies anxious to learn type-setting, in order to earn a decent support for themselves and those dependent on them." The *Sentinel* separated women in a building apart from men. Still, the printers' union went on strike.[30] When the men were let go and the women kept on—and more hired—the *Chief* cheered from Fort Atkinson, where Emma Brown could only chuckle at the change. "We see that our brethren of the press have found women fit for such work," wrote the woman who had been putting out a paper, from writing copy to setting type, from selling ads to balancing the books, for almost fifteen years.

For women like Emma Brown, marooned in small-town Wisconsin, far from fighting on the front or Sanitary Fairs in the cities, the press was a source of information on the battlefield of woman's rights. But women knew better than to rely on the Wisconsin press alone. The *Chief*'s "exchanges" regularly included eastern women's papers, and a poignant letter to *The Sibyl* from a Whitewater woman, Louisa T. Whittier, attests to its importance as a source of moral support.

> Two years have elapsed since I reported myself to your readers, yet I still answer to the call . . . to manifest my love for freedom. I think it not alone those who enlist under the United States Government that have fighting to do. . . . While woman is by law and public opinion denied legal rights and privileges with man—shut out from the most lucrative employments,

and but half paid for what she is allowed to do, so long will "marrying for a home" be the legitimate result. . . . Women of America, it is to you that I make an appeal to . . . make yourselves worthy of a higher position in life than the darling, angel, pet, slave of any human being.[31]

Whittier also called on women to "throw off the fetters which a false public opinion has fastened upon you," symbolized by the popular fashion of constrictive corsets and pounds of petticoats. Apparently alone in Whitewater, and perhaps in Wisconsin, Whittier was an advocate of the dress-reform movement and wore the much-derided "bloomers," or tunic and "trowsers," promulgated by Amelia Jenks Bloomer, editor of another eastern women's paper, *The Lily*.

Despite Emma Brown's presence in the press, Wisconsin did not yet have a "women's paper"; the *Chief*'s joint masthead mirrored more acceptance of women in reform, but the paper appeared to be run much like the movement, with the male Brown in charge. Their noms de plume implied a relationship which was unequal if affectionate: He was "The Senior," she "The Junior." But it was Emma who bore the burden of getting Thurlow and the paper into print. While he toured the country, she set columns into type. While he pleaded the cause, she pleaded for copy. One request from Emma, sent from the Fort Atkinson office to the family farm nine miles away, elicited an exasperated reply. "Scarcely time to eat, sleep, think, much less to write," wrote Thurlow. "Why *will* you send that remorseless cry for copy? Spring planting, cattle to run out of fields, and you still call for copy! I avail myself of this opportunity of saying to you, that I will not write a word. Crustily, T. W. B." When the accompanying weekly diatribe on "demon rum" ran short, Emma slyly put Thurlow's scolding rebuke in the paper as well.

Emma's role as the *Chief*'s real editor became public only in 1865, when Thurlow's wartime pace took its toll. A last lecture tour east to his boyhood home was a "trip full of light and shade for him," she later wrote. When her brother came home bedridden, men in the movement became uneasy about the health of the *Chief*.

The *Chief*'s future was a crucial concern for the Templars at war's end. With the return of soldiers to the state, the order's rolls rebounded to more than thirteen thousand members, and lodges doubled to almost two hundred. For the *Chief*, retaining the designation of "Official Organ of the Order" was critical after wartime paper shortages and circulation declines forced a cutback to monthly publication. By 1865, the *Chief* was semimonthly but the Browns were in debt.[32] They anticipated—and desperately needed—a subscription boom.

But some men in the movement predicted the *Chief*'s imminent demise under Emma Brown. Her ability and the paper's prospects were discussed at the order's annual meeting in 1865 in Fort Atkinson. In a rare display of emotion, Emma publicly thanked "many personal friends who read the *Chief*" and defended the Browns in a ghoulish debate which only added to the distress of a woman already overwhelmed by work and worry for her beloved brother. Thurlow was in attendance but could not speak; he "mustered strength to climb the two stairways," collapsed, and was carried home to The Oaks.

For months, Emma Brown continued to cover for her brother by putting his byline on almost every page of the paper, until she had to run his obituary. In May 1866, Thurlow Weed Brown was buried in "full Grand Division regalia" and eulogized by editors from Wisconsin to New York who hailed him as "heroic." Many quoted his farewell missive, sent from The Oaks to his sister at the *Chief* office. The few sentences ended, "The battle is over. The Senior."

Emma Brown's battle was only beginning. Thurlow Weed Brown was buried amid bickering over his editorial remains by men in the movement who worried whether a woman could match his invective or even meet a deadline. While the men debated her ability to run a paper, Emma Brown got the paper out.

The era of a rabble-rousing reform press in Wisconsin seemed over in 1866, its best "agitators" gone to other states or a better world. The Reverend Ichabod Codding, called to a Baraboo pulpit, also died in 1866, while the Reverend Edward Mathews was preaching Reconstruction in the South. Sherman Miller Booth was a government publicist and press agent in Illinois, and three decades away from his return to Wisconsin. In 1897, at the age of eighty-five years, he would address the Wisconsin Editors and Publishers Association. To many an editor not even born by the end of the war, Booth proclaimed that he had never regretted the price he paid for his cause.[33]

The *Chief* survived, but under Emma Brown it would not be the same. Long the silent partner in the *Chief,* she soon found her own voice. At the same time, women nationwide "gained new authority and a new public voice in the midst of wartime devastation," writes historian Sara M. Evans, and "women in many different voices prepared to claim new liberties in a postwar world." With their campaigns in abolition and temperance, the Sanitary Commission and the Loyal League, women had exhibited "an energy and level of organization never before seen in American public life."[34]

Emma Brown and her *Chief* would give a "public voice" to other women who had gone unheard and unsung for so long, whose silence also was almost over in 1866—another year of significance for the woman's rights movement, as well as for women in Wisconsin. The woman suffrage campaign, born in 1848 in Seneca Falls, at last would be borne west.

2

Women's Crusade, Press Crusaders
Temperance and Suffrage, 1866–1874

B EFORE Thurlow Weed Brown's death in 1866, his sister's presence on the *Wisconsin Chief* was barely visible beyond the masthead, which suited the Templars—until she became sole editor and publisher. Ironically, Emma Brown never planned to be either, or even a writer; she was a typographer first and always, for forty years. Near the end of her career, with typical candor, Emma recalled her happenstance entry into the field in 1849, when she helped her brother found the *Chief:* "We volunteered to learn the mechanical part of the business, and thus save the expense of one hand, with never a thought of using scissors or pen. We set type, learning to do this work when it was so much of an innovation upon established practices as to call out press comments far and wide. . . . We have done all the work on the paper except the press work; the 'type-setting' of the approved standard." Emma's commentary on other papers always noted the quality of type. However, her critiques would become bolder and encompass far more than the set of a serif; soon, Emma Brown would judge not just the journalism but also the leadership—the men—of the movement.

In part, the enduring impact of Emma Brown was the result of her apprenticeship in the pressroom as well as the newsroom, in an era when many a male counterpart also mastered tasks from setting type to selling papers. The production side of the business had been the downfall of Emma's predecessor in Wisconsin, Mathilde Fransziska Anneke, when her paper was boycotted by male printers because she hired and trained woman typographers in 1852. A decade later, woman typographers hired by the *Milwaukee Sentinel* during the Civil War outlasted a strike by the men's union, only to be sent home upon soldiers' return. Elsewhere, woman typographers who entered the workforce in wartime also worked for less than prewar wages, and only for the duration. To forestall postwar firings, a woman journalist and typographer organized the first women's labor union in the nation in 1869 in New York City, where woman typographers composed as much as twenty percent of the field.[1]

Emma Brown was not the first woman in the Wisconsin press, but she was the first to last. She also was in the first wave nationally of "literary women,"as woman journalists were known in the nineteenth century. The first woman on a mass-circulation paper was Margaret Fuller, author of the influential *Woman in the Nineteenth Century,* who was hired in 1845 by the *New York Herald's* Horace Greeley. But he was a noted antisuffragist. Editors, not known for altruism beyond the editorial page, were not the reason for women's entry into the newsroom before other male bastions, according to historian Eleanor Flexner. Instead, the "literary field" was one of the few fields for which women could educate themselves. The "learned professions"—law, medicine, and the ministry—required licensing or schooling still closed to women, while "writing and editing involved training and discipline that was largely individual and self-acquired."

Far more women found a welcome in the reform press, where they were no neophytes to making news, than at the *New York Herald.* By 1845, when Fuller was that paper's first woman reporter, Jane Elizabeth Hitchcock already was a co-editor of the *Anti-Slavery Bugle* in Ohio. As early as 1841, L. Maria Child edited the *Anti-Slavery Standard,* a national newspaper in New York. The leading "literary woman" in the country, she already had edited a children's magazine and also was an influential author and freelance writer. And, from 1834 on, *The Advocate of Moral Reform* was edited and published entirely by women.

The earliest paper to welcome women's news may have been the *Female Advocate,* an organ of the moral reform and temperance movements which had openly solicited "communications from good writers of both sexes" since its inception in 1832 in New York City under the Reverend William Goodell. His wife and co-worker clearly had an influence on the *Advocate's* agenda; Clarissa Cady Goodell was a founding member of the Female Moral Reform Society and the local Ladies' Temperance Society. Her versatile husband also published the *Genius of Temperance Lecturer* and later edited the abolitionist *Principia.* There, he raised their younger daughter to run the office when she was only fourteen, and Lavinia Goodell would be an assistant editor for *Harper's New Monthly Magazine* before she was thirty. By then, she would follow her family to Wisconsin and turn her talent to temperance—and would turn to Emma Brown's *Wisconsin Chief.*[2]

Like Emma Brown, women were most welcome on "temperance sheets" such as *The Lily,* the first "women's paper" published and edited by women, and a favorite "exchange" in the *Chief.* Both papers began publication on the same day, New Year's Day in 1849, and both in upstate New York, only miles apart: the *Chief* in Auburn, where the Browns shared the masthead as co-publishers and co-editors from the first, and *The Lily* in Seneca Falls under the auspices of the local Ladies' Temperance Society and the editorship of Amelia Jenks Bloomer. Previously a correspondent for the *Seneca Falls Courier*—the paper which had publicized the first woman's rights convention a year before—Bloomer became publisher of *The Lily* in 1850, when her "temperance sheet" became a "suffrage paper" as well.

Similar papers soon arose across the East, and across the spectrum of women's causes from pay equity to dress reform, but always for suffrage—unlike the *Chief,* at least until 1866. And, unlike the *Chief,* none of the first "women's papers" survived to 1866.[3] But Emma Brown would endure in Wisconsin, and on her own, while new "women's papers" arose in the East, for the same reason: male dominance of reform.

From the first woman's rights convention at Seneca Falls through the Civil War, women reformers deferred to the urgency of ending slavery, with the understanding that men in reform would work for universal suffrage—for women as well as freedmen—once abolition was won. After the war, women who held hope that men would fulfill their vow helped to found the American Equal Rights Association. At the first meeting in New York City, men shared the podium with Elizabeth Cady Stanton, Susan B. Anthony, Lucretia Mott, Lucy Stone, and the Reverend Olympia Brown. One of the first woman ministers in the country, she was making her first public stand for woman suffrage. More than a decade later, Olympia Brown would be one of the first woman ministers in Wisconsin, where she would sacrifice her pulpit for the woman suffrage campaign. More than five decades later, Olympia Brown would be the only woman left of the women on the podium in 1866—the only one who lived to vote.

In 1866, the same men who sought women's support acquiesced to writing them out of the Constitution for the first time, with inclusion

of the word "male" in the Fourteenth Amendment. Even Frederick Douglass, the staunchest supporter of Stanton and of woman suffrage at Seneca
Falls, stood firm for enfranchising freedmen first. Enraged and forever
embittered, Stanton and Anthony "solemnly vowed that there should
never be another season of silence until woman had the same rights
everywhere on this green earth, as man."

Stanton, Anthony, Stone, and Olympia Brown crossed the country
from East to West against ratification of the Fourteenth Amendment
in 1867, a futile campaign which only underscored the need for women
to win suffrage on their own and in their own press. All the women
were expert on the podium, and Olympia Brown was experienced in
the pulpit; stumping New York State and the new state of Kansas, she
gave more than three hundred speeches in three months alone. But the
pulpit and podium were overpowered by the Republican party and its
press in both states. Both drives ended in defeat; in Kansas, according
to Stone's husband, Henry Blackwell, "the negroes got but a few more
votes than did the women."

By 1868, the already-bitter and divisive debate between women and
men in the movement escalated to direct confrontation between Frederick
Douglass and Olympia Brown, both officers of the American Equal
Rights Association. At the annual meeting in New York City, when
Douglass called on women to honor "the negro's hour," Brown demanded
that he explain "the difference in *principle*" between "the enfranchise-
ment of two million negro men" and "the emancipation of seventeen
million women." She resigned to help found the New England Woman
Suffrage Association, a regional organization whose first president was
Julia Ward Howe. However, unlike Brown, the author of "The Battle
Hymn of the Republic" said in acceptance that she was willing "that
the Negro shall get the ballot before me."

In 1869, after the Fourteenth Amendment became law, Stanton and
Anthony founded the more militant National Woman Suffrage Association for a federal-amendment campaign. Within months, Lucy Stone
and Henry Blackwell founded the more conservative American Woman
Suffrage Association for state-by-state campaigns. Not for the first
time—nor the last—woman suffragists were split over apparently opposing strategies to achieve the same end.

Woman suffragists were in accord on the primary tactic for influencing public opinion: the press. In 1868, Stanton and Anthony started
a suffragist journal, *The Revolution,* which folded in 1870. But Stone
and Blackwell's *Woman's Journal,* founded in 1870, would endure for

fifty years until suffrage was won. The "suffrage Bible," the "torchbearer of the cause," the *Journal* immediately attracted a substantial number of subscribers and contributors from across the country, including Lavinia Goodell. The *Woman's Journal* later would be emulated by dozens of state suffrage papers which "sprang up, and died, with great regularity" in the latter nineteenth century, according to a historian. One would "spring up" in Wisconsin under Olympia Brown, but not until she went to the West.[4] By then, Emma Brown would be at the end of her pioneering career in the press, after forty years—and after welcoming Olympia Brown, Lavinia Goodell, and other press crusaders to Wisconsin and into her columns.

In 1869, when Stanton and Anthony first toured Wisconsin, the presence of a woman publisher and editor in the state press was still a phenomenon. However, had some men in the reform movement had their way, even her solitary voice for women in Wisconsin would have been silenced years before. Emma Brown's battle for her press presaged women's larger struggle for leadership in reform—and their success. Despite her gender, she would endure to preside over the country's longest-lasting "temperance sheet." Owing to her gender, Emma Brown would be uniquely positioned to cover women's temperance crusade, a major story missed by most papers because it was women's news. When women and temperance gained coverage in the larger press at last, crusading temperance publishers and editors would become a part of the story because they were on the beat from the first—none longer, and few better, than Emma Brown.

In 1866, in the Wisconsin press, Emma Brown was unusual but no longer unknown, as she had been a decade before. In 1856, the Browns' first year in the state, when the *Daily Wisconsin* had credited the *Chief* to a husband-and-wife team, Thurlow had to explain that his "better half" was his sibling—and his equal in "the sanctum" of the *Chief* office. By 1866, press colleagues knew Emma Brown. At a memorial service for her brother at the annual meeting of the state Editors and Publishers Association, the men welcomed Emma—without irony—as a "worthy compeer in our journalistic fraternity."

But few Templars outside of Fort Atkinson knew Emma Brown or the extent of her editorial contribution to the temperance cause, and a female in the "inner sanctum" was exactly what some feared. Only months after Thurlow's death, Templar leader J. M. May of the Janesville *Western Advance* lost a first bid for the order's lucrative patronage;

in fall 1866, the annual meeting of the state Grand Lodge awarded a sentimental renewal of its sponsorship to the *Chief*. But even the grave was not beyond the grasping May, who claimed the Brown farm for the Templars in repayment of alleged debts by the deceased, an attempt to force Emma Brown to sell the *Chief* to save The Oaks.

At first, Emma Brown demurred from the fray. Her father placed "A Card"—an advertisement—in the *Chief,* defending the settlement of his son's estate and denouncing the order for allowing May "the despotic power of an autocrat." May's claim apparently was groundless, and was not mentioned again. However, in January 1867, his *Advance* received designation as the "official" organ of the order at an unsanctioned meeting in Janesville. In effect, state Templars had two official papers, a situation which suggests that if Emma Brown was no longer unknown, she still was underestimated by May and his men.

Rather than spare the order from public scrutiny, Emma Brown aired the internal fracas in the *Chief*. With pride, she ran an "'unwritten' history of 'organ grinding'" and proclaimed her paper as the order's "Organ —Unofficial." With pathos, she ran reprints and reminiscences of her late brother's work in "remembrance of one now beyond the reach of stinging taunt or treacherous friends." She also retained his name on the masthead for months, at last removing it "sadly and tearfully" to establish her sole ownership. But May only intensified his attacks on Emma as a "fighting editor"—an epithet which she took as a compliment—for rallying readers to debate which paper was the "true temperance banner in this state." The invitation violated unwritten policy of the Templars, but Emma's editorial policy argued against an increasingly "closed society" on principle and for pragmatic reasons: In "crystallizing and combining public sentiment, the more we simplify our work, the more we commend it to the masses outside of our organization."

Emma Brown's democratic way of running a paper nearly was her downfall. At the Templars' annual meeting in fall 1867, she had her defenders, "representatives from every portion of the state who came to present the claims of the *Chief*" to designation as official organ of the order, to no avail. Only afterward did they and the *Chief* discover that the order already had awarded the designation to May's *Advance*. A desperate Emma struck a deal with the order, and conceded sole control of the *Chief* to save it.

Briefly, the *Chief* bore the name of a Templar newspaperman from Milwaukee on the masthead, ahead of Emma's, and his imprint on every page. As co-publisher, A. H. Burdick made some improvements; printed in Milwaukee, the paper was larger and cleaner, with full-size pages and more modern typeface. The content was no better, but decidedly different: a "Milwaukee Department" shared the front page with temperance fiction and poetry; on inside pages, a "Base Ball" column and statistics from local leagues almost eliminated Fort Atkinson news items. Burdick returned the paper to a weekly schedule, doubled the longstanding subscription price of a dollar per year, and offered volume discounts for Templar subscribers in return for the editors' "having learned the wants and wishes" of temperance readers. The *Chief* was the "size and general style of a temperance paper they would sustain," wrote the obsequious Burdick, "now a first class journal, and coming fully up to the standard."

A month later, the masthead again listed Emma Brown as sole editor and publisher, independent of the order. She retained weekly publication but returned the paper to its previous price and to Fort Atkinson, without explanation; apparently, the Brown-and-Burdick combination was as uncomfortable in the office as in print.

From December 1867 forward, Emma put out her idea of a paper, not the Templars', and would endure two decades more without patronage and with editorial autonomy. The loss of official status was unnoticeable in print, since she continued to publish Templar news and ads for Templar regalia, and remained active in the order. She later would hold offices in local and district lodges and serve on a committee conducting a sensitive inquiry into a Madison lodge—which, of course, she reported in full. The state lodge also published its proceedings in the *Chief* and again subscribed in bulk, sometimes. At times, Templars had no choice: Emma Brown and her *Chief* would last to 1889, outlasting almost all her competitors in the temperance press in the state and, indeed, in the country.

Over time, Emma's personality emerged in the paper, if at first imperceptibly and only stylistically. Her brother had used the press as his pulpit, to preach and exhort; she relied less on invective than on information and more on news than on opinion. His editorials had been witty but verbose, replete with personal examples and pathos; hers often consisted of a single, incisive line—but Emma's sentences could sear. Her editorial commentary accompanied "exchanges" clipped from an extraordinary number of periodicals and other papers, from the *New York Herald* and *London Telegraph* to the *Deaf Mute Times* of the Wisconsin Asylum for the Deaf at Delavan. "Exchanges" replaced temperance tales, tunes, and poetry, except for her brother's, which Emma

would reprint almost weekly; decades later, correspondents still wrote
to "T. W. & E."

In the most significant change under Emma Brown, the *Chief* became
a collective effort reliant upon press correspondents. In part, their contributions helped to fill the vast space once reserved for her brother's
opinions. However, Emma also clearly enjoyed a means of communication with a world far from Fort Atkinson. Her *Chief* reflected changes
in journalism in the latter nineteenth century, as newspapers became
less partisan — or, at least, less the personal platforms of their publishers, if only for the sake of profit.[5]

Emma Brown took pride in journalistic progress and felt a professional bond with the "press fraternity," downplaying any discrimination by her "brothers of the press." When she entered the field, Emma
recalled, "both publishers and printers, with a single exception, gave
us the most kindly and fraternal greetings to their ranks." A member
of the Wisconsin Editors and Publishers Association which had welcomed her in 1866 as a "worthy compeer," Emma looked forward to
the camaraderie of "shaking hands across the inky chasm" at meetings
which occasioned her few absences from Fort Atkinson. Other members also made a point, when passing through Fort Atkinson, of visiting Emma. In the typically transient journalism of the nineteenth century, her press colleagues came to treat Emma Brown and her *Chief*
almost as a shrine, or a miracle.

Only late in her career did Emma Brown state a longing for a professional sisterhood, but it long was evident between the lines. The *Chief*
ran news of and by women, especially from early women's papers, from
the paper's first days in the East where access to women's news was easier. Yet even in small-town Wisconsin, Emma's avid monitoring of "exchanges" ensured that the *Chief* rarely missed a landmark in the woman
movement. For example, in 1868, Emma Brown gave front-page play
to a seemingly minor slight to New York woman journalists, an incident which historians credit with causing the spread of the women's club
movement which, in turn, would enlist wider support for woman suffrage, half a century later.[6]

Emma Brown's bias for women's news was even more evident in 1867,
when Susan B. Anthony and Elizabeth Cady Stanton first toured the
West to fight ratification of the Fourteenth Amendment. The tour caused
a "suffrage commotion" in Wisconsin, where "the women, both German and American, awoke to action and organized a local suffrage society at Janesville" variously called the Equal Rights Association or the

Impartial Suffrage Association, according to Dr. Laura J. Ross, a later leader of the state suffrage movement. In 1867, Ross and other suffragists were encouraged when she received the first state-level political appointment for a woman in Wisconsin, as commissioner to the World's Exposition in Paris, from Governor Lucius Fairchild—also a suffragist, but not yet openly.

In 1867, a freshman assemblyman from Rock County named John T. Dow introduced a bill for a referendum on a suffrage amendment to the state constitution—the highlight of his legislative career, which would be over before the bill died. A temperance lecturer of some renown in local reform, Dow presided at the first meeting of the new suffrage society in Janesville. But suffragists faced competition; for the same night, the Janesville Young Men's Association had secured Senator Charles Sumner of Massachusetts, a nationally renowned orator, to speak on temperance. The *Chief* balanced its coverage by according equal space to Sumner and suffrage speakers, including two ministers and a Racine farm wife. But Madison's *Wisconsin State Journal* explained—in a soon-familiar refrain—that women didn't want the ballot.

Still, in 1868, woman suffragists had reason for hope in Wisconsin. Dow's bill had passed both houses in 1867, by votes of fifty-seven to twenty-four in the assembly and nineteen to nine in the senate. But the bill required second passage in the next biennium. In the interim, suffragists planned a statewide campaign, and contacted Stanton and Anthony. "I saw your notice . . . in that banner of freedom, the Boston *Investigator*," wrote R. F. Mills of Kenosha, who forwarded "a few extracts" of favorable coverage from the Racine *Advocate* and the Milwaukee *News,* the latter "the leading Democratic paper of the State." In return, Mills requested "some pamphlets containing the best arguments for universal suffrage" and "some of your best speakers in the Wisconsin field," where "we, in this state, intend to make a determined fight next year for female suffrage." Mills was optimistic, reporting that the bill had passed "by more than two to one" in both assembly and senate. "Yet you must not suppose that our cause is so favorable as that," she cautioned. "Certainly the great car of progress is under motion, and no bigoted, conservative fogyism can long stay its progress."[7]

"Fogyism" prevailed over progress in the "Wisconsin field" in 1868, and the campaign came to a swift end. So did the political career of the brave but foolhardy Dow, who lost his bid for reelection but nobly returned to Madison to lobby for the bill. The suffrage bill and women's petitions were presented this time by another Janesville legislator, William C. Whitford, president of Milton College. But before the bill came on the floor, concurrent ratification by Congress of the federal Fourteenth Amendment made the question moot at the state level, at least in the minds of most legislators. The second reading of the suffrage bill did not survive even the assembly.

But suffragists rebounded by 1869 when Anthony and Stanton came to Wisconsin for the first statewide suffrage convention. The call came from Milwaukee, a comparative mecca for women in the professions: it was signed by Mathilde Franziska Anneke, by then a teacher at her Tochter Institute, a German girl's academy; the Reverend Augusta Chapin, pastor of a Universalist church and the first woman minister in Milwaukee; Lila Peckham, a law student; and Dr. Laura J. Ross, the first woman physician in the city—and one of the first in the country—who had been denied admission to the Milwaukee Medical Society for more than a decade. Ross soon would be the first president of the Wisconsin Woman Suffrage Association, which would survive for more than fifty years, until the Nineteenth Amendment was won.[8]

The organizational convention of the WWSA, held on February 24 and 25, 1869, drew standing-room-only crowds to Milwaukee City Hall for Stanton, Anthony, and Mary A. Livermore, past head of the Civil War Sanitary Commission and publisher of the Chicago *Agitator*. In the recollection of an editor "who as a lad strayed into the convention," he had to "flatten himself against the wall because the chairs were all occupied, the audience being made up mostly of women." Gentlemen of the press also were in attendance; the *Milwaukee Sentinel* printed proceedings, and the *Evening Wisconsin* countered suspicions that the convention drew "only that class known as strong-minded." *The Revolution* claimed that "Milwaukee papers teem with accounts . . . most of them very friendly in tone and spirit, even if opposed to the objects under consideration."[9] Even Stanton's controversial "Bible argument"—a revision of chapter and verses cited as divine sanction of women's submission—"was published in full in daily papers," she reported. Stanton fared well with Wisconsin papers, in comparison with "the twaddle of the Western press," as she called their counterparts in Chicago.

The most colorful account of the convention, the women in attendance—and, especially, the men—was Stanton's report to *The Revolution*. "The platform, besides an array of large, well-developed women, was graced with several reverend gentlemen—Messrs. Dudley, Allison, Eddy, and Fellows—all of whom maintained women's equality with eloquence and fervor," she reported. However, two "reverend gentlemen" in the hall—local ministers with the memorable surnames of Love and England—"profanely claimed the Bible on the side of tyranny." Stanton engaged in elevated debate, to the approval of "the rest of the learned D.D.'s," until England strayed from theology and Stanton stooped to the personal level.[10]

> Mr. E. is a small, thin, shadowy man, without much blood, muscle, or a very remarkable cerebral development. . . . We would advise always to avoid the branch of the argument he stumbled upon in the Milwaukee Convention—"the physical superiority of man." Unfortunately for him, the platform illustrated the opposite, and the audience manifested, ever and anon, by suppressed laughter, that they saw the contrast between the large, well-developed brains and muscles of the women who sat there, and those of the speaker. Either Madam Anneke, Mrs. Livermore, or Dr. Ross, could have taken the reverend gentleman up in her arms and run off with him.[11]

Her irreverence toward men of the cloth was hardly new to readers of *The Revolution,* but Stanton's slur on men of short stature required clarification. She intended "nothing invidious," wrote Stanton. It simply was "not politic or in good taste for a small man to come before an audience and claim physical superiority; that branch of the argument should be left for the great, burly fellows . . . who illustrate the assertion by their overpowering presence."

Stanton's presence at the Milwaukee convention, she was pleased to report, won unanimous approval of her "pet resolutions" on woman's rights, which had been voted down in Washington and Chicago. So successful was Stanton, Anthony, and Livermore's stop in Milwaukee that Madison women "heard of the great enthusiasm" and telegraphed an invitation for the trio to extend their stay in the state. Escorted by "a large delegation," they were delighted when met at the Madison depot by a onetime *New York Tribune* reporter who escorted the women to a reception. They were feted by Madison's finest, whom Stanton listed— apparently, in order of importance—as "lawyers, judges, senators, generals, editors, Republicans and Democrats," all "alike ready to break a lance for woman." One lawyer, general, and Republican, all in one, was Wisconsin Governor Lucius Fairchild, who later presided in the assembly over their impromptu address to "a splendid audience." The invitation was unexpected and the women were exhausted. "We all said the best things we could think of, with as much vim as we could command after taking all day in the [train] cars and every moment until we entered the Capitol, without even the inspiration that comes from a good cup of tea or coffee," Stanton wrote. But Madison papers praised the performance, printed in full in the *Wisconsin State Journal,* and the governor won her over when he subscribed to *The Revolution.*

Stanton's whirlwind tour ended with an education, en route to Chicago, on women's struggle for political status in the state. At Janesville, the local postmaster boarded the train on his way to Washington, D.C., where he hoped to win back by patronage his lucrative sinecure lost in a popular election to a woman, possibly the first to win political office in Wisconsin. The affronted incumbent confronted Stanton, who later pieced together the story. For his corrupt postal practices, he had been turned out at the polls in favor of an underling, Angeline King. "This was a bomb shell in the male camp," wrote Stanton, "and half a dozen men started for Washington, to show General Grant that they had, one and all, done braver deeds during the war than Angie could have done, and that their loyalty should be rewarded." However, his cagy opponent already had arrived in Washington, D.C. and "stole the march on all of them," Stanton wrote with glee. "If the people of Janesville prefer Angie, as they have shown they do by their votes, we think it would be well for the powers that be to confirm the choice of the people." But "the powers that be"—the president and her congressmen—would not intervene on behalf of the duly elected postmistress, as Stanton reported in a follow-up story. It seemed to be the end of the story. However, years later, the remarkable Angie King would have her revenge. While her opponent remained as postmaster, she would become the third woman lawyer in Wisconsin.[12]

Another setback to women's political progress in Wisconsin had occurred concurrent with the Milwaukee suffrage convention. A bill for limited "school suffrage" had been scheduled to come before legislators, but after the convention, to allow women an opportunity for lobbying. Opponents had the bill brought up on the calendar too soon, and it was defeated in the senate on the day before the suffrage meeting at the Capitol. The only progress in the biennium would be passage of a bill allowing women to run for school offices, although they could not vote for themselves—and even that law would lack enforcement for several years, except to restrict women from running for any other elective office.

An apparent victory for woman's rights came in 1869, when women first graduated from the University of Wisconsin. However, regents had endorsed coeducation in 1851, in conflict with the university charter, an oversight that legislators left uncorrected for fifteen years while women were relegated to the Female College on campus. The WWSA's Dr.

"Girls can be defrauded of their rights to a thorough education by narrow, bigoted men entrusted with a little brief authority."—Dr. Laura Ross Wolcott, a pioneering woman physician in Milwaukee and a founder and the first president of the Wisconsin Woman Suffrage Association. Photo courtesy of the State Historical Society of Wisconsin.

Laura J. Ross called the separate system one of "the petty ways in which girls can be defrauded of their rights to a thorough education by narrow, bigoted men entrusted with a little brief authority."

Ross sent an even more searing statement penned by Lila Peckham to Stanton and Anthony, which they included in the *History of Woman Suffrage*. In 1866, Peckham wrote, "it was declared that the University shall be open to female as well as male students," at least in some schools—but not for long. "At first the students recited together, but Mr. Chadbourne made it a condition of accepting the presidency that they should be separated," she wrote. The regents acceded to the man whose name, decades later, would adorn a women's dormitory—allegedly a suggestion by women students with a sense of humor as well as history. But in 1866, the result of the regents' vote already was evident in Peckham's research comparing women's and men's curricula, as described in the "catalogue"—which, even then, was filled with "facts that are confused, contradictory and obscure," as Peckham wrote.

> The [female college] course does not amount to enough to add any reputation to the college. . . . We find a long account of the A.B., A.M., P.B., S.B., S.M., L.B., Ph.D., to which the fortunate gentlemen are entitled after so much study. Lastly, the students of the female college may receive "such appropriate degrees as the regents may determine." I wonder how that solemn body deliberates as to whether a girl shall be A.B., P.B., or A.M., or whether they ever give them any degree at all. It makes little difference. With such a college course a degree means nothing, and only serves to cheapen what may be well earned by the young men of the college.[13]

In 1869, when six women completed the regular college curriculum, President Paul Ansel Chadbourne threatened for weeks to withhold their degrees until regents forced him to relent.

Among the first group of women graduates was the class valedictorian, Clara Bewick Colby of Windsor, who would become a leader in the national suffrage campaign after leaving the state in 1872. Another member of the pioneering class of '69 who did not graduate but would earn numerous honorary degrees was Dr. Ellen Sabin, also from Windsor but born in Sun Prairie, where she returned to start a teaching career which would take her to a leadership role in women's education in Wisconsin two decades later.

But as Olympia Brown wrote, "owing to prejudices it was not until 1873 that complete coeducation was established" at the state university, a decade after several private colleges in the state and three years after stockholders of Milwaukee Female College elected three women to the board of trustees. The first college for women in Wisconsin, the school was founded and endowed by eastern educator Catherine Beecher, sister of the antislavery author, who had sent Mary Mortimer to Milwaukee in 1851 as principal. A remarkable woman, Mortimer was an English immigrant, orphaned young and denied an education by her oldest brother. She began seminary at the age of twenty-one and completed a four-year course in two years, but claimed she had no sympathy for "so-called women's rights," or so she wisely said. However, her students would have an impact on women's history beyond their relatively small numbers.[14]

With few women college graduates in Wisconsin, even fewer were in professions. Of founders of the WWSA, for example, Lila Peckham died young, a "great loss to the suffrage cause." The Reverend Augusta Chapin left her pulpit in less than a year to return to Iowa. Dr. Laura J. Ross was left to run the state suffrage organization almost alone, as Mathilde Fransziska Anneke became more prominent in the national movement.[15]

Suffragists could look to the East for signs of progress, where Anneke gave the major address at the annual meeting of the American Equal Rights Association in 1869. In English and in German, she pleaded with men who had acquiesced to the Fourteenth Amendment and its inclusion of the word "male" in the Constitution: "Don't exclude us — don't exclude woman — don't exclude the whole half of the human family. . . . from the ballot-box, which is the people's holy palladium." To men who called Stanton and Anthony "imprudent" for allegedly imperiling the proposed Fifteenth Amendment to enforce freedmen's suffrage, Anneke replied, "Whether it be prudent to enfranchise woman is not the question — only whether it be right." Most of the men repudiated Stanton, their president, while woman after woman spoke in her defense. Significantly, the only woman who supported Douglass over Stanton was African-American journalist Frances Harper. According to historian Paula Giddings, Harper "suspected that the white feminists . . . were less than genuine" in their claim of support for universal rights regardless of race.

Still, with Stanton and Anthony, Anneke quit the organization and stayed in the East to represent Wisconsin at the founding in 1869 of their National Woman Suffrage Association, which would outlive them all and lead the drive to victory half a century later.[16]

In 1870, to win support for the new national organization, Stanton again went on a tour of the West, and Wisconsin. At a suffrage convention in Janesville in March, women reported much apparent progress made in organization since the Milwaukee convention of a year before. Dr. Laura Ross Wolcott, wed in the interim to Wisconsin's foremost physician, listed WWSA branches at Baraboo, Boscobel, Evansville, Fond du Lac, Richland Center, Union Grove, and Milwaukee, all represented at the "large and enthusiastic convention." Wolcott was reelected president and would hold the post for a dozen years, but by default; no statewide suffrage conventions would be held for a decade, until Stanton and Anthony returned to the state.[17]

Without assistance from "the National," the WWSA was not self-sustaining, and suffragists held little hope for the state. Instead, by 1873, in Wisconsin and across the country, they would organize for woman's rights again, but under the guise of another cause: women's next campaign would be for temperance. But the woman suffrage movement would benefit more in the long run, at least in Wisconsin, where women would learn how to take the law in their own hands—all the laws won so hard, and enforced so little.

Most in the press missed omens of the coming women's temperance crusade, and rarely would crusaders encounter a press as hostile as in Wisconsin. The sorry record was redeemed only by Emma Brown and her *Chief*. Few papers were as prescient in anticipating the story because few editors were as astute as Emma Brown in welcoming "women's news." From the "exchanges" she read, from the correspondence she ran, and from her own run-ins with men in the movement, Emma knew that women made news. Her cultivation of woman correspondents gave the *Chief* the "inside story" of the crusade. More important, access to the *Chief* gave women power—the power of the press.

But well before Emma Brown brought the *Chief* to Wisconsin, women's frustration with unenforceable laws was evident. In 1854 at Baraboo, battering of wives by drunken husbands enraged townswomen. Storming a saloon and a beer seller's home, spilling barrels and bottles onto the streets, the women withstood a gun-toting saloon keeper and a mob of men. The women were arrested and convicted, but won their case on appeal. A similar case occurred in 1857 in Richland Center, where "from the very beginning, the temperance question was a vital civic concern," according to an early account of the town. The "advent of 'John Barleycorn'" in the village, in the form of both a "Bowling Saloon" and a "rum shop," led the Ladies' Temperance Society to lead the way in "mobilizing public opinion," writes historian Twylah Kepler. Women enlisted a new organization, the local Templar lodge, to ensure that "the saloon's stock was seized and poured onto the ground" and "the rum-shop 'spirits' were . . . emptied into Pine River"—although the women did not intend the "discharge of firearms, and tense feelings" that followed. But they learned a more valuable lesson. Because "the liquor question and local politics lent impetus to almost every election, making the women keenly aware of their inability to wield any power at the ballot box," Kepler suggests that many townswomen were "temperance workers prior to becoming suffragists."

Wisconsin women were not alone in increasing awareness of their powerless status. In 1857, the *Chief* also applauded women in Ohio who "demolished a rumseller under strong provocation" and were arrested for inciting riot but won dismissal of charges, to the "vociferous cheering of a crowd" in the Sandusky courtroom. Similar incidents were increasing and widespread across the country, according to historian Jack S. Blocker, Jr. He suggests that the "growing willingness of temperance women in the late 1850s to organize separately from men suggests that something like the Women's Crusade might have developed much earlier than it did, had not war intervened." However, after the Civil War, more isolated uprisings were reported in the *Chief*.

After the war, nowhere did women have more cause for provocation than in Wisconsin, where intemperance was on the rise. While per capita alcohol consumption stabilized across the country, drinking soared by thirty percent in Wisconsin because of beer. Hundreds of breweries arose across the state; brewing was Milwaukee's leading industry but also pervaded rural areas, long the stronghold of temperance, because a staple of the brewing process—hops—became a lucrative commodity, if briefly.[18] Many farmers who formerly were temperance men had yielded their fields, and the "hops question" raged in the *Chief*. As a Templar wrote, "some who stood in the front rank when the Order was in its glory, have laid aside their armor and are raising hops quite extensively."

At the same time, women's frustration with the Templars also increased. The order did not maintain the postwar momentum in membership owing to lack of leadership; no resident organizer replaced Thurlow Weed Brown, and state rolls dropped steadily from thirteen thousand in 1865 to eight thousand in 1870. That year, at a lackluster lodge meeting in the *Chief*'s own Jefferson County, women seized control. A *Chief* report from one of the "earnest co-workers" on the incident was innocuous until the end, which took an ominous turn: "Our sisters, silent heretofore, are . . . now determined to move heaven and earth if need be to come off victors in the strife. They are preparing for vigorous action."

But Emma Brown was not the organizer her brother had been, the crucial combination of what she called an "organ-grinder" and "touring agitator" which women in Wisconsin needed. Lacking the temperament for the lecture circuit—and the time—Emma Brown stayed put because she had a paper to put out. Instead, she and her *Chief* would serve as a means of communication for another press crusader, and for the Wisconsin women's temperance crusade.

Lavinia Goodell of Janesville not only was an experienced journalist but also had the mobility and organizational ability which Emma Brown lacked—and alone of women in Wisconsin, Lavinia knew the law. By 1871, at thirty-one, she had left a promising career at *Harper's Magazine* in the East to care for her parents in Wisconsin. She continued as a "press correspondent" for the national *Woman's Journal* but, in Janesville, she could find only freelance work for the *Gazette.* To "occupy her mind," Lavinia learned law on her own—the only way for a woman to learn law in Wisconsin. She "wanted to go into a law office, like any other student." However, as she wrote to her sister, "human nature in these regions is not educated up to that." Local lawyers "suffering for the want of students to help . . . would not let me in, because I was a woman," and "would sooner hire shiftless incompetent boys . . . than take my services gratis, when they know how steady I am and anxious to learn." Lavinia learned to "enjoy Blackstone and Kent even more than anticipated" but was "lonesome having no one to talk them over with."

Lavinia's father deemed her "cut out for a lawyer," but her mother disapproved, as did Janesville. "It is quite an innovation for me to go into court in this small, conservative, gossipy town, and requires some moral courage. But I think of the primitive Christians, who had to fight with wild beasts in the amphitheatres, or live in the catacombs, or be beheaded, or buried alive, and conclude I can stand it," she wrote. Lavinia's solution was to act the "lady" as well as the lawyer. "The community looks at me a little doubtfully as not knowing what kind of a woman I may be, but as [I] develop no other alarming eccentricity than a taste for legal studies, wear fashionable clothes, attend an orthodox church, have a class in the Sunday school, attend the benevolent society, and make cake and preserves like other women, I am tolerated." To the list of her activities, Lavinia later added "keeping house, making my own clothes," and serving as "a member of the Woman's Board" and "Secretary of the Temperance Union."[19]

"There are so many timid ladies who are afraid they shall do something 'unwomanly.' . . . It is the women who are untrammeled by
husbands who must do [the work]."—Lavinia Goodell of Janesville,
a leader of women's crusades for temperance and prison reform, and
later the first woman admitted to the State Bar of Wisconsin. Photo
courtesy of the Berea College Archives.

Lavinia Goodell enlisted in the movement at a fortuitous time in
Wisconsin, or so it seemed at the time. The Republican party needed
to woo back the temperance electorate abandoned almost fifteen years
before for "slavery—and its spoils," as the *Chief* had put it. Ever since,
the German vote had helped the Grand Old Party hold the "spoils," the
governorship and legislature, which dutifully voted down annual prohibition petitions. However, in 1871, the gubernatorial election had gone
to Cadwallader Washburn. Called out of retirement from an exemplary
career in both houses of Congress where he had served both reform and
the Republican party, Washburn was a rarity in Wisconsin as a Republican who put principle above politics. In one of his first acts in office,

he recommended passage of an annually tabled temperance bill. Germans turned to a Liberal Republican party, panicking lawmakers in the Grand Old Party who suddenly passed the Graham Law. Named for its Templar sponsor, the statute resurrected earlier temperance laws, with similarly disastrous repercussions for reform.

The Graham Law was neither enforceable nor enforced, and backfired when Milwaukee brewers organized. In Madison, an acting mayor ordered enforcement of a long-ignored Sunday-closing law in every saloon in the city. Germans organized in protest, a jury acquitted the violators, and the mayor hurried home to send his ambitious substitute back to oblivion. In Milwaukee, predictably, the mayor led defiance of the law despite his Republican party affiliation; Harrison Ludington had won in a Democratic stronghold by winning over the German vote which he had no wish to lose. He did lose a test case but defied the court and became a local hero—especially with Milwaukee brewers Valentin Blatz, Joseph Schlitz, and others who would make him Wisconsin's governor. First, they founded and funded the Wisconsin Association for the Protection of Personal Liberty to campaign for repeal of the Graham Law.[20]

Compliance with the law was low even in rural areas such as the *Chief*'s own Jefferson County. In 1872, temperance women sued a saloon keeper for flouting the law and won the first round, only to lose on appeal. Women continued to campaign against other saloons but closed none, owing to repeated delays in the courts. An angry Emma Brown began her own press campaign against a legal system closed to women in Jefferson County, where Lavinia Goodell would win her first court case for temperance women—in 1874. In 1873, she still was reading the law to ready herself for admission to the bar in Rock County, but Lavinia Goodell also was reading the *Chief*.

Emma Brown would be the conduit and Lavinia Goodell would lead the way, but the catalyst for the Wisconsin temperance crusade came in 1873 from men in the movement who would not let a bad law alone. To strengthen the Graham Law, already widely defied, Templar legislators unwisely added an amendment usurping municipal home rule. By fall, the Graham Law debacle would bring down Governor Washburn— the hope of the movement, he would leave Wisconsin disillusioned and disgraced—and would bring the Democratic party into power for the first time in more than a decade, and the only time for two decades more. But in the summer of 1873, the Graham Law debacle brought only a small-town backlash across the state, by local officials determined to retaliate against the state.[21]

In Janesville in July 1873, councilmen voted to grant more tavern licenses by unanimous vote—including two men voted in on a "temperance slate" who reneged on campaign promises. Women turned to the town's temperance men, but they were "too busy" or "too timorous or too apprehensive of detriment . . . to interfere in a dubious contest," as the Reverend Goodell reported to the *Chief*. But the "ladies lacked not courage, resolution or perseverance" and "felt impelled" to organize, he wrote; as a result, his daughter, too, was too busy organizing temperance women to relay their news to Emma Brown. Lavinia had recruited her father to forward her "considerable reporting" in the local *Gazette*, and the retired reform editor could not resist adding his own information and insights to her accounts of the Janesville temperance women's campaign.

The campaign initially combined publicity and press agentry for immediate impact. Lavinia and a cohort called a Saturday teatime "parlor consultation" at which women set a "Ladies' Mass Meeting" to be held the next Tuesday, and delegated duties. A petition to the town council, already written, was handed to a woman who went off in her waiting carriage to secure signatures of "highly respectable ladies in different parts of the city" and also arranged free use of the local opera house. Another woman "busily engaged in writing notices . . . with names of [petition] signers appended" as they came in, to be read from pulpits on Sunday and to run in the *Gazette* on Monday with an "advance"—a news release—on the mass meeing. Copy also went to printers for handbills to be distributed on Monday, deliberately coinciding with press publicity.

Success was ensured when two hundred townswomen turned out for the first meeting. After prayer and Scripture reading, they elected officers; Lavinia Goodell, apparently pleading law studies, agreed to serve as vice president, while the top post went to co-worker Dorcas Amanda Hadley Beale. The members adopted resolutions, already drafted, which called for the protest already planned. Goodell gave lessons on "legal aspects" of drafting a constitution, bylaws, and petitions and "some practical advice" on law pertaining to nonviolent direct action.

The next night, only four days after their first planning session, Lavinia Goodell led thirty women "in procession" down Janesville streets to the city hall to present their petition in council chambers filled with waiting women. As Lavinia reported in the *Gazette*, "the visit of the delegation and their petition gave rise to varied remarks" by the men. The petition included 1,250 signatures; only 42 townswomen had refused to sign. However, officials went ahead with licensing of three new taverns.[22] "If those 1250 names represented 1250 ballots," Lavinia wrote privately to her sister, "those licenses would not have been granted." But women took solace in a lesser victory. Returning to rally where the march began, women persuaded the hotelier to tear up his tavern license. Emboldened, women began "talk of establishing a temperance coffee house, to draw off customers from the saloons," she wrote.

Janesville women moved swiftly to a more "permanent organization," the Ladies' Temperance Union, to promote "a healthy public sentiment." At a second mass meeting, a week after the first, leaders reported to an overflow crowd that all applicants for licenses had withdrawn. The women also withdrew from public view, wisely; despite the overwhelming response, they had met widespread resistance even among their own gender. As Lavinia Goodell confided to her sister, "there are so many timid ladies who are afraid they shall do something 'unwomanly' that I fear they will never do anything womanly, and there are many who would join in the work gladly but their husbands hold them back. It is the women who are untrammeled by husbands"—women like herself and Dorcas Hadley Beale, a widow—"who must do this thing."[23]

The Janesville crusade moved forward more cautiously, with "untrammeled women" like Lavinia Goodell instructing others in organizational skills to instill self-confidence. Putting off more mass meetings until "advisable," women met weekly for training from organizers of the first petition drive. Sessions included reports of "amusing and instructive as well as some affecting incidents," followed by classes in public speaking and "literary exercises," a euphemism for writing for the press. Once trained, women again went public. Regular reports to the *Gazette* and *Chief* described more mass meetings and more "affecting incidents," as when liquor dealers yielded their licenses, publicly, to women's applause.

By then, with word in the *Gazette* and *Chief* that women were organizing—and how they did so—the temperance crusade had spread swiftly across Wisconsin. Early in 1874, the *Chief* reported that uprisings were under way in more than a dozen towns including Fond du Lac, Appleton, Ripon, Whitewater, and—of course—the *Chief*'s own Fort Atkinson. The collaboration of Emma Brown and the Goodells had wrought the result for which Lavinia's proud father had hoped. Women statewide had a "specimen of decision and action" that saw "prompt imitation by many more . . . the more and the sooner the better."

There would be many more, and soon; the Janesville uprising was a harbinger of the women's temperance crusade to come across the country—and possibly was a causal factor in similar incidents that would erupt in the East before the year was out. The later crusade would be better served by history; neither Lavinia Goodell nor Emma Brown— nor even the role of the reform press—received credit in accounts by crusaders at the time, or historians since. Crusaders, like historians, tended to rely primarily on eastern urban papers, where women's news would win coverage at last.

But word of the Wisconsin crusade would reach at least some "would-be crusaders" across the country because Janesville leader Lavinia Goodell also was a regular contributor to the *Woman's Journal*. With an apology for having been "too busy to jot down" her work for "many months" until August, she sent an account of "new fields for womanly activity" that had lain fallow for too long.

Within a month of the Janesville women's first march, but more than six months before the first repercussions in the East, the report on the Wisconsin crusade ran in the *Woman's Journal*. In a letter headlined "Women Waking Up in Wisconsin," Goodell wrote of woman speakers on the western lecture circuit in the previous spring who had planted the "seed" of suffrage and temperance fervor among "many of the 'first' ladies of Janesville." Those who had held "strong prejudice" against "the principle that Woman's sphere may extend to the platform, and that she may labor for the State as well as for the family," soon found themselves "converted to . . . faith in the propriety of Woman's preaching." They also were the first in line in the "powerful revival which took place" when, as Goodell wrote, "several things occurred within a few months . . . [that] served to broaden and deepen thought on the subject of Woman's duties, and her relation to the community."

For *Woman's Journal* readers, Goodell reported on the events of July in Janesville "as this town is doubtless a fair sample of many others throughout the Union" where temperance women and city fathers were in "irrepressible conflict." As to "the 'unwomanliness' of public speaking, that bulwark of ancient prejudice is swept away," wrote a gleeful Goodell, although "license aldermen were of course intensely disgusted by such 'unwomanly' conduct" as mass meetings and "marches in procession through the principal business street."

Again, as in the *Gazette* and *Chief,* Goodell gave step-by-step instruction in the strategies and tactics of a crusade, culminating in the critical work of creating a "permanent women's organization." But the hardest work may have been overcoming what modern-day theorists call "cognitive dissonance," as the "first ladies" of the town found themselves in conflict with concepts of "women's place."

> The next step in progress was taken . . . in the shape of a movement of the ladies of Janesville themselves—yes, even the most dignified and conservative among them. . . . are quite enthusiastic in the new movement, and intend to continue and extend their influence by permanent organization labor. Some of the most conservative among them are a little anxious about their "womanliness," but they are so much interested in the work that I think they will rather readjust their ideas on the question of "womanliness" than give it up.[24]

In closing, Goodell issued a fateful call-to-arms for *Woman's Journal* readers: "So we are marching on."

At the end of 1873, the East erupted in marches, mass meetings, and other tactics that were eerily similar to those in earlier uprisings in Wisconsin—and for the same reason as in Wisconsin: women's frustration with lack of enforcement of temperance laws. Unlike incidents in the 1850s and 1860s, the 1873–74 crusade was consciously nonviolent and attracted legions to the cause. By the autumn of 1874, as many as 142,000 women would conduct crusades in more than nine hundred communities in thirty-one states, including at least thirty crusades in Wisconsin. Crusade activity in Wisconsin would be among the highest in the country, following only far more populated states, in what historian Jack S. Blocker, Jr., calls "the first women's mass movement in the country."

Across the country, as in Wisconsin, women turned to the press as a means of communicating strategies and tactics of their crusade. In the eastern press, first reports came from crusaders' correspondence which ran verbatim, as had Lavinia Goodell's in the *Gazette, Chief* and *Woman's Journal*. Similarly, "local newspapers in first crusade towns spread word" in the East through "exchanges and out-of-town subscribers," according to Blocker. Historian Ruth Bordin suggests that editors could not resist the story because its "spontaneity, its color, and its female participation and leadership, was excellent copy," which provided "sources of information and encouragement" to "would-be crusaders."[25]

However, as with Emma Brown and Lavinia Goodell, the larger crusade was legalistic, logical, and hardly spontaneous; instead, it was a calculated campaign by women who encouraged the press, serving as sources and providing stories. In Adrian, Michigan, women published a guidebook which included instruction on use of the press, and distributed a thousand copies of a call for a national day of prayer. From women in Hillsboro, Ohio, churches in five hundred towns received a "crusade kit" with copies of pledges, a call to action, an appeal to liquor sellers and a petition to the Ohio legislature, and a "press circular" on origins and progress of the campaign.

In the East, crusaders' correspondence soon persuaded major dailies and even international papers to send their own staff to cover the story, sometimes to amusing result. In Osborn, Ohio, a horde of reporters from the *New York Tribune,* Cincinnati's *Gazette, Enquirer* and *Commercial,* and the Sandusky *Register* descended on the tiny hamlet in a single day. From Ohio, where most uprisings included hymn-singing "street processions" on saloons,[26] a *London Herald* writer expressed patronizing dismay at the impropriety of "this odd fashion of seeking to secure sobriety" in America. He regaled his readers—and those of the *Chief*—with the "novel scheme of the women of Southern Ohio," whose "curious means and appliances" included "'picketing,' private inquiries, and public prayer."

The puzzlement and provincialism of the eastern press amused Emma Brown, whose "Crusade Roundups" reveal a press long inattentive to women and the West—which to New Yorkers apparently started at the Ohio state line. One reporter from New York, no longer the center of reform, went for a closer look because in "the East, we only catch echoes of the great commotion." A baffled colleague predicted in the *New York Herald* that "something will come of this immense moral excitement in the West, surely," but admitted, with unintentional candor, "exactly what, no man as yet can tell." As historian Jack Blocker, Jr., suggests, even papers "closed to the temperance cause" had "made an essential contribution to the spread of the crusade," if unwittingly—and, if they reported on it at all.

If readers had relied only on the men of the Milwaukee press, word would have spread slowly to Wisconsin. The *Christian Statesman* "regularly reported the skirmishes" of the state's women, according to a historian. However, the city's largest-circulation paper, the *Daily Milwaukee News,* first told of the eastern crusade a full month after other major papers in the Midwest. Even then, the *News* ran only episodic, unfavorable reports and represented crusaders as religious fanatics or criminals, as in its coverage of the crusade in Illinois. The most violent incident in the country erupted in Chicago when a peaceful "street procession" of sixteen thousand women withstood thousands of men, and mass arrests were made. Just a day's train ride away, Milwaukee's

News could not ignore the story but did editorialize against the crusade—and anyone who might attempt similar "street marches" in Milwaukee. Women heeded the warning, according to Blocker's analysis, because "a strong liquor industry and a hostile press" combined to make "militant tactics . . . ineffective or even counterproductive" in Wisconsin, where no incidents on the order of the one in disorderly Chicago would be tolerated—or even attempted.[27]

Nowhere were women and brewers in "sharp war" more than in Wisconsin, according to the *Chief*, and nowhere were the "liquor interests" as well organized. Emma Brown denounced Chicago police for arresting only women, not the men in the "howling whisky mob" that "assailed women with jeering and insulting language." But the *Chief* primarily, correctly, blamed the "liquor interests" for literally feeding the mob frenzy. Emma long had accused front groups and "friends in the press" alike of being in the brewers' pay, and put her own perspective on publicity from their Personal Liberty Association. For example, when the *Daily Wisconsin* applauded the contribution of liquor dealers and tobacconists to Milwaukee's wholesale trade, $10 million of the $50 million total in 1873, the *Chief* was appalled and called for development of less devastating local industry, a decidedly unpopular stand. Among her "exchanges," Emma Brown found the numerous newsletters and other publications published by brewers' groups, and excerpted damaging quotes from members and politicians who pandered to them. But Emma battled alone in the state press and, duly warned, Wisconsin women rarely took to the streets and stressed less strident activity.

Still, the militancy and religiosity of eastern campaigns made for the most colorful coverage, as is evident in a reporter's account reprinted in the *Chief*.

> First reports gave rise to a suspicion that the religious exercises were somewhat of a ruse or pretense. . . . But it is not a brazen irruption of "women's rights" agitators prostituting singing and prayer to undevout uses . . . not technical "reformers" but simply the female members of our Christian churches. The atmosphere is that of a religious revival. . . . When Christian women go from a prayer meeting in the very spirit of Jesus, and tearfully entreat men not to ruin themselves and others, and then kneel in the very barrooms to pray for their salvation, and do this day after day . . . the hard hearts yield, and women and Christ conquer.[28]

Repudiating such effusive and revivalist readings of the crusade, Emma Brown lashed out at "the men who legislate and make powerful an infamous traffic and then expect the women to pray it down" through moral suasion rather than political action.

Pious rituals reassured many gentlemen of the press, but not all men of the cloth. As the *New York Herald* noted, "the movement does not run in any regular church groove, and is not the product of any single denomination," but was "bigger than all the ministers of the land." In Cincinnati, where Catholicism was the single largest denomination, the archbishop's denunciation of the "excess of the lady league" led a more receptive minister to respond that clergymen, politicians and legislators alike were "worthless" to women "working in the only way that Providence has left open to them. . . . Because the men of America have failed to do their duty, the whole business has thus been left to God and the women."

In Wisconsin, women like Emma Brown and Lavinia Goodell called for more than a moralistic crusade. They contradicted the accepted wisdom of the press then, and historians since, that the temperance movement drew its members and "moral code" from organized religion. Goodell, for example, knew churchgoing would be good for business but would resist formal affiliation with a faith until fatally ill. Brown was a lifelong, admitted agnostic whose preference was for military metaphors, although hardly those of a holy war: crusaders were "'camped on the field of battle,' 'calling the roll anew,'" according to the *Chief*. "Women have enlisted for life, and . . . there is no disposition to give up the fight. Our good brothers may as well step into their places and do their share of the work."

Both Brown and Goodell called for a far more politicized women's crusade, for woman suffrage. Brown was subtle by comparison, stating that "whether the good accomplished will prove permanent . . . remains to be seen. Our good brothers—with the legal power to crush the traffic—have failed by voice and action, and now seem more than willing to have a hard job taken off their hands, while women have not the same advantage." But Goodell was more forthright, in private and in public. To her sister, she wrote that the crusade was women's only resort because "we have not the influence a ballot would give us." To the *Woman's Journal*, Goodell wrote that "conservatism" constrained women in Wisconsin, where "to affirm one's faith in Woman Suffrage is about as much as one's social position is worth, and for a woman actually to declare that she desires to go to the polls and vote, produces an effect not unlike that which might be produced should she express a desire to commit burglary or arson."[29]

Still, Wisconsin women other than Brown and Goodell also were willing to risk societal ostracism for the sake of winning suffrage. Dr. Laura Ross Wolcott wrote the *Woman's Journal* that she was "intensely interested in the speedy enfranchisement of women" because "we have so many abuses of long standing that demand immediate attention." She called on "every friend of the Movement, man or woman," who had "begged, prayed, entreated, and petitioned" to plead no longer. "Let us form 'Woman Suffrage Political Clubs' all over the country, to resist taxation without representation," she wrote. "Let us treat every husband, brother, son or friend as we would an entire stranger, if he oppose us"—and even "if he does not use his best endeavors to help us."

Women's temperance unions, leagues, and bands went forward across Wisconsin with a combination of political action and press crusading. Appleton crusaders reported to the *Chief* that they had closed half of the saloons in the city and to the *Woman's Journal* that "our city fathers granted license but our city mothers are determined to spoil the saloon-keepers' business by getting their customers to sign the total abstinence pledge, and by some other ingenious modes that women know so well how to invent." Their leader in Appleton was Susan J. Swift Steele, spouse of Lawrence College's president. The author of the state's chapter in the *History of the Women's Temperance Crusade,* she also reported on the results of women's ingenuity elsewhere in Wisconsin. In Ripon, she wrote, women created coffeehouses and reading rooms, confronted dealers and druggists with a petition signed by nearly six hundred residents, and organized a boycott of dealers' businesses.

Some women were more direct. Julia Hosford Merrill, a member of the Ripon College faculty and president of the local Woman's Temperance League, "stepped into the untried waters" of saloons, while less courageous women watched in "solemn awe." Soon, Steele wrote, "a rumor that the ladies were going to make rounds was sufficient to empty every saloon in the city," as "women who had never even tried to speak . . . outside of their own homes were moving rough men to tears with words of tender eloquence." Steele also quoted an unnamed "Milwaukie paper" which described a Ripon intersection in chaos: "men of low desires" were "reduced to the state of teachable children" on one corner, while "excited gentlemen" met on another to pledge more than a thousand dollars "to protect and defend the sisters" and "devise ways of baffling the traffic at the polls."

Ripon women's first foray into political action even made a martyr of one unfortunate male voter. On election day in April 1874, wrote

Steele, crusaders were "quietly visiting voters and circulating tickets" until encounters with a "saloonist and his satellite" escalated to "warm combat." Women vied for the vote of an "old man, sick, poor, and intemperate," who had intended to sit out the election, but his room became a battleground as crusaders and saloon keepers debated and departed, each returning with a carriage to transport him to the polls. The women's tenacity won out, and wore him out. They delivered the "poor man too weak to ascend the stairs" to the polls and had the ballot box carried down. But voting was his "last work" before grateful "crusaders cared for his comfort a few weeks, then followed him to his burial." Worse, he had voted in vain. The temperance ticket lost in Ripon, where "whiskey was jubilant."[30]

Despite defeats at the polls, Steele was encouraged by "the tone of the press," at least the small-town press where crusaders' accounts still ran verbatim. For example, a correspondent reported to the Fond du Lac *Commonwealth* on a Women's Temperance Band which first met in March. By the summer, women had held ten public meetings, secured a thousand pledges, and hired touring lecturers — and townswomen "who heretofore had taken no part in public meetings" also "developed into impressive and effective public speakers." The *Commonwealth* expected that "the experience will be of great value to them in the prosecution of their work."

Women could "prosecute" — and win — by the summer of 1874 because Lavinia Goodell became the first woman in Wisconsin to be admitted to the bar — and the first candidate for the Rock County bar who had to argue for her own admission. However, her examiners were courteous and her fellow candidate "very cordial and gallant"; he was Joel B. Dow, a past publisher and editor of the Beloit *Journal* and son of the sponsor of the ill-fated suffrage bill seven years before. Goodell also was welcomed by "most of the prominent lawyers" and the press; the *Milwaukee Sentinel* praised her "pleasing and modest address and sufficient intellectual vigor." In jest, she wrote to her sister of the "danger of becoming intoxicated with success." But the new member of the bar was in no danger of succumbing to the attention; she was intent upon doing well "for the sake of *other women* as well as my own."

Only collection work came Goodell's way until women hired her to prosecute two dealers in Fort Atkinson where, the crusaders claimed, the district attorney was a "liquor man." As Goodell wrote, they could not "get any lawyer who had courage enough" to take the cases and thought "perhaps the *lady lawyer* might have!"[31]

Goodell won both of her first cases and, on appeal, won the first again despite a desperate subterfuge by the defense attorney. He sent word that the case was rescheduled, causing Goodell to almost miss her train. However, she saw through the ruse, met her clients in time, and planned her revenge. Women "laid their plans so quietly and carried them out so effectually," reported the *Chief,* "that the first inkling the dealers had" of the failure to forestall her "was the official call for their appearance in court." Goodell returned "on the evening freight train covered with glory," but the second appeal went against her clients. Still, the dealer "was so discouraged that he gave up his business," she wrote, so "it was a moral victory after all." More victories awaited her: a Janesville judge commended the "lady lawyer" on behalf of the local bar, the *Chief* reported that Fort Atkinson women "were much pleased with her tact and ability in managing the suits," and women of her hometown hired Goodell to prosecute a Janesville dealer, a case which carried her through the summer.

Goodell did become demoralized days later, discovering that women were no better than men about payment of bills. The news that the Fort Atkinson clients wrote "grudgingly of her fees" left Lavinia Goodell "quite disheartened" until she shared her lament with another Janesville lawyer. He "was quite amused" at her naiveté, but she "felt better" for his lesson about a side of law practice which had been omitted from her "Blackstone and Kent."[32]

Emma Brown offered a more encouraging report on the women of Fort Atkinson, who entered politics to the extent that they could. Fort Atkinson women held half of local Templar offices—the maximum allowed—and had organized a Ladies' Temperance League and a Temperance and Literary Society. Both set aside weekly "study meetings" as election day neared, and "districted" the town to ensure that "every voter was personally asked to give his influence and vote for temperance. During the canvass, large mass meetings were held on Sunday evenings, and a number of our women added to the interest of these gatherings by talks well timed." On election day, "a delegation of women was at the polls . . . closing up their work bravely and well." The temperance ticket lost, but "the sisters" were undaunted, continuing to "participate as efficient co-workers in the year's campaign which opened when polls closed," according to the perennial corresponding secretary of the local Templar lodge and now the Ladies' League: Emma Brown.

Women's press crusade still was not welcome among temperance men. As the crusade summer closed, state Templars met in Fort Atkinson and passed a resolution to "hail with joy the movement among the women of our land in behalf of our cause, seeing as we do the effect of their prayers." However, lest "the sisters" miss the implicit disapproval of political action, the Grand Lodge passed another resolution explicitly warning them that the "most important and pressing work" was to "educate the people," not to secure laws — for temperance or woman suffrage — ahead of "public sentiment."

The Templars were too late. In 1874, three-fourths of temperance tracts, pamphlets, and other publications were written by women, and most were published by women's organizations. As one woman wrote, in the combination of prayer and pragmatism which came to characterize the crusade, "The Lord giveth the word . . . but the women that publish the tidings are a great host." Yet even after 1874, another wrote, many men "declared they *would not take, or read, a paper published or edited by a woman!*"[33]

However, readers of the only paper published and edited by a woman in Wisconsin would stay ahead of the story. Most papers were prone to "wilful and flagrant misrepresentation of the facts," according to the *National Temperance Advocate,* and many misread the lessening of women's activity at summer's end as the end of their temperance crusade. But readers of the *Chief* knew better.

In July 1874, a year after the Janesville uprising and well before the last crusade in Wisconsin, Emma Brown reported "talk" among women in Watertown of a call for a Women's State Temperance Convention to be held in the fall. The call signaled the end of scattered local campaigns and the start of more permanent organization statewide — the next stage of women's crusade, in the press and into the "public sphere."

3

Women's Alliances, Press Allies
Temperance and Suffrage, 1874–1882

CRUSADERS from across the state came to Milwaukee in October 1874 to organize the Wisconsin Women's Temperance Alliance, at the same time that their counterparts organized elsewhere. Temperance women everywhere recognized that their "true grass-roots movement" could not continue in "size and intensity unprecedented with no planning, minimal coordination and no central control," according to historian Jack S. Blocker, Jr. Centralization offered women the means of internal communication which would be less possible in the press without the press agentry—from street processions to poll watching—which guaranteed publicity for the crusade.[1]

The organizational meeting of the Women's Alliance, like the crusade, opened with prayer but moved quickly to political action. Among the speakers was Janesville crusade leader Lavinia Goodell, presenting a paper entitled "What Shall We Ask of Our Legislature?" The *Milwaukee Sentinel* called her address "very able," although "very long and severe on liquor and liquor dealers." Before long, Lavinia Goodell would become the bane of liquor dealers in courtrooms across Wisconsin, but she would not be a leader in the Alliance. Her next crusade, once again with widespread publicity, would be for admission to the Wisconsin bar.

The full proceedings of the Women's Alliance were reported in the *Wisconsin Chief*, which continued to serve women as a means of internal communication. With the Alliance, women had an organization of their own, but they would not need an organ of their own for years, because women in Wisconsin had Emma Brown. After the crusade, as before, the *Chief* publicized their work and was rewarded with "exclusives," if by default, because Emma Brown remained the state's lone woman editor and publisher for a decade after the crusade.

But the rise of the Alliance and of Lavinia Goodell would be slow, steady, and almost unseen in Wisconsin, except in the *Chief,* because the ongoing crusades of a few women were not newsworthy until far more women turned to the Alliance as an organization of their own, only later in the decade and only as a last resort. In the beginning, the crusade brought record numbers of women, and men, into more traditional temperance organizations. Indeed, in the postcrusade fervor, many temperance men joined any and all organizations, including the new Prohibition party.

Women, of course, were not welcome in politics, but some crusaders participated to the point of getting men to go to the polls. The *Chief* cheered women's work in town after town which elected "temperance tickets" and "went no-license" after 1874, from Shawano to Lake Mills. In Richland Center, a Ladies' Temperance League was "headed by the wife of the editor and backed by almost *every* lady in the place," according to the local *Republican and Observer,* which published an anti-licensing petition with signatures of 175 women that was submitted by the Ladies' League to village trustees. Closer to home for the *Chief,* the Whitewater women's league worked with the local *Register* to elect a "dry" village president. "There were before the election some eleven or twelve saloons . . . serving something besides Kalckoff Bitters or Chicago Pop," he proclaimed to a mass temperance meeting, and also cited less anecdotal evidence of success from a local railroad agent who reported that liquor shipments were "not one hundredth part" of those of the year before. The *Chief* applauded the political action by "the people of Whitewater who demonstrated that temperance voting is a good element to add to 'moral suasion.'"

Women also attempted legal action, and employed Lavinia Goodell, until the judicial process tried their patience. In Whitewater, the women's league launched a campaign to close saloons, with popular support from free advertisements in the *Register* to free use of the local grange hall where they met to plan monitoring of local liquor dealers' compliance with the law. When they served citations on four dealers, the defense subpoenaed two "leading women of the town" and the league to appear in court. The dealers' "petty spite and malignant purpose," as Emma Brown put it, only rallied the public. The women appeared in court with "about forty ladies and gentlemen representing the very best social and business elements" and with the formidable Lavinia Goodell as their lawyer. Goodell reduced the defense to "a most pitiful fiasco" and the dealers capitulated, vowing to "discontinue the business entirely." But Brown's joy was muted a month later when one dealer simply moved his saloon to the *Chief*'s hometown. Soon, all four reneged on their vow to the court and appealed the decision. A year later, they finally paid fines from $78 to $190—stiff penalties, since five dealers nearby in Edgerton paid just $10 each for the same offense, but not sufficient to put booming saloons out of business.

Across the state, women soon became disenchanted with local campaigns and legal tactics. For example, Emma Brown's own women's league in Fort Atkinson was in the forefront, at first, as even leading men enlisted and the league won enforcement of Sunday laws and occasional suits against dealers. But the town stubbornly refused to vote a "temperance ticket." The *Chief* followed a similar story in Janesville, where "saloons succumbed" to Lavinia Goodell, whose litigation skills "created a sensation" and "astonished" defense attorneys. However, saloon keepers' adept use of the appeal process to delay enforcement and fines, or even overturn decisions, forced demoralized Janesville women to go forward with their cases "one at a time." The *Chief* also told of the travails of a Green Bay woman who "suffered from the traffic." The day after defeat of a "temperance ticket," she entered a complaint against all saloon keepers in the city for flouting the law, and won. Then dealers simply paid the fines and stayed in business. She sued again in 1874 and twice more in 1875, "walking to town, a distance of nine miles, with a little barefooted child in her arms to make the complaint." When four dealers finally paid $5 fines, the *Green Bay Gazette* applauded "the plucky little woman" for "true temperance reform." The *Chief* disagreed. "We might 'reform' in this way for ages," wrote Emma Brown. She would loyally endorse a later campaign by a "temperance attorney" in Wausau: her nephew and the late Thurlow Brown's son, Neal Dow Brown, namesake of the national reform hero. Elsewhere, Emma advised women to abandon hope of progress through the courts.

Although politics was closed to women, many expected progress from men in the new Prohibition party. However, in Wisconsin the party would be plagued by incompetence from the initial call to convene. For example, Emma Brown castigated the men for sending publicity only ten days before the first date set for the convention; it was rescheduled. Then, when their claim of a large turnout turned up in the *National*

Temperance Advocate, Emma Brown begged to differ. "We have it from good authority that only 18 or 20 were present," she reported. "We think a large number of temperance people in the State favor a move of this kind, but no effort was made to combine their influence." With "sharp criticism" for men's "management"—or lack of it—the *Chief* could not "commend the ticket to a large class of temperance people." As a temperance man put it, "For God's sake, put a stop to it. Cold water"—a popular euphemism for prohibitionism—"cannot win this fall."[2]

The Prohibition party embarrassed state temperance men, although neither major party drew well in 1875. Repercussions of the Graham Law debacle—the temperance law which led to the election of a Democratic governor and, indirectly, to the crusade—gave Republicans a lasting abhorrence of reform. Repudiating the Graham Law, they ran as their gubernatorial candidate the Milwaukee mayor who had defied the law. Harrison Ludington ran a campaign founded upon repeal of all temperance laws, a campaign funded by the Milwaukee brewers' Wisconsin Association for the Protection of Personal Liberty.[3] Republicans won back the governorship but lost the legislature, although not because of "the third ticket men, who made no difference in the result," according to Emma's county-by-county analysis of returns. Elsewhere, temperance men were more organized, Emma reported. She watched from afar as "a staunch temperance man" narrowly won the contested presidential election in 1876 and applauded Rutherford B. Hayes for his refusal to schedule his inauguration on the Sabbath. Emma later gave front-page play to his First Lady as well, who "withstood a year of social ostracism in Washington" and actually "dried up the White House."

But in Wisconsin, the embarrassment of repeated scandals in the Grand Old Party would not break its grip on the governorship. The Prohibition party drew negligible numbers even in 1877, despite widespread publicity for the first introduction in Congress of a Constitutional amendment for prohibition—and equally widespread coverage in Wisconsin of corrupt practices by Republican party officials on the brewers' payroll. The *Chief* blamed brewers and "pig-headed" politicians for the sorry state of state politics, but Emma Brown put the blame for the Prohibition party's problems on temperance men. Regretfully, the *Chief* endorsed "the Republican party whisky ring," as an appalled reader put it. He demanded that she "answer as you think Thurlow W. Brown would." Emma answered, for herself, that Prohibitionists could not win, and was right.

Emma Brown especially took party leaders to task for late publicity, and was right again; one convention in Milton drew seven delegates and adjourned for lack of a quorum. Prohibition party men would never win a single state office or a significant share of the electorate; even their presidential candidate would win fewer than seventy votes in Wisconsin by the end of the decade. Then, the men would ponder ways to enlist women in politics, too late.[4]

The majority of temperance women and men turned—or returned—to traditional organizations, which reaped the greatest rewards from the revived interest in temperance following the crusade. The example of Fond du Lac alone suggests the fervor for temperance even a year after the crusade came to town. A *Chief* correspondent counted the "pledged army of the city" as almost three thousand, half the total population of the town. Clearly, membership overlapped among eight hundred members of the City Open Temperance Society, seven hundred members of the Catholic Total Abstinence Society, three hundred members of the Women's Temperance Band, more than two hundred members of the Cotton Street Church Society and one hundred members of the First Baptist Temperance Society. Significantly, while the Sons of Temperance listed a respectable membership of more than one hundred men in two lodges in town, Fond du Lac Templars reported more than five hundred in the regular ranks, the Temple of Honor, and the juvenile auxiliary.

Even the long-moribund Sons of Temperance witnessed a brief revival everywhere, reporting a net gain nationally of six thousand new recruits. In 1875, the Sons' thirty-first national convention celebrated a total membership of more than eighty-eight thousand. But by 1880, the order would be forced—pending bankruptcy—to admit women.[5]

No organization, old or new, would succeed so well as the Templars in the postcrusade decade, and nowhere so well as in Wisconsin. Yet no organization would decline so swiftly, in part because of internal power struggles among men in the movement over the wisdom of political action. Primarily, their problems would result from their reluctance to empower women at all. Although the later rise of women's organizations can be explained by their experience of achieving only limited progress in the Templars, women also gained invaluable experience which explains their own later progress because the order excelled in the strategies and tactics of reform.

The Templars achieved remarkable prestige and power as well as record membership in Wisconsin, where the Grand Lodge would claim to be the largest in the world and the State Chief Templar would rise to lead the international order. In Wisconsin in 1875, the order had more than forty Temples of Honor and more than two hundred lodges, almost half organized in 1874 alone; in the same year, state rolls nearly doubled to almost fifteen thousand at a rate of growth more than double the national rate. As State Grand Worthy Secretary B. F. Parker of Mauston exuberantly reported to the *Chief*, with "more men and women of influence . . . there seems to be nothing in the way to mar our happiness as an Order."

The order happily issued its first full financial report in the *Chief* in the fall of 1875, when the Wisconsin Grand Lodge was out of debt and in the black for the first time in the decade. As Parker wrote, "we have the means to pay our way without begging." His superior, State Chief Templar Theodore D. Kanouse of Watertown, counted "on our books, to the exclusion of doubtful members and lodges," more than two thousand new members and fifty-eight new lodges in 1875. The increase was noteworthy "notwithstanding the financial depression of the people"—the Panic of 1873—"and their consequent hesitancy in undertaking any new enterprise which would increase their annual expenditure of money, even a trifle" such as dollar-a-year dues. He paid heed to the public's fiscal "hesitancy" by opening the books, introducing a new accountability into the notoriously secretive—and lucrative—business of running the order, revealing that receipts of $9,720.49 ran ahead of $8,966.80 in expenses.

Templars targeted recruitment campaigns at the traditional small-town core of temperance support, and employed the first organizers to work the Wisconsin circuit with any regularity since Thurlow Weed Brown's death a decade before. A *Chief* correspondent attested to the work of Templar agent Jack Warburton in 1875 in the town of Mukwonago, where the stalwart Sons still numbered almost one hundred but were outnumbered by town boosters who won a liquor license for the local hotel. The Templar agent drew "a crowded house," "spoke and sang for about three hours," and started a Temple of Honor "with 16 members, and some of them the rumseller's best customers. *They*, the first, stand firm and by their enthusiasm have added at least 20 more." But when Warburton returned to town in "a driving snowstorm, the worst of the season," to rally hardy Templars, the rum-selling hotelier refused to stable their horses. "Drinking as well as non-drinking men thought that went a step too far," the correspondent wrote. Horse lovers filled the next town hall meeting, elected a "dry" slate, and turned the hotel into a "temperance house." The chastened owner "accommodated the traveling public as heretofore," including Warburton, whose repeated tours held Mukwonago in the ranks of "no-license" towns.

While reinforcing their rural strongholds, the Templars also cultivated new urban constituencies, even in Milwaukee, where a lodge started in 1875, at last. Sixteen charter members, some recruited from remnants of the Sons of Temperance, held a membership drive which resulted in 128 members and a "handsome new hall"; a little more than a year later, Milwaukee Templars numbered more than three hundred in six lodges and three Temples of Honor. A *Chief* correspondent attributed the sudden rise in "sentiment" to a valiant Women's Temperance Band, the "originators of the public temperance meetings in this city." The organization "gave root" to twice-weekly gatherings at the YMCA and mass revival meetings. But the combined work of women, Templars, and the YMCA had little effect on Milwaukee Germans' deep-rooted resistance to temperance.

Outside of Milwaukee, Templars made new efforts among ethnic groups, even Germans. The State Chief Templar inaugurated eight Welsh lodges in 1875 and called on members to recruit immigrants by "going to them with their own language," especially Germans and Norwegians. A German lodge soon "prospered beyond expectation" with fifty members in Fond du Lac, according to an "exchange" in the *Chief,* and a correspondent reported a new Scandinavian lodge near Milwaukee. Eventually, Templars maintained a German lodge in LaCrosse, two Native American lodges at Keshena and "Brotherhood"—probably Brotherton—as well as twenty Welsh lodges, and five of only a dozen Scandinavian lodges in the country. The Wisconsin Grand Lodge was among the most ethnically diverse in the order, according to the national *Temperance Journal.* Scandinavians even had their own national temperance paper "in their own language," Emma Brown reported—half in apology and half in exasperation—to explain why the *Temeltjenarnes Nykterhetssallskap* was "untranslatable in this office" and would not be among the *Chief*'s otherwise wide range of "exchanges."

Wisconsin Templars also took a liberal stance on racial equality, a cause which would catapult the State Chief Templar to the top of the international order. It was not the first time that Wisconsin was in the forefront on the issue; as early as 1850, some state lodges had seceded from the Sons of Temperance for excluding freedmen. Wisconsin Templars also defied their order to start a "colored lodge" in Madison in 1867 and a Native American lodge in 1876, during a decade of international debate in the organization over the racial ban.[6] In 1876, at the international convention, Wisconsin's Theodore Kanouse stood firm for racial equality and succeeded, which resulted in his election to national office, but British lodges seceded from the order in protest.

In 1877, when Kanouse ascended to the international order's highest office, Right Worthy Grand Templar, the *Chief* exulted at the honor to the state. But Emma Brown, typically, saw a downside: "Templars have so long worked under Mr. Kanouse . . . that they hardly know how to accept the situation, and congratulations over his promotion are inclined to stick in the throat."

Emma Brown's foreboding was correct; Kanouse came to power just as the order peaked. From 1878 on, international membership declined steadily, and national numbers dropped nearly nine percent in the next two years, in part because of the British secession and resultant internecine warfare. However, in Wisconsin, the *Chief* reported that British infiltrators tried and failed to win away Wisconsin's Welsh lodges for a foothold in "the States." In the state, the order declined less dramatically but steadily, and never again reached the record numbers of 1878 when Templars surpassed twenty thousand adult members in more than 450 lodges and more than eight thousand members in almost 150 juvenile auxiliaries. Still, well into the 1880s, Wisconsin's Grand Lodge remained fourth largest in the world—after only New York, Sweden, and Maine—with more lodges active for twenty-five years than any state, according to the national *Temperance Journal*. Although membership fell almost a third in the early 1880s to few more than fourteen thousand, the international order remained a force in reform with more than six hundred thousand on the rolls.

The Templars' decline was a blow for business in the state because reform was big business. In 1878, receipts totaled more than $10,000 and expenditures were $8,800. The major expense was a "tax" of twelve cents per member paid to the national order, of which two cents was returned to districts. Other budget items included reimbursal of $34.70 for expenses and under $200 for services by the Chief Templar, although he was salaried at $1,200; under $100 for services of the secretary, who also asked less than his $500 salary; and $50 for office rental. A decade later, well after the order peaked in Wisconsin, receipts were down one-fifth to almost $8,000, but the Grand Lodge was still in the black by $183.31.

Reform leaders also became increasingly businesslike. As one State Chief Templar reported in the *Chief,* in a single year he "traveled by railway, highway and water 12,523 miles, addressed 153 public meetings, visited 132 Lodges and 6 Juvenile Temples, attended 30 conventions, organized and reorganized 16 Lodges, initiated 255 members, instituted 1 Degree Temple, conferred degrees on 69 members, dedicated 2 halls and attended to office duties," including "receiving 1,600 letters, all of which I have answered, and . . . 725 letters and postcards." In total, leaders traveled more than 54,000 miles in the year; one toured at least twenty Wisconsin lodges in less than three weeks.

Members, none salaried and many of them women, also sent in meticulous and even more staggering "reports of work." In a single year, "the 12 G. T. districts" presented 1,251 lectures to 120,580 listeners including 5,813 children in 94 Sunday schools and 4,699 children in 114 day schools, visited 425 lodges and 62 Temples of Honor, organized 131 lodges with 2,867 charter members and 65 temples with 1,516 charter members, received 1,974 "propositions" and wrote 4,630 letters. To the total of 1,424 public meetings, the *Chief* suggested that the reader add more than 21,000 weekly lodge meetings plus uncounted picnics, sociables, and "entertainments." The *Chief* tallied 34,456 miles traveled by members, to which "the writer"—Emma Brown, recording secretary of Fort Atkinson's lodge—"added over 2,000 miles to this item outside of her own District."

Emma Brown also reported annual distribution in Wisconsin alone of more than a million pages of Templar tracts and other "literature" which had "the advantage over all other methods." In her district, expenses included $22 for five hundred copies of the *Chief,* $3 each for ads in the *Chief* and *Western Good Templar,* $12 for four thousand "platform cards," $9.25 for five thousand "dodgers," one thousand "letterheaps" and envelopes—pledge cards, flyers, and stationery—and $9.25 for four dozen recognition pins. Income of $342.45 in tract sales and collections left a surplus of $18.44 at year's end. Never one to miss a chance to dun for dues and ever a good soldier in the temperance war, Emma ended with a fund appeal in the militaristic metaphor so prevalent in reform: "We are a drilled army, and regular dues assure continuance of our forces at the front" without "a day's furlough" and "no waiting in camp for the paymaster."[7]

But desertions in the ranks only increased, as did Templars' ingenuity in recruiting and rallying temperance forces. A Templar Mutual Benefit Association advertised reduced rates in the *Chief,* with a plug by Emma Brown who claimed that "all others have to pay a whisky loss . . . estimated at from 20 to 25 percent, the direct result of intemperance."

At county fairs, "temperance tents" with "dry" refreshments doubled as recruiting centers. A "ribbon movement" swept the state as devotees — "ribbon men" and "ribbon ladies" alike — adorned lapels with white or blue bows as public badges of sobriety. In the *Chief*'s Fort Atkinson, a Ribbon Club Reading Room was "carpeted and fitted up very tastily" by local "ladies" and located near the depot for temperance people to "wait for work, the mail, or trains"; women staffed the facility fourteen hours daily during the week, and four hours on Sundays. But Emma Brown editorially discounted the "raging Ribbon epidemic" as "like measles. People are not liable to have either disease a second time."

Templars' still-healthy numbers concealed a fatal weakness for social activity. At their most serious, lodges sponsored lecturers of renown or "10-cent entertainments" from Neal Dow of "Maine Law" fame to the Janesville lodge's touring production of a two-act drama, "The Last Loaf." The *Chief* reported more frivolous activity such as Fort Atkinson's recurrent "sociables" which advertised "new maple sugar to be saucered out" for an admission of "5 cts. Sugar, extra." However, temperance crowds became harder to please. In a *Chief* review of a "very pleasant Sociable arranged on short notice," Emma noted that "of course, the purely critical found some loop-holes. Those who did not expect *perfection* enjoyed the 'comedietta,' the singing, the fun and good time generally."

State leaders soon unofficially reversed the order's official resistance to political action, another significant factor in the decline worldwide and in Wisconsin, where Theodore Kanouse was an outspoken proponent of moral suasion — until he was willing to try almost anything to stem the defections from the ranks, and until he ran for governor. His successor, State Chief Templar B. F. Parker, also called for more "instructive" meetings, admonishing members who were too "slow to learn the wisdom of carrying our temperance principles into our politics as well as in our Lodge rooms." But the emphasis on "entertainments" continued in many a rural enclave, especially the ever-popular Templar picnics billed in the *Chief* as "dry" but rained out with regularity.

The weather was a standard excuse in Wisconsin for anything gone wrong, and a popular explanation of the order's problems. Kanouse wrote in 1881 that "the worst snow in 20 years," a brief spring, and an early summer of "the most extreme heat" had conspired to restrict "field work and organization." But record blizzards did not deter the order's indefatigible "professional agitator," Jack Warburton. The *Waukesha Freeman* reported that the "brave temperance lecturer" so agitated two men in Sussex that they trailed him to Hartland and "succeeded in disturbing the meeting to a considerable extent but their program of whipping was not carried out." Justice was carried out when the men were convicted of battery and fined. In Jefferson in 1881, a single "field visit" by Warburton spawned a Temple of Honor, a Common Sense Club, a Law and Order Club, and a Ribbon Club, according to a *Chief* correspondent. But Emma Brown was skeptical of organizational longevity in Jefferson, where "lodges have come and gone before, twice."

Far more important was the opposition by the Brewers Congress, which showed its might in Milwaukee in 1882. A "Sunday law" petition drive to close theaters on the Sabbath in Milwaukee "frightened" the brewers, who organized a boycott of merchants who had signed the petitions for the Sunday law. "The condition of things promises to bring serious injury to the business interests of the city," warned the *Waukesha Freeman,* with the ill-concealed enjoyment which accompanied its exposés of urban blight to the east. When the *Freeman* assailed the biggest business in Milwaukee for "the attempted suppression of public opinion," the Waukesha paper won "wholesale denunciations from the German press of Milwaukee" and quickly backtracked. Attempting balance by castigating a Milwaukee minister who was behind the "boycotting idea," the *Freeman* opined that, "undoubtedly, doctors of divinity have the same right to make asses of themselves that brewers have." But the *Freeman* was caught off-balance when the "blue law" drive was extended to curtailing delivery of Sunday mail; postal privileges were regarded as basic rights in the newspaper business. "The spirit of intolerance is just now more dangerous than distilled spirits, even," the *Freeman* intoned, and faded from the debate. The drive for the Sunday law lost.[8]

The Templars' comparative lack of political clout was evident in long-overdue legislative redistricting in 1882, which sealed the fate of temperance forces, dismayed by the loss of more than a dozen seats in their rural strongholds to urban—German—population centers. Although immigrants and first-generation residents now outnumbered "natives" two to one in Wisconsin, the redistricting engendered cries of corruption and gerrymandering. The *Chief*'s Emma Brown offered a more domestic metaphor for the result: "A Committee of women skilled in old-fashioned 'patch-work' would have made a better and more symmetrical piece of work."

In a rare attempt at more than anecdotal research, Templars conducted an early example of an opinion poll and discovered other significant demographic trends in the state which did not bode well for reform. State Chief Templar B. F. Parker's "postcard survey" was a radical step for the authoritarian order because leaders asked lodges where they had gone wrong. Most had gone west.

Some lodges did not respond; they no longer existed. Almost two hundred did reply, reporting that more than twenty-four hundred Templars had left the state in 1882 alone. Worse, they were the core of the order or, as Parker put it, "the class of people from whence we derive our membership." Leadership left, too; among emigrés to the Dakota Territory would be "Sister" and Theodore D. Kanouse, the glory of the Wisconsin Grand Lodge. Parker's panic was understandable but his prose unintelligible: "Our organizers planted Lodges in small rural communities where the only hope of their continuance rested in the certainty of a continuance of residence on the part of those who took part in the organization." His findings on "unprecedented emigration from the rural districts of Wisconsin" would be verified by demographers. However, Parker's "postcard survey" also disclosed a disturbing psychographic trend: "a strange apathy among the temperance people of Wisconsin in regard to *organized* effort."[9]

The apathy which so puzzled Parker may have been the result of repressive tactics among small-town despots who took vigilant adherence to their vows too far, and turned vigilante. John M. Barlow, later a New Lisbon legislator, recalled near-ostracism in "no-license" Mukwonago as a youth. On a visit to the wicked East where he first tasted sweet cider, Barlow described "'dissipated' doings away off in New England" in an "indiscreet letter" to a more indiscreet friend, who passed it around town. Barlow returned to a "red-hot lodge trial." He "defended himself through numerous trials and much fine figuring" and was "cleared of the disgrace of dismissal from the order" but had his revenge; "the friction occasioned did not leave a large amount of harmony among the members of the lodge, which languished, and finally collapsed."[10]

An unacknowledged reason for the order's losses in the ranks, where women languished, is exemplified by Wisconsin's Theodore Kanouse, a champion of racial equality who was ambivalent regarding women's role. Only late in the 1870s did he allow a woman—his wife—to head their home lodge in Watertown, for a six-month term. A *Chief* correspondent reassured readers that the lodge survived "under the successful leadership of a lady." More often, "Sister Kanouse" was in charge of children's temples. The Fort Atkinson lodge followed and also endured the "experiment" of a three-month term under Helen E. Brown, widow of Thurlow Weed Brown.

In sum, the Templars did not lose the postcrusade momentum in the temperance movement; they gave it away, to women. In 1874, Wisconsin Templars had hailed women's crusade and called on the "sisters" to support the "right men" with "all the honorable means which womanly ingenuity can devise"—a term distasteful to Emma Brown, for one; she called it simply "the power of organized work."

The order once in the vanguard of woman's rights had held back from leadership the very members who showed the most initiative, or "womanly ingenuity," from the crusade forward, through the painful debacle of the Prohibition party and the protracted demise of the Templars. And lead women would, on their own; it was the Woman's Christian Temperance Union which would excel in the "power of organized work"—and in influencing the power of the press.

In Wisconsin in 1874, as elsewhere, crusaders organized statewide in anticipation of the founding of the national Woman's Christian Temperance Union. In October in Milwaukee, the Wisconsin Women's Temperance Alliance was organized by women who came from every corner of the state; the first slate of officers represented Beloit, Brodhead, Eau Claire, Eureka, Fond du Lac, Fox Lake, Madison, Milwaukee, Racine, Ripon, and Waupun. Although Lavinia Goodell was not a leader of the Alliance, women elected her co-worker in the Janesville crusade, Dorcas Hadley Beale, to serve as corresponding secretary, and Appleton crusader Susan Swift Steele was elected president of the Alliance.

Steele was one of ten women in the country—and the only one from Wisconsin—to sign the call for a national women's temperance convention in August 1874, which led to the founding of the Woman's Christian Temperance Union. At the convention, held in November in Cleveland, Ohio, "the Mecca of the Crusade," Steele was one of 135 delegates from sixteen states. Another member of the Alliance, Mrs. J. A. Brown of Milwaukee, also attended and was appointed to constitutional and business committees. Steele was appointed to committees on credentials and publications, and was elected a vice president of the WCTU.[11]

The first president of the WCTU, Annie Turner Wittenmyer, was the editor of the Methodist *Christian Woman* and well known for her work with the Sanitary Commission in Iowa and on battlefields from Shiloh to Vicksburg, where her "heroic service" was commended by Union

General Ulysses S. Grant. Her experience in the war would be invaluable to the WCTU, which she made a "tightly knit but democratic organization," according to historian Barbara Leslie Epstein. However, Wittenmyer's prominence in the press was even more useful, according to historian Ruth Bordin. Her "tremendous importance" and "prestige" came from "control of an established newspaper . . . which could be used to assist the temperance cause."[12]

Press coverage of the first national WCTU convention was considerable, but reporters stressed the novelty of women speakers and the reassuring religious overtones of the gathering, missing the more significant story: the WCTU adopted a "Plan of Work" with lessons on the power of the press learned in the crusade. The longest section, "On Making Public Sentiment," instructed women to seek publicity and stage events, contribute press columns, publish and distribute literature, and carry their campaign into the schools with temperance instruction and essay contests, "glee clubs of young people to sing temperance doctrines into the people's hearts as well as heads," and displays "on the walls of every schoolroom" of an "engraving known as 'The Railroad to Ruin.'"

Despite her distaste for the "prayerful sisters" of the East who dominated the organization, Emma Brown welcomed WCTU news—especially news of a newcomer to the temperance campaign, but not to Wisconsin or the woman's rights movement. Frances E. Willard was a native of Janesville whose abolitionist father had served in the first state legislature. A distant cousin was Emma Willard, a pioneer in women's education, and an aunt and a cousin were on the faculty of the forerunner of Milwaukee Female College. Frances Willard enrolled in 1857 in Milwaukee Female Seminary where, after her "rearing on the prairie," she reveled in the "clear and invigorating moral atmosphere" and found many "noble mates," notably classmate Marion Wolcott, later the stepdaughter of Dr. Laura Ross Wolcott, a pioneering suffragist in the state.

Despite her "devotion to Milwaukee," Willard left after only a year when her father sent her to a new Methodist women's college at Northwestern University in Evanston, Illinois. By 1871, she was president of her alma mater, a speaker at the annual Women's Congress in Washington, D.C., and a successful freelance writer for magazines and newspapers; among her lesser accomplishments, Willard later was the first woman editor and publisher of a major metropolitan paper, her brother's Chicago *Daily Post,* after his death—from alcoholism.

In 1874, Willard was employed by the new WCTU in Illinois, where

"Ideas are our bullets. The evolution of temperance ideas is in this order: The People are informed, convicted, convinced, pledged."—Frances E. Willard, an alumna of the Milwaukee Female Seminary and the president of the largest women's organization in the world, the Woman's Christian Temperance Union. Photo courtesy of the State Historical Society of Wisconsin.

her rise was inevitable, and immediate. Within months, she was promoted from president of the Chicago union to secretary of the Illinois union and then to national corresponding secretary.

Willard wrote a remarkably prescient handbook in 1874, *How to Organize a W.C.T.U.*, possibly the first textbook on public opinion campaigns. Sections of the handbook included "Opening Exercises," "Rules of Order," "Remember the Music," "Look to the Enrolling Tablets," "Entertain Your Speaker," "Roll of Honor," and "The World Wants Facts;" in modern terminology, meeting planning, special events, volunteer recognition, and opinion research. The longest section, "The World Wants Facts," included a short course on publicity with sample news releases and advice on editors' schedules and psyches—with sympathy for women who, despite heeding format and deadlines, "have gone hundreds of miles . . . only to find a single stray line in the corner of one newspaper."[13]

Emma Brown promoted Willard's press-wise practicality as a relief from the religious tone of the rest of the WCTU's publicity. Although the *Chief,* like the Alliance, officially remained distant from the WCTU for the rest of the decade, Willard won front-page play from the first. In September 1874, her inaugural temperance address was reprinted in the *Chief,* in full, with an admiring line on Willard's grasp of "making public sentiment." In Willard's words, "Ideas are our bullets. The evolution of temperance ideas is in this order: The People are informed, convicted, convinced, pledged." Decades later, in as many words, communication theorists would identify similar stages of public opinion formation.[14]

In the same address, Willard adroitly appeased more evangelical women while sending a subtle message to others well versed in the history of the woman's rights movement. She called on women to "use our influence in all suitable ways to enlist the pulpit and the press," echoing the Declaration of Sentiments and Resolutions from the first woman's rights convention, in 1848 at Seneca Falls.

Willard's gender was sufficient to win coverage in general papers, still unaccustomed to women on the podium or in the press, but her ability was not unnoticed. Early in 1875, the WCTU's debut in the temperance movement came when Willard, Wittenmyer, and other women addressed a national temperance convention in Chicago. A *Chief* "exchange" from the Portage *Advance,* newly the official organ of state Templars, described their enthusiastic reception.

> Never in America was a convention constituted so liberally in this respect. Never has woman in a deliberative assembly so participated on an equal footing with her brothers. . . . Our own Miss Willard, and many more, demonstrated that woman could master the situation and thrill an audience without losing anything that was "pure womanly." If some spoke with more heat and haste than wisdom—the same criticism is justly applicable to the men. When it is considered that but recently woman has trod the

platform or broken the silence of centuries, is it not surprising and significant that our sisters bear themselves with so much poise and ability?[15]

Less press attention went to the convention's endorsement of at least limited woman suffrage, a compromise offered after the convention initially tabled a resolution for full suffrage "amid an uproar." Then Wisconsin's Lavinia Goodell proposed that "the question of the prohibition of the liquor traffic should be submitted to all the adult citizens of this country, irrespective of sex."[16] The motion carried a majority of the "large and spirited gathering" of 688 delegates, as reported to the *Chief* by a correspondent.

Emma Brown led with the suffrage angle on the story, and was critical of coverage of the convention by the "secular press," which emphasized resolutions that endorsed "the power of prayer as an agency" and "the religious element" among women. "More than would be gathered from the secular press, the convention was a unit" on suffrage, and had taken a significant step, she wrote. However, after a quarter of a century in the reform press, Emma was weary of reporting the passage of paper promises. "Resolutions, if put in practice, would revolutionize our work, but we long ago lost faith in bombarding the liquor traffic with resolutions," she wrote. "Still, we suppose it is the proper thing to do — pass resolutions at a temperance convention — so that they need not go home feeling as if they had forgotten something."

But back home in Wisconsin, the wisdom of tying temperance to woman suffrage was still doubted, and apparently not even debated at the second convention of the Alliance. From October 19 to 21, 1875, in Fond du Lac, women convened to conduct business including election, without debate, of a conservative slate headed by Dorcas Hadley Beale, who had served as corresponding secretary but succeeded to the presidency in midterm when Susan Swift Steele resigned the post for personal reasons.

The Alliance earned compliments from the press — a critical audience — for convention planning, a complex task in an era when women rarely traveled alone and could not consider commercial lodging. Editors praised women in host cities for arranging housing in private homes. They also extolled prompt "advances," although publicity apparently was sent to — or used by — only papers in host cities and the *Chief*. At conventions, women officially resolved to send reports to the press — but, again, only to the same papers and only with resolutions which often were not newsworthy.

However, in 1875, resolutions for political action by women were sufficient to earn ridicule from the editor of the Fond du Lac *Commonwealth*. A. F. Watrous, head of the state Templars' Temples of Honor, initially hailed the convention as "one of the most interesting gatherings ever held." Then he read their resolutions. Women first voted the usual avowal that their purpose was to organize women's and children's auxiliaries, which the *Commonwealth* commended. The next resolution revealed women's new role: "That as moral suasion alone has failed to reach the rum power, we pledge ourselves to use our influence in every laudable manner, for the enactment and enforcement of prohibitory laws." Delegates also determined to circulate petitions for a prohibition amendment, to be delivered to legislators "by a committee of three ladies."

The Alliance's audacity in claiming political action as within women's purview, if only for prohibition, engendered a press debate between the *Commonwealth* and Emma Brown. Watrous belittled the Alliance by writing, "if in the place of the second resolution the women had said: Resolved, That we make a delicious chicken pie of chickens yet in the shell; or that the best way to harvest wheat is to take it before it heads out; or, that every three year old girl should wear long dresses . . . they would have done themselves as much credit." Emma lashed back at his "usual homily on the benefits of purely moral suasion" with a blistering attack in the *Chief:* "We have known something of prohibitionists and their work—and we never yet have met one who did not believe in thoroughly organized societies with pledged members, and the power of press and platform to mold public opinion. . . . The women of the Alliance mean to reach the traffic as well as its effects."

Despite Emma's defense, the women of the Alliance went into retreat. They did not pursue the proposed petition drive and disappeared from public view, with only convention advances in the *Chief* but no further correspondence for the next two years.

A month after the Alliance convention, in November 1875, delegates to the second WCTU convention came from fifteen states, one fewer than the year before; Wisconsin was not represented. A reason may have been the religiosity of eastern crusaders who initially dominated the WCTU; significantly, the proposal for nationwide organization first arose at a National Sunday School Assembly in Chautauqua, New York, in 1874. The evangelical emphasis had continued at the first WCTU convention and became a point of contention when inclusion of "Christian" in the organization's name was opposed by some temperance women from states other than New York and Ohio; as in Wisconsin, their crusade had been far less moralistic and more oriented toward political action.[17]

However, in Wisconsin, press reaction to the Alliance's relatively innocuous resolution for political action was a significant reason for temperance women to wait so long to endorse their own suffrage or even affiliate with the WCTU. Alliance president Beale would hold the post into the next decade and hold the organization apart from the suffrage campaign because she saw the Alliance as a single-interest organization, and perhaps wisely; temperance was a cause sufficient to occupy women for decades to come, in Wisconsin.

Even the WCTU would not endorse full woman suffrage in 1875 or for the rest of the decade, the tenure of Annie Turner Wittenmyer. Like Beale, she would hold back her organization to support of partial, "temperance suffrage"—too bold a stand for the Wisconsin Alliance, which would not affiliate with the national organization until 1880. By then, the WCTU would be the largest women's organization in the world,[18] in large part because of new "plans of work" undertaken at its 1875 convention.

The WCTU, like the Alliance, impressed the *Chief* with proficiency at convention planning and publicity. Advances arrived by September, with two months' lead time. Well in advance, states were required to send "scientific statistics" on "juvenile work, saloon-visiting, and friendly inns" free of alcohol. Delegates avoided "inns" of any kind in Cincinnati, where women provided housing in private homes and even entertainment, in the form of "Sabbath Gospel temperance meetings throughout the city."

The 1875 convention also marked the introduction of an innovative and sophisticated lobbying strategy that explains the WCTU's later political influence. Organizers in 1874 had called for a single delegate from each congressional district, but did not turn away others. In 1875, the *Chief* reported, women enforced the plan for equal apportionment and instructed conventioneers to apply pressure on congressmen upon returning home. A historian suggests that the strategy was "the basis for most special-interest lobbying ever since." Emma Brown also saw its significance: without the vote, she wrote, lobbying was women's only resort.

Although the Alliance was not represented in the WCTU, that Wisconsin women continued unofficial communication with national leaders is evident in coverage in the *Chief.* Emma Brown continued to rely on "exchanges," including WCTU publications, but many items came courtesy of a complex network of correspondents nationwide who relayed clippings or reported on events. For example, an eastern woman's colorful account of the "harmonious and dignified" WCTU convention in 1875, "quite equal to the one in Cleveland" the year before, was forwarded to Emma Brown in Fort Atkinson from a woman in Appleton, probably Susan Swift Steele. The Wisconsin leader also was in contact with national leaders; Wittenmyer's *History of the Women's Temperance Crusade* included a chapter by Steele on Wisconsin, where "public sentiment has been and still is fast deepening and widening."

But "public sentiment" was slow to change in Wisconsin, in comparison with surrounding states. In 1875, to the east and west, Michigan and Minnesota women won "school suffrage"—the right to vote, but only on school issues—which had been held by women in Kansas since 1861 and in Kentucky since 1838. In 1875 in Wisconsin, legislators did pass a bill strengthening the earlier law which accorded women a role in the schools—a law even more limited than "school suffrage" and less logical: women in Wisconsin could run for school office but could not vote, even for themselves. Still, four women ran and won races for county school superintendent in the first year, and nine would be elected to office by the end of the decade.[19]

The status of Wisconsin's first woman lawyer also lagged behind that of women in surrounding states in 1875, when Lavinia Goodell was denied the right to pursue a case on appeal to the Wisconsin Supreme Court because she did not belong to the state bar, a courtesy automatically extended to any lawyer admitted to a lower bar. The first woman to be admitted to a state bar, Arabella Babb Mansfield in Iowa in 1869, had met no resistance. However, in Illinois in 1870, Myra Colby Bradwell was denied admission to the bar because she was married; her marital status meant she could not enter into legal contracts, according to the Illinois Supreme Court—and the United States Supreme Court, which upheld the decision in 1872. By then, Bradwell was an ardent advocate of woman's rights and publisher of the *Chicago Legal News,* and led a successful press campaign for a state law outlawing occupational sex discrimination. The first woman lawyer was admitted to the Illinois bar in 1873, a year before Lavinia Goodell was admitted to the Rock County bar.[20]

After Goodell was refused admission to the state bar, she sued for admission and gained a hearing before the three-man Wisconsin Supreme Court in December 1875. The high court was headed by Chief Justice Edward G. Ryan, a foe of woman's rights since the first state constitutional convention almost thirty years before. As Goodell wrote, Ryan "bristled all up when he saw me, like a hen when she sees a hawk. . . . It was fun to see him!" She was not optimistic, but she was pragmatic and saw an opportunity to advance women and her law practice at the same time. "If they don't admit me, I shall try the legislature with a bill to have me admitted," Goodell wrote to her sister. "It will advertise me splendidly."

In February 1876, in an opinion by Ryan, the Wisconsin Supreme Court ruled that a woman lawyer violated "natural law." As the chief justice wrote, "the law of nature destines and qualifies the female sex for the bearing and nurture of the children of our race and for the custody of the home. . . . All life-long callings of women, inconsistent with these sacred duties of their sex, as is the profession of law, are departures from the order of nature; and, when voluntary, treason." Ryan detailed "peculiar qualities of womanhood" that made women unfit for the law; for example, they might be exposed to "unclean issues . . . unfit for female ears."

However, Goodell had the ear of Emma Curtiss Bascom, wife of the University of Wisconsin's temperance-minded president, John Bascom, and a reformer in her own right. Both became prominent in the movement after arriving in Wisconsin in the crusade summer of 1874. At Emma Bascom's invitation, Goodell went from the hearing to the president's manse where the women planned a press campaign for public opinion. Bascom had contacts in the capital press, while Goodell had cultivated editors from Fond du Lac and Edgerton to Pardeeville and Portage on lecture tours for suffrage, temperance, and prison reform, and was a correspondent for national papers under the byline, "Lavinia Goodell, Attorney at Law." Soon, papers from Goodell's hometown *Gazette* to the national *Woman's Journal* joined in ridicule of Ryan's ruling. The *Wisconsin State Journal* published Goodell's brief and jested that "if her purity is in danger, it would be better to reconstruct the bar than to exclude the women." In a similar tone, the *Chicago Tribune* wondered "if the latter phrase of the decision"—on the "unclean" nature of law—"was satisfactory to Wisconsin lawyers."[21]

In a *Chief* roundup of press reactions to Ryan's opinion, no editor was more insightful than Myra Colby Bradwell of the *Chicago Legal News*. In March 1876, the woman who had been banned from the Illinois bar ran Goodell's own "admirable review of the decision," and appended an editorial commentary that called the "especial attention of readers" to Ryan's opinion, reprinted in full, "because it could only hasten the day when the right of suffrage shall be extended to women in Wisconsin."

Goodell appealed the high court ruling but could do little to hasten her suit, which would not be reheard until the end of the decade. Her case already had become a cause célèbre in the East, where she addressed the Women's International Temperance Convention in 1876 and met with Lucy Stone, William Lloyd Garrison — a friend of Lavinia's father from the abolitionist press — and Charlotte Ray, the first African-American woman lawyer in the country.

Goodell attended the Centennial Exposition in Philadelphia in July 1876, where a "women's centennial exhibit" included her certificate of admission to the Rock County bar and her brief for admission to the Wisconsin bar. The exhibit caused considerable comment, but was overshadowed by the denial of women's request for participation in the official Fourth of July festivities for the national celebration of the nation's hundredth anniversary. Susan B. Anthony interrupted the event with a reading of a Women's Declaration of Independence which was widely reported in the press, and reawakened interest in suffrage among women nationwide.[22]

By 1877, even Wisconsin saw a resurgence in suffragism when Elizabeth Cady Stanton returned to Milwaukee for the first time since 1869. On tour to promote a proposed sixteenth amendment to the Constitution, the "Anthony amendment" for suffrage, she was aided in securing signatures on a memorial to Congress for the amendment by "prominent women in the city" and "entertained by the leaders of social affairs." One may have been Mary Blanchard Lynde, who had become one of the first three women trustees of Mary Mortimer's Milwaukee Female College in 1870. A leader in the prison reform movement, with Lavinia Goodell, Lynde also became the first woman appointed to the State Board of Charities upon its creation in 1871. Her husband was Milwaukee's member of the House of Representatives, William Pitt Lynde, who presented the petition to Congress with the signatures of 477 Wisconsin women and men, led by the names of Lavinia Goodell and Mathilde Fransziska Anneke.

Another Wisconsin leader's assessment of the 1877 campaign, almost fifty years later, was complimentary. Women's tactics would change little in decades to come: "Suffrage literature was distributed, suffrage petitions were circulated, money was collected to help in support of national work, and delegates were sent from Wisconsin to the national conventions in Washington. So suffrage work done in the beginning was of substantially the same character as in later years."[23]

But there still was substantial "suffrage work" to be done in the state, if judged by the delicately worded edicts of the board of regents of the University of Wisconsin. Relying on the collective wisdom of the medical profession, the regents reneged on admitting women to the regular degree program in one proclamation.

> Every physiologist is well aware that, at stated times, nature makes a great demand upon the energies of early womanhood and that at these times great caution must be exercised lest injury be done. . . . Education is greatly to be desired . . . but it is better that the future matrons of the state should be without a University training than that it should be produced at the fearful expense of ruined health, better that the future mothers of the state should be robust, hearty, healthy women than that, by over-study, they entail upon their descendants the germs of disease.[24]

No official reply from "the future matrons of the state" to the regents of the state university was recorded. The response, instead, was a steadily increasing enrollment of women students who "greatly desired" the regular education still denied them.

However, Wisconsin women did not respond in like numbers to the call for suffrage. That the campaign still was characterized by a lack of consistency at the state level was evident in the enthusiasm which greeted national leaders like Stanton on their infrequent visits, and in the inevitable ennui soon after. Only when women coordinated strategies and tactics at national and state levels would the "Anthony amendment" finally win passage—more than forty years after its first submission to Congress, in 1878.

By 1878, the flurry of interest in Stanton's tour and woman suffrage had abated in Wisconsin, and temperance women had regrouped after press reaction to their relatively innocuous resolution to political action for prohibition. In 1878, they were so emboldened that the Alliance returned to Fond du Lac, home of the *Commonwealth* which had caused the press uproar. Women also guaranteed publicity by planning a keynote address by Lavinia Goodell and, well ahead of the convention held in October, again sent advances to the *Chief.*

The Alliance also expanded efforts on the podium and in the press in 1878. For example, Alliance president Beale spoke to a statewide convention of Congregationalists in Waukesha, on the same podium with renowned rhetoricians, where her address was applauded as a "triumph" and secured the church's endorsement of a proposed state prohibition amendment. The Alliance also began a monthly organ "edited and entirely managed" by Beale, reported Emma Brown, who recommended the *Messenger* as a bargain at thirty cents a year.

The Alliance's entry into the Wisconsin press was one of numerous "temperance sheets" which arose in the postcrusade era. Before 1873, the *Chief* had been joined by the *Western Advance* of Janesville and then Portage, and a *Wisconsin Grand Templar* was the "official organ" of the order in 1873 but lasted only briefly. In 1875, the order adopted the *Advance* under a new editor whom Emma recommended as "a temperance worker who did not need to change his faith to fill his new position." In 1875, Mineral Point men began a *Wisconsin Temperance Journal,* a weekly which soon went semimonthly. The semimonthly *Northwestern Prohibitionist* in Ripon moved within months to Oshkosh and on to Milwaukee, where ten men ran the paper for a few months until they ran it into the ground; the paper moved to Madison before its demise. In 1876, a Fond du Lac *Commonwealth* editor started the monthly *Appeal,* later sold and moved to Chippewa Falls where it failed. In 1877, the *Son of Temperance* started in Racine with a woman as associate editor; she lasted less than a year, the paper little longer. Two Sons started the *Temperance Herald* in Milton Junction in 1879. Another revived the Mineral Point *Temperance Journal,* later a local insert in a national paper's "patent outside"; the short-lived experiment was a precursor, in reverse, of the common modern-day practice by small-town papers of purchasing preprinted mass-produced national "magazines" to serve as inside sections. In Oshkosh, a *Signal* changed hands often, as did a *Western Good Templar.*

Newspapers were only part of the postcrusade boom in the temperance publishing business. The size and scope of the National Temperance Society and Publication House in New York were evident in an 1877 annual report summarized in the *Chief* by Emma Brown. The organization "stereotyped and published over 450 books, tracts, and pamphlets, upon every phase of the question. Of tracts, a total of 38,171,800 pages; of books and pamphlets, a total of 129,242,092 pages; of all publications, an aggregate of 239,294,290" with costs for "stereotyping, copyrights and engraving, $57,478.48." However, as Emma wrote, "few publications are sold at a profit, some are sold at cost, many more are sold at less than cost, and many are given away." The organization "gratuitously distributed" temperance literature worth over $25,000 in a single year.

The diversity of reform publishing, merchandising, and marketing also was evident in the National Temperance Society's advertisements in the *Chief*. Readers could choose among "over 300 varieties of Temperance Tracts and Leaflets, from 1 to 24 pages each. Four page tracts, 40 cents per hundred, $4.00 per thousand; 4 page tracts in German, same price. Children's Illustrated Tracts, $3.00 per thousand. Packages of 50 tracts, 25 cents; Leaflets, 10 cts." In addition, the society offered a new monthly magazine, a new edition of "the hand-book, 'Liquor Laws of the United States,'" and items such as a seventy-two-page desk calendar called the *National Temperance Almanac and Teetotaller's Year Book,* available for ten cents.

The competition in the temperance market contributed to a high rate of transiency in the temperance press, which was not a Wisconsin phenomenon; the *National Temperance Advocate* ran a trade column called "Chips," which Emma Brown perused for "three-line obituaries" of "papers that passed on." Each, of course, only underscored the longevity of the *Chief* and Emma Brown, who had little to fear from competitors and sincerely welcomed "companions in the cause," which could only benefit from more "temperance banners." Emma recommended the newcomers to readers; reported their inevitable moves, management changes, and mergers; and regretted the demise of each in turn—although another always turned up. As Emma noted, it was not surprising that a "strong temperance man" in the New York reform press invented the "newspaper-addressing machine."

The only "temperance sheet" to endure into the next century would be the Alliance's *Messenger,* which would continue publication as the *Home Guard* after Wisconsin women affiliated with the WCTU. The *Guard* would outlast all other "temperance sheets" in Wisconsin, even the *Chief,* because the WCTU would outlast all other temperance organizations in the world—and would become the largest women's organization in the world, under Frances Willard.

The rise of the WCTU and Willard in the latter 1870s was the direct result of her ability to exploit the postcrusade popularity and profitability of print media. Initially, the WCTU went out for printing of its *Our Union* and purchased other print material from the National Temperance Society and Publication House, which made the profit. Printing and purchasing costs put the WCTU in fiscal distress, until Willard maneuvered into leadership of the publishing committee, the "literary arm." In a brilliant move, she created a parent corporation, the Woman's

Temperance Publishing Association, which was "conducted by women, its types set by women compositors," as Emma Brown reported with professional pride. The publishing company soon became the WCTU's major source of income—and Willard's source of power.

Willard won editorial control of the WCTU's *Our Union* from the more conservative "Wittenmyer faction," and became a household word in temperance homes. The circulation of *Our Union* neared ten thousand in 1877, reported Emma Brown, who found it "much improved typographically" under Willard. More important, the news content was increasingly prosuffrage, which brought a protest from the *Our Union* staff but established a following for Willard. Her campaign for the WCTU presidency was deferred briefly when she had to rescue her brother's Chicago *Daily Post* upon his death, an episode which only increased Emma Brown's identification with her heroine.

However, journalism was just a sideline for Willard, who soon revived her run for the WCTU presidency against Annie Turner Wittenmyer in a power struggle which would send both women to Wisconsin to seek support. Wittenmyer came first, to Appleton in June 1879. But, whether by design or unavoidable delay, the Alliance would not affiliate with the WCTU until Frances Willard's triumphant return to Wisconsin, another six months away.

In the interim, in June 1879, a far longer delay came to an end for Lavinia Goodell in her four-year battle for admission to the state bar. When the state high court's ruling against her was upheld, Goodell began a legislative campaign with the help of the respected John B. Cassoday of Janesville, the speaker of the assembly. Other Janesville colleagues joined him, and a petition with signatures of every lawyer in Rock County was submitted by Cassoday with a bill drafted by Goodell prohibiting denial of admission to the bar on the basis of gender. Goodell came to Madison to lobby legislators, testify in hearings, and cultivate the press. The *State Journal* promised to "make favorable notices of my bills," Goodell wrote; in all, she had drafted eight bills for causes from prison reform to protection for battered wives. In Madison, she also enlisted the aid of Emma Bascom again. By March 1877, Lavinia Goodell's bill for the bar had been made law. However, owing to her ill health and her parents' deaths, she had not attempted admission for two years.

In 1879, Goodell was not the only woman lawyer in Wisconsin. That year, the Rock County bar also admitted Angeline King, the Janesville woman whose election as postmaster a decade earlier had enlivened

Elizabeth Cady Stanton's sojourn in the state, and had caused consternation as far away as Washington, D.C. Goodell and King opened a law office in Janesville, adorned by lithographs sent by Stanton of herself and Susan B. Anthony.

By 1879, women had been admitted to the bar in almost a dozen states and the District of Columbia. Even the United States Supreme Court rescinded its earlier refusal to hear arguments by a woman, Belva Lockwood. She had lobbied a bill through Congress in February 1879 which forced federal courts to admit women, and was the first to benefit from the new law. However, no precedent would sway Wisconsin's irascible Chief Justice Ryan.

When Goodell again applied for admission to the Wisconsin bar, her most able ally was not a male colleague but Emma Bascom. By then, Bascom was an officer of her local temperance league and president of an Equal Suffrage Association founded in Madison in 1878. In April 1879, at Goodell's second hearing before the high court, Bascom was in the courtroom. Historian Catherine B. Cleary suggests that her presence "could hardly have been overlooked by Madison's social and political elite" as "a gesture of support for Goodell that reminded the court of the public interest in its decision," while Ryan also may have been reminded of "remarks" made by Bascom's husband "on the ethics of the judiciary," which "must have added to his unhappiness" at the hearing. Despite the legislative fiat for Goodell, the unhappy Ryan still dissented when the Wisconsin Supreme Court ruled in her favor in June 1879.[25]

By 1880, women like Goodell and Bascom had new hope for woman's rights in Wisconsin, buoyed by the affiliation of the Women's Alliance with the WCTU—and with Frances Willard. At the national WCTU convention in October 1879, as Emma Brown put it, "Miss F. E. Willard was elected President. That means work." It also meant Willard's return to her native Wisconsin in January 1880 to induct the Alliance into the WCTU in Madison, where Emma Bascom was elected corresponding secretary of the new state chapter.

Affiliation with the WCTU ensured the wider publicity and preeminence which had eluded temperance women in Wisconsin, where the Alliance was overwhelmed by the Templars and ignored by the Prohibition party. Although the new state chapter's first meeting in Madison drew only sixty-seven delegates, they now were the local representatives of the largest women's organization in the world, with twenty-seven thousand women in more than eleven hundred locals in twenty-four states

"Will [the Republican party], as so repeatedly in the past, turn a deaf ear to reason, and still continue to deny the rights of half the human family? If so . . . it [will] continue deaf, dumb and blind."—Emma Curtiss Bascom of Madison, a president of the Wisconsin Woman Suffrage Association and the Wisconsin Woman's Christian Temperance Union, at the same time. Photo courtesy of the State Historical Society of Wisconsin.

and almost sixty thousand members in more than three hundred juvenile auxiliaries and children's legions.[26]

Identification with Frances Willard also had immeasurable benefit for Wisconsin temperance women. After the state chapter's induction, Willard offered a public address before a large audience in the Capitol. The *Chief* reprinted an effusive review by Madison's *State Journal* of Willard's dress and address. "Remarkably graceful and dignified," in stark dress which added to her stage presence, Willard gave an address "of great beauty of thought and felicity of expression brilliantly illustrated with anecdotes," which "proved her to be one of the foremost lecturers of the Northwest."

However, at least in Wisconsin, affiliation with the WCTU would not help women win temperance. In giving up local autonomy for the greater good, the Alliance gave up the goal of temperance closer to home in Wisconsin, where the WCTU never would gain ground against the best-organized opposition in the country, the brewers.

Temperance and woman's rights were linked everlastingly after the crusade, which did not bode well for either cause—especially in Wisconsin, whose women were only the first to face a countercampaign which spread across the country almost as swiftly as had their crusade. By 1880, the brewers' Personal Liberty Association became a model for the industry; under the aegis of a new, national Brewers Congress, the tactics used in Wisconsin would be adopted and expanded to include an "Agitating Committee" and a "literary manager"—a publicist—in New York City, a lobbyist in Washington, D.C., and "vigilance committees" in several states.[27]

Elsewhere in the country, women's crusade and the WCTU had succeeded in achieving their overt purpose: overall, consumption of alcohol dropped precipitously in 1874, while per capita consumption of "hard spirits" was cut by half, never again to reach the record levels of precrusade years. The number of liquor dealers declined to a lesser degree and would recover in less than two decades.

But adherents of beer drinking rebounded by 1880 to previous levels of consumption and conviviality—especially in Wisconsin where Milwaukee's brewers encouraged many a tavern keeper and even entire towns to backslide. The *Sentinel* summed up the decade as disheartening for women owing to a "general disinclination—among the Teutonic races at least—to be dictated to by those who have not the power to enforce their will," without the ballot.[28] With the brewers, Wisconsin women were only the first to face the strongest opposition to temperance—and, soon, to woman suffrage.

In the spring of 1880, Wisconsin witnessed a surge of political action at the polls and in the press by temperance women. The *Chief*'s "exchanges" included women's columns in several papers such as the Whitewater *Register*'s "temperance department" by a "ladies committee" which reported regularly on progress of a two-year campaign by "leading women" for a "no-license ticket." When the women turned up at the polls to monitor turnout, the village board moved balloting to the town jail. As they reported in the *Register,* the board was "quite correct in supposing that the women would not follow such a crowd into the lockup; but the insult to decent men, compelling them to go there or lose their votes, brings discredit on our village government." When the election eventually was contested, the court agreed and ruled for the temperance slate.

Wisconsin women also watched as their "sisters to the south" in the Illinois WCTU won legislative approval of limited suffrage on liquor laws. Emma Brown regaled readers with correspondence from women who marched to the polls, literally; on election day in one border town, fifty women met for a prayer meeting at dawn, then "processed two by two" to the polls where they were greeted by the town band, all men, who played "in honor of the great event of the women's casting their first vote." Some "proselytized" near the polls all day, meeting "no rudeness" from men, while others organized carriage caravans to transport elderly and infirm voters. "It was a touching sight to see the aged women with their gray hairs and feeble footsteps coming so grandly to the rescue," wrote the president of the Illinois WCTU. "The result was a triumphant victory for no license—not a woman's vote on the other side."

With "temperance suffrage" in Illinois and "school suffrage" in Michigan and Minnesota, stalwart remnants of the Wisconsin Woman Suffrage Association attempted to revive support in the state. In March 1880, Marion V. Dudley of Milwaukee testified before a state senate committee on behalf of a suffrage bill. But the men refused to grant suffrage by legislative enactment, as in other states, and gave only grudging approval to a referendum on an amended "partial suffrage" bill, for married women only. The bill would exclude Lavinia Goodell, as Emma Brown noted: "Imagine Judge Ryan's grim smile when he thinks of Miss Goodell as debarred from voting!" Emma did not note that she also would be excluded, and endorsed the bill anyway, as did the *State Journal* and small-town papers such as the *Palmyra Enterprise.* More typical of press opinion was the *Milwaukee Sentinel*'s prediction that the bill would die in the next biennium.

Lavinia Goodell, the state's strongest proponent of woman's legal rights, did not testify; she died within days of the bill's passage, and only three weeks after word that she had won her first case before the Wisconsin Supreme Court. Goodell battled cancer as well as the court throughout her campaign for admission to the state bar but remained active until 1880 on the podium, in the press, and in her practice, by then in Madison. Her death in March, when she was only forty years old, was reported in the press across the Midwest. The *Milwaukee Sentinel* eulogized "the lady lawyer" as "a prominent advocate of woman suffrage as well as temperance reform," who "was associated with some of the leading women of America in raising the condition of her sex." In the *Chief* obituary, Emma Brown added only a single line: "She will be deeply mourned."

Not all members of the state bar mourned Goodell's passing. The president of the bar, Moses M. Strong, would note "as a matter of proper satisfaction" in his "tribute" to deceased members that only one other woman had been admitted before the bar, and she had "wisely selected so circumscribed a sphere as New London" for her practice rather than encroach upon the male bastion of Madison.[29]

Still, the state again "attracted the attention" of Elizabeth Cady Stanton and Susan B. Anthony, who toured together in Wisconsin for the first time — and the first suffrage convention — in a decade. On June 4 and 5, 1880, Stanton, Anthony, and other national leaders met in Milwaukee with twenty-five women from several local organizations that had arisen on their own. Marion Dudley spoke on her testimony, reprinted in pamphlet form for delegates to distribute statewide, and women talked of reviving the moribund state suffrage association. As a later state leader wrote, Wisconsin seemed in a "promising condition" — at least, until Stanton and Anthony left.

Once again, suffragists' lack of sustained organization let legislators renege on reform. The limited-suffrage bill did not receive the required second approval, and another bill was submitted but also lost. As Laura Ross Wolcott recalled, the "successive defeats discouraged the women. They instructed their friends in the legislature to make no further attempts for a constitutional amendment, because they had not the slightest hope of its passage." The press as a whole was hopeless as well; the *Sentinel* somehow deduced that "the only successful opponents to woman suffrage are women themselves" and that "nobody really cares about the issue."[30]

Some suffragists seeking political action turned a last time to the equally hopeless Prohibition party. In 1881, party leaders started an

auxiliary—a standard strategy to enlist women—called the State Prohibitory Amendment Association and elected Emma Bascom as corresponding secretary, the same position she held in the state WCTU. The
Chief received regular correspondence on recruitment schemes such as
sale of "stock" at a dollar per share, rather than dues, to "investors"
in the association. The *Chief* also reported, with relief, that party leaders
decided "not to run a separate ticket in the coming gubernatorial canvass." Then the men reversed themselves and ran another futile ticket.
The *Chief* and other temperance papers stayed with the GOP, as did
most voters; the Prohibition party's claim of a forty percent increase
over the previous slate still amounted to only one-ninth of all votes cast.

At the Prohibitory Association's next annual meeting, in the Capitol
in Madison, Emma Bascom ran for reelection but was voted out. Leaders
promised improvement, passing resolutions to "employ an organizer"
to "devote considerable time to the consideration of the methods to be
used in raising money" and to conduct publicity. But the organization's
publicity suffered, according to Emma Brown, who criticized "advances"
sent only after the next annual meeting.

In another portent of the political future for temperance and for
women in Wisconsin, the new WCTU relied on the Prohibition party
in a campaign that won for the wrong reason and went down to widespread ridicule. An Anti-Treat Bill, outlawing the common saloon courtesy of standing drinks, was passed by lawmakers as a joke—until outraged public reaction led to swift repeal.[31]

An item in the *Chief* in 1882, unrelated to legislative campaigns, offered a more telling insight into most women's plight. A correspondent
from Christiana reported progress made since the women's temperance
crusade: the "traffic flourished unmolested and unreproved" no longer,
nor were "horses and wives beaten without remonstrance"—apparently,
in that order of importance.

Although women's crusade for temperance had run aground in Wisconsin by 1882, the Alliance and the WCTU—and even the Templars
and the Prohibitionists—served women as crucial training grounds in
strategies and tactics of statewide organization and political action. A
subtle but more significant impact of the crusade was as an impetus
for women to organize, ostensibly for temperance but inevitably for the
ballot. The covert purpose of their crusade, suffrage would be the stated
cause of their next public campaign in the state.

4

Women in the Newsroom, Women in the News
Temperance and Suffrage, 1882–1890

THE Wisconsin Woman Suffrage Association was revived in 1882 in reaction to legislators' burial of the limited-suffrage bill, but women initially welcomed male leadership in the movement. Leading the list of illustrious gentleman suffragists was General Lucius Fairchild, the Civil War hero and former governor who had introduced Elizabeth Cady Stanton and Susan B. Anthony in the assembly on their first tour of the state in 1869. In all, fifty-five prominent Wisconsin men and women issued the call in August for a statewide suffrage convention to be held in Madison in September.

This time, significantly, Stanton and Anthony were not invited; their militant tactics, such as Anthony's interruption of the nation's centennial celebration in 1876 to read women's Declaration of Independence, may have been too scandalous to some midwesterners, women or men. This time, the WWSA program was led by Henry Blackwell and his spouse, Lucy Stone, cofounders of the American Woman Suffrage Association, the conservative counterpart to Stanton and Anthony's National Woman Suffrage Association.

The conciliatory mood of the 1882 convention applied across generations as well as genders. Although those attending stressed their "independence of the former [state] association," they proposed a list of officers that was intended "to preserve a connecting link" with the previous organization. The slate was led by Dr. Laura Ross Wolcott; the pioneer-

100

ing woman physician and first president of the WWSA in 1869, she had been wed and widowed—her husband was General Erastus B. Wolcott, a Civil War hero and surgeon general of Wisconsin until his death—in the intervening decade. In that decade, Wolcott held the presidency by default because the WWSA had not even convened.

The new leadership came to the new WWSA from crusades across the state. Emma Curtiss Bascom—whose husband, the University of Wisconsin president, presided at the 1882 convention—was elected a vice president of the WWSA, the same post she held in the state WCTU. Alura Collins of Mukwonago, elected WWSA corresponding secretary, also held state WCTU office. Active in the WCTU at the local level were Marion V. Dudley of Milwaukee, elected a vice president of the WWSA, and Edna Phillips Chynoweth of Madison and Vie H. Campbell of Evansville; both would be officers of both organizations at the state level. Others among the thirty-five WWSA delegates came from "temperance towns" of Grand Rapids, Mosinee, Berlin, and Richland Center.

Richland Center, the village where temperance women had led a violent attack on "John Barleycorn" in the form of a "Bowling Saloon" a quarter of a century before, would provide suffrage leadership in the state for the next four decades—the legacy of Laura Briggs James, also elected a vice president of the new WWSA in 1882. She was the second wife, and sister of the first wife, of a Civil War hero and prosperous store owner in Richland Center. The widower had wooed his "eclectic sister-in-law," a former teacher, by financing her return to school at Oberlin College "for the cause of pioneering women's employment in the telegraphy profession." In 1873, Laura Briggs James had returned to Richland Center, where she would found a family dynasty soon renowned for suffrage reform.

Richland Center women would play a significant role in the new WWSA's reorganization, a part that required courage in small-town Wisconsin. Early in 1882, twelve women met at the James home to found a "suffrage club." But they took precautions, according to historian Twylah Kepler—if not to the extent suggested by local myths that surround the founding, such as "that the first meeting was held 'behind drawn blinds.'" Still, "these women were well aware that they were committing a controversial act, for many then considered it quite radical to advocate woman's right to vote."

The women dealt with organizational details without any difficulty until they came to naming the club. Despite approval of "the idea of a suffrage club," several women suggested that "by omitting the word"—

suffrage—"they would be more free to work for other reforms" whose reputations might suffer by association. Their new president, "a charter member of the WCTU," agreed. Arguing that "there was nothing to be gained by a name that might cause instant antagonism . . . she warned the group, 'We must be as wise as serpents and harmless as doves if we are to make converts to our cause.'" A "lively discussion ensued," but in the end, according to Kepler, "the new organization was named the more acceptable title of, simply, 'The Woman's Club'" because "surely the most prejudiced husband could not object to an organization whose constitution sought 'to suggest and develop plans for social, intellectual, educational and philanthropic interests.'" However, they "did not define 'intellectual interest,'" and "members knew it meant female suffrage." Men also knew what the women meant to accomplish. The next week's *Republican and Observer* published a member's report under the headline "Suffrage Club Meets."

Despite publicity, or because of it, the Woman's Club went forward with "tact and judgment," according to Laura James. Even she later admitted that "we each felt a shrinking fear" for a time. However, James worried less about "outside criticism" than that "elements of inharmony within our circle" might cause the club to disband—and her greatest fear was that "we might wish ourselves safely back forever in the seclusion of homes." But membership soared. Within a month, a branch in nearby Sextonville was organized by a charter member of the Woman's Club—Mary Hurlbut, Laura Briggs James's mother.

By the summer of 1882, the Richland Center club was the largest suffrage organization in the state, and was asked by Madison women to assist in reorganization at the state level. Fourteen Woman's Club members went to Madison "with pencils sharpened at both ends," as one reported in a Richland Center paper, to assist in writing the call for the convention in the fall of 1882. However, women in the capital had already honed a publicity campaign that pinpointed "sympathetic papers" with remarkable accuracy. For almost six months prior to the convention, women sent articles on suffrage every two weeks to eighty papers in the state. As Helen Olin of Madison reported in the *Wisconsin State Journal,* "with only one exception, the courtesy and kindness of the press have been universal," and almost half of the eighty editors had "personally assured" her committee of space for a regular suffrage column.

The rebirth of suffrage organization in Wisconsin owed much to temperance crusades and the WCTU for training a generation of women in the strategies and tactics of reform. But these women would not lead the WWSA for long—and men would never again so dominate a suffrage convention in the state—because another first-time WWSA officer in 1882 was the Reverend Olympia Brown of Racine.[1]

This time, because of Olympia Brown, the WWSA would endure until woman suffrage was won—twice. But, because of the trials and errors of Olympia Brown, woman suffrage would be won and lost in Wisconsin by the end of the decade, and for decades to come. So notoriously single-minded for suffrage was Olympia Brown that she had not participated in the women's temperance crusade, and had never learned its crucial lessons on the use of the press.

The Reverend Olympia Brown was one of the most remarkable and radical women of her time, or since. Since 1868, when she had stood down Frederick Douglass and stormed out to help found the first regional suffrage association, Brown refused to affiliate with either Stanton and Anthony or Stone and Blackwell but became a charter member of both organizations. Brown also refused Anthony's offer of a full-time post as a professional organizer, at double her ministerial salary, and decided to stay in the pulpit. But Brown had lost her pastorate in Connecticut when elders decided—only after her marriage and the birth of her first child—that they preferred a "gentleman preacher." By 1876, an embittered Brown testified before a congressional subcommittee for Anthony's federal suffrage amendment. "Our interests are still uncared for," she said, "and we do not wish to be thus sent from pillar to post to get our rights." In 1878, after a two-year search for a pulpit, Brown was called by a Universalist congregation in Racine, where her husband, John Willis, purchased a part ownership in the *Times-Call.* Although she was not the first woman minister to serve in Wisconsin—the Reverend Augusta Chapin had helped to found the WWSA before returning to Iowa—Brown was the only one at the time. But she rarely sought press attention, and then primarily in the *Chief.*

In her early years in Wisconsin, Brown avoided the notoriety which she had earned in the East for her pioneering ministry and suffrage campaigning. She concentrated on building her congregation and rebuilding her career, refraining from work in the limited-suffrage campaign and restricting her suffragism to out-of-state activity; in 1880, for example, she had only shared a podium with Stanton and Anthony at the Milwaukee convention but had spoken for Wisconsin at their National Woman Suffrage Association convention in Indianapolis. By 1880, when Brown wrote a chapter on her 1867 Kansas campaign for the second

"Our interests are still uncared for, and we do not wish to be thus sent from pillar to post to get our rights."—The Reverend Olympia Brown of Racine, a pioneering woman minister, the founder and publisher of the *Wisconsin Citizen* and the president of the Wisconsin Woman Suffrage Association for almost thirty years. Photo courtesy of the State Historical Society of Wisconsin.

volume of their *History of Woman Suffrage,* her own painful suffrage past seemed buried in history books. As Brown's biographer writes, "none of [the contributors] could have dreamed how many more volumes"—four—"still would have to be written before women won the right to vote."[2]

When women did vote, Brown would be the most venerable of "first-generation" suffragists who survived to cast a ballot and would be venerated by "second-generation" suffragists elsewhere. However, in Wisconsin, her organizational style would alienate younger women. Brown was a spellbinding speaker—"the female Beecher of the rostrum," according to an admirer—and an experienced organizer, but elevated centralization to the extreme. That Brown would run the state movement almost alone was understandable; it was the way she always had worked, against great odds. But Brown's inability to adapt her style to the collective effort of the postcrusade era was regrettable, and put her at odds with the public, the press, and many women within the WWSA, to its detriment.

Only two weeks after the 1882 WWSA convention, at the first executive committee meeting in Madison, Brown's impact already was evident when members approved a wide-ranging campaign far beyond any previously attempted in Wisconsin. If Brown was not the sole architect, she controlled the campaign's outcome by being its author; her name, not Laura Ross Wolcott's, was on press correspondence datelined Racine. The tactics were those Brown had used before: the long-term goal was a petition drive to the state legislature for a referendum, "although many of the suffragists"—Brown among them, or she would not have mentioned it—went "still further" and wanted to petition legislators to pass a resolution to Congress for a Constitutional amendment. The WWSA's short-term "object" was "to work up a sentiment" for suffrage, with priority put on a statewide canvass to "insure vigorous presentation of the matter to the public." The executive committee appointed an agent, Sarah A. Richards of Milwaukee, "reputed to be a shrewd and capable businesswoman," to "work up the feeling, organize clubs in the various towns, travel from place to place and attend to the affairs of the suffragists." Addresses were planned statewide by Richards, Brown, Alura Collins, Marion Dudley, and a "Mrs. Haggert, of Indiana"—Mary E. Haggart—"one of the ablest female speakers in the country."

Characteristically, but unfortunately, Olympia Brown listed publicity as the WWSA's last priority; she used the press only when she could preach to the converted. Brown's wary attitude toward the press traced to earlier experience in the East where, after initially enjoying the attention paid to her pioneering ministry, Brown had learned that being a newsmaker meant being at newsmen's mercy. Reporters taunted her in print on retaining her own name after marriage and behaved like "small boys" regarding woman's rights, she recalled.[3]

Brown attempted to extend internal control of the organization to controlling the news—an impossibility, and bound to backfire. Her reports most often went to the press after the fact, with release restricted to "friendly papers" such as the *Chief* and the *Waukesha Free-*

man. Editors opposed to suffrage or even neutral rarely received advances which invited press attention. The only advantage was a savings for the WWSA's postal budget; as a policy, it could only doom a public opinion campaign to defeat. In her defense, woman suffrage undoubtedly was doomed in Wisconsin, where only indomitable women like Olympia Brown would withstand the well-organized opposition.

Within weeks, Brown's aversion to publicity was reinforced by press response to the proposed suffrage campaign, which won statewide attention from the very papers she had attempted to circumvent. The *Milwaukee Sentinel* conducted an "independent investigation into the Woman Suffrage movement" that was picked up by the press statewide; even once-sympathetic editors were caught up in what later media theorists would call the bandwagon effect. The *Freeman,* for example, said that "the *Sentinel* shows that suffrage does not move, in this state, at least. If women generally should ask for the suffrage they would most probably get it, but the fact is that women generally have too much sense."

The WWSA attempted to implement Brown's plan. Suffragists canvassed and spoke in several counties, and one, John Bascom, earned an interesting compliment from the Elkhorn *Independent* for an address "as unanswerable as it was profound." But neither Indiana's able Mary Haggart nor the petition drive was mentioned again, and no statewide WWSA convention was held for two years.[4]

For the next two years, the WCTU would take the lead in Wisconsin reform, if for the last time—a time which temperance women would use wisely to move the organization toward suffrage in the state as well as nationwide. In the interim, women in the WWSA and WCTU, trained in temperance and more comfortable with publicity than was Olympia Brown, cultivated the press on their own. For example, the Whitewater Woman Suffrage Club arose after the 1882 convention, enrolled more than one hundred members, and contributed a column called "Equality Before the Law" in the local *Register,* one of the first papers to welcome women's temperance columns in the 1870s. In Richland Center, a "firebrand" member of the Woman's Club was a frequent "temperance correspondent" to local papers, including one that had headlined the story of the "Suffrage Club" only six days after its founding, and Laura Briggs James's sister-in-law Georgianna had a regular column in the *Richland Rustic.* From Mukwonago, Alura Collins exhibited reportorial flair and astute news sense in correspondence in the *Chief* as early as 1877 and in the *Freeman,* too, after 1882. Collins established considerable credibility as a news source by sending useful items on the WCTU and other organizations as well as the WWSA and by sending advances well in advance—a rarity noted by an appreciative Emma Brown. Collins also signed her name to her work at a time when many women still used pseudonyms or initials.

The WCTU's preeminence in the press was underscored at the state convention in Milwaukee in October 1882, only weeks after the WWSA's. By 1882, forty papers ran women's temperance columns in Wisconsin, and the success of their press campaign was the news of the convention for the *Freeman*. Women "reported that the sentiment of the press in the State was more favorable to the temperance cause . . . and the number of papers which advocate prohibition was said to be constantly increasing," said the *Freeman*. As significant as the number was women's control of the news slant; papers were "pleased" to run copy as "edited by ladies," which "allowed them a candid expression of sentiment through their columns."

The WCTU continued for another year to be less than candid on increasing suffrage sentiment within the organization. At the 1882 convention, Frances E. Willard laid the foundation for women to widen their work and concerns with her "Do Everything" slogan—which also allowed women to do less than more militant suffragists in the WCTU. As historian Sara M. Evans suggests, the slogan symbolized "a brilliant organizing strategy" to encompass a spectrum of women and their causes, although Willard continued to work from within to bring more reluctant members to the suffrage cause and forged ties with politically minded temperance men whose support would counter public criticism. She also continued to cultivate an increasingly worshipful press—always the most reluctant to alter the status quo—in order to withstand editorial criticism which was bound to come whenever women were bound for the ballot.

In 1883, most temperance women and men seemed bound for Lake Monona, where the WCTU's "temperance camp" established leadership in the Wisconsin movement only ten years after women's temperance crusade. Planning began at the 1882 convention with the first turnover at the top since the organization's founding as the Women's Alliance. Dorcas Hadley Beale of Janesville had stepped down from the presidency to serve as corresponding secretary and coordinate publicity. The new WCTU state president, Isabella H. Irish of Madison, issued a call to all "temperance people" to attend a three-day temperance camp at Lake Monona in July 1883. The women won the endorsement of the Templars and enrolled more than a hundred attendees who heard speakers including the ever-popular past leader of the international order, Theodore D. Kanouse, and a physician who spoke on "physiognomic" effects of alcohol. The main draw was Mary B. Willard, editor of the WCTU's new *Union Signal* and sister-in-law of WCTU president Frances E. Willard. With activities for children and tent housing for all attendees, including Emma Brown, the *Chief* pronounced the camp "well done."

Still, membership in the state WCTU remained low until Willard launched a national recruitment drive capitalizing on the tenth anniversary of the 1873–74 crusade. By November 1883, the national convention reported a record membership of one hundred thousand women in every state and territory. Another measure of success was the *Union Signal,* the result of a merger by Frances E. Willard of her Illinois chapter's stronger paper with the national publication. With a circulation of fourteen thousand, the weekly *Union Signal* already was the most popular "temperance sheet" in the nation and soon would be one of the largest-circulation papers in the world. The WCTU's publishing company also was one of the largest in the country with a list of books, manuals, tracts, pamphlets, and periodicals as well as the *Union Signal.* [5]

At the 1883 national WCTU convention, women from thirty-three states and territories reveled in elaborate rituals which recalled their origin in the crusade and the organization's remarkable rise. Local unions in Wisconsin also reported celebrations to the *Chief* but received mixed reviews, surprisingly, from Emma Brown.

Emma Brown disapproved of the WCTU's new direction for its second decade because she read Willard's "Home Protection" campaign correctly as a calculated subterfuge for suffrage. The first report surfaced in October 1883 in one of Emma's "exchanges," the Illinois WCTU *Lever,* in which the chapter resolved to "work for woman suffrage as well as prohibition." The *Chief* retorted that it supported "woman suffrage as a measure standing upon its own merits" and as women's "by right," not by means which compromised either cause. Emma railed at the WCTU again in November when Willard won the national convention to her campaign for "Home Protection," a slogan she had coined earlier which impressed press and politicians alike and won limited suffrage in Illinois. Now the national WCTU convention approved a "sixteenth amendment" petition campaign to Congress for woman suffrage. As Emma sternly reminded readers, "there cannot be but one amendment submitted at a time" and the next was supposed to be for temperance. "We want the steady, persistent and untiring work for 'this one thing'"—temperance—"and no wasting of power in carrying along a lot of other reforms."

Willard's "Home Protection" slogan signaled a turning point not only for suffragists but also for temperance women, marking the end of a generation—Emma Brown's generation. It was a difficult juncture for Emma, an early and ardent admirer of Frances Willard until her dilution of the *Chief*'s paramount cause. Emma and her cohort had seen temperance made secondary in reform before, when abolitionism led the antebellum agenda. But the abandonment of the "first generation" of temperance women in 1875 has been ignored by historians who see only the impact on the suffrage cause; for example, Eleanor Flexner suggests "that the work of WCTU members for woman suffrage raised obstacles out of all proportion to the help they contributed," because they only raised the ire of "liquor interests." As Emma knew, espousing suffrage would similarly split "friends of temperance so much divided on the question."

Emma Brown also had been in reform long enough to recognize that Willard's slogan signaled a shift in the suffrage movement which could only compromise the suffrage cause as well, by conceding the ballot as an inborn right and acceding to the concept of suffrage as a privilege to be earned. According to biographer Ruth Bordin, Willard saw neither temperance nor suffrage "as a right" and regarded "considerations of strategy as more compelling than ideology." Willard was early in her willingness to barter for the ballot by touting women as a protemperance bloc; according to Aileen S. Kraditor, the shift in ideologies from "justice" to "expediency" was more characteristic of the post-1890 period. Then, many women would emulate Willard's use of "domestic imagery," in historian Sara M. Evans' words. However, Willard has not received credit—or blame—as a pioneer in mass persuasion history as well. Her "Home Protection" slogan also is one of the earliest examples of the shift from rational argument to emotional appeal, which historian Merle Curti dates to the turn of the century.[6]

Willard was a "second-generation" suffragist born too soon, while Emma Brown was a temperance ideologue before Willard was born. "In the thickest of the fight for prohibition for more than thirty years," Emma refused to sacrifice principle for progress—and she foresaw strategic and tactical problems, too. "It is unfortunate for both questions that the effort should be made to support both in one organization. Both are weaker together than either would be apart," she wrote. "Women's work for temperance will be far more effective without being yoked with the work for woman suffrage, and woman suffrage will be infinitely stronger when sought to be obtained from principle and on its merits, rather than from expediency." The journalist in Emma Brown also had a few things to say about the "facts" of the situation facing woman suffragists. "Facts are stubborn things which all the enthusiasm and zeal in the world cannot move," she wrote from long experience.

Stubborn resistance to temperance had never stopped Emma Brown, but reason gave way to emotion for her as well; she could not put suffrage ahead of the cause which had consumed her brother's life, and her own. The *Chief* continued to carry suffrage news because Emma Brown never could turn down a good story. But she would wage editorial warfare on the WCTU campaign to the end—and, in the end, she was right; both suffrage and temperance would suffer. However, at the time, Emma Brown felt wronged.

Emma Brown and other temperance women of the crusade era were replaced by new WCTU leadership that emerged in 1883. Madison's Isabella H. Irish was reelected as president in 1883 at the annual meeting in Sparta. But Irish would soon be succeeded by Emma Curtiss Bascom, whose tenure also would be brief. The news in 1883 was a newcomer to office in the state WCTU, Amy C. Kellogg, president of the Fort Atkinson union—a local angle played large in the *Chief*. Emma Brown vouched for Kellogg as "raised in temperance"—and on the *Chief*—and saw hope of a return to the primacy of temperance in the WCTU. She would be disappointed.

In 1884, Kellogg rose to the presidency of the state WCTU on a wave of support for woman suffrage with the success of the tenth-anniversary drive, and Willard returned to Wisconsin. Statewide, the WCTU reported more than twenty new local unions for a total of seventy-five, with more than fifteen hundred members. A record number of the "cold-water army" gathered in September in "the city of healing waters," as Kellogg called the resort town of Waukesha for the fabled therapeutic power of its natural springs. The "representatives of the grandest society ever organized and conducted by woman" were in a celebratory mood, giving ovations to every speaker. But women were waiting for Frances E. Willard.

Willard came before the state WCTU to win endorsement of her "Home Protection" campaign and won headlines as well. She "spoke to a crowded audience as they had never before heard a woman speak. Every sentence which fell from her lips electrified her hearers and sunk

"It must be confessed with sorrow that our Badger State is behind the sister states in the onward march of reform."—Amy Kellogg Morse of Fort Atkinson, a president of the Wisconsin Woman's Christian Temperance Union. Photo courtesy of the State Historical Society of Wisconsin.

deep into their hearts," according to the *Waukesha Freeman*. The charismatic Willard won the convention's unanimous endorsement of her pledge in favor of "the platform and principles of the Prohibition Party," which included planks for woman suffrage.

From 1884 on, the Wisconsin WCTU openly emulated Willard's methods, which transformed a movement into a bureaucracy—but the methods worked to win numerous women, if not temperance. Willard's thirty-eight "departments of work" conducted campaigns for causes from equal pay for equal work—in "respectable occupations"—and inclusion of women on juries to hiring of female officers in women's prisons and inclusion of women in official church positions. Under Kellogg, the state WCTU soon included two dozen departments. "Press Work" and "Franchise and Legislative Work" were both under Alura Collins whose publicity, combined with Kellogg's recruiting tours, would double WCTU membership to three thousand women in only three years.

Like Willard, Kellogg was careful to disavow direct ties between temperance and suffrage for her Wisconsin constituency. In a typically conciliatory comment, she wrote in her annual report that some in the Wisconsin WCTU "thoroughly believe in woman's suffrage" but "others, and some of our best workers, too, have not yet come to the point that woman needs or should have the ballot."

Neither WCTU followers nor its foes were fooled at the time, at least in Wisconsin, where temperance women and suffragists often were one and the same. As one wrote to Laura Briggs James, all eighty members of her Marathon County WCTU were suffragists by 1884—the year when James, Collins, and others in the WCTU and the WWSA would revive the suffrage campaign deferred since 1882.

But in 1884, women also witnessed a sobering reminder of the influence of the brewing industry with the loss of the leader of both the WCTU and the WWSA, Emma Curtiss Bascom. In 1884, she had stepped in to serve as interim president of both organizations upon the resignations of Isabella H. Irish from the WCTU and Dr. Laura Ross Wolcott from the WWSA. The double burden for Emma Bascom may account for her decision not to seek election to either post by the fall of 1884, but a more likely explanation is that she reduced her prominence in reform because of her husband's differences with university regents, especially brewers.

John Bascom's proclivity for temperance apparently was not known before he accepted the University of Wisconsin presidency but accelerated after his arrival in Madison—understandably. The excessive incidence of undergraduate inebriation was denounced from the pulpit, even then; one outraged reverend wrote the *Chief* that he witnessed more alcohol consumption in a week in Madison than was seen elsewhere in a year. Similar scenes witnessed by Bascom led him to write a temperance tract distributed nationwide, unsettling regents with a stake in one of the state's leading industries.

Regents' unhappiness with John Bascom increased by 1884, when he became the "moral leader" of Madison's Law and Order League. Bascom also was unhappy, but with dilatory enforcement of liquor laws by a former student, Dane County district attorney Robert M. La Follette. Bascom founded the Madison league in emulation of an earlier vigilante effort in Milwaukee, where posses of "special policemen" had been hired to enforce "blue laws" banning liquor sales on the Sabbath. However, they were surpassed by the private force hired in Madison, where sixty saloon keepers were arrested and fifty convicted in only eight months. The league soon expanded its campaign to closing down gambling in the capital, causing some grumbling among cardplaying legislators. But Bascom went too far when he tried to enforce "blue laws" on barbershops and livery stables as well as saloons. Enraged Germans enlisted the brewers' Wisconsin Association for the Protection of Personal Liberty, won press support, and pressured Bascom's league to disband. But brewers—and the Board of Regents—were not appeased.

In historian David Thelen's oblique words, the Bascoms would be "compelled to leave Madison," a loss not only to the University of Wisconsin but also to the WCTU and the WWSA—and the coming woman suffrage campaign. In a letter to Susan B. Anthony, "listened to with interest and prized" by national leaders, Emma Bascom decried state politics as corrupted by brewers: "Will [the Republican party], as so repeatedly in the past, turn a deaf ear to reason, and still continue to deny the rights of half the human family? If so . . . it [will] continue deaf, dumb and blind."

The reasons behind Emma Bascom's decision not to continue leadership in the temperance and suffrage movements in Wisconsin may have been on one successor's mind in 1884. Before the WCTU convention in Waukesha and Frances E. Willard, Amy C. Kellogg admitted that "it must be confessed with sorrow that our Badger State is behind the sister states in the onward march of reform."[7]

The 1884 WWSA convention made for colorful coverage. In Richland Center on September 9 and 10, the Woman's Club festooned a local hall with flowers and far from flowery slogans such as "the chivalry which prompts men to represent women at the polls should extend to the prison and the gallows." They also had built "polling booths" where a "mock trial" of suffrage was staged to demonstrate to doubters that women did want the vote, a public stand known as the "Indiana plan." After a welcoming address by Laura Briggs James's mother, Sextonville member Mary Hurlbut, women voted for the Prohibition party and resolved to publicize results in the "friendly press": the *Prohibitionist*, Richland Center papers, and the *Chief*. Residents were not all as friendly — Laura Briggs James dismissed "outside criticism" until a teacher lashed out at her daughter — but local papers reported a "packed" hall for the public session, despite "intense heat" which caused hardy suffragists to resort to "the old-fashioned hand fan." The "very earnest session," as Emma Brown wrote, "showed plainly that women were deeply interested in politics."

In the festive ambience, women celebrated the growth of the WWSA since 1882 when state organizer Sarah Richards had been "sent out to develop suffrage sentiment." In addition to associations in Racine, Richland Center, Berlin, Grand Rapids, Madison, Mosinee, and Mukwonago in 1882, women had held a "special meeting" in Janesville and had organized two associations in Milwaukee and one each in Bay View — later within Milwaukee city limits — and New London, North Prairie, Oshkosh, Rochester, Waukesha, Wauwatosa, and Whitewater. The only mournful moment of the convention, apparently, was to note the death of a founder of the WWSA: Mathilde Franziska Anneke, another loss for the cause on the eve of the suffrage campaign.

Encouraged by the spread of support, the convention again approved a campaign for full suffrage, as in 1882, and reinstated the plan deferred for two years. At last, the long-awaited Mary E. Haggart of Indiana would come to Wisconsin — and with her an amazing slate of speakers, including Mary A. Livermore, Julia Ward Howe, and May Wright Sewall, for "a course of lectures . . . on subjects relating to women" arranged by Olympia Brown, but only in Racine. Olympia Brown's town was becoming an annual stop on the circuit for national suffrage lecturers; Sewall had spoken in Racine the year before at a Woman's Council, reported as well run without "a hitch or a jar" by Brown. The meeting indicated her impatience with the WWSA's inaction in 1883, when no convention was called.

In 1884, the WWSA reelected Brown to a vice presidency — not the presidency, as she apparently wished. In her WWSA history, Brown claimed that she was elected president in 1884 to succeed Emma Bascom. However, contemporary press coverage and other accounts in the *History of Woman Suffrage*—by Laura Ross Wolcott, who was in the WWSA, and by Theodora Winton Youmans, who was in the press—state that Bascom was succeeded by Hattie Tyng Griswold of Columbus, whom Brown would have denied her brief place in history for reasons unknown. The discrepancy does not entirely discredit Brown as a source but is revealing because when she couldn't make history happen her way, Olympia Brown simply rewrote it—as she would be accused of doing, unjustly, in the suffrage campaign.[8]

Two other vice presidents newly elected at the 1884 convention who would play pivotal roles in the coming suffrage campaign were Alura Collins and Laura Briggs James. Collins would write the bill and lobby it through the legislature, where it would be submitted by the new state senator from Richland Center, who was the well-connected husband of Woman's Club member Georgianna James and brother-in-law of Laura Briggs James. Because Norman L. James was newly elected, women initially relied on promises of assistance from "sympathetic lawmakers," men with more legislative experience to ensure the law's legality.

Alura Collins also was new to legislative work. As Olympia Brown wrote, "the first woman lobbyist in the state" was "a young woman wholly unfamiliar with the routine of legislatures." Few women were, although Alura Collins also was the WCTU lobbyist but had accepted the appointment only recently, and would recall the WWSA campaign as an "experience very bewildering to a novice in such work." Contributing to her bewilderment might have been the lack of a budget; as Collins later wrote to Laura Briggs James, the $25 allotted for expenses by the WCTU had been expended on costs of lobbying for the WWSA, and she still owed $5 for postage which she could not cover. In closing, Collins begged the WWSA for a "regular arrangement."

For a novice in lobbying, Collins exhibited considerable initiative, and improvised well. First, she surveyed candidates for the legislature by "hectographed letter." Few but favorable replies convinced Collins to relocate to Madison to learn the legislative "routine" and to write a rough draft of a bill—a full-suffrage bill—for lawmakers to review and revise. However, after fruitless weeks, she abandoned hope of promised help from "those who professed themselves friendly." As Collins recalled, the men "thought school suffrage was all we ought to ask for and had no advice or suggestions to make for even that. I made up my mind that I must depend upon myself and I then gave up the legislature."

Collins "betook" herself to the University of Wisconsin law library to study other states' laws and draft a bill for full suffrage by legislative enactment—on that means of avoiding a referendum of the voters, she and Olympia Brown were adamant, even decades later. The legislative route was logical and followed precedent; it was the way women had won the ballot in other states, while a referendum required persuading a majority of the state's men. On advice of legislators, and almost as an afterthought, Collins also drafted a bill for school suffrage only—and only to be submitted after defeat of the first measure.

Her drafts done, although "very doubtful about the correctness in wording," Collins "trusted that the several lawyers" in the legislature "of national reputation even then, would discover any mistakes and correct them." But the "busy men" barely glanced at her work, especially the limited-ballot bill. "They thought since it was school suffrage that it wouldn't upset anything very much," Collins recalled. Women also considered the school-suffrage bill insignificant, as she later admitted. "I was so deeply engrossed by my work for the constitutional amendment," she recalled, "that I paid but little attention to the fate or meaning of the School Suffrage bill" as "the bills came safely through committees."

When the full-suffrage bill went into committee hearings, the WWSA went en masse to Madison. "Pioneer suffragists from around the state" testified, with many more women in attendance. Left to Collins was the less eventful side of lobbying, a "slow, tedious affair" which afforded "time for educational work." She arranged for legislators to introduce at least one petition per day, because "even if a petition contained but two or three names, its record in the minutes counted for us." Daily, lawmakers found her "hectographed copies" of suffrage arguments on their desks so that "in some way . . . the subject was placed before every member at every morning's sessions, briefly and forcibly."

As interminable weeks went by, Collins also allowed time for excursions into Madison to escape the tedium, and to regale *Waukesha Freeman* readers with accounts of life in the Capitol and on campus. Escorted by a university student, the younger brother of the *Freeman* editor and publisher, Collins attended classes by famed professors and was enthralled, although "crowning all was a view of the eclipse through the telescope" on Observatory Hill. She also covered a concert, carefully citing musical selections, but could not find words to describe the Madison fashion scene. "I suppose I ought to tell how some of the lovely ladies were dressed, but I am the worst person in the world to notice any such thing," Collins wrote. "Someone had to tell her" the hues of women's gowns, but for the few that were black. She also entertained legislators' wives, which she especially enjoyed. However, "it wasn't all pleasant," as Collins recalled with ladylike restraint. Madison's "girl lobbyist" endured "many unpleasant experiences but these were mostly due to ignorance and I've long ago forgotten most of them," or so Collins would claim long decades later.

After weeks of inaction, unpleasant events occurred with a suddenness which stunned women. The legislative campaign had been conducted according to Olympia Brown's policy of downplaying publicity, an inclination reinforced by a sympathetic lawmaker who advised women to conduct a "still hunt" out of sight of a press overwhelmingly opposed to suffrage. The WWSA "avoided publicity as much as possible," Brown wrote, "while working quietly to create a public sentiment in favor," providing printed material upon request such as "leaflets and information generally" which Collins sent to University of Wisconsin students staging a suffrage debate.

But the hearings brought the campaign to the notice of the *Milwaukee Sentinel,* still the leading paper in the state, which deduced once again that women did not want "the privilege," on the basis of a rather informal survey of one state with suffrage, and on the word of one anonymous, male source. The *Sentinel* would not have had to look far to find women who wanted the vote. Marion Dudley wrote a column for women in the *Milwaukee Telegraph* which included prosuffrage material, while the *Waukesha Freeman* ran Alura Collins' editorials and endorsed at least limited suffrage, as did the *Whitewater Register* and *Wisconsin Chief.* Arguing with the *Sentinel* as to the "privilege" of suffrage, Emma Brown wrote that "it would be but simple justice to give the amendment a unanimous vote."

But "simple justice" would elude women as press and public pressure mounted on politicians. At an evening hearing on the suffrage bills, attendance was high; "no other question during the session had drawn out so many town people," Collins wrote. However, the question drew only one legislator, assemblyman Frank Nye, to speak for suffrage. The mood of most legislators was made more apparent when the committee attached a requirement for a referendum to the school-suffrage bill as well as to the joint resolution for a full-suffrage amendment to the state constitution, although only the latter required a referendum by law—a point which Olympia Brown later would use to "show the purpose of the framers to have been to grant State or national suffrage," not school suffrage, as "was pointed out by some of the men instrumental in its passage."

Passage was swift in the senate which, within a week, sent both bills on to the assembly where Frank Nye again was women's hero. As Collins reported, when the assembly unexpectedly passed the school-suffrage bill first—the bill submitted only as an "afterthought"—and the joint resolution for full suffrage came up for a vote afterward, only Nye "urged that, as the assembly had just concurred in school suffrage . . . how could the same assembly refuse to, at least, submit the joint resolution to the people." The assembly did refuse, and left women with a limited-suffrage law subject to a referendum at the polls—and worse, as women would discover when the law was subjected to interpretation by the courts.

Although the flaw in the law would not be found by the courts until three years later, the women already were disturbed by rewording which had been substituted by the assembly. Collins wrote that she had originally, and "unfortunately, worded the bill for clear understanding by all"—at least, all other states where similar wording worked well. Her bill had required that any woman registering to cast a ballot "in the *school district* where she offers it in the ten days next preceding any election pertaining to school matters, shall have a right to vote at such election."

Two words were critical: "It originally read School District instead of Election District; at least that was the meaning," as Collins later recalled. Her version survived the senate by a vote of twenty to eighteen, "but the bill was amended while in the Assembly in such a way as to further add to its indefiniteness." In the assembly, "someone proposed a substitution" of the new wording—"Election District"—which was passed by a vote of sixty-seven to thirty-three, "and then by the Senate upon being sent back to that body."[9]

As Collins wrote at the time, "although there are some very clear-headed lawyers in the Legislature," the lack of clarity in their law was surprising—or perhaps not, given politics.

> Why they allowed such indefinite wording to pass both houses unchallenged, I cannot understand. Rev. Olympia Brown and a good many others believe that it was done purposely. A prominent gentleman in Republican politics said to me in Madison that he could not understand why the Legislature allowed the bill to pass in the form it did, except on one supposition—that the friends of the measure in the Legislature hoped to get at least municipal suffrage by means of it, and that the enemies hoped to defeat all suffrage for women by the wording of it.[10]

With the rewording, even she was unsure of her bill's meaning, Collins wrote, and "a number of the Wisconsin Woman Suffrage Association wrote to gentlemen who were opposed to suffrage in any form for women, and asked them what the bill meant, and they responded that if it meant anything, it meant very much."

Olympia Brown also received reassurances that the law, as reworded, would allow women to cast their ballots in more than school races. "Many, and among them the men who voted for the law in the legislature, urged that the law did not indicate what we were to vote for but only the election at which we were to vote. They showed that nearly every election 'pertained to school matters,'" Brown recalled. But Collins remained concerned about the rewording of her bill and protested the proposed alterations, to no avail. "I was told I ought to be very thankful to get so near school suffrage," she recalled. "Several members of the legislature spoke to me about its wording and were sorry, for they felt sure there would be trouble about it; and there was trouble."

At the least, the law gave women limited suffrage. At best, as Senator James told Olympia Brown, the "law is all you need. Take it and work it for all it is worth."[11] But women would discover that the suffrage law, as worded, was worthless.

The WWSA clearly was unprepared for a public opinion campaign, but Olympia Brown and the WWSA cannot be blamed either for not anticipating a referendum or for rewording the law; that was the work of legislators who should have known what they were doing—and, perhaps they did. The WWSA's lack of preparation is evident in the lack of even an adequate roster of members for internal communication; the first step taken after passage was a "suffrage directory" to "ensure more concerted action among suffrage workers," as Alura Collins wrote in a press announcement of the project. The directory also served as a promotional piece as written by WWSA organizer Sarah A. Richards, a former Schofield schoolteacher who acted as office manager—although without an actual office—for the campaign, from Milwaukee. With names and addresses of WWSA members and "others known to favor the cause," the directory was primarily of use to the WWSA but also was advertised as available to individuals or other organizations, at a discount if ordered in bulk. Richards also provided a brief history of the state movement, profiles of leaders, and sketches of "auxiliary associations, temperance societies and women's clubs in the state"; the "backgrounder" also became the basis for Olympia Brown's later account in the *History of Woman Suffrage*.

The scope of the project was admirable, and the tactic of compiling a directory of members would become a standard means used by many organizations for ascertaining and sustaining support. But the canvass came too late, months after the legislative campaign, while the directory was delayed owing to upheaval within the WWSA.

Scant records of the WWSA convention in September 1885 suggest considerable internal disarray, even schism. The first official announcement was a rousing call "for all friends of equal rights to active duty" in the campaign to abolish "the aristocracy of sex which still exists" in child custody laws and similar "vestiges of barbarism, such as denying women the "school ballot." The call was signed by Harriet Tyng Griswold as president and by three other officers but not by officers Laura James, Alura Collins, and Olympia Brown, who were listed only as speakers. Nationally known speakers included Susan B. Anthony and Clara Bewick Colby, the valedictorian of the first University of Wisconsin class that included women. Colby had left the state fifteen years before for Nebraska where she founded the state suffrage association and the *Woman's Tribune,* the unofficial organ of Anthony and Stanton's suffrage organization. Colby made the *Tribune* "a most interesting and profitable family paper" offering "versatility and variety," according to Olympia Brown, in part because the editor was a "born teacher" who "wanted to help everybody and instruct everybody. Unfortunately many people do not wish to be instructed and some cannot be helped."[12]

Apparently neither Anthony nor Colby came to help the WWSA convention—either convention. Contemporary press accounts and WWSA histories again conflict, and rival meetings may have been held in Madison and Whitewater. However, only one side survived, and no more was heard of Hattie Tyng Griswold. The WWSA's new—and now officially elected—president was Olympia Brown.

The WWSA's disorganization, or Brown's distaste for the press, resulted in almost no publicity for the suffrage referendum for a full year, even in the *Freeman* and *Chief.* The WWSA's lack of support was apparent in a *Freeman* editorial by the recently married Alura Collins Hollister: "Can we not find workers everywhere to help carry this law? Our efforts should be constant . . . from now on, and at the polls." The lack of a cohesive campaign strategy is clear in her conclusion. All that was needed to win, wrote the newlywed, was for "every earnest woman" to "convince some man."

Finally, in the fall of 1886, with little more than two months until election day, the WWSA launched a campaign at the annual convention. Advances on the meeting hardly were heartening; one speaker, vice president Vie H. Campbell of Evansville, promised an address entitled "The Indifference of Women to Political Equality." However, the meeting held September 28 to 30 in Racine at Olympia Brown's church was reported as "the best ever held in the state" by a *Chief* correspondent. Nationally known speakers included Elizabeth Boynton Harbert of the Chicago *Inter-Ocean,* "celebrated English reform leader" Frances Lord, and, at last, Susan B. Anthony.

The 1886 convention came twenty years after Anthony brought Brown into the suffrage movement, and almost as many years since Brown refused Anthony's request to resign her pulpit for the sake of suffrage. However, soon after the WWSA meeting, Brown quit her hard-won ministerial career to preach full-time for the cause.

When the WWSA went public, the campaign continued to rely on the podium rather than the press. The effort kicked off with a mass meeting in the Capitol, in the assembly chamber, where Anthony gave an address. At the state fair, a WWSA exhibit featured women's organizations, but, according to the *Freeman* and *Weekly Wisconsin,* few papers received publicity and response was low. Through the fall, Brown toured Wisconsin and rallied women to be ready to vote. One even ran for statewide office: Fort Atkinson schoolteacher Carrie J. Smith declared her candidacy for state superintendent of schools, with the *Chief*'s endorsement of her scholarship and "practical knowledge of teaching" compared with the incumbent—whom Emma Brown found only "satisfactory." However, he was reelected.[13]

In November 1886, the WWSA actually won woman suffrage in Wisconsin, at least until women went to the polls. The referendum was approved by a narrow margin of only 4,583 ballots—43,581 in favor and 38,988 against—of more than 80,000 cast, and turnout was low; only thirty percent of voters in the gubernatorial race also voted on the referendum, on a separate ballot. The victory also resulted from the law's ambiguity. Most men—at least, those who later wrote outraged editorials—were willing to let "the ladies vote at school meetings to the extent that they desire," opined the *Freeman,* until the "ladies" let it be known that they desired more.

The woman suffrage law that women had won at the polls would be lost in the press, where Olympia Brown was at her worst. Within a week of the election, to counter the inevitable claim that women didn't want the ballot, she undertook a new and aggressive canvass of Wisconsin with Susan B. Anthony, Clara Bewick Colby, Mary A. Livermore, and other national leaders. The tour was intended to "awaken women to the necessity of voting at the first opportunity," but apparently only awakened the press to what women had wrought.

The tour apparently also caused dissension within the WWSA because Brown appeared to be "high-handed" in handling arrangements alone. However, as Brown wrote, she had "a very short time in which to prepare for a campaign" after receiving word from Anthony and her cohort "that they would join in holding conventions in all the congressional districts." In only a week, "by the president's deciding on places and dates without consultation, sending posters to the different towns selected and announcements to all the papers of the State, and then going in person to secure halls and make local arrangements," the tour began with "a tolerable degree of preparation." In her defense, Brown acted decisively. However, it is suggestive that, years later, she still was defensive.

In a whirlwind tour of Wisconsin, the women held "suffrage conventions" in each of the state's nine congressional districts in only three weeks, with as many as three addresses a day scheduled for Waukesha, Ripon, Oshkosh, Green Bay, Grand Rapids, Eau Claire, LaCrosse, Evansville, and Madison, and unscheduled stops in Acadia, Milwaukee, Neenah, Richland Center, and "other points," according to news accounts. The tour ended with addresses in the Capitol "to a distinguished audience," Brown wrote. "The effect of these meetings was marked. Many members were added . . . branches were organized and an impetus given to the work such as never was known before."

But the tour backfired and became the impetus for belated press reaction against the suffrage law. The bandwagon effect began within a week of the election in Waukesha, with the *Freeman*. Theron W. Haight—an open and ardent antisuffragist—dismissed the "convention" as a failure for not "exciting great apparent interest on the part of more than a very few people." However, Haight was sufficiently excited to interrupt the speakers and insert himself into the story. As he reported, when Anthony spoke "in favor of the so-called reform" and "seemed particularly anxious to hear anything that anybody could consider a 'reason' in opposition to woman suffrage," Haight "called out remarks on the other side of the question"—and then quoted himself, without the slurs and quotation marks which made Anthony's stand appear questionable.

The *Freeman*'s slanted antisuffrage coverage undoubtedly had an impact on others in the state press. Not only was Waukesha the site of the first stop on the tour, but Haight also had been publisher of the *Freeman* and editor of the *Sentinel,* and was widely read and respected by his brethren in the press. And they could not miss the story; for the first time, the *Freeman* played woman suffrage on the front page, and followed the story with reports of similar press outrage on Olympia Brown's postelection tour.

Although the press reaction was unwarranted, Olympia Brown undoubtedly alienated many a Wisconsinite with her increasingly nativist rhetoric. After canvassing the state through the winter, Brown returned to Madison in March 1887 when the bill for a full-suffrage amendment to the constitution again came on the calendar. Before a joint committee — including German legislators — at a hearing "attended by women from all parts of the State" that also was heard by "corridors filled with people anxious to learn," Brown made an intemperate speech. According to Alura Collins Hollister's account, Brown "said, among other things, that American born women exceeded all uneducated foreigners in the United States."

A month later, when Wisconsin women went to the polls for the first time, political pressure had mounted and many were refused. As election day dawned, according to Olympia Brown, Wisconsin Attorney General Charles B. Estabrook — whose wife would be an outspoken antisuffragist — "sent out telegrams to those places where he supposed women would be likely to vote, ordering the inspectors to reject their ballots, which was done; but where they were not advised by him the ballots of women were accepted." The attorney general had not anticipated the extent of interest by "likely" new voters; according to Alura Collins Hollister, "over two thousand women throughout the state voted, or tried to vote."

In rural areas, many women met no resistance and voted in municipal races as well as in school elections. At Sturgeon Bay, for example, two hundred women were accompanied to the polls by a state legislator who "reported to his constituents at home that the law gave women full suffrage," as Olympia Brown recalled. Emma Brown reported in a *Chief* roundup that "quite a number of women voted in Palmyra," where they were credited with tipping a hotly contested race for town chairman to a temperance man.

Some small towns even competed to make women welcome at the polls and were rewarded with record turnouts, especially for temperance. In Whitewater, 135 women went for the Prohibition ticket of 256 protemperance voters who cast ballots — and outnumbered men at the polls. The *Register* applauded the "sensation produced by women voting" as "notable in the history of our city" and as irrefutable evidence that women really did want the vote, editorializing that "the personal interest which women take in the suffrage privilege has been underrated. That more than one-fourth as many women as men . . . go to the ballot box as voters in spite of all the hesitancy and reluctance which naturally would be felt on taking a first step, is a significant proof of the earnestness with which they welcome the privilege, even as limited as it is." The turnout so impressed Republican men in one ward that two women served as delegates to the citywide party caucus to select candidates for school races. "Surely a grand beginning has been made," rejoiced the *Register,* while scolding other wards for not taking similar "concert of action." The *Chief* also praised the ward officials, if noting huffily that Fort Atkinson men had inaugurated the practice of inviting women into party caucuses twenty years before.

In 1887, some women had "practically full suffrage," as Olympia Brown would recall, but not all. The attorney general's telegrams had reached most urban areas with municipal races, where officials were confused and many women were refused the right to vote in all races. In Fond du Lac, according to Collins, a woman who "went to the polls with her husband, and he a lawyer"—luckily—had to "argue before the [polling] inspectors her right to vote the whole ticket" before she could cast even a limited ballot.

For many first-time voters in the spring of 1887 it would be the last time, although women's interest in politics continued to surprise a press persuaded for so long that few wanted suffrage. Even the *Sentinel* evinced some support for suffrage, according to historian Robert C. Nesbit, although coverage was "often enlivened by light-hearted comment or downright burlesque." In Waukesha, the *Freeman* reported "the best attendance in fifteen years" at the annual school meeting because of the turnout of women, including an octogenarian who was "one of the oldest persons in town." However, editors reassured readers that women voted apolitically, with "purely an interest in the welfare of the school."[14]

But the *Freeman* became uneasy by fall 1887 when Olympia Brown brought her tour back to town to promote a new and aggressive campaign to test the limited-suffrage law to its limits, or beyond. The *Freeman* gave a glowing review to Mary Livermore's address, more than two hours long, but found fault with Brown, "a rather small, sharp-featured lady with a strictly pious, tract-distributing air." When Brown talked of testing the "possible comprehensiveness of the school law" in court, the *Freeman* urged women to "use sensibly and prudently these lesser rights in order . . . to use greater."

Press debate followed Brown across the state as she organized women to test the extent of the suffrage law. "Soon there was a determined effort to find the full meaning of the law," Collins wrote, as "little groups of women all over the state prepared to offer their votes at a regular fall election." When they did, many women were refused at the polls—including Olympia Brown.

In Racine in fall 1887, the city attorney denied Brown the right to cast a ballot in any race. Alerted to her plan to vote in every race, he declared the law unconstitutional by turning her own argument against her, a petty cruelty. If women had the right to vote in school races, he reasoned—in her reasoning—that the city "could not see at what elections they would *not* have the right, as all elections pertain to school matters." Instead, he read the law to mean that women could vote only in school races, with separate ballots in separate boxes—which neither he nor the law provided.

Brown sued the city of Racine, demanding $5,000 in damages and beginning a long and costly court battle which only lost the law in the end. Brown claimed that she acceded to the WWSA in undertaking the suit against her own better judgment and the advice of Susan B. Anthony, who had lost an attempt to win suffrage in the courts. Brown's intent was "to instruct the people in the law and the circumstances of its passage" and, for suffragists, "to inspire confidence in spite of the refusal of the ballots." Time also was a factor; with a "presidential election near at hand, politicians would not leave it uncertain as to whether or not women were entitled to vote" but would seek a ruling "without proper argument and presentation of the facts," unless women acted first.

But Brown later admitted that she risked the lawsuit in part for personal reasons, to answer press attacks. Brown hoped to stop reports that she had been belligerent at the polls and attempted to physically "force" her ballot in the box. She sought a forum other than the press to deny an alleged "exclusive interview" published by a paper with which she had never dealt. Above all, Brown wanted to end the most hurtful press speculation: that she was neglecting her husband and children while touring the state for suffrage.[15]

Olympia Brown would appeal to the press only late in the long court battle, and only owing to financial desperation. First, she went directly to the public on yet another tour with Stanton and Anthony. As Brown later wrote, "it was necessary to keep the people interested [which] meant

a continuous canvass of the state until the next session of the court."
It also was necessary to pay legal fees; the "long litigation cost the little
band of suffragists" $1,500 to $2,000, according to WWSA records, and
women found fund-raising for suffrage "a difficult task," which finally
forced Brown to issue public appeals in the press. Decades later, Brown
admitted that the task was made more difficult because of the WWSA's
undoubtedly demoralized and "unorganized condition."

Olympia Brown was jubilant when the first court decision came
down for her and for full woman suffrage, or so she announced. Racine Circuit Court Judge John B. Winslow—later chief justice of the
Wisconsin Supreme Court—not only upheld her right to vote in school
races but also construed the law to allow women at least municipal suffrage and left open the possibility of more. The ruling was immediately
appealed to the state high court, but Brown could not wait to claim
a complete victory and vindication. Her manner apparently offended
behavioral norms for a matron. As the *Freeman* put it, "Mrs. Olympia
Brown, alias Willis, a preacheress of Racine, was especially conspicuous in her exultation."[16]

Brown had won with a hidden agenda, or so some in the press saw
it. The *Freeman* reported editorial distaste across the state for her attempt "to defraud a legislature into a practical revolution in the ballot."
In its favor, the *Freeman* continued to support the "school ballot" but
claimed that "Olympia and her followers fell to studying the law more
closely, and only after a time decided that more could be got out of
it than they imagined." Warning women that a "tricky and double-dealing
policy" of "pushing the law to its extreme limit in order to take advantage of oversight in the wording" was not "the best idea of courtesy"
and "hardly honest," the editors admitted that neither good manners
nor "perfect truth and honesty" were common practice in Madison. But
women's "primal aim" was to "purify politics," not to play it so well.

The local "lady lobbyist" and *Freeman* correspondent from the Capitol
lashed back with a lengthy and detailed defense of her work, of the
WWSA, and of Olympia Brown. Rebutting "the many unkind and un-
true things said of her in the papers lately" and reviewing legislators'
role in rewording her bill, Alura Collins Hollister argued that if anyone
"fell to studying" the law too late, it was men. "Directly after . . . the
law was declared carried, it seemed that men had just begun to study
it and opinions for and against the broad meaning were freely published
about the state," she reminded the *Freeman*. "It became evident very
soon that a law so variously understood must be submitted to the Su-

preme Court. It became still more evident after the elections that a test case must be made." Her reply was not published for more than a month, and not by *Freeman* editor Henry Mott Youmans. The letter finally was printed by a *Freeman* newcomer, the paper's first woman reporter.

If Alura Collins Hollister was devastated by the result of the rewording of her law, she could take comfort in knowing that she had chosen her words well when they persuaded Theodora Winton of the *Freeman*. Although Winton would write that she was "always a suffragist," she had not yet taken a stand on suffrage in print or stood up to Youmans, her editor and publisher—and husband-to-be.

Publication of Hollister's letter was a turning point for woman suffragists as well as for Winton; from 1888 until suffrage was won, Winton would print women's news and present their views as no man would, or could. With Hollister's letter, for example, Winton appended her opinion that "if women vote, they will often vote ignorantly or angrily or selfishly as men do; and they have the same right to commit these errors and to learn by them."

The emergence in a Wisconsin newsroom of a new editorial voice for suffrage came too late for the campaign but was welcome because women could no longer count on Emma Brown and her *Wisconsin Chief*. Dying of cancer, she struggled to meet deadlines during the suffrage campaign. By 1888, the last full year of publication, her *Chief* was missing for months at a time when suffragists needed it most, and was almost silent by the end of the WWSA's court battle.

But Emma endured to voice her disdain for the Wisconsin Supreme Court when, in January 1888, justices reversed the lower court's ruling on Olympia Brown's suit and "decided against the 'broad' construction given the law by advocates of woman suffrage." The high court handed down the strictest interpretation possible: women could vote only on "school matters," only on separate ballots—and only in separate boxes not specified by the suffrage law.

Emma Brown never knew that she had written the obituary of the nineteenth-century Wisconsin woman suffrage movement. She managed to carry her *Chief* to January 1889, marking the fortieth anniversary of the country's longest-lasting "temperance sheet." The issue included the state Chief Templar's annual report, which reiterated the importance of "organ grinding," as Emma called it. "We have grown up in ignorance of the great work being done not only in our own State, but in the whole world, if 'we could not afford' to spend one or two cents a week for the *Wisconsin Chief*," he wrote.

"The foolish woman suffrage movement was founded on an abstraction [but] if abstractions were capable of enforcing legislation, the suffragists would be right."—Henry Mott Youmans, the publisher and editor of the *Waukesha Freeman,* "the mouthpiece of the progressive movement." Photo courtesy of the State Historical Society of Wisconsin.

128

"If women vote, they will often vote ignorantly or angrily or selfishly as men do; and they have the same right to commit these errors and to learn by them."—Theodora Winton Youmans, an editor of the *Waukesha Freeman* for almost forty years, the last president of the Wisconsin Woman Suffrage Association, and a founder of the Wisconsin Federation of Women's Clubs and the Wisconsin League of Women Voters. Photo courtesy of the State Historical Society of Wisconsin.

It was a fitting epitaph. Emma Brown conscientiously transferred her subscription list to the *Western Good Templar* before she died in June 1889, when the Chief Templar ordered that the "charter and regalia of each lodge in the state be draped in mourning for three months" in honor of "Sister Brown, a brave-hearted woman"—an honor rarely accorded any woman by the order.

This time, no "temperance sheet" of similar stature arose in the state to take the place of the *Wisconsin Chief.* According to an analysis of the state press after Emma Brown's demise, most editors "simply did not devote articles to temperance activities" because "most thought such material pedestrian or insignificant."[17]

But Olympia Brown ensured that Wisconsin had a "women's paper." After the court decision, she despaired of the state press and determined to state her side of the story. "Dear Sisters," she opened her first issue of the *Wisconsin Citizen* in 1888, "I have never struggled to force my ballot into the box, or to get it in by any illegitimate means." The account of her treatment at the polls and in the courts "entreated" readers to discount "newspaper sensationalism and idle or malicious gossip."

The psychic wounds suffered by Olympia Brown in the suffrage campaign were evident in the *Citizen,* and her "little sheet" never matched the *Chief* in readership or readability. Even her admiring biographer admits that the *Citizen* was less a women's paper than one woman's personal pulpit, which Brown used to "take issue with whatever struck her as unfair." Notably unwise was her continued nativist campaign against men who could vote soon after arriving by boat in a country where native-born women were denied the ballot. In 1888, an embittered Brown escalated attacks in print and in person on the "serfs and slaves from the old world" for whom "we enfranchise the saloon and the poorhouse," while "we disenfranchise the home, the church, the school," and the "daughters of America."

Only years later could Olympia Brown assess the high court's ruling on the suffrage law with the wit which her early *Citizen* lacked. When the court determined "that the legislators did not 'intend it,'" Brown wrote, "this was a poor compliment to the committee that recommended it and the legislators who voted it."

Even after the court ruling, some legislators advised women to continue test cases in the courts for two years, to no avail. In the final case, women voted for school superintendent in the fall of 1888 in Oconto County, where sympathetic officials provided separate ballots and boxes.

But the election was contested and went to the Wisconsin Supreme Court, which went against suffrage again.

In January 1890, justices sent the suffrage law back to the legislature for rewording, but lawmakers delayed for more than a decade. Lacking provision for separate ballot boxes, "the law became practically a dead letter except in a few instances," Brown wrote; women still voted in some towns and villages, dependent upon sympathetic officials. But major municipalities held to the court ruling, and she recalled virtually no support for suffrage. As Olympia Brown wrote, so long as even one woman was denied the vote, in Wisconsin or elsewhere, enfranchisement was ensured for none.[18]

The crushing setbacks in the Wisconsin Supreme Court almost eradicated the suffrage movement for the rest of the century in the state, where women would wait long for even limited suffrage. In 1886, Wisconsin was only the thirteenth state to grant any form of suffrage. By the time that Wisconsin women won school suffrage again, their state would be one of the last to allow them into the polls at all—and women in four states would have full suffrage, by legislative enactment.

Long years later, when women finally won full suffrage, Olympia Brown looked back at lessons learned on conduct of a public opinion campaign. "As we now know," she wrote, "it is one thing to get a bill passed by the legislature and quite another thing to get it passed by a majority of the electorate." Despite the passage of decades, Olympia Brown would always regret an opportunity lost for women not only in Wisconsin but also beyond state borders. By the time that legislators would rush to ratify the Nineteenth Amendment, "women would have been voting in Wisconsin for thirty-three years," she wrote. "Other states would have found means to enfranchise their women, and the world would have been better for it."

Wisconsin's record on woman's rights actually worsened by 1890 when the state went backward in statutory protection of minors who were victims of sexual assault—the girls without hope of the vote or a voice in the press, except for the *Citizen*. In 1887, before the defeat of suffrage and ahead of most states, Wisconsin had raised the "age of protection" for girls from ten years of age to fourteen. But in 1889, Senator P. J. Clawson of Monroe won passage of a bill which lowered the age to twelve and reduced the punishment for rape from life imprisonment to as little as a one-year sentence if a child could be "proved" to be a "common prostitute." As Olympia Brown wrote in indignation, Wisconsin's law was "believed to be the only case on record where the age of protection has been lowered" rather than raised.

The fate of temperance women, too, was sealed in 1890 by another law backed by a temperance editor and Republican governor, William Dempster Hoard of Fort Atkinson. His nativist Bennett Law made the English language compulsory in every classroom and became intertwined, in astute Teutonic minds, with the WCTU's campaign for compulsory temperance education. Germans and Scandinavians were an "unholy alliance," in historian Robert C. Nesbit's words, but also were organized in greater numbers than ever before, electing only the second Democratic governor since the Civil War and winning repeal of the Bennett Law. Republicans once again renounced reform—and Hoard and the WCTU. While the WCTU won compulsory temperance education in public schools in almost every state, Wisconsin long remained among the most resistant to the WCTU campaign.

In the void between the decline of the WCTU and the WWSA and the next wave of suffrage support, the *Citizen* had little in the way of good news for women. The WWSA at least was free of debt from court fees as a result of the work of "leading spirits" among Wisconsin suffragists, Brown reported. Significantly, she singled out the "excellent service" of the Richland Center Woman's Club which had pledged $200 for legal fees, and raised the sum with oyster suppers and self-sacrifice. For example, club founder and first president Julia Bowen had donated a necklace given her by her husband, who was displeased to discover it gone. As descendants recalled, "he would have given her whatever amount of money she wanted for the cause," but "she felt asking and receiving was not a sacrifice" for suffrage.[19]

A decade which had opened with hope ended in despair for Wisconsin suffragists of the "first generation," who were devastated by loss of leadership. The 1880s had opened with the untimely death of Lavinia Goodell and closed with the demise of Emma Brown and her *Wisconsin Chief*. Midway through the decade, women mourned the death of Mathilde Franziska Anneke and the departure of Emma Bascom. While Alura Collins Hollister stayed in the state after the decision which rescinded suffrage because of the wording of her bill, she never rose to higher office in the WWSA.

However, the "second generation" of suffragists was watching and learning from their heritage of reform. The means by which women handed down strategies and tactics through the generations is best exemplified by the suffrage dynasty founded in Richland Center by Laura Briggs James. She served as a link between movements, as a leader in the women's temperance crusade and the WCTU in the 1870s, in the woman suffrage campaign of the 1880s—and in the next movement, in which a new generation would learn the strategies and tactics of public opinion campaigns, because Laura Briggs James also was a founder of one of Wisconsin's first women's clubs.

Laura Briggs James's major legacy to the movement would be her daughter Ada, who later recalled attending suffrage meetings as a child in Richland Center in the 1880s. Motivated to complete "the unfinished work my mother did," Ada L. James would lead her generation of Wisconsin suffragists out of the despair which descended upon the state movement by 1890—but not for two decades.[20]

First, Ada James and her "second generation" followed their mothers into women's clubs, a movement so sedate in comparison to those before—for abolition, temperance, and suffrage—that few observers in the nineteenth century could foresee its outcome in the next, except for the Richland Center *Republican and Observer* and the few others in the press that relied on women in the newsroom to report on women in the news.

5

Ladies of the Clubs
Municipal Reform, 1890–1898

I N 1890, Theodora Winton Youmans of the *Freeman* opened an all-out press campaign to bring the women's club movement to Waukesha. Calling for more than reading circles, magazine clubs, and church aid societies, she also provided the agenda for progress in what would become clubwomen's "sphere": the schools. In her new "Woman's World" column, Youmans questioned the *Freeman*'s editorial praise for the county school superintendent's self-congratulatory annual message and issued her own reading of the report. At first, she slyly complimented officials for employing women in twenty of twenty-three teaching positions. Then, her editorial hit the hiring policy as accruing a considerable savings for the county, and turned into an exposé of "sex precedence"—gender inequity—in teachers' pay: the average monthly wage of women was "$28 nearly," compared with almost $56 per month for men, Youmans wrote, "and yet, some women are so averse to making themselves odious as reformers that they sit idly by."

Women were not idle in Waukesha. As annual school meetings neared, Youmans escalated her exposé of local education policies and rallied women to exercise their citizenship to the limit of the law. Although they lacked a voice in school elections, women could vote at school meetings; the turnout of sixty Waukesha women set a record attendance for the city. Their work and that of "Woman's World" won applause on the *Freeman* editorial page by the publisher, Henry Mott Youmans—the new columnist's newlywed husband.

134

Within a year of the call to action in "Woman's World," women organized clubs in Waukesha at the same time that thousands of clubwomen were organizing across Wisconsin and the country. In 1890, upon the founding of the nationwide General Federation of Women's Clubs, the new movement enrolled more than twenty thousand women, more women than ever enlisted for suffrage — or ever would. Even after 1890, when Wyoming became the first state with full woman suffrage and the two rival national organizations merged, the new National American Woman Suffrage Association still totaled few more than ten thousand members — and, eventually, the new General Federation of Women's Clubs would eclipse even the WCTU.

In numbers as well as influence, the club movement would surpass the WWSA and WCTU far sooner in Wisconsin, where the suffrage and temperance movements already were in eclipse. During the decade, the WWSA declined to as few as seventy members — fewer than the number of clubs which would enlist in the next statewide women's organization — while the WCTU never enrolled more than four thousand women in Wisconsin. The next national temperance organization never attempted to start up in the state: the Anti-Saloon League would lead the later, successful drive for the Eighteenth Amendment and actually achieve prohibition, but in the 1890s leaders wrote off Wisconsin as a "wet stronghold" beyond hope for reform — for temperance, or for woman suffrage.[1]

As Theodora Winton Youmans wrote of the devastating defeat of woman suffrage in the state's highest court, "active political ladies" anywhere in Wisconsin had nowhere else to turn in 1890 but to women's clubs. As historian Nancy F. Cott writes of women's "voluntaristic politics" and the club movement, "where one large or vital pre-1920 women's organization declined or ended, more than one other arose to take its space, if not its exact place."

The sad irony of the *Freeman*'s call for women to organize was that Waukesha was the city once known as Prairie Village, the site of the first organization of "political ladies" in Wisconsin almost sixty years before. Women in the "feminist tradition" had organized again and again, first in female moral reform, abolition, and soldiers' aid societies, and then in temperance crusades which trained the "first generation" of suffragists to campaign for the ballot — but too soon, especially in a Wisconsin unmoved by the justice of their cause.

The "second generation" would retrace their steps, learning the same tactics of public opinion campaigns but this time for municipal reform, a town at a time, and with a different strategy: clubwomen worked to change their communities, not the Constitution—or not at first. This time, because of the lessons left by the generation before, women in the "benevolent tradition" would learn the requisite skills in far less time and would come to suffrage sooner. But unlike earlier suffragists enraged by the injustice of being denied the ballot, clubwomen would come to suffrage because they became vexed by the inefficiency of working without the vote.

The clubwoman's catchphrase, "municipal housekeeping," made their campaigns more palatable at the time—much like the WCTU's similar slogan, "Home Protection"—and would legitimize the woman suffrage movement in the minds of men, and many women. As Theodora Winton Youmans wrote, "club women were headed for the ballot box from the beginning." But she wrote of their yen for the vote long decades later. If Youmans was "always a suffragist," as she said, as a clubwoman she was too wise to admit it too soon.[2]

In the beginning, before the club movement came to Wisconsin, forerunners existed as early as the frontier era; the movement simply formalized a means by which women found sisterhood for decades—the women who would come late to suffragism, long after their more outspoken sisters. Precursors such as scattered reading circles and sewing circles had organized in the East in the 1820s, and in Wisconsin soon after settlement. Although some organized for reform far sooner, the informal "circles" remained and served far more women—the more conservative women who refrained from "the struggle" until almost the end of the century, but women with access to the press from the start.

Women's clubs first became a movement because of a press campaign by the first woman journalist with a nationwide audience, Jane Cunningham Croly, better known by the pen name "Jennie June" on her column syndicated by the *New York Dispatch*. In 1868—the same year that passage of the Fourteenth Amendment radicalized women who started the woman suffrage movement—a far lesser slight infuriated Croly. She and other New York City newswomen helped plan an event for the local press club but were excluded by male colleagues, and Croly started a club for women in professions.

Sorosis was not the first women's club, as Croly claimed, but she does deserve credit for causing the spread of the club movement through her column by publicizing the men's rebuff, which received widespread press attention.[3] In Wisconsin, for example, "Jennie June" was a favorite among Emma Brown's "exchanges," and the *Chief* ran in full, on the front page, the running press debate between Croly's attackers and her more gentlemanly defenders. One *Atlantic Monthly* article ridiculed New York newsmen's claim that they wanted only to spare women colleagues from "wine and smoke." The writer envisioned an "equality banquet" where, instead of "wine and cigars, there will be at every table its due proportion of ladies, the ornaments of their own sex, the instructors of ours, the boast and glory of the future Press of America." He expected the utopia for women to occur in, exactly, 1893.

Although word of the movement reached Wisconsin swiftly, few women's clubs formed in the 1870s. Sparta's Clio Club claimed to have started in 1871, and the Richland Center Woman's Club traced its origins to an organization that met informally as early as 1875, with Laura Briggs James—later a leader in the WCTU and WWSA—among its members.

But the center of early club activity was Milwaukee, where the first club's roster read like a social register. In 1874, charter members of a study club called the Ladies' Art and Science Class included leading "ladies of the city" with surnames of Allis, Chapman, Cudahy, and Ilsley—names which adorned the city's first bank, department store, and factories, and even entire suburbs—who asked the president of Milwaukee Female College to "lecture to them on the physical sciences" and, later, on the subject of art. The scholarly level of study attracted the attention of the Milwaukee press, which printed papers presented. The study club would continue for two decades, but by 1876 younger members and other women with similarly illustrious surnames founded a more formal organization, the Woman's Club of Wisconsin.[4]

The story of the founding of the Woman's Club in Milwaukee suggests the significance of nationwide women's networks in the nineteenth century, and of the nation's Centennial Exposition in 1876. According to a club historian, the "great centennial" was "a large influence in awakening the minds of many American women." Several Milwaukee women attended the event where Susan B. Anthony read women's Declaration of Independence, and the women's exhibit included the certificate of admission to the Rock County bar sent by Wisconsin's first woman lawyer, Lavinia Goodell. However, the Milwaukee contingent apparently was most impressed by meeting prominent eastern clubwoman and suffragist Julia Ward Howe.

If the Milwaukee women were not ready for suffragism, they did return determined to organize a counterpart of eastern clubs. The "intelligent, alert, mentally acquisitive women" met "to discuss ways and means of advancing their knowledge, of extending their outlook, and of the possibility of forming a woman's club to further the purpose," a "bold move." However, "with very few precedents in the country to guide them," they contacted Howe, who came to Milwaukee in October 1876 to meet with thirty women in a Grand Avenue mansion. As could be expected, the author of "The Battle Hymn of the Republic" offered "an inspiring talk" and promised to send her club's constitution and bylaws. Less than a week later, the women organized the Woman's Club of Wisconsin.

Women at the Milwaukee club's first meeting were "emboldened by the experience," according to their historian. None was bolder than the head of the organizational committee, Mary Mortimer. The founder and president of Milwaukee Female College, who once had claimed no sympathy for "so-called women's rights," now presented a paper which "took courage and a forward outlook." Comparing ancient and modern civilizations, she concluded that the world had made little progress, at least for women. "We have heard, to weariness, of the 'Sphere of Woman,'" said Mortimer. "We have grown not only weary, but rebellious, and have come out in the Nineteenth Century to declare that we have as much right to dwell in the sunlight and make a noise as our brother man."

The Woman's Club never would be noisy but worked quietly to achieve the "object of the Club," which was "primarily to elevate and purify our civilization"—although a club historian admitted that civilizing even their own city was "a large order." But women undertook a series of classes comparable to college coursework, and "the Club took itself very seriously," as did Milwaukee papers which reprinted the lectures. Mortimer apparently was unusual in her level of education, although other members had attended the Female College—the school attended by Frances E. Willard twenty years earlier—which had been the first institution in the state to welcome women onto its board of trustees fifteen years before, including club member Mary Blanchard Lynde. However, as historian Theodora Penny Martin writes, early study clubs "*were* education until women, through education, learned what education was." As much as suffrage work, study clubs contributed to women's education for the "public sphere" through the opportunity to gain skills in public speaking and to hear "the sound of their own voices."

The level of Milwaukee clubwomen's self-education also is attested by the expertise of lecturers. Most came from local colleges' faculties,

"We have grown not only weary, but rebellious, and have come out . . . to declare that we have as much right to dwell in the sunlight and make a noise as our brother man."—Mary Mortimer, a founder of Milwaukee Female College and of the Woman's Club of Wisconsin. Photo courtesy of the Milwaukee County Historical Society.

but a course on parliamentary procedure was taught by a "Major Roberts" who was "stationed in Milwaukee," the author of *Robert's Rules of Order,* who spoke for no charge. However, grateful for their "great good fortune," the women sent a check for $25 for his favorite charity— but only after considerable debate. With initiation fees of $3 and annual dues of $2, the club "could hardly feel affluent," and "some ladies thought that the Club needed the money quite as much as any charity and, anyway, it was a bad precedent to establish." Monetary concerns also may have made some members uncomfortable; for a second series of courses, Robert received a pair of cloisonné vases.

Milwaukee clubwomen rapidly became more confident in the realm of finance and even fund-raising. The Woman's Club increased initiation fees to $10 and annual dues to $1 per quarter, and the Ladies' Class adopted a fee structure to cover expenses for use of Milwaukee College's meeting hall and library. At first, the class spent any surplus on an art collection and "rare and beautiful" books for the college, but by 1884 women contributed nearly twenty percent of the cost of a new annex for a reading room and library.[5]

Milwaukee clubwomen expanded the nineteenth-century notion of "women's place" early on, and their influence soon reached twenty miles west to Waukesha, the next wellspring of club activity in Wisconsin. Other study clubs founded in the interim included the Green Bay Shakespeare Club in 1877 and Fort Atkinson's Tuesday Club, which also focused on Shakespearean literature, in 1880. But Waukesha's first "mutual improvement club" in the 1870s lasted only "a couple of seasons"— a standard unit of time in the town touted as the "Saratoga of the West" for the restorative power of the area's mineral springs.[6] Although not a metropolis like Milwaukee, Waukesha was unusual for a combination of small-town ambition and cosmopolitan ambience by 1890, because the booming resort business lured many a famous and near-famous name to "take the waters" or take in symphonic concerts, not one but two "scrub base ball clubs" by "omnibus line," or dusk-to-dawn dancing in the seven-hundred-room Fountain House, which seated five hundred for dinner. Hotel and boardinghouse registers and other "society news" ran daily "in season" on the front page of the *Waukesha Freeman*. "Out of season," it reverted to weekly publication.

Rare evidence of the spread of clubs from town to town can be traced in the *Freeman*'s "society" columns, which called by 1883 for a "literary society to add interest to local social life." A Ladies' Literary Society formed but met intermittently until "a dozen Waukesha ladies" invited the president of Milwaukee College to describe "the rise, growth and workings" of the Ladies' Art and Science Class and to "discuss the feasibility of a similar undertaking" and "different methods of best forwarding such an enterprise" in Waukesha. The "enterprise" went forward, for a while; the *Freeman* reported—prematurely—that the Ladies' Art Class of Waukesha was "a definite settled thing" within a week, when thirty women met at Carroll College "to form themselves into a society and arrange all details pertaining to such an association." A "Miss Fanny Ells was made president," and a recruiting committee announced "excellent success" with forty women pledged and twenty more "looking with favor upon the project." Meetings were set for late afternoons so that teachers could attend; the first, in two weeks, was to be a "tour of Italy." But whether women ever met is unknown; no further word appeared in the *Freeman*.[7]

The *Freeman* would have many a further word on women's news from the mid-1880s on — and for nearly the next four decades — owing to the hiring of the first regular woman reporter, Theodora Winton. By the turn of the century, she would lead the state club movement and the campaign for the "school ballot." The consummate clubwoman and "second-generation" suffragist, Winton would have an extraordinary impact, owing to her rise in the press and her role in the woman's rights movement.

The only Wisconsin native ever to rise to leadership of the state suffrage movement, Winton was raised in reform politics. Her parents came west before the Civil War from upstate New York to Waukesha County. Theodora, their first child, was born in a log cabin in Ashippun in 1863 but was raised in Prospect Hill, a crossroads between Waukesha and Milwaukee. Emily Winton, a schoolteacher in the East, taught her daughter to read and write while Theodore Sumner Winton tutored his namesake in politics. An early proponent of the Republican party, he was a prosperous storekeeper and postmaster, a prestigious federal post awarded as patronage — "frankly by favor," as his daughter put it, and lost only under the infrequent "Democratic cloud" when the lucrative post office still stayed in his store. The stage driver's thrice-weekly deliveries were among Theodora's earliest recollections; a voracious reader, the postmaster's daughter consumed dozens of papers, secular and religious, in English and in German — the last because residents of "Coffee Road," a nearby settlement, soon so outnumbered "Yankees" that the area became known as New Berlin.[8] Early familiarity with Germans tempered Winton's "Yankee" origins and upbringing, enabling her to escape the nativism so endemic in the suffrage movement.

If Theodora Winton's childhood was prosaic, her education and career were atypical of leaders in either woman suffrage or women's clubs in Wisconsin. Although she was valedictorian of her class — of five — at the state's first college, Carroll College, the school had by that time been reduced to academy status and offered the equivalent of only a high school degree.[9] By contrast, most suffrage leaders of Winton's era

or even earlier—Lavinia Goodell, Emma Bascom, Olympia Brown—
had earned college degrees or studied ministry or law. Clubwomen also
were "strikingly well educated," according to a study of sixty-six early
state club leaders. They were more than seven times as likely to have
a postsecondary education than women of the time; a third attended
college or normal school, and several completed graduate work, medical school, or other advanced study. Many were pioneers in the professions; a third had worked for pay, primarily as teachers, although one
was a physician, another a librarian, and several were in business or
sales. However, Winton was the only journalist among Wisconsin club
leaders—and one of only a handful who would continue her career after marriage.[10]

Well before her marriage to the publisher of the *Waukesha Freeman*,
Winton was hired in her own right at the paper which long had been
influential in Wisconsin's politics and press. Founded as an abolitionist
organ on the eve of the Civil War, the *Freeman* had first earned a reputation for excellence under one of the most respected men in the state
press, Theron W. Haight—a scholar, historian, lawyer, and founder of
a small-town journalistic dynasty in Wisconsin which would endure for
more than a century, but not under his name. Haight also had been
a schoolteacher in Mukwonago, where he married a student, Annie Youmans, whose family name was known in medical circles in Wisconsin,
where her father was the first president of the state medical society. However, the name of Youmans was better known in the East from the bylines
of family members, women and men, in the field of journalism.

Decades before the first formal education in the field, the *Freeman*
became known as a "school of journalism" which launched many a
notable newspapering career in Wisconsin. For example, one of a series
of apprentices who were taken on at the *Freeman*, and taken into the
Haights' home, was a Mukwonago boy who started as a "printers' devil"
at the age of twelve in 1872 and founded the *Milwaukee Journal* a decade
later. Another Mukwonago native who came under Haight's tutelage
in 1872 was his brother-in-law, Henry Mott Youmans. He bought a half
interest in the business and bought out his mentor in 1874, although
Theron Haight continued to pen witty editorials for which the *Freeman*
was famed.[11]

Whether by Youmans or Haight, *Freeman* editorials hewed to the
Republican party line against woman suffrage but were not opposed
to women in the "public sphere." For example, the *Freeman* asserted
in 1883 that the "foolish woman suffrage movement was founded on

an abstraction," although "if abstractions were capable of enforcing legislation, the suffragists would be right." However, when women campaigned more pragmatically to clean up the dirt streets of the town—long a topic of much talk but no action by local men—the *Freeman* commended "the ladies for being more enterprising than the gentlemen" in a civic improvement "once more due to ladies' work."

The selection of "exchanges" and "telegraphic news"—wire services, a phenomenon new to the *Freeman*—was similarly skewed against woman suffrage. Disparaging editorial commentary accompanied a *North American Review* article by "a Mrs. E. C. Stanton" while another *Review* excerpt ran without comment on a former federal surgeon general's statement that women were unfitted for the "public sphere" by "smaller brain capacity" and "peculiarities of their nervous organization." However, the *Freeman* also ran national WCTU "circulars" and Frances E. Willard's speeches, coverage of eastern suffragist and clubwoman Julia Ward Howe, and even news favorable to suffrage from the West, especially from Wyoming, where the press reported "results of thirteen years' experience of woman suffrage in that territory." The *Freeman* also editorially deplored "sad cases" of wives and mothers left penniless or childless owing to "dower rights" and custody laws which did women "a great wrong"—although the editors seemed more incensed when Milwaukee papers "handed a hard deal" to local "female base ballists."

By 1885, the *Freeman* was torn between small-town boosterism and antisuffragism when its editorial-page stance conflicted with front-page promotions of "exclusives" from the legislature provided by the "lady lobbyist" of the WWSA, Alura Collins. Her connections with the editors were impeccable; like *Freeman* publisher Henry Mott Youmans, Collins was the offspring of a medical man in Mukwonago, where she had been a student of Theron Haight in his schoolteacher days. Now she taught the men of the *Freeman* a lesson on "women's news." When her reports were well received by readers, Henry Mott Youmans endorsed school suffrage and, within a year, hired the first woman on the *Freeman* staff.[12]

Theodora Winton came to the *Freeman* in time-honored fashion as a freelancer and "campus correspondent" who enterprised her way into the newsroom and soon captured the front page. In an era when bylines were few, she may have freelanced for the *Freeman* as early as 1880. By 1885, Winton clearly was the writer of a column called "College Items" which gave equal coverage to women as well as men at her alma mater. In 1886, "Miss Theodora Winton" won her first byline for "wielding the pen in a very pleasing manner" in accounts of her "journeyings" around the state, a series which hinted at her independent nature because she traversed the North Woods alone. By then, the *Freeman* was eager for a "women's column," but experiments with anonymous local freelancers and an unnamed if "talented earnest lady" failed—until July 1887. Although still unsigned, the style of "Women's World" was unmistakably that of Theodora Winton.

The title of "Woman's World" suggests the networking of newswomen nationwide. The same title topped a column begun the year before in Iowa by another Wisconsin native, Carrie Lane Chapman, a Ripon-born schoolteacher who started her journalistic career after marriage to the editor of the *Mason City Republican*. Decades later, Carrie Chapman Catt would lead the national woman suffrage movement to victory, but she became Winton's idol long before for her leadership in women's clubs and for her column. Both women were influenced in both their journalism and suffrage careers by a mentor whom they then knew only through "exchanges": Elizabeth Boynton Harbert, columnist of "Women's Kingdom" in the *Chicago Inter-Ocean* from 1877 to 1884.[13] A generation of woman journalists faithfully read Harbert, and each other; for example, Winton's innovative press campaigns for working women would be picked up by other woman columnists in at least the *Inter-Ocean* and Indianapolis papers.

Appropriately, Winton's first "Woman's World" opened with quotes from "Jennie June" Croly, "the most industrious woman in literature" and the most influential woman journalist, and by then the editor and part owner of *Godey's Lady's Book*. Winton also ran "exchanges" on business education for women in "short-hand" and "type-writing," word of a "marvelous new invention in a New York restaurant called a dishwashing machine," and an editorial defense of local "girl graduates" whose attire caused a debate on college dress codes, in which Winton reminded readers that "brains are what count."

Fashion commentary was a constant in Winton's column, but as a serious health concern, in contrast to the tendency of the press to ridicule women's campaign for dress reform. Winton was well dressed but had a no-nonsense style. An early enthusiast of bobbed hair—which emphasized her eyes, her best feature—she was not a beauty, nor did she want to be; Winton was "stately," a word she applied to women she admired. She was not so courageous as to wear "trowsers," but applauded "sensible" clothing; one "exchange" on "lighter walking dresses"

—ranging in weight from ten to forty-nine pounds—spurred Winton to call for local women to report their "own experiments" in literally lightening the burden of being in style.

But Winton most often wrote of women's progress in politics. In 1888, only weeks after the loss of Wisconsin's school-suffrage law, she ran an item on "A Coming Voter" which reported the result of "municipal suffrage" in Boston where twenty-five thousand women cast ballots in the mayoral race. Winton applauded women in political posts as well as those at the polls, from the first woman appointed to a federal position—lawyer and suffragist Phoebe Couzins, a United States marshal in Missouri—to candidates in Wisconsin, where women retained the right to run for school office, although few won: only three served as county school superintendents by the late 1880s, although as many as nine had held the post earlier in the decade. Winton also praised a woman in Pleasant Valley, Wisconsin, "who was elected town treasurer and has just secured her office in spite of vigorous opposition on the part of the male office-holders of the town."

Interspersed with political items in "Women's World" were "bits and pieces" on women's progress around the world. Winton called on her countrywomen to follow the practice of French "feminests" who preferred the all-purpose "Madame" to "Mademoiselle," which denoted marital status or lack of it, "because we think it is nobody's business . . . and lacking in dignity." Winton demanded a "more decorous title" than the "diminutive Miss" in the English language as well. Winton also recommended the status of woman's rights in Alaska, where matriarchs of the "Tlinket tribe," or Tlingits, owned property and married—or simply purchased—younger men. Her purview extended even to the world of sports; although Winton was enamored of "the base ball game," she gave equal space to all girl athletes, as in an item entitled "Basket Ball, as She Is Played."

The column invited correspondence from "every woman who has a question to ask, an experience to relate, or a suggestion to offer," but did not exclude men willing to brave Winton in her "World." A farm wife sent a copy of her speech to a local Farmers' Institute, where she had called on rural women to lighten their labor rather than "accept a nineteenth-century interpretation of women's destiny and duty." An "Amos B." responded with a maudlin account of his farm-worn mother and sisters who "talked much of *duty,* not so much of *rights*" in his recollection, although he conceded that "distance may lend some enchantment to this view." He closed by begging "edification" from "well educated" women on the "philosophy of suffrage. I want to know—do tell." Winton invited replies to "Amos B.," whom she identified as the source of "treasonable inferences he has long been suspected of harboring" that came to light only at the height of suffragists' court battle in Wisconsin. The WWSA's Alura Collins Hollister sent a scathing rejoinder, suggesting that men regress to farming without steam threshers, cultivators, and twine binders. The debate raged on in the *Freeman* until "Amos B." went too far; when he called organizations from the "W.C.T.U. to the W.X.Y.Z." only "occasions for mere gossipping," Winton ended the contretemps. By then, her correspondence came in at such a rate that her beleaguered co-workers began a column called "Stories About Men." It lacked Winton's flair, and lasted only a few weeks.

Winton even had the effrontery to correct errors elsewhere in the *Freeman,* including her publisher's pronouncements on the editorial page. Unfortunately, her column began after the WWSA's attempt to expand the school-suffrage law and only as Olympia Brown became embattled in the courts. By then, the *Freeman*'s editorial stance on suffrage had become poorly reasoned and almost unanswerable—but Winton found a way. When Henry Mott Youmans would not run the letter by Alura Collins Hollister on the legislative perfidy that had doomed her suffrage bill, her rebuttal ran in the *Freeman,* in full, but in "Woman's World." The next week, Winton slyly praised papers which "give suffrage a good deal of space, and without doubt rightly, for any question so important to so large a number, whether men or women, certainly deserves at least a thorough agitation."

Winton often must have been agitated when reading her own paper. If the *Freeman* was a training ground for journalists, it was a proving ground for the paper's first woman reporter. However, Winton stood her ground, and although the *Freeman* would not stand for woman suffrage until the turn of the century, her influence soon extended beyond her column. From 1888 on, only wars or elections pushed women's news off the *Freeman*'s front page.

By 1888, readers' response convinced the *Freeman* to make Winton's column a regular feature. One of the first papers in Wisconsin with a women's column by one who knew the beat, as the publisher was pleased to note, the *Freeman* "at last obtained on a substantial and lasting basis" an "editor in charge who is a woman," he wrote. For her part, Winton promised local investigative journalism as well as "items" from elsewhere. Within weeks, Winton's hard-hitting series, headlined "Her Daily Bread," exposed working conditions in "women's occupations" from servants and seamstresses to compositors and, of course, schoolteachers. By 1888, when few women ran for school office, even fewer were running schools; almost eighty percent of Wisconsin teachers were women, but only one former schoolmarm was among 175 principals in the state.[14]

The column contributed to a sudden rise in *Freeman* size and circulation, and its writer won a weekly byline, the only one in the paper—and the best-known byline in the *Freeman* for nearly the next forty years, but not by the name of Winton. Henry Mott Youmans, a widower, announced his impending honeymoon in January 1889 in an uncharacteristically lighthearted item on the editorial page—"the boys in the office" would accept payment on accounts due in the "absence of the publisher of the *Freeman* for four or five weeks"—which went unexplained. Elsewhere on the page, he mentioned his marriage to "Miss Theodora Winton of this paper."

Theodora Winton and Henry Mott Youmans would have a long and apparently happy alliance, perhaps because they did their arguing in the paper. However, their honeymoon was hardly peaceful. The newlyweds' tour of the West extended to six months, with travelogues wired to Waukesha on Mormon polygamy in Salt Lake City, on opium dens in San Francisco's Chinatown, and on women's labor unions in California. The stories started in only the second week of the tour; all were signed, with studied nonchalance, "T.W.Y." The byline may have been a concession by the bride, because the *Freeman* wedding banns had implied that she would retain her maiden name.

Theodora Winton Youmans was promoted to associate editor of the *Freeman* by 1890, which made her the second-in-command of an increasingly influential paper in Wisconsin. Editorial influence was not measured by size of circulation; at about two thousand, the *Freeman*'s circulation was equaled by only four other "country papers" in the state, but was far less than those of papers in Eau Claire, Fond du Lac, Janesville, LaCrosse, and Oshkosh as well as Madison and Milwaukee. In Milwaukee, circulations of the *Sentinel* and the *Wisconsin* each reached about twenty thousand, and *Peck's Sun* topped thirty-three thousand, the largest English-language paper in the state. Several German-language papers matched the *Sentinel* and *Wisconsin* in circulation, and a few surpassed the *Sun:* the largest of almost five hundred papers in Wisconsin, at a circulation exceeding seventy-five thousand, was the *Haas and Bauernfreund.*[15] But more important than circulation in measuring the power of a nineteenth-century paper were the political connections of its editor and publisher.

A Republican organ from its founding and highly respected under

Theron W. Haight, the *Freeman* remained a paper read by other opinion leaders for Henry Mott Youmans' ability to gauge the electorate, and the elected. In 1890, for example, his estimation of Representative Robert M. La Follette was widely quoted—"a very bright and clever young fellow" who, "after he has had time to grow some, may be invited into the Senate but must not be hurried"—and was recalled a few months later when Wisconsin's boy wonder lost his bid to return to Congress. When a more mature La Follette returned to politics, he would win an endorsement from Henry Mott Youmans, who would be in the inner circle of the governor's advisors—another alliance from which the *Freeman*'s new editorial status, and all Wisconsin women, would benefit.[16]

Theodora Winton Youmans' rise was helped immeasurably by her marriage and her promotion to editorial status. Called the "first lady of the state press" at conventions of the Wisconsin Editors Association, she was one of only about half a dozen women in news management in Wisconsin in 1890, by her own count—and even more unusual as one who had entered the press on her own. In a survey for the *Milwaukee Sentinel,* she found as many as thirty newswomen in the state, although "most were running reform papers." By 1890, only two women held the post of publisher, both in Green Bay and both owing to their husbands' demise. Only one other Wisconsin newswoman at the time also had entered the field on her own, and also worked in what Youmans called the "country press." Youmans won her point: neither the *Sentinel* nor the *Journal* employed newswomen full-time until 1890— the year that Youmans conducted her survey. The *Journal* promoted a part-time book reviewer to full-time, although she worked as an editorial writer in the mornings, and tutored an office boy in the afternoons.

Youmans' article contradicts assumptions about women in the newsroom, and about all working women. Historian Robert C. Nesbit calls her career "less conspicuous professional employment" than others "since women provided the bulk of the popular novels of the time [and] it was probably less traumatic for men to see them in newspaper offices." But newsrooms never were known for tolerance of outsiders, whether novelists or not, and journalism was a job which often took reporters out of the office. *Milwaukee Journal* historian Robert W. Wells downplays but does not deny the discrimination which the first newswomen faced. Even in the office—at least, in the *Journal* office—"it was generally believed that a woman's place was not in the newspaper business." Hiring of women after 1890 caused "much shaking of heads," he writes. "The old days, when a newsroom was as reliably masculine as a saloon, were gone forever."[17]

Some historians also assume that Youmans and other newswomen of her era were ignorant of their past, and were "doubtless unaware of the others" who had paved their way, in Nesbit's words. Yet Youmans' chronicle in 1891 acknowledged the debt owed to pioneering women in the press, including Mathilde Fransziska Anneke and Emma Brown. Youmans also knew that the presence of women in newsrooms was a national trend. The census reported thirty-five woman journalists in 1870 but almost three hundred by 1880, a number which tripled by 1890 when, she noted, nearly two hundred newspapers had women "on staff." Their numbers would double again to more than eighteen hundred in the 1890s, although women still would make up only seven percent of all journalists. Yet Youmans advised that "the girl that is fairly intelligent, is active and earnest, and able to write a clear narrative and not afraid of anything in the world, can generally get a good position with good pay"[18] — an apt self-description of Youmans and her career.

However, Youmans' generalization was unfair to her gender in an era when many an intelligent, courageous woman found any career closed. One in ten Wisconsin women worked in 1890, a total of eighty-one thousand, but most were domestics — most often, Irish women who did "Bridget-work," as the *Sentinel* put it — and only one-tenth of one percent worked in stores or offices. Youmans' status made her an anomaly in a state where, so the *Sentinel* opined, only "gentlewomen in reduced circumstances" and unmarried women needing "pin money" could be excused for competing for employment with men. As Nesbit writes, "the hired girl" remained "the greatest bargain of the time" in Wisconsin, at the same time that working women were seen as "a threat to the workingman" by the public — and by some men at the *Sentinel*.[19]

Although atypical in her access to power, Youmans was typical of many women of her time and place in turning to the club movement as a route of political influence; the press, after all, could only editorialize for reform. Clubwomen were accomplishing it — although at first for themselves, as self-improvement clubs gained the confidence to reform the popular perception of "women's place."

Milwaukee clubwomen exhibited the most enterprise in raising funds for a place of their own. Members of the Woman's Club of Wisconsin tired of meeting in their "parlors which was delightful for a time, but it grew irksome," a club historian wrote. Women held meetings in "public places," "ill-fated" hotels and Milwaukee Female College but "felt they could not accept its hospitality all the time" and kept "moving from place to place." They were deterred from building even a small "Club House" owing to the cost of upkeep until a member proposed an ingenious plan for a building on a larger scale, with self-supporting rental space. The "level-headed, far-seeing and clever group of women" created "The First Stock Company of Women in the World" by incorporating to sell a thousand shares at $25 each to members and "a few carefully selected friends"—all women. The Athenaeum opened in 1888, at a cost of $9,400 for the site and more than $14,000 for facilities including a ballroom, reception halls, and dressing rooms for rental to the public. The audacity of the project "naturally attracted a great deal of attention and publicity" and soon was copied by a club in Cleveland, Ohio, which invited Milwaukee clubwomen to the opening of its Propylaeum.

Milwaukee clubwomen moved from self-improvement to improving educational opportunities for all women. In 1890, "younger members" of the Ladies' Art and Science Class started the College Endowment Association "for the express purpose of raising funds for [Milwaukee Female] College" and, soon, for its successor. The new club soon eclipsed the Art and Science Class, which would close its books by the end of the decade. One of the most dynamic "younger members" would be Dr. Ellen Sabin, one of the pioneering woman students in 1866 at the University of Wisconsin, who had started her teaching career in Sun Prairie. Since then, Sabin had served as a principal in Madison and in Portland, Oregon, where her pay was cut almost ten percent because of "her being a female" but she had been promoted to superintendent of public schools. In 1890, Sabin returned to Wisconsin as president of Downer College. Like Milwaukee Female College, Downer was in fiscal straits. Sabin soon engineered the merger of Milwaukee-Downer College, with the assistance of the College Endowment Association.

The College Endowment Association, soon to become the largest women's club in the state, would issue the call to organize statewide—and also would ensure that the new organization that ensued would adopt Milwaukee-Downer, the only women's college in Wisconsin.[20]

But statewide organization still was six years away as the decade opened, and clubs still were scattered from Sparta to Richland Center, from Green Bay to Fort Atkinson and Whitewater, where the Emerson Club arose by 1890—the same year that the *Freeman*'s "Woman's World" issued the call for women to organize in Waukesha.

The overwhelming response to Theodora Winton Youmans' call, and her exultant record in the *Freeman*, allows examination of the rise and evolution of the club movement in Waukesha—not a typical Wisconsin town in many ways, but more so than Milwaukee. The first club to answer the call, by 1891, bore the unusual name of the Beacon Lights. Previously a "reading circle," probably the Ladies' Literary Society begun a decade before, the club dated its founding to 1885 when two women—one was Anne Youmans Haight, Henry's sister and Theron's wife—were walking home from church, talking about books, and decided to continue their discussion in a more organized manner. Upon the call for formal organization, club founders took their unusual name from *Lords' Beacon Lights of History,* a popular series on the history of civilization, "which they were reading at the time." According to a club historian, meetings soon became so formalized that women practiced public speaking "complete with a critic who checked members for mispronounced words and faulty diction," and stressed attendance with rules so rigid that "only illness or death were accepted excuses for absence." Soon, "no other clubs in town" attempted to meet when the Beacon Lights met.

Many another club soon arose in the town, for women and men, including a Woman Suffrage Club in 1894. The same year, a Magazine Club formed that soon was renamed the Women's Club and claimed to be "the first club in Waukesha to organize with the social element as incident rather than aim." The first president of both clubs was Marion V. Hamilton, also an officer of the WWSA. Hamilton had "a genius for club work," according to Youmans, her successor as president of the Women's Club, which formalized to the extent of printing programs in pamphlet form for a full year ahead.

Soon, clubs that were founded for less scholarly pursuits filled the *Freeman*'s new "Social" column. The Women's Relief Corps, an outgrowth of the charitable work begun by the Civil War Sanitary Commission on behalf of soldiers, veterans, widows, and orphans, organized a Waukesha chapter. Churchwomen had a Christian Endeavor Union and an Episcopal Ladies' Society. Coeducational clubs included the Mikado and the While-Aways. A Business Men's Association also was "flourishing finely"; the Waukesha Men's Club rented an "elegant suite of rooms" on the order of an upper-class Englishman's club for "the principal object of providing a place of amusement, recreation and rest"; and the Wheelmen sponsored bicycling tourneys and more sedentary sporting events such as smokers with cards and billiards.

Outnumbering all were women's study clubs including a History Class, an Art Class, a Music Club, a Drama Club, an Owl Club, and a Horticultural Society. By 1895, the Beacon Lights and Women's Club were rivaled by the Ideals, an "outgrowth of a small reading club organized by six ladies for a little social pastime" who soon adopted a more serious agenda. Later, a Teachers' Club also organized to undertake coursework akin to graduate study.

Club membership and programming overlapped considerably—understandably—in a small town. For example, Youmans was a charter member of the Women's Club and later joined at least two others, as did other women. The clubs often read the same works, although only the Women's Club went on record with "immoral literature" as a program topic. The result of the discussion was a stride for free speech, although Youmans' report in the *Freeman* reflects discomfort with the topic: "The weight of opinion seemed to be that while such books deal with immoral subjects they are not harmful because they present immoralities not in an attractive form but as something to be feared, leading to inevitable punishment and unhappiness."

Clubs also welcomed lectures by college presidents and professors, leading local business and professional men—and by the few women in the professions, although the latter's scarcity led to overexposure. Especially popular was Dr. Maybelle Park, a prominent Waukesha physician who addressed several clubs on public health and was called upon to present, repeatedly, her 1896 WWSA convention paper, "Does the Professional Woman Need the Ballot?" No doubt to the relief of Dr. Park and her audience, clubs soon cosponsored programs which led to their first cooperative civic campaigns.

Four women's clubs launched the first cooperative campaign for municipal improvement in 1896, when Waukesha surpassed seven thousand in population and prided itself on city status—yet still lacked the hallmark of civilization, according to the *Freeman:* a "circulating library." Clubwomen formed a Library Association with a membership fee of twenty-five cents per quarter, donated and "carefully covered and labeled" their own books, and opened the library in their parlors on a rotating basis under Beacon Lights founder Fanny Ells as volunteer librarian. In little more than a year, weary clubwomen were overrun by as many as seventy borrowers a day perusing twelve hundred books in their parlors. In a campaign to make the library "self-supporting," women arranged a public meeting with speakers including the mayor, the Carroll College president, and local author Theron Haight, who commended clubwomen for founding a library after "failed efforts of young men to start one" and recalled "other noble accomplishments" nationwide which women achieved "after they had been abandoned by men." But the women were abandoned again. "The heroic management," as they were hailed by the *Freeman,* was forced to run the library for years—years of "patient and self-denying efforts" and "round-about" fund-raising, with endless rounds of "card parties and whist" and "book socials."

Increasingly, clubs also cooperated for instruction in skills required for the "public sphere." The Ideals "early abandoned the idea of study for the line of civic betterment and public welfare," wrote a club historian, while the Women's Club now held only one "distinctively social meeting" a year. Both clubs and the Beacon Lights cosponsored a woman lawyer's lecture entitled "Laws of Wisconsin Affecting Women as Wives, Mothers, and Property Owners," reprinted in full in the *Freeman.* The Suffrage Club secured a local lawyer, the Prohibition party candidate for governor, to "address the club on organization of the township and county," which led to a "series of lessons" open to other clubwomen on conducting campaigns.[21]

Clubwomen elsewhere also cooperated in campaigns to improve their towns and cities as well as their organizational skills, and had organized nationwide in 1890 as the General Federation of Women's Clubs. The first call for a national convention, issued in 1889 by Jane Cunningham Croly's Sorosis club, drew delegates from two hundred clubs representing twenty thousand women across the country. They used the GFWC as a means to share strategies and tactics of municipal reform in some "lines of work," but not all. Imitating the concept of compartmentalization in the WCTU and "department clubs," the GFWC encompassed concerns from self-improvement to community service and soon was emulated in a frenzy of "federating" at the state level.[22]

Upon federation in Wisconsin, women would only formalize an agenda already set by local clubs which long had shared strategies and tactics. For example, the Alexandrian Club in Sparta conducted inspections at the State School for Dependent Children and uncovered deficiencies which officials corrected. Other clubs in proximity to institutions were prompted to do the same, and to campaign for appointment of women to the State Board of Control of Reformatory, Charitable and Penal Institutions—again.

The issue of prison reform seems incongruous with the image of clubwomen, but women in the "benevolent tradition" had provided charitable care well before governmental intervention and welfare, from temperance women's aid to families impoverished by alcoholism to the Sanitary Commission's campaign for wounded veterans, war widows, and orphans. Nationwide as well as in Wisconsin, an early leader in the prison reform movement had been Lavinia Goodell, whose contact with incarcerated clients led her to campaign in the state and national press for improved conditions in institutions.

Another early leader in prison reform who rose to national prominence was Mary Blanchard Lynde of Milwaukee. A founder of organizations for the incarcerated and a force in the campaign for state intervention—and the wife of Congressman William Pitt Lynde, one of Wisconsin's most prominent lawyers—her work helped in establishment of a State Board of Charities and Reform. One of the first appointees to the board upon its formation in 1871, she also was one of the first female appointees to a political post in Wisconsin. Lynde served with distinction, and considered employment of women to be a part of her mission; by 1880, Sarah F. C. Little was superintendent of the State Institution for the Blind at Janesville.

In 1880, at the National Conference on Charities and Corrections, Lynde presented a paper entitled "The Treatment of Erring and Criminal Women" that exposed unequal treatment of prostitutes and their clients by police, courts, and prison officials in Milwaukee. After a police raid, "the male inmates are suffered to escape, or under an *alias,* fined and discharged," she wrote, while women were "dragged through the streets" before innocence or guilt was determined, and then "into open courts for trial!" Without patrons—"protectors"—to pay their fines, women were subject to sentencing by male judges and strip searches by male jailers and, sometimes, to sexual assault. Lynde campaigned for woman matrons and won appointment of a police matron in 1884 in Milwaukee, the first city in Wisconsin with a woman supervising care of incarcerated women—and the only one until the next century, despite Lynde's campaign for similar reform statewide through her position on the state board.[23]

But Lynde was the last woman on the board for decades. The agency's reorganization, and the rise of professionalization of social work, resulted in exclusion of women. Their incarcerated sisters were overseen by a five-member, all-male Board of Control which had become a sinecure for the press by 1890, when newspapermen held three of the patronage posts. There were women with similar credentials, as the *Freeman* pointed out in 1895, campaigning for the appointment of Flora Beall Ginty, publisher of the Chippewa Falls *Herald* and treasurer of the Wisconsin Newspaper Association. Some editors endorsed the *Freeman* campaign, but to no avail.

In another campaign, clubs statewide endorsed vocational education

"The male inmates are suffered to escape, or under an *alias,* fined and discharged, [while women are] dragged through the streets, and into open courts for trial!"— Mary Blanchard Lynde, one of the first Wisconsin women on a state board, one of the first woman trustees of Milwaukee Female Seminary, and a founder of the Woman's Club of Wisconsin. Photo courtesy of the State Historical Society of Wisconsin.

and established classes in domestic science, or home economics, in their communities. Few were as enterprising as the Women's Club of Oconomowoc, formerly a "cooking club," which raised funds for domestic science and manual training with events which the *Sentinel* described as "like a 'recipe swap,' only on a big scale." At a nickel fee, they drew one hundred patrons a week and, in only three months, raised sufficient funds to rent rooms and purchase equipment. The "Saturday school" soon served two hundred children, with waiting lists for boys' classes in carpentry and girls' classes in cooking and sewing.

In the campaign which would take priority on their agenda, Milwaukee clubs worked for appointive posts for women at the municipal level. In 1895, they cooperated to win a seat on the school board for Mary Freeman Merrill, a former teacher and past president of the Woman's Club, and started a campaign which would secure the same right for women in cities statewide.[24]

That Milwaukee clubwomen increasingly won acceptance of their entry into the "public sphere" is evident in one of the earliest examples in the country of a phenomenon new to the press as well as women, a "clubwomen's edition" of a newspaper. In 1895, Milwaukee clubs edited and sold ads for the February 22 edition of the *Journal,* a one-day experiment which nearly revolutionized the newsroom. As described in the *Journal,* in "a scene never before witnessed in the city, the business manager's office was taken possession of and the counting room was filled with women who have been busy taking orders for advertisements, copy orders and looking after the thousand and one details of that part of newspaper work."

Clubwomen proved adept at every part of putting out a paper, "canvassing the city, state and country for weeks" for news and even arranging for a male escort when covering prizefights. While newsmen in some towns tried to trick the "novice reporters," the gentlemen of the *Journal* provided china teacups for pastepots and banished pictures bordering on the profane, "all because of the invasion of young women which happened today," according to the anonymous contributor. "The truth compels me to admit that the present condition of affairs cannot last. Newspaperman['s] nature could never stand the strain of so much decorum."

Even the *Journal* editorial cartoonist was enlisted for the cause. An illustration entitled "In Possession" featured a woman in an office with signs proclaiming "Positively No Men Will Be Admitted Today" and "No Smoking." She wore protective cuffs to prevent printer's ink from marring her leg-o'-mutton sleeves, and scissors slung by a ribbon to her wellcorseted waist. At her side was a wastebasket overflowing with clippings from "women's papers" and the WCTU *Signal*. At the door, a mustachioed caller peered in with trepidation—and flowers for the editor-for-a-day.

The *Journal* "clubwomen's edition" was not all in fun, and raised $3,775 for the Milwaukee Welfare Fund through auction of "silk editions"—limited runs that were printed on silk or similar fabric—and advertising commissions. With women from the social register soliciting advertising, the fifty-six-page paper was the largest ever seen in the city—and possibly the first in the city with a prosuffrage editorial sent by Susan B. Anthony.

The serious news content of the women's *Journal* argues against the tendency, then and since, to dismiss "club editions" and their "editresses" as symptoms of the "stunt journalism" era. As historian Ann Colbert suggests, even a transitory place in the press was a once-in-a-lifetime opportunity for women—most women, when woman journalists were few—to "write what they believed to be important contributions toward understanding of what they aspired for themselves and their communities." The clubwomen "took their tasks seriously . . . to challenge and change—perhaps for all time—the nature of what a newspaper could and should be."[25]

The press was slow to change, but Wisconsin was transformed by clubwomen's most popular project, their beloved free libraries, because of a lobbying campaign by Lutie E. Stearns of Milwaukee. She later wrote of her "first plea for Woman Suffrage at ten years of age from the top of the woodshed in the backyard of our Milwaukee home," after hearing her mother's firsthand report of a speech by Susan B. Anthony in 1876. By 1886, Stearns was a schoolteacher. Frustrated by lack of material for her students, she filled market baskets with books from the Milwaukee Public Library—which hired her in 1888. But the city was well served by comparison with small towns, and Stearns helped to organize a Wisconsin Library Association in 1894 and to draft legislation which created the Wisconsin Free Library Commission in 1895. By 1896, the number of libraries in Wisconsin had doubled since 1893—the same span in which more than half of the seventy clubs soon to "federate" statewide were founded.[26]

The Wisconsin Federation of Women's Clubs was the project of a visionary from Berlin, Lucy E. Smith Morris, who saw the potential of women's political clout if clubs organized statewide. So did the General Federation of Women's Clubs, by then with a membership of more than

"I made my first plea for Woman Suffrage at ten years of age from the top of the woodshed in the backyard of our Milwaukee home."—Lutie E. Stearns, a founder of the Wisconsin Free Library Commission and a president of the Wisconsin Woman Suffrage Association. Photo courtesy of the Milwaukee County Historical Society.

one hundred thousand women and almost five hundred clubs. The GFWC named Morris its Wisconsin correspondent in 1895, when she organized a "correspondence committee" of a dozen women to promote statewide federation by "acquainting clubs with each other, and the value of contact and cooperation." In August, the College Endowment Association—the state's largest club, and the successor to the Ladies' Art and Science Class—officially "issued a call to the women's clubs of the state to assemble" in Milwaukee in fall.

Significantly, resistance was evident even in Waukesha. Youmans, a member of Morris' committee and district vice president, the top post, campaigned for federation from the first. More than a year later, only the Waukesha Women's Club sent delegates—one was Youmans, the club president—to the first meeting of the WFWC.

Some clubwomen were feminists from the first and welcomed the potential influence of federating statewide. The political savvy of some clubwomen was evident in organization by Morris of her committee and the WFWC by congressional districts, the lobbying strategy introduced by the WCTU. Other WFWC leaders would include Vie H. Campbell of Evansville, a past WWSA vice president and state WCTU president from 1892 to 1898, and Edna Phillips Chynoweth of Madison, a corresponding secretary of the WWSA and a treasurer of the state WCTU. Clubwomen's "domestic feminism," according to historian Karen J. Blair, long had been an "ideological cover" for instruction in the skills needed —writing, public speaking, parliamentary procedure—for municipal reform, and soon for the suffrage campaign.[27]

While some clubwomen wanted to change the world—to "Do Everything," in the words of Frances E. Willard, a pioneer in women's clubs as well as the WCTU—some wanted only to change their communities, or themselves. Protestations of apolitical purposes were sincerely made by many Wisconsin clubwomen who would not be easily persuaded to endorse suffrage or even to organize statewide. Some service clubs worked almost as adjuncts of the WCTU, cooperating in campaigns for temperance education, homes for unwed mothers, and an adoption agency.[28] Others continued as study clubs. As a clubwoman wrote to Youmans and the *Freeman* from a Woman's Council in Washington, D.C., "if it is true that thousands of different women are doing the same things, it is equally true that hundreds of the same women are doing different things."

The club movement was not monolithic, not even after some clubs "federated" statewide. In 1897, the Wisconsin Federation of Women's

Clubs' first directory would list three thousand members—but the roster reflected only a fraction of the clubwomen in the state.

In 1896, the WFWC's organizational meeting drew delegates from sixty-three clubs to hear Ellen M. Henrotin, president of the national GFWC and a leading suffragist in Illinois. The women met October 20 and 21 at Milwaukee's Pfister Hotel, where they identified free public libraries as a priority and elected officers. The first act by the first president, Lucy Smith Morris, was a promotional ploy to recruit more clubs —"social, literary, scientific, artistic"—by listing all as founders of the WFWC in the first directory, if they enlisted within a month. Seven clubs signed up in time, and dozens more sent delegates to the first convention, in 1897 in Oshkosh.

At the first WFWC convention, the contrasting status between the suffrage and club movements could be read between the lines of a speech by Lucy Morris. The WFWC's founder exulted in clubwomen's combined strength and newfound sense of sisterhood, the "spirit of loyalty of women to women," and the "larger sources of happiness thereby opened unto us." That clubwomen composed a large source of support for reform already was evident in a progress report on the WFWC's first campaign: since 1896, more than one hundred libraries had been founded statewide, Morris had been named to the Free Library Commission, and Lutie Stearns had become its first—and only—paid staff member. However, as a historian writes, Stearns "actually had a staff of hundreds: Wisconsin clubwomen."

The state of Wisconsin also had a staff of clubwomen by the hundreds who monitored the care of incarcerated women and children, always with official sanction but not always to prison officials' delight. In 1897, at the first convention of the WFWC, clubs from Milwaukee, Sparta, and other cities in proximity to institutions reported on inspections conducted and deficiencies corrected—in some cases—and called for a statewide campaign for prison reform. The WFWC endorsed a campaign for appointment of two women to the State Board of Control, its "first foray into the political arena."

There would be many more political campaigns by the WFWC, which so easily reached accord in 1897 on clubwomen's agenda for years to come—public schools, prison schools, domestic science schools—that the coming campaign for school suffrage seems inevitable, in hindsight. However, within the WFWC, the first official allusion to suffrage was yet a year away.

Members now made only nominal pretense of maintaining an apolitical, "ideological cover." An address on "club philosophy" by Rose C. Swart of the Oshkosh Normal School faculty was revealing—and condescending. "It is not as the rivals of men but as their loyal assistants that we should undertake public service. Men are really wonderful beings," said Swart. "They have made the world a good place to live in. But they haven't made it so good but it might be better." Her address suggests the confidence—or overconfidence—that women gained from their newfound strength in numbers.[29]

In 1897, clubwomen returned to their communities to campaign for appointment of women to political posts at all governmental levels. Some campaigns already had begun before the convention, as in Waukesha, where clubwomen came home to celebrate the appointment of one of their own as county physician: Dr. Maybelle Park, the first woman in the position in Wisconsin. The jubilant clubwomen planned further cooperative effort at the local level, in campaigns that came to be formalized as civic federations. The first were founded in 1897 by clubs in Beloit and Berlin as well as Waukesha, where women would work en masse with the new county physician for an agenda that ranged from founding the city's first hospital and Red Cross chapter to gaining access for women to a local gymnasium.

Word of the success of the first civic federations spread swiftly in the Wisconsin Federation of Women's Clubs, including Richland Center's Alpha Circle. In 1898, it issued an invitation to federate to four other Richland Center organizations including, of course, the venerable Woman's Club, which hosted the first meeting in its rented rooms above the post office. The rooms also housed the club's lending library that was "stocked at first solely with suffrage books and tracts," according to historian Jerry Bower, but the "arrangement grew more and more awkward" as the collection grew to almost five hundred volumes. The county board refused to lend the club an unused room in the courthouse, allegedly because rural members bowed to their wives, who opposed city women's ways.

A public library was the first item on the Richland Center Civic Federation's agenda and would be approved five years later in a referendum. But resort to the polls brought angry retorts by women both "publicly and privately," according to Bower, because "the fate of the project to which they had devoted much energy would be decided by *male* voters." With the library won, the women went on to establish domestic science classes, intended to counter "intemperance and many other vicious habits . . . largely due to poorly cooked and unnutritious food," according to the minutes. They also would conduct a turn-of-the-century temperance campaign that kept the city "legally dry" for more than eight decades, and would build parks and playgrounds, public health clinics, and the first municipal auditorium in the state, where the federation met.

Women's success in lobbying, publicity, and fund-raising led one city councilman to interrupt a meeting with an appeal "for the ladies to come upstairs" and lend their support to his latest cause. They did. But two months later, at a civic federation luncheon for city fathers who lauded themselves in speech after speech on local progress, the men slighted women's work. Among angry clubwomen was Laura James's daughter Ada, who wrote in her diary that "we were getting in the municipal fathers just what we get in the home."

However, some Richland Center Woman's Club members recalled considerable support from the men—even for suffrage, the club's primary cause. "Several of the members found that their husbands were even more heartily in favor of [woman] suffrage than they were," according to one account in a local paper. Another report claimed that, "surprisingly enough, when most men were opposed to giving the vote to women, the husbands of most of the club members gave their support to their wives and became ardent workers themselves." Some women even wanted to extend membership to men but were overruled when their co-workers argued "that the women needed the discipline and education they would acquire by depending on themselves," "that the work should be done by women alone"—and "that the men who would join, would help the women anyway."

In Waukesha, women also "federated" with the local suffrage club from the first. As president of the Woman's Club, Youmans had called a "mass meeting" of six clubs to form the Civic Federation—where she presided to ensure inclusion of the Suffrage Club, whose eligibility was in question owing to its unusual status. As a "mixed club," it included dues-paying members who were denied office and operated "under certain other disabilities": they were men. As Youmans wrote, "speakers for the club insisted that since it was devoted to the interests of women, and since a large proportion of its membership was made up of women, *and since it was managed by women,* it might properly be called a women's club." With men only suffered as members, the Suffrage Club successfully "defended itself as a women's organization" and, by unanimous vote, was welcomed as a founding member of the Civic Federation.

By 1898, many clubwomen clearly were preparing for full citizenship, and in Waukesha the first club avowedly for woman's rights from its inception was organized. Although called a study club, the Practical Club never aspired to the classics; its purpose was instruction in "practical skills." Members enlisted local men to speak on banking and writing wills, and "a course in Parliamentary Practices and Civics was started immediately." The Practicals "federated" in their first year, the club historian boasted, because the term connoted support of woman suffrage. Soon, "woman's rights became the topic of many a program. We were looking forward to when we would be free to use the ballot."[30]

By 1898, clubwomen's potential political clout already made them sought after by woman suffragists. Nationwide, after Wyoming entered the union as the first state with full woman suffrage, the movement had been set back by the deaths of Lucy Stone and Elizabeth Cady Stanton early in the decade. Susan B. Anthony had assumed the presidency of the National American Woman Suffrage Association in 1892 at the age of seventy-two but reinvigorated the movement with more victories in the West. By 1896, Colorado, Utah, and Idaho had enacted full suffrage. There were losses, as well, but the optimism of the movement was evident in Clara Bewick Colby's ebullient account in her *Woman's Tribune* of a defeat for women in 1898. Even then, she could write that "every vote cast for suffrage is a victory over ancient custom, prejudice and conservatism, gained by education and agitation."[31]

In Wisconsin, as ever, the only events which had attracted attention to the suffrage cause were visits by national leaders. In 1896, the WWSA "kept open house" at a ten-day Chautauqua "tent assembly" where the Reverend Dr. Anna Howard Shaw—a physician, a minister, a NAWSA vice president, and a famed rhetorician in an era which prized podium performers—lectured to an audience of more than four thousand at Lake Monona. But in Madison, the WWSA submitted only two bills in the 1890s, both in a single biennium. Membership also declined, while the WFWC was in its ascendancy. In 1898, the WWSA convention appointed Morilla Andrews of Evansville to assist in editing the *Citizen* with "different departments added to the paper in an effort made to make it of value to all club women." The WWSA also voted to "put an organizer in the field," the Reverend Alice Ball Loomis, to contact women's clubs.

However, clubwomen's wide agenda did not appeal to the Reverend Olympia Brown. As president, she won a resolution to retain the WWSA's single-interest orientation or, as Brown wrote, to "keep the one object in view and whack away at that alone instead of dividing our forces by taking up other issues."[32]

"Every vote cast for suffrage is a victory over ancient custom, prejudice and conservatism, gained by education and agitation."—Clara Bewick Colby, a native of Sun Prairie, the valedictorian of the first graduating class to include women at the University of Wisconsin, and a founder and the publisher and editor of the national *Woman's Tribune*. Photo courtesy of the State Historical Society of Wisconsin.

164

The WCTU, too, cultivated clubwomen in 1898, a time of concern for temperance women owing to the death of Frances E. Willard. Coincidentally, her last public speech had been in her hometown of Janesville, in January. A tour de force entitled "A White Life for Two," the talk "dealt with the liquor question in a way that impressed all present," according to the *Gazette*. With her impressive command of statistical evidence, Willard linked the evils of alcohol and wife-beating, even by husbands who counted on their wives for income; she cited data including the three thousand deaths of women at their husbands' hands in 1897, nationwide, and the four million women supporting themselves and their families. But her speech ended early, after only an hour. As a companion later recalled, Willard had been unwell—and was almost sixty years old—but had no foreboding of her collapse in the pulpit. Still, Willard first bid farewell to "the friends of her childhood days" among two thousand people in the pews of the Congregational church. Before departing Janesville, she departed from her schedule for a brief family reunion, returning to her first schoolhouse and her first home, Forest Home. Upon her return to Chicago, Willard canceled her itinerary, including a working tour of Europe for the cause. Six weeks later, Willard lay in state in Chicago, where thirty thousand mourners passed her bier in a single day amid press predictions that the WCTU would not survive. However, among temperance women it was well known that, true to her managerial standards, Willard had trained her staff for the inevitable transition in leadership of the international WCTU.

In Wisconsin, survival was a standard concern for the WCTU. In 1898 in Milwaukee, temperance women could not be roused to battle even for sobriety at the Soldiers' Home built by women after the Civil War. A bill to "limit the forty-nine saloons that besot the twenty-five hundred old soldiers at the Milwaukee home was finally buried," as were several inmates due to drink, a *Freeman* Capitol correspondent reported. "Good men"—there was no mention of women—"concluded that as long as federal authorities sell drink inside the grounds, it was not the business of the state." The state's Prohibition party men did rally to reestablish a temperance press in Wisconsin, but the paper faltered despite the aid of the WCTU's Amy Kellogg Morse. In 1898, the state WCTU convention called on clubwomen to "keep the crusade fires burning."[33]

In 1898, even Wisconsin's governor encouraged clubwomen's political crusade with the appointment of Theodora Winton Youmans to a state-level post, on the semicentennial committee. Youmans immediately enlisted the WFWC to assist in organizing a "Congress of Women" as part of Wisconsin's semicentennial celebration of statehood, and Lucy Smith Morris would proclaim to the WFWC that "the kingdom of women has newly acquired territory." But clubwomen were only reclaiming the realm won by the first generation of women in reform; Youmans' position resembled Dr. Laura Ross Wolcott's post on an exposition committee more than thirty years before.

WFWC convention planners clearly considered politics within clubwomen's bounds by 1898. The headliner was Jane Addams, founder of Chicago's Hull House and a national suffrage leader, who spoke on "city housekeeping." Another speaker was Beatrice Webb, a Socialist and suffragist whose address on industrial conditions led to a WFWC resolution to campaign for limits on work hours of women and children. Better known to Wisconsin women was Belle Case La Follette, a clubwoman and wife of the former congressman and undeclared candidate for governor, who left their "country-fair crusade" across the state only long enough to seek the WFWC's support.

The most significant political action reported at the first WFWC convention came in a progress report from outgoing president Lucy E. Morris on the campaign for appointment of women to the Board of Control: a bill had been submitted, had won first approval, and awaited only the next legislative biennium for final action.

At the 1898 convention, clubwomen also promoted one of their most political members to the presidential track: Theodora Winton Youmans. With election to the WFWC's third-ranking office, recording secretary, she would rise to the top in two years. Advance was not automatic but seemed assured; Youmans received 108 of 117 ballots cast, far surpassing the votes for vice president or president—an indication not only of her personal popularity but also of clubwomen's support for her outspoken advocacy of suffrage.

The only unsettling occurrence at the 1898 WFWC convention apparently came in the education committee's progress report on the number of women in school offices, as school superintendents and on school boards, primarily because of clubs' campaigns. The report was self-congratulatory and received well by clubwomen until, in conclusion, the education committee encouraged members to exercise their "school suffrage" won a dozen years earlier.[34]

The resultant confusion is not recorded, but more astute members apparently called for a point of order—and only then did many stunned clubwomen discover that the limited-suffrage law had been lost a decade before. And only then did the "ladies of the clubs" learn that their education in politics had only begun.

The enterprise of early clubwomen in Wisconsin must be placed in the larger context of women's progress—or the lack of it. In the early 1870s, while women in Sparta, Richland Center, and Milwaukee started the state's first clubs, other women in Wisconsin conducted temperance crusades and organized the Women's Temperance Alliance and the WCTU. By the mid-1880s, when clubwomen began fund-raising for Milwaukee Female College, the WWSA was lobbying for full suffrage in the state legislature. By 1887, when some women went to the polls, only to be refused and forced to file suit for their rights under law, clubwomen considered the act of legally incorporating to "boldly embark on their own building" to be "a very precarious and daring enterprise." And in 1888, when Milwaukee clubwomen celebrated the opening of their Athenaeum, three stories high, all Wisconsin women lost even limited suffrage in the state's highest court.

If clubwomen did not enlist in the "century of struggle" until the end of the nineteenth century, they would bring the suffrage campaign to an end in the next—and they already had brought civilization to Wisconsin. Campaigns may seem miniscule at the local level—a hospital here, a lone library there—until writ large as the hundreds of hospitals, libraries, playgrounds, parks, and less visible good works accomplished by women's clubs. However, as historian Janice Steinschneider concludes of Wisconsin clubwomen's work, "while the civic contributions were remembered, sometimes the club origins . . . were forgotten." Many historians belittle the "middle-aged, middle-class" "mainstream of American womanhood" and denigrate the "benevolent tradition" of "do-gooders."

If "municipal housekeeping" hardly measures up to the majesty of movements for abolition, temperance, and woman suffrage—and is harder to measure—civic reform had an extraordinary impact on the mundane life of the country. Even less measurable, although as important in women's lives, was the liberating impact of "housekeeping" outside the home. As Youmans wrote, club work offered an "outlet for their energy and ability," when the only alternative was a "career of uselessness." Whatever their reasons, writes Steinschneider, "Wisconsin women together found their public voice" through the good works accomplished in the club movement before they won the vote—again, and for good.[35]

By 1898, clubwomen would come to the fore of the suffrage campaign but for reasons far different from those of the "first generation." Newly awakened to the need for the vote, now a well-organized special-interest group skilled in strategies and tactics of public opinion campaigns, they spoke with the powerful voice of the WFWC—and with their voice in the press, Theodora Winton Youmans of the *Waukesha Freeman*. In the same way that they had won municipal reform, a town at a time, the "ladies of the clubs" would school themselves to win back the ballot, a little at a time.

6

Schooling for Suffrage
Progressive Reform, 1898–1910

I N 1898, clubwomen embarked on their first significant campaign for
political influence statewide, but not for suffrage—not yet. No formal action would be taken for more than two years on the issue first
raised at the 1898 convention of the Wisconsin Federation of Women's
Clubs. The WFWC's priority remained the appointment of women to
political posts, a campaign in which their baptism by fire in politics would
leave clubwomen smoldering with unseemly anger. But the campaign
would be rescued by the political rebirth of Robert M. La Follette, who
would take many tenets of municipal reform to state and national
levels—not surprisingly, since his agenda was to a considerable extent
scripted by a WFWC member, his co-worker and wife, Belle Case La
Follette. With "Fighting Bob" to battle for their causes in the backrooms
of politics, as historian William Chafe suggests, well-connected clubwomen were "a decisive voice in the progressive coalition."[1]

In Wisconsin, from 1898 forward, no woman's voice would be more
decisive than that of Theodora Winton Youmans of the *Waukesha Freeman*. And no one would give other women a greater opportunity to be
heard as well. As early as 1888, she had opened her paper to "every
progressive woman" who needed to "know what the women of the world
are thinking and doing." Only decades later would it be evident that
what clubwomen were doing at the turn of the century was educating
Wisconsin for woman suffrage again, and again.

By 1898, hundreds of women worked in the governmental sector in

Wisconsin—as clerks, copyists, and stenographers in the legislature, as notaries and court commissioners in the legal system, and in state, county, and city offices—but few were in supervisory positions, even over women who were wards of the state. By 1898, women "entirely managed" the Milwaukee Industrial School for Girls, which relied on their fund-raising as well as public funding, but it was an exception. Women primarily worked as "teachers, matrons, bookkeepers, supervisors, State agents for placing dependent children, etc.," according to Olympia Brown. No woman, she noted, was among the physicians for women and children incarcerated in state institutions.[2]

The cause of prison reform had been adopted by individual clubs even before federation and by the WFWC in 1897 at its first convention. By 1898, a bill to put two women on the five-member State Board of Control had been passed by lawmakers. But the bill still required a second round of approval. In the interim, clubwomen proceeded with caution, politely securing the Board of Control's approval before touring a dozen institutions and asylums in the state.

But in 1899, with a new legislative biennium, the WFWC's Board of Control campaign began in earnest. The bill was submitted again by an assemblyman from Green Bay, home of WFWC president Ella Hoes Neville, and went into hearings within a week. "About twenty club women" went to the Capitol to present their research, as Neville recalled, and "received the most considerate attention." But legislators stalled for a month on the Board of Control bill.

Clubwomen increased the pressure with a press campaign which suggests the range of their assertiveness in the "public sphere." The *LaCrosse Chronicle,* for example, featured the favorable opinion of the Reverend Nellie Mann Opdale, a "tall slender woman with a pale intellectual face." Only recently moved to town from Mukwonago, where she had been a protégé of Olympia Brown, Opdale had won headlines in the *Freeman* as "an enthusiastic wheel woman," one of the first female bicyclists in Waukesha County. The *Chronicle* story ran in the *Freeman* as a sidebar—coyly headlined "Has Faith in Her Sex"—to a front-page survey of opinions on the bill held by "prominent local ladies." Whether in the professions or homemakers, all endorsed the bill—although Youmans was not likely to solicit opposing views. However, the range of endorsements from tentative to emphatic was revealing. Most assertive were a lawyer, two physicians, librarian Fanny Ells—who called the issue "too obvious for argument"—and the president of the Suffrage Club. Less strident were a high school assistant principal, the principal's wife, and the president of the City Federation of Women's Clubs.

The least assertive comments came from leaders of the town's two oldest clubs. The Ideals' president, discomfited by a foray into politics, averred that she was "not in favor of the ballot for women" but "still felt the bill now before the legislature to be an excellent one." The Beacon Lights' president was even more tentative, although she applauded women in the "public sphere" as an apolitical influence: "Women would bring to the work minds more intent upon bettering their fellow men and less interested in pleasing 'the powers that be,' in other words more heart and less politics. I should like to see them given a trial anyway."

But lawmakers would try women's patience, not their ability. While clubwomen awaited the outcome of the Board of Control bill, the men stooped to fraternity house humor in the face of a serious cause. A wag in the assembly submitted his own woman's rights bill for an "anti-tight lacing law," allegedly to liberate women from repressive lingerie but more to amuse his colleagues. The laughter was not shared by the "ladies," according to the *Freeman*'s Capitol correspondent. He did not report how women's own brand of humor was received when "a gift for the author of the anti-tight lacing bill came from the ladies of Watertown and was a tightly laced corset full of roses and carnations, accompanied by a sarcastic note."

More serious, and subtle, was an "anti-lobby bill" before the legislature. The bill apparently had its impetus in progressive reform but, as an astute reporter wrote, was amended to make lobbying almost impossible for "the women who want the ballot or representatives of their sex on the board of control" as well as other grass-roots groups. The "anti-lobby bill" also was killed, but undoubtedly distressed clubwomen and divided their energies.

Clubwomen repeatedly attempted to enlist the attention of the legislature. Two petitions from federated clubs were entered in the assembly record, as was a resolution from the WFWC's ninth district convention. However, the first committee halved the proposed two posts on the Board of Control to a single nonvoting "observer" before forwarding the bill to a second committee which postponed it, indefinitely. Perplexed by the legislative process, the WFWC let the bill die. As historian Janice Steinschneider writes, "the immature Wisconsin federation" could not "wage a systematic campaign" which "involved behavior that was clearly political, a problematic situation for clubwomen at the turn of the century"— although immaturity was a more serious behavioral problem for some men in the legislature. At least clubwomen, with experience, "would become more comfortable in the political realm."

The experience of the Board of Control campaign was enlightening, and embittering. At the 1899 WFWC convention, Neville had to calm some clubwomen who "did not intend to forget the Board of Control episode" and vowed to continue visiting state institutions "until we are strong with power to act, with our two women on the Board of Control." But the campaign would continue for years.[3]

In 1899, the stalemate on the Board of Control bill might have left the WFWC's agenda clear for suffrage, but for a momentous event—and an enormous undertaking: Wisconsin was selected as the site of the next national convention of the General Federation of Women's Clubs, a coveted honor for 1900 when the organization would mark its tenth anniversary. Milwaukee would be the "temporary center of the club universe," effused Theodora Winton Youmans, who would cover the event in her dual roles as an editor of the *Freeman* and as the chair of the convention press relations committee. But her enthusiasm would be tempered by the end of the "Milwaukee Biennial," which would consume more than a year in the planning.

Women were not alone in anticipating a windfall of publicity from "the Biennial." Ever the town booster, Youmans admonished Waukesha city fathers to "advertise its advantages as a summer resort among the most desirable kind of patrons." Milwaukee city fathers already had awakened to the lucrative potential of women's sizable conventions and even attempted to solicit suffragists' business. A Citizens' Business League sent a delegation across Lake Michigan to Grand Rapids, where clubwomen and the WCTU had worked with suffragists to lure the annual meeting of the National American Woman Suffrage Association. But Milwaukee's bid, apparently hastily assembled, did not win serious consideration.

Had the home of the original Milwaukee brewers hosted a national suffrage convention at the turn of the century, women's history for the next two decades might well have been written far differently—or so the impact on women in Wisconsin of the national clubs' convention would suggest. According to historian Janice Steinschneider, "the WFWC traveled a long road from defeat in 1899 to its more self-assured, ready and successful response" in the next century, as state clubwomen displayed a "more organized and well-developed machinery" and less "cautious, defensive tone."

In 1899, the WFWC already had taken a small but historic step, breaking with the tradition of housing out-of-towners in host members' homes—to Youmans' approbation. An inveterate traveler before her marriage who still took separate vacations without her husband, Youmans long had been impatient with women more sheltered than she and less skilled in "little details" of life on the road. "Madame Clinging Vine," she wrote, "who feels burdened with the ticket and check her husband procures for her and who never in her life wrote her name in a hotel register, must brace up and look after herself at the club conventions, or she will fare badly."

Now Youmans wrote with admiration of how far women had come—literally and figuratively—in coming to women's conventions. "One result of the club conventions not generally considered is the practical self-reliance developed in . . . delegates when not entertained by resident club women, but who look after themselves at the hotels and duly pay their bills." The WFWC, she wrote, set "an example which other conventions could follow."

However, clubwomen had not come far enough in breaking down social barriers and would set an example at the 1900 Biennial which made Milwaukee infamous as a turning point in women's history—but not a turn for the better. According to historian Gerda Lerner, the confrontation to come was the culmination of "the shattering of the old abolitionist-feminist alliance" by "a new generation . . . who shared the nativist and racist ideas of men of their class" and "followed the spirit of the times in turning away from the race issue." To win wider support, the "constant compromise of suffrage leaders with the Southern viewpoint on the race issue inevitably led to discriminatory practices and racist incidents"—notably the "Ruffin incident" at the Milwaukee Biennial, where clubwomen would give the wrong answer to the "color question," in Youmans' words.[4]

Wisconsin clubwomen were oblivious to the issue early in 1899, and overwhelmed, with convention planning already under way under Ellen M. H. Peck. A longtime leader in "Cream City clubs"—an appellation for Milwaukee due not to its Dairy State locale but to light-hued local brick—Peck promised a "harmonious gathering" of "the most well-known, the most gifted, the most able women in all the United States," Youmans wrote. Based on previous Biennials, they anticipated attendance of two thousand, including observers and "unusually large delegations from the South," because a southerner was president of the GFWC for the first time.

At the time, Wisconsin clubwomen felt no foreboding about the expected influx of southerners. However, in July 1899, Youmans reported a revealing interview with an officer of the Alabama state federation, vacationing in Waukesha, who intimated that southern women were organizing to make a stand for segregation.

> It is not improbable that the matter will be brought up at the next state federation convention. The fact that the present president of the general federation, Mrs. Rebecca Lowe, is a southern woman [from] Atlanta . . . will probably have an influence in bringing Alabama into the fold. The Alabama federation has not joined the general federation for a specific reason marked out by the color line. Some years ago two colored women were sent as delegates to the Biennial of the general federation and this so incensed the southern white women that they have looked with disfavor on the national organization since.[5]

The alleged attempt to gain admission apparently was southern mythology, but in Milwaukee would be self-fulfilling prophecy.

Most accounts imply that the GFWC did not anticipate a request for admission by African-American women, but Youmans began "advances" on the issue almost a year before the Biennial. She interviewed another prominent southern clubwoman, a Georgia compatriot of GFWC president Rebecca Lowe who had come to Waukesha to "take the waters." Youmans even crossed the Mason-Dixon line for the story, contacting an "informant" in a Florida club which had been inspired to organize a "colored kindergarten" after an address by Margaret Murray Washington, wife of Booker T. Washington and the "lady principal" of the Tuskegee Institute—and a leader in the National Association of Colored Women's Clubs.[6] She had been given "a warm welcome," according to the "informant," whom Youmans confronted on the "color question": "I asked if Mrs. Washington would be received on terms of social equality by the white club women working with her, and was told that at club functions she was so received in this city but would not be in private homes—a hard dispensation." However, Youmans also supported segregation in suggesting an understanding of southerners' "sound principle of keeping the two races separate and distinct, one from the other."

Even before the confrontation at the convention, the GFWC expected controversy over a proposal which was a smokescreen for segregation: reorganization of the system of delegate selection which made Biennials "unwieldy," Youmans wrote. Convention planners in Milwaukee, where clubwomen were scheduled to vote on the issue, also foresaw a rift over reorganization of the GFWC. Well before the Milwaukee Biennial, rumors of internal warfare among clubwomen were rife, and a regional split was apparent. Disgusted by the internal dissension, Jane Addams called a press conference in Chicago to announce the Hull House Club's boycott of the event in protest against "ineffective" conventions—a "startling situation," Youmans wrote, which would "doubtless have an important influence on the reorganization proposal." Women allied on the issue "along regional lines," reported Youmans, with opposition centered in the South and East and proponents in the North and West—a sectional split resembling a "states' rights" controversy which caused a war between North and South before.

Only later would the relevance of the reorganization issue be evident to many members because the ban on clubwomen of color was not in national bylaws, and in Wisconsin the state federation officially practiced open admission. But racial segregation was an unwritten law. The WFWC convention program committee chair later reiterated that "if a colored woman should come to the convention as a regularly accepted delegate, there is no doubt that she would have all the rights and privileges of a white club woman," and claimed to be unaware of any application by African-American clubs—and may not have been. But, at the same time, the WFWC convention credentials committee rejected the Phyllis Wheatley Club of Racine. According to the WFWC, the application arrived too late. According to the club president, "this is an old fight all over again. Years ago the men in the south fought our men. Now the women are fighting us."[7]

If some Wisconsin clubwomen were unaware of the de facto racial segregation and its connection to the reorganization isssue, leaders in the GFWC saw the coming conflict—and may even have encouraged it. In 1899 in Chicago, Jane Addams and past GFWC president Ellen Henrotin of Illinois both addressed the convention of the National Association of Colored Women's Clubs, founded in 1897 as a counterpart to the GFWC. According to an NACWC historian, delegates in Chicago resolved to win "recognition by the General Federation of Women's Clubs."

Spearheading the campaign was a founder of the NACWC, the remarkable Josephine St. Pierre Ruffin. An editor of the black weekly *Boston Courant* in the 1890s, she had founded *Woman's Era* magazine for "organizing the colored women of the country to do systematic work for the uplifting of their race." Not just a journalist, Ruffin also was the strategist who plotted the NACWC's path to cross the "color line" in the women's club movement. The founder—and the first and only president—of Boston's black New Era Club, Ruffin also belonged to several "mixed race clubs," including the prestigious New England Women's Press Association and the venerable New England Woman's Club, was a charter member of the Massachusetts School Suffrage Association, and served on the board of the Massachusetts Federation of Women's Clubs.[8]

Ruffin's credentials were impeccable, as the woman who had recruited the New Era Club for the GFWC would recall. "I can safely say that none of us think of the color line in connection with her," wrote Anna D. West, president of the Massachusetts Federation, in response to later reports that Ruffin deliberately attempted to deceive the GFWC by hiding her club's orientation.

> Why, I thought absolutely nothing of Mrs. Ruffin being a Negro woman or that the club was made up of colored . . . women when I wrote asking it to join the Federation. I sent out a circular letter to all the clubs in the state asking them to join us. When I forwarded the New Era Club application to [GFWC president] Lowe, I no more thought of explaining that it had a mixed membership than I should think of telling that a club was made up of Jewish women or Irish women. I sent the constitution along. It read plainly that the New Era Club was devoted to helping the Negro race.[9]

Youmans verified with a GFWC officer the rumors that a "colored delegate" would come to the convention, and GFWC president Lowe later admitted that she knew the composition of the New Era Club.

But in 1900 in Milwaukee, even before the Biennial convened, the GFWC turned Ruffin away at the door of the elegant Pfister Hotel. Her credentials were accepted, but Ruffin was denied the routine courtesy of representing all her clubs—including the New Era Club. Ruffin "regretted that the question of race had been advanced," writes historian Charles Wesley, but resisted "endeavors made to compel [her] to give up her badge" and stood firm while the GFWC board conferred. The board finally reversed accreditation of the New Era Club but offered to admit Ruffin with "every courtesy as a delegate at large"—from her predominantly white clubs.[10]

According to Youmans, Ruffin was not "obstreperous" but open and aboveboard, while the GFWC acted in panic when "her presence disclosed the existence of the color line." Youmans did not allow "courtesies" to cloud the issue, writing bluntly that "the New Era club was thrown out and dues returned to Mrs. Ruffin." Although "the board apparently had a perfect right to adopt such procedure," Youmans offered no apologia for the GFWC. "The judgment of such procedure may be questioned," she wrote, and it was, when "the delegation from Massachusetts, where the old abolition spirit still holds sway, was insistent, but to no avail." With ill-concealed satisfaction, Youmans wrote of the resulting fracas, "I judge it made life miserable for the board of directors for several days."

Contrary to accounts which suggest that the "color question" was not raised on the floor, clubwomen submitted a flurry of resolutions which brought the issue into the open—resolutions for reconsideration, resolutions for recounts of votes on resolutions for reconsideration—and brought the GFWC to the point of schism because the South was ready to secede again. Youmans later described a scene which resembled a political convention in chaos, as the president of the Georgia state federation and her floor managers "stood prepared," poised for "the moment the colored club was admitted to membership," and "never absent from the convention at the same time, one being always present, ready to voice her resignation" from the GFWC. "There is not doubt that the admission of the New Era Club would have caused the secession of the whole southern contingent at Milwaukee," she wrote. Despite herself, Youmans admitted admiration of Lowe's adroit use of parliamentary procedure to rule out of order any discussion of membership rules, averting a southern walkout. But Lowe did not go unopposed.

When Lowe came up for reelection, a ritual courtesy accorded to incumbent presidents, pandemonium erupted on the floor and the press had a heyday. "Repeated disturbance by noise of members" interrupted "stormy meetings where business became complicated and the parliamentary critics were out in force" to force out Lowe. "The opposition to her re-election doubtless came from her position on the color question. It was strong opposition, too," Youmans wrote, "nearly one-third of the whole vote being cast against her." However, Lowe was reelected, and the South at last had its revenge.

As clubwomen's customarily sedate proceedings escalated into unseemly debate, reporters from across the country reveled in GFWC infighting—to delegates' dismay. "Sensational articles" led Youmans to reply, "lest some readers may have a wrong impression." She did not give an impressive defense, explaining that clubwomen were in a quandary between "questions of expediency as well as principle"—and expediency won out. "It must be understood that the acceptance of one colored club might very possibly result in another southern secession and another civil war." Youmans abandoned the restraint of her straight-news reports "apropos the New Era club embroglio" only on the editorial page, yielding to a caustic comment: "There appears to be no reason for naming a woman's club 'The New Era,' judging from some of the results of the convention at Milwaukee. We are in the same old era."

Editors, too, were in the "same old era." Youmans vented her displeasure at their tendency to treat the Biennial as a fashion show: "I don't believe, as has been stated in print, that delegates brought an average of seven trunks each, and I didn't notice how often any particular woman changed her gown." She admitted that "it was what we women call a dressy affair"—and could not resist noting that, by Milwaukee standards, eastern women were overdressed, with "elegant and modish toilets" even in the morning. Yet, Youmans wrote, "it was really a democratic gathering in dress as in other ways, and a place where brains counted. As far as I could see, it made absolutely no difference whether brains were dressed or not."

Youmans also mused on benefits of the Biennial which escaped her brethren of the press: "'And what did it amount to? What did you get from it?' are frequent questions. Well, personally, I got inspiration and information I consider valuable. Further, I brought home from the Biennial an increased respect for the American woman," which her male colleagues apparently did not share.

Youmans reported the close of proceedings with relief as well as regret; as chair of the convention press relations committee, she had good reason to wish good riddance to the Biennial. The WFWC had been overwhelmed by attendance which exceeded all expectations: the total was almost four thousand, double that of the Biennial before, because of the southern contingent which doubled the number of delegates to nearly one thousand—and women were outnumbered almost three to one by "observers," primarily the press corps.

But women nationwide never would put the Milwaukee Biennial behind them, in the press or in history books. "The incident led to discussion of the race issue in clubs and the nation's newspapers," according to historian Gerda Lerner. The *Evening Wisconsin,* for example, ran a favorable interview with Ruffin. But the white press soon went on to other stories while debate raged in the black press. The *Wisconsin Advocate* adhered to Booker T. Washington's credo and seconded "wise and thoughtful counsel" that the "colored race . . . forever cease trying to force itself where it does not belong," even praising the GFWC's Rebecca Lowe as "a noble woman, charming lady and true friend to our race" for her care of her "old black mammy and four colored servants." According to historian Joe William Trotter, Jr., lack of support for Ruffin from their paper enraged Milwaukee's miniscule African-American community, whose leaders "engineered a 'great indignation meeting'" and "denounced the actions of the Federation and the *Advocate*'s editor as well."

The Milwaukee Biennial was a watershed for women in the black civil rights movement at the turn of the century. According to historian Paula Giddings, despite Ruffin's "numerous appeals" and those of Margaret Murray Washington, her husband "refused to use his influence in her behalf or take any stand on the matter." As a result of the refusal of the "Washington machine," many women of color rebelled against male leadership, and the ramifications of the "Ruffin incident" were significant within the "race movement."

The Milwaukee Biennial also was significant in the woman's rights movement because the GFWC set a precedent long followed by other women's organizations. As Gerda Lerner writes, "the color bar in national women's organizations did not drop until several decades later"—six decades later. In 1900, in Milwaukee, the "color line" in the woman's rights movement was drawn so indelibly that it rarely would be crossed by the "second generation" of suffragists and for generations to come, as racial segregation would continue to prevail over gender solidarity.[11]

But Wisconsin clubwomen—the white, mainstream, middle-class clubwomen—rebounded within months from the hubbub of the Biennial and its unhappy aftermath, and got back to "old business" on the agenda: suffrage. At the WFWC convention in November in Racine, familiar faces from the Biennial included author Charlotte Perkins Gilman Stetson of New York—who had added Houghton to her name, having married the day after speaking at the Biennial—and *Club Woman* editor Helen Winslow of Boston. Jane Addams of Chicago returned to address the WFWC for the second time, this time to speak on industrial conditions of working women. Their concerns came together in "a new departure" for the WFWC, Youmans reported. A session "devoted to reviews of recent literature on the social and economic position of women" led to a "literary reference committee" to promote a list of readings to clubs and libraries statewide as well as research on the issue. "The time has come," departing president Ella Hoes Neville said in her farewell address, "when it is not enough that woman should be alone a homemaker. She must make the world itself a larger home."[12]

Low in the *Freeman* follow-up story on the WFWC convention was a modest mention—in eyestraining agate type—of the mandate which clubwomen accorded their new president: Theodora Winton Youmans. In Waukesha, her cohort of more than two hundred women, almost the entire membership of the town's clubs, turned out for a reception in Youmans' honor. It was held in one of the few local facilities large enough to hold them—the Young Men's Christian Association.

Clubwomen's vote for a president was a vote for her platform, and Youmans' precipitate rise to the WFWC presidency ensured a return to the deferred school-suffrage campaign and more "new departures" for the WFWC. Under Youmans, the executive committee immediately endorsed a policy of publishing all proceedings—not only of conventions but also of the executive committee—in the press. Editors received lists of committees and objectives for the coming year, including a "legislative committee which is not a standing but a temporary committee," whose "object is to secure such legislation as is necessary to make effective a law now on the statute books permitting women to vote for school officers."

The WFWC policy contrasted with that of the WWSA in its ill-fated 1886 campaign when the press had accused women of "fraud" and "conspiracy" in attempting a "practical revolution" rather than partial suffrage—and when men had been even more offended by the "exultations" of Olympia Brown. Instead, with canny awareness of the importance of image, clubwomen promised openness—although, in reality, their publicity was incredibly understated and implied that the WFWC intended only a minor improvement on an established law. The posture of high accountability and low visibility was a pose, and not quite principled—but neither was politics, as they had learned in the Board of Control campaign. As historian Janice Steinschneider suspects, clubwomen's strategy "may have been a public relations device, to insure that public criticism of their activities remain low. It is difficult to assess just how much placating of possible critics [and] how much posturing was going on, and how much of it clubwomen really believed."

This time, clubwomen were prepared to act as a pressure group, mobilizing members and deploying tactics which the WFWC would implement whenever political action came within their expanding purview. As Steinschneider writes of the "well-developed machinery" of the WFWC, "members attended legislative hearings in favor of bills, petitioned government officials and boards, and attempted to arouse and direct public opinion. They enlisted clubs' aid, and sent clubs letters asking, for example, that they inform local legislators of their opinions on a particular bill."[13]

This time, too, the women's timing was exquisite. Within a week of the WFWC announcement, a newly elected governor publicly—if implicitly—endorsed clubwomen and their agenda as his own, in his inaugural address. Although La Follette wisely did not specify school suffrage, he ensured that what he said about women would be irresistible to the press—as wide dissemination of a wire-service report attests—by citing the press: "La Follette's suggestion in his inaugural that bright women be pushed to the front is generally commended, and papers instance cases (as on school boards and in charities) where women acquitted themselves well." La Follette admitted that "here and there, questions are raised" on women's ability, naming the *Mineral Point Tribune* and noting "Milwaukee editors" notorious for catering to a German constituency. However, he skillfully positioned backward papers as opponents of progress and progressive reform: "So-called foreign elements in our state oppose these recurring efforts to put women to the front, as some say, to 'take them out of the home.' While they are conservative, as shown by the fact that not many of their women are in the club movement, yet there is a breaking down of this absurd tradition."

Clubwomen could not have written the governor's inaugural address better, because one clubwoman probably did. Belle Case La Follette was said by some to be her husband's equal as an orator and had helped with his speechwriting since their student days, when she had been the scholar of their University of Wisconsin class while his poor grades had almost cost him a diploma. Ever after, speeches and publicity by and about her husband had to "get by Belle," and La Follette later referred to his years in the office as "when we were governor." He credited Belle for his appeals to the legislature which enabled him to appoint women to the Board of Control, to the Boards of Regents of the University of Wisconsin and State Normal Schools, and to the Board of Factory Inspectors, which oversaw working conditions of women and children. All were clubwomen's causes, and undoubtedly the doing of Belle Case La Follette, who would write—for one of her own speeches, for suffrage—that "government is considered as men's exclusive province, a limitation that has narrowed the lives of the women, that has robbed the children, and that has reacted most injuriously upon the state."[14]

Despite the gubernatorial endorsement, and the impact of an inaugural speech widely covered by the press, clubwomen went forward with caution in their legislative campaign. The WFWC was not officially connected with the Board of Control bill, which was killed, but other bills went through in 1901 that would add women to the Boards of Regents

"Government is considered as men's exclusive province, a limitation that has narrowed the lives of the women, that has robbed the children, and that has reacted most injuriously upon the state."—Belle Case La Follette, the first woman graduate of the University of Wisconsin Law School, a co-founder of *La Follette's Magazine,* and a leading publicist for the progressive movement. Photo courtesy of the State Historical Society of Wisconsin.

of the University of Wisconsin and of the State Normal Schools and one to the Board of Factory Inspectors. The last was submitted by the Consumers' League, which had been almost synonymous with the WFWC since national organizer Florence Kelley spoke at the 1899 convention on women's working conditions.[15]

Clubwomen kept a low profile by lobbying as individuals rather than en masse, carefully avoiding any appearance of alliances which could suggest a "conspiracy" of women, and wisely so. Despite overlapping leadership, the WFWC especially remained distant from the WWSA, which in 1901 — at the same time that clubwomen were seeking school suffrage — suddenly submitted a bill for support of a federal full-suffrage amendment. The mild memorial to Congress, sponsored by assemblyman David Evans, literally sent legislators fleeing from the floor for their political lives. As Youmans recalled, "legislators whose especial aim was to avoid making enemies found woman suffrage a stumbling block in the path." She quoted the *Wisconsin State Journal,* which "tells us that 'the sergeant[-at-arms] was ordered to bring in the timid members who sought to dodge the vote. Half a score of half-ashamed men on whom female constituents had brought pressure came trooping to their seats." It was progress, of a sort. Fear had replaced ridicule — if not forever, for a while — and lawmakers at last saw suffrage as a serious issue. Indeed, it was a sign of progress that the press saw women as a "female constituency," a pressure group, at all.

But the WWSA was not yet a significant constituency, and the assembly killed the bill by a ballot of more than three to one, while the senate registered only one vote in favor. The bill died so swiftly that it merited little more than a one-line obituary. Fortunately — for the historian, not the editor — the *Freeman*'s Capitol correspondent, who clearly was paid by the inch, filed a far wordier report: "Woman's suffrage was quickly done for in the senate the other day. . . . In the house a letter from some good mother in the Israel of Ripon was read, evidently the indignant pleas of some woman who pays taxes and is allowed to see drunken loafers go to the polls and decide how her money shall be spent. It was softened by that pathetically helpless vein with which a sad minority, especially the standard-bearers of unpopular causes, address the great, powerful, reckless legislature." The writer milked even more out of the story by means of editorial commentary and crystal-gazing, predicting that "someday the intelligent women of Wisconsin will come into their own," and sagely informing readers that "only in their infancy do great forces seem small."

Clubwomen would "come into their own" while Brown and her "small band" continued to fail in attempts at even partial suffrage and in almost every biennium, wrote Youmans. "Organization, public speaking, press publicity, conventions, in those days as later, had one object, suffrage legislation in state and nation. . . . Measures embodying full or partial suffrage continued to pour in at each session of the legislature and frequently that body was urged to use its influence to secure the passage of legislation by Congress. These measures received some favorable consideration during the first decade of the new century, but not enough to secure their passage." As Youmans later summed up the discouraging decade for the WWSA, "so the cause advanced, with no appearance of advancement sometimes, from one year's end to another."

But appearances—"image"—counted as much as substance in the new century when, in contrast with the WWSA, the WFWC constituted a sizable workforce of women who had compiled a record of success in municipal reform. Clubwomen also concentrated effort rather than diluting their demands and conducted a campaign so constrained that press attention was low even after passage.

In May 1901, clubwomen won the only bill submitted by the WFWC in the biennium and won back school suffrage. For public consumption, the WFWC president called the success a "slight" coup. Youmans filed a report in the *Freeman* which balanced justifiable pride with judicious wording: "Only one bill was introduced at the instance of the State Federation, that providing for the slight additional legislation necessary to permit women to vote for school officers. . . . This bill is now a law. Hereafter separate ballot boxes will be provided and Wisconsin women may vote for school officers." Only twenty years later, after full suffrage was won, would she exult on the record at reviving a law which had been "practically a dead letter" since passage, in Olympia Brown's words. Even then, ever the diplomat, Youmans did not name the WFWC but graciously deferred to the WWSA as "an important factor" in winning back the school-suffrage law lost a dozen years before.[16]

By 1901, clubwomen had become so adept in their political maneuvering that, as subsequent events suggest, the WFWC may have conducted a bit of pork-barreling behind the scenes for school suffrage. The bill had been introduced by a legislator from Milwaukee, which stood to benefit the most from their next campaign: a fund drive for a $10,000 endowment for Milwaukee-Downer College. The college long had been a cause of Milwaukee clubwomen, including Downer president Dr. Ellen Sabin, and benefitted by her statewide connections through the WFWC.

A Neenah clubwoman and paper mill heiress, Helen Cheney Kimberly, had issued a challenge grant of $5,000 for a chair in domestic science at Downer, to be matched by double the amount from clubwomen. However, owing to the amount, a decision had been deferred. Now, at the WFWC executive committee meeting after passage of the school-suffrage law, leadership approved the Downer College endowment campaign by a unanimous vote.

Women's schooling in fund-raising would be crucial in the suffrage campaign, and the Downer endowment drive was a significant test. However, membership had yet to be convinced, at the next WFWC convention. The board slated speakers who were guaranteed to sway the most timid of members, with a program of domestic science educators from Downer College and across the country, including Nellie Kedzie Jones of Berea College, Kentucky, a pioneering school in home economics whose president was the brother-in-law of the late Lavinia Goodell. Jones also was a pioneer in the field and, a decade later, would join the University of Wisconsin Extension.

One of the most persuasive WFWC members, Rose C. Swart of the Oshkosh Normal School faculty, chaired the fund drive. At the convention she noted that "there is now no place in the West where women may be trained as teachers in this line of work" and spoke fervently in favor. Clubwomen overcame their trepidation—although only after a two-day, "long and vigorous discussion." In the end, they not only approved the Milwaukee-Downer College endowment drive by a wide margin but also voted to undertake a petition campaign for a similar chair at the University of Wisconsin.[17]

Discussion of domestic science aside, the 1901 convention—the first since the school-suffrage campaign—was conspicuously political. In October in Madison, in the assembly chamber where national suffrage leaders had addressed lawmakers for decades, clubwomen now "enjoyed the distinction of occupying the seats of legislators," Youmans wrote. Women also were made welcome at an "at home" at the executive mansion hosted by Belle Case La Follette, and the official convention welcome was extended by the University of Wisconsin president. Speakers included the state superintendent of schools, the husband of WFWC leader Lettie Brown Harvey.

The convention was the largest in the history of the WFWC, with more than 250 delegates, a third more than the year before. Membership topped 5,500, half again that of the first year, while the number of clubs had more than doubled to 145 in five years, reported Youmans.

Presiding at the convention, she stressed the "special power" of club-women's potential: "Think of the power in the hands of these five thousand women who are fairly representative of the intelligent and progressive womanhood of the country, and who are thoroughly organized for work. Their special power lies in their organization, never lose sight of that." As historian Estelle B. Freedman writes, clubwomen were well aware that they had created a "separate public sphere." In Janice Steinschneider's words, it was "an organization of women, organized as women."[18]

Conspicuous by its absence was any celebration of the school-suffrage victory. In the legislative committee's progress report, passage of the law was mentioned only in passing. Clubwomen would not gloat, but they could not be complacent. In Richland Center, in one of Laura Briggs James's last letters before her death, she wrote that "we do not now consider the old objections that women should not vote because they can't fight." She had a favorite anecdote about Susan B. Anthony: when confronted by reform editor Horace Greeley as to "what she would do if she voted and there should be war, Miss Anthony answered, 'I would do just as you do—stay at home and advise others to go.'" James reminded her readers that women's work was crucial in wartime, but "you expect patriotism and heroism from men. I look for it among women and find lots of it." James also had an answer for "every objection now urged against the franchise for woman [that] was once used against her employment outside of the home and against coeducation." As James asserted, "since it is found that five-sevenths of our graduates are girls and that three-fourths of our teachers are women, that argument is squelched." In conclusion, Laura James noted that "latterly, we are told that we would neglect our homes if we were to be interested in politics, but we have only to remind such croakers that it would take much less time to vote."

To remind women to vote, Youmans went on a statewide tour until the next election—their first in fifteen years. But then, and always, she would be disappointed by voter apathy. "On April 1, 1902, Wisconsin women voted on the question of issuing certain school bonds. The number of women voting at that time was small, a precedent generally followed while the franchise of women was limited," Youmans declaimed in their defense. That few women voted on school questions "was frequently occasion of reproach to those seeking wider suffrage for women." Yet, as Youmans said, school races tended to draw low turnouts of men, too. Given good reason, women made good voters, she wrote in her column. "On occasions of especial interest a large women's vote was cast at these elections. . . . When the control of the Milwaukee school board depended on the election of new members, forty thousand Milwaukee women are said to have voted."[19]

However, many clubwomen had to be cajoled into the polls. In an address to the WFWC, Youmans minimized the significance of school suffrage to maximize voter turnout—a turnabout, but possibly for the benefit of men in the press who were present.

> Please do not feel that in voting on school matters you are committing yourself to any advanced suffrage theories or to the vicissitudes of a political life. . . . Your vote is simply an expression of your practical interest in the school, an interest that you have often expressed in other ways. . . . As an abstract idea, voting indeed has its terrors, but when you remember that in this case your vote means simply a voice in the selection of the officers who direct the education of your children and in the settlement of other pertinent educational affairs, it seems only normal and rational.[20]

For one for whom life held few "terrors," at least not at the polls, Youmans' speech seems incongruous. However, her caution is understandable in the context of a simultaneous resurgence of the WWSA.

The WFWC went forward from the school-suffrage campaign with caution, restraining more ardent members while reassuring reluctant women—and any onlookers—that they were satisfied with the partial ballot. Not so the WWSA, which resurfaced in 1902 with "suffrage headquarters" in "a little room in the State House" in Madison "for distribution of literature and knowledge," hardly an activity to cause concern. However, Brown also announced a petition campaign and protest by taxpaying women, "by whatever method may seem best"—the sort of threat which had lost school suffrage once before.

As proof that clubwomen would not seek more than the law meant, and as promised, Youmans dissolved the temporary legislative committee—although not without a wistful comment that some state federations fearlessly maintained standing legislative committees. Members knew what that meant. As Youmans put it, counterparts "boldly proclaimed an interest and an intention that most club women recognize, but that some think best to keep quiet about," lest they lose the partial-suffrage law, again.

The specter of the 1888 defeat would haunt Wisconsin women, whether "ladies of the clubs" or less subtle suffragists. If some clubwomen also found settling for partial suffrage painful, it was the politic thing to do—and wisely done, considering Wisconsin's suffrage past. By keeping its word, the WFWC preserved its image of integrity—and, as important, its political viability—for many a campaign to come, as clubwomen sallied into the "public sphere" with increasing success.

However, clubwomen could not make headway in the WFWC's next campaign, the Downer College endowment drive, for years. The campaign had advanced little in a year, by the 1902 convention, where Youmans scolded clubwomen for lack of progress. "When you give your voice, give your hand to help along," she said. "Moral support that doesn't do anything is not worth much."[21]

Wisconsin women first overcame their discomfiture with fund-raising at the local level, where none could rival the women of Neenah, among them the paper mill heiress who had issued the Downer challenge grant. According to a *Freeman* rewrite from an "exchange," the women "broke all records in the way of raising funds for the improvement of their city"—and, no doubt, their state. In Neenah, a public library long had been a low priority, until clubwomen lost patience with city fathers. "Committees were appointed, the society leaders of the city visited the business men, retired lumbermen and papermill owners," and women "soon had the desired sum secured"—in excess of $20,000, in a single week. At the same time, they raised the last of $10,000 for another "proper building" desperately needed in Neenah, a public theater, since "the city had no place for public entertainments" other than a roller rink of low repute.

Clubwomen also became increasingly comfortable with taking credit for their work by publicizing their fiscal prowess, thus making fund-raising and publicity "respectable" work for women. Small-town editors welcomed clubwomen's self-promotion, as evidenced by a *Freeman* "exchange" from the *Beloit Free Press*.

> The club is a more important factor in the life of our city than the uninformed have any idea of; some say it has in a large degree done away with the old time "calling" and other social functions. Nowadays our women do not meet to gossip . . . for education and philanthropy are most interesting subjects to discuss. They are taking what might be called a post graduate course [and] good effects are everywhere visible for [they have] more comprehensive knowledge of public and business affairs. . . . Beloit has many public benefits due to the energy of the club women. The City Federation of Women's Clubs has done so much general good that it needs no explanation of its aims.[22]

With a brief, requisite mention of the beneficial effect of club work on women become "better wives, mothers and companions," the writer concentrated on "the main line of work for the year" to come. Beloit clubwomen's "worthy subjects" included "school room decoration, furnishings for the hospital or an emergency fund for the same, a girls' sewing school and a boys' reading room."

Across Wisconsin, many a clubwoman refined her skills in the explosion of activity after the school-suffrage campaign — and would put them to use in the suffrage campaign to come. Oshkosh women emulated the ingenious "Athenaeum plan" first devised by the Woman's Club in Milwaukee, legally incorporating as a stock company and raising $13,000 for the second self-supporting club facility in the state. The Twentieth Century Club House grand opening brought congratulations from clubs nationwide — although some, Youmans admitted, were "apt to give a little sign of envy along with their enthusiastic appreciation." In the later suffrage campaign, she would have even more reason to appreciate Oshkosh clubwomen, especially Sophie Gudden and Jessie Jack Hooper.

Sophie Gudden was an early activist in the Consumers' League. A Bavarian immigrant whose accent was complicated by a stutter, she also was crippled but conquered her self-consciousness and physical disabilities and became an accomplished public speaker. Gudden soon rose to the presidency of the state Consumers' League and later served as a vice president of the national organization, "a model of social feminism" and "one of the most effective social reform agencies in the Progressive era," according to a historian, as well as one of the most political of clubwomen's affiliations. From 1900 to 1910, Gudden also chaired the WFWC consumer affairs committee which included early suffragists Edna Phillips Chynoweth of Madison and Vie H. Campbell of Evansville. Relentlessly but persuasively, Gudden urged clubwomen to the ballot by suggesting that if their concern for education justified school suffrage, the needs of working women and children necessitated full suffrage.

Jessie Jack Hooper would rise to even greater prominence in the suffrage campaign, in the state and at the national level. A leader of Oshkosh's Twentieth Century Club, she also was an officer of the Woman's Parliamentary Law Club and Business Woman's Club as well as the city plan commission and the WWSA. Youmans' most faithful co-worker to 1920 and beyond, Hooper also became a member of the board of the National American Woman Suffrage Association and one of its best lobbyists in Congress.[23]

In Waukesha, too, Youmans and other clubwomen refined their fund-raising and organizational skills in a series of municipal reform campaigns. Their proudest accomplishment, a dozen years after the first "reading circles" formally organized, was forcing the city to take responsibility for the public library in 1901. For years, clubs' "round-about fundraising" supported an annual library budget of $300, while aldermen continued to refuse women's requests for annual subsidies of as little as $25. Finally, women announced a plan "to go directly to the public, especially businessmen," a process of "personal solicitation" which was "not entirely pleasant either to the solicitors or the solicited," as the *Freeman* put it. The city swiftly relieved beleaguered merchants of the financial burden, and clubwomen of their books.

In Waukesha, as across the country, newly public libraries continued to rely on clubwomen for leadership. A *Freeman* campaign for "some of the ladies who have been prominent in library work to be recognized in appointments" resulted in the naming of four women to the nine-member library board and hiring of the long-suffering Fanny Ells as the first city librarian. The city more than recouped her salary when Ells helped lure to town the national convention of the American Library Association in 1902, which drew eight hundred delegates to programs such as a "club session" on fund-raising and tactics to train women as "a real force in public affairs."

Repeatedly, Waukesha clubwomen initiated and funded needed municipal projects until city fathers were persuaded of their worth. The Ideals supported the city's first hospital through fund-raisers such as the club's "literary" work, a cookbook called *The Ideal Way to a Man's Heart*. Women and their civic federation also established a children's library, a school nurse program, a Young Women's Christian Association to serve as safe lodging for working women, and a "civic housekeeping campaign" for supervised playgrounds, the forerunners of the municipal park system. In their province of the schools, Waukesha clubwomen campaigned in 1902 for the election of one of their own, Julia Rockafellow, as county superintendent of schools and supported her efforts to fund improvement of rural schools through centralized purchasing.

Fund-raising campaigns educated women to the need for varied new skills for the "public sphere," especially public speaking. Abandoning the comparative security of prepared scripts, the Waukesha Women's Club debated whether a professional career was "desirable for girls" and decided in the affirmative. After a Practical Club debate, "Resolved, That

Literary Women Are Good Home Makers," the *Freeman*'s literary woman smugly reported that, again, "affirmative had the best argument." At the same time, suffrage did not fare so well with the Athletic Base Ball Club in nearby Menomonee Falls, where clubwomen spoke in favor but judges —three men—ruled unanimously for the "two boys in the negative."

The "great achievement" of the Women's Club's second president—Youmans—was a series of "seven lessons in parliamentary law" which captivated the public as well as clubwomen, who opened the course for a twenty-five-cent fee and were forced to find a larger site. Instruction in parliamentary practice seems an unlikely crowd pleaser but was welcomed by women unaccustomed to running public meetings—and unwilling to be ruled out of order ever again. A *Freeman* correspondent's testimony to women's ability at the podium suggests, between the lines, how often it had been doubted: "It is obsolete to think that women cannot run a meeting according to parliamentary rules; cannot make their voices heard in a large hall [and] cannot discuss matters of finance in a way to make average congressmen turn green with envy." The significance of clubwomen's self-instruction in organizational skills cannot be understated. A decade later, for example, Youmans' knowledge of parliamentary law would lead to a coup for the suffrage campaign.[24]

Waukesha clubwomen adopted another tactic which later would be adapted for the benefit of suffrage coffers but raised funds in 1902 for the WFWC's Downer College endowment drive: a "Club Women's edition" of the *Freeman*. For months in advance of the February 14 publication date, "the management"—Youmans—ballyhooed "the most notable number of the *Freeman* ever to be issued . . . from an entirely unprejudiced point of view." However, the edition lived up to her hyperbole. As Milwaukee clubwomen had done seven years before for the *Journal*, Waukesha clubwomen established a record for the *Freeman* which endured for decades, doubling the paper's size and almost doubling circulation to thirty-five hundred.

Compared with the earlier *Journal* edition, the *Freeman* counterpart was a more confident adventure in journalism and offers a perspective on the sort of paper women wanted to run, and to read: more coverage of arts and education—led by "The Value of Business Education to Women"—as well as a "literary department" and a "domestic department." In sum, the edition looked and read much like any women's section, then and since.

However, clubwomen also knew how to sell a paper and offered state, national, and international news, business, and sports—which, even in turn-of-the-century Wisconsin, included bowling and "ladies leagues"— and an advice column with an unusual twist. The best-read department undoubtedly was "For the Gentlemen: Sweet Sisterly Advice," a satire on "sob sister" journalism—and a witty send-up of the standard view of "women's news." Mythical husbands were aided in regaining spouses' affections, two-timing bachelors were told to mend their morals, and all men were advised to mind their manners by not "expectorating in the streets." Chubbier "chappies" were admonished to help around the house as better exercise than bowling, while "modish men" were advised on "A Few of the Season's Fads" with "Heart to Heart Talks on Waistcoats and Neckties."

The department deserving most comment was a wide-ranging editorial page which led with "Our Platform." Clubwomen stood for a conservative approach to income taxes, tariffs, trusts, the gold standard, and temperance. An editorial on women's place in politics artfully avoided the topic of suffrage but adroitly answered the argument that women would only vote with their men. The writer—Youmans—pointed out that sons also inherited their fathers' politics and "not one in a hundred calmly studies and weighs the principles advocated by each party and then makes up his own mind."

The "Club Women's Edition" of the *Freeman* raised more than $1,000 for the Downer endowment drive, causing the editor-in-chief—Youmans—to comment for her staff of thirty women that "we could do as well as this every week, but it would ruin every other newspaper in Wisconsin." On the potential impact on journalism if "two hundred or fifty-five hundred or four hundred thousand women should go into the newspaper business"—the number of clubwomen in Waukesha, in the Wisconsin Federation, and in the General Federation—she wrote only that "the imagination totters."

Despite such efforts, the Downer endowment drive dragged on. But the related lobbying campaign, to establish domestic science studies at the University of Wisconsin, succeeded sooner. In 1903, legislators appropriated funds for a department at Madison which would be a pioneer in the field of home economics and one of the best in the country under clubwoman Abby Marlatt. The Downer drive ended in 1904 when Helen Cheney Kimberly not only honored her challenge grant but doubled it, netting a total of $20,000 for a chair in domestic science and for a loan fund for "poor girls." At the 1904 WFWC convention, clubwomen were so delighted with the success of their first statewide solicitation— or so relieved to know that they no longer would be subjected to annual scoldings—that they founded a permanent fund for introducing home economics curricula throughout the state public school system.

From 1904 forward, clubwomen gained increasing confidence in the "public sphere" and were increasingly welcome in state politics, none more so than Theodora Winton Youmans. Governor La Follette appointed her to the Wisconsin Board of Managers for the St. Louis World's Fair and to a state committee for tuberculosis prevention—a political controversy—in 1904, and to the Board of Regents of the State Normal Schools in 1905. But she was not the only beneficiary of the La Follette largesse. Also in 1905, he appointed Kate Sabin Stevens of Windsor to the University of Wisconsin Board of Regents and—after intervening with lawmakers to win the compromise of a single seat—at last appointed a woman to the Board of Control. However, clubwomen continued to monitor state institutions and their seat on the board, which repeatedly faced repeal or reduction in status or salary.

Still, the La Follettes' influence lasted long after his election to the Senate and their return to Washington in 1906. The WFWC worked on an Industrial Commission pamphlet on working conditions of women and children, worked with the University of Wisconsin Extension in a promotional campaign for community education, and assisted other state agencies from the Bureau of Child Welfare to the Pure Food Commission. Although the WFWC now served as a "readily available pool of talent," lest hard-won gains be lost the WFWC went "on record as favoring the appointment of the *right woman only*" and "much better no woman at all than the wrong woman," according to a WFWC committee report which identified the primary characteristic for women in public service as "tact"—only because "ability, both natural and cultivated," was assumed.

The WFWC became a sought-after source of expertise for nongovernmental organizations, which soon realized that every clubwomen represented an unrivaled, unpaid campaign staff of thousands. For example, as a founder of the Wisconsin Anti-Tuberculosis Association, Youmans enlisted the WFWC in campaigns for prevention of contagion such as the drive for safer public drinking fountains—"bubblers," in the Wisconsin idiom. Youmans also was a founder of her county historical society, enlisted the WFWC in preservation campaigns for the State Historical Society, and served on its board. However, the major force on the WFWC landmarks preservation committee was historian Julia Lapham of Oconomowoc, the daughter of Increase Lapham and archivist of his pioneering scientific studies.

The WFWC proved crucial in campaigns for pure food laws, nurse certification, visiting nurses, and free medical examinations for children. Through the GFWC, Wisconsin clubwomen also worked with national organizations including the Consumers' League, the American Association of University Women, the National Council of Jewish Women, the National Conference of Christians and Jews, the American Civic Association, and the American Red Cross. In sum, as historian Janice Steinschneider suggests, the WFWC "often acted as a clearinghouse of many progressive reform causes and special interest associations" indicative of clubwomen's wide interests.[25]

But the coalition most significant to the suffrage campaign would be that of clubwomen and the Wisconsin Teachers Association. They shared not only a commitment to education but also mutual membership, and leadership; the first two women to serve as WTA presidents were WFWC officers. The first was the outspoken Rose C. Swart of the Oshkosh Normal School, and the second would make the WTA and WFWC almost synonymous: Mary Davison Bradford, who would be the superintendent of public schools in Kenosha and president of the National Council of Administrative Women in Education. Already a respected educational reformer and longtime chair of the WFWC education committee, she had enlisted clubs' support of innovations from summer schools to facilities for disabled students.

Bradford and clubwomen had become most identified with the kindergarten movement, endorsed by the first WFWC convention a decade before. But they were not the only important constituency on the issue. As a Capitol correspondent to the *Freeman* reported on passage of a bill to lower the school age at the turn of the century, the law was "hailed with glee by mothers the state over." By mid-decade, the movement seemed so secure that the WFWC's annual progress reports were a matter of routine—until introduction of the unlikely bill which would be clubwomen's impetus to suffrage.

In 1907, a misguided assemblyman named Roderick Ainsworth offered an amendment to the state constitution to raise the school age from four years old to six, ostensibly to reduce disbursements to school districts. In effect, despite his denials, the bill would prohibit kindergartens—or at least make them too prohibitive to fund. Still, the bill passed both houses of the legislature and seemed destined for a required second approval in the next biennium.

But the Ainsworth bill was doomed. The kindergarten campaign would be the first test in the political arena of the alliance of the WFWC and WTA—and the last test of clubwomen's patience with the political process without the ballot.

The heroine of the kindergarten campaign, Gertrude Cushing of Milwaukee, called the WFWC to battle at the 1907 convention. A member of the College Endowment Association—a legacy of the city's earliest study club, the Ladies' Art and Science Class—Cushing not only alerted clubwomen to the pending bill but also outlined a strategy of attack which employed every pressure tactic in their arsenal from publicity to lobbying the legislature. The plan was especially astute in exploiting the WFWC's strength: its structure, which corresponded to congressional—thus, legislative—districts.

The WFWC immediately moved to effect a coalition with the WTA and to ensure internal communication, while preparing to survey public opinion and conduct lobbying and publicity efforts. For the first time since the school-suffrage campaign, clubwomen reinstated a legislative committee—temporarily—as a liaison with district officers and the education committee in a two-pronged plan aimed at politicians and the press. As Cushing put it, incumbent candidates who had backed the bill were to be "convinced of the error of their ways, by moral suasion when possible" but by more coercive means if necessary. Clubwomen planned a systematic canvass of each district to determine public support and promised release of results to candidates—and the press— prior to primary races, to "prove that although we have not been granted a franchise," as Cushing asserted, "we are able to make or unmake the laws."

By the spring of 1908, the kindergarten campaign made headlines, and headway. Within weeks of the WFWC convention, the WTA's annual meeting was addressed by clubwoman Carrie Morgan, superintendent of schools in Appleton, who enlisted educators. Enlisting the press, clubwomen released the results of their public opinion poll research. By March, Milwaukee's *Daily News* and *Evening Wisconsin* reported that the campaign was having an effect. Although they refrained from editorial support, several education associations allied with the WFWC and WTA. In hope of appeasing clubwomen, the hapless Ainsworth accepted invitations to appear before both the WFWC and the WTA at their 1908 conventions.

In the fall of 1908, the WFWC and WTA conventions received extensive coverage because of Ainsworth's public debates with women who bested him and doomed his bill. First, at the WFWC convention in October, Ainsworth faced an array of educators and lawyers who demolished his statements on student ability and on the bill's impact. The WFWC's bold move won leading state papers to the women's side. With kindergartens at stake, as the *Milwaukee Journal* crowed, "Women or Men Win."

The combative mood of the WFWC convention was evident in a report from Cushing's legislative committee, which never would be "temporary" again. "The twelve women forming this committee" were "impelled to assert that the law makers of Wisconsin are going to have a hard time of it next winter, unless they agree with the women on the kindergarten question. . . . Here then is a golden opportunity. To agitate and to educate [is] a combination of strong power." The convention took the opportunity to establish the first WFWC standing legislative committee, with Cushing as chair—a significant step for clubwomen who had disbanded a similar body but six years before, when a permanent lobbying committee seemed too "bold" a step toward the ballot and "best to keep quiet about."

One farseeing clubwoman spoke up, according to the *Sentinel,* to raise a significant point of order regarding the WFWC's hard-won school suffrage. In the event of legislative approval and the referendum required for the bill to become law, she wondered whether women would be entitled to vote on the Ainsworth amendment to the state constitution since the kindergarten issue was a "school matter." The answer exposed the limits of school suffrage: the answer was no.

Within a month of the WFWC convention, clubwomen statewide distributed thirty thousand pamphlets printed by Cushing's Social Economics Club and won the majority of the state press to their side, according to teachers at the WTA convention. Teachers also did their part to put Ainsworth on the defensive at the WTA debate by inviting Cushing and scheduling her presentation first. A sizable contingent of clubwomen at the WTA convention heard the educators acknowledge their power and potential as "the intelligent women in the state. . . . who have been the most ardent advocates of the kindergarten and most thorough students of its principles."

The WTA overwhelmingly endorsed a formal protest of the pending bill. By the opening of the 1909 biennium, the Wisconsin Association of School Boards also had allied with the WFWC and WTA. The Ainsworth bill was not resubmitted for second approval.

At the next WFWC convention, in 1909, the first report was from Cushing's legislative committee. In a strongly worded criticism of the political process, it detailed legislative chicanery and ignorance witnessed by women and denounced the men's "ill-considered, ill-drafted bills" and "shockingly mismanaged official housekeeping." It was the worst epithet in the clubwoman's lexicon, and an indication of the impact of the kindergarten campaign on women in Wisconsin who never would be the same.[26]

By 1908—the height of clubwomen's kindergarten campaign—the Reverend Olympia Brown belatedly "detected a new grass roots interest in suffrage" in Wisconsin. On a tour of campuses with NAWSA organizer Dr. Maud Wood Park, Brown captivated coeds with the saga of her battle to be admitted to a college half a century before. Students formed five campus suffrage leagues. However, after Park left the state, all lapsed for lack of support.[27]

An indication of the "new interest in suffrage" in 1909 was the WWSA's first statewide suffrage petition campaign in decades—prompted by a nationwide effort for a federal amendment conducted by NAWSA. "The National" was more systematic than the WWSA, and "blanks were sent all over the State to schools, libraries and other public institutions and to individuals. The members took up the matter with enthusiasm and worked faithfully. [They] did all that could be done in the six weeks allowed and about eighteen thousand names were signed," according to Youmans. However, five thousand names were secured in a single canvass of Brown's hometown of Racine, where one woman was solely responsible for securing, door to door, over one thousand signatures—a "Mrs. Wentworth, over eighty years of age," the same Elizabeth R. Wentworth praised in the *History of Woman Suffrage* by WWSA founder Dr. Laura Ross Wolcott as "an earnest and excellent writer" who had "kept up a healthy agitation through the columns of her husband's paper at Racine," more than two decades before.[28]

For decades, the WWSA had been so disorganized that Brown was unable to pay national dues in 1900. Dismayed, Susan B. Anthony donated to NAWSA the few dollars needed and wrote to Brown—her coworker for almost four decades—"I cannot bear to have the national records of 1900 go down to history without your name standing at the head of the Wisconsin suffrage society." Brown would serve as president for a dozen years more, but she and the WWSA led the state suffrage movement in name only. By 1901, the leadership of the campaign had gone to clubwomen, by default.

The WWSA's inactivity was not unusual in the first decade of the century; since 1896, when women in four states had won full suffrage, not a single campaign had succeeded of hundreds across the country. In 1906, Susan B. Anthony's death only sent NAWSA deeper into what suffragists called "the doldrums."

In Wisconsin, "the doldrums" had descended sooner than elsewhere. After the defeat of school suffrage, Brown almost abandoned Wisconsin, understandably, stumping South Dakota in 1890 and Iowa in 1892. However, upon her husband's death in 1893, Brown inherited his publishing company in the midst of a nationwide financial panic which ruined his *Racine Times-Call.* For the rest of the century, until she found a buyer, Brown served as publisher and editor of the paper—a bitter irony; she never would conquer her preference for the pulpit and the podium over the press. By the turn of the century, Brown again was often absent from the state and seemed little interested in—and less attuned to—women in Wisconsin. She spoke at NAWSA conventions and lectured in the East where she lived with her son, a journalist. Brown sent copy for the *Wisconsin Citizen* to her daughter and other on-site editors in the state, monthly missives which were "weighty with news and advice to Wisconsin workers," according to her biographer. Brown returned for annual WWSA conventions, but turnout was dismal. Other than the *Citizen,* the WWSA issued only two publications in the decade—during the WFWC's two-year kindergarten campaign.[29]

In 1910, "the doldrums" ended at the national level with the first victory in almost fifteen years—again in the West, where women in Washington State won full suffrage—and NAWSA membership soared to seventy-five thousand. However, the number of women in NAWSA still was far less than the quarter of a million women in the WCTU—and the GFWC would surpass one million members soon after 1910. Similarly, in Wisconsin, the WFWC enrolled more than seven thousand women, compared with fewer than two thousand in the WCTU.[30]

But by 1910, the WWSA was down to a few dozen members and fewer active local associations under Olympia Brown, who was out of touch with the state and the "second generation" of suffragists—including her second-in-command, Ada L. James.

Ada James was a strikingly literal example of a "second-generation" suffragist, a clubwoman for whom "women's place" had always been in politics—in her home and her hometown. She called suffragism the "religion" of Richland Center where she recalled attending suffrage meetings with her mother, the late Laura Briggs James, and with her grandmother, the late Mary Hurlbut, both among founders of one of Wisconsin's first women's clubs. As historian Lawrence L. Graves writes, Ada James was "imbued with Progressive doctrines early." By 1909, she had helped to found a new and explicitly suffragist organization in Richland Center, the Political Equality Club, for the purpose of examining "the lives of women who have been instrumental in obtaining for us the educational and political rights we are now enjoying"—and pledged to continue "the works." Ada James embodied "the surge of support for women's rights beginning about 1910," when "the daughters of the women" who founded women's clubs "grew to maturity and carried the whole matter a step further," according to historian Karen J. Blair.

For Ada James, the next step in 1910 was the same step taken a quarter of a century before by her uncle, the legislator from Richland Center who in 1885 had submitted the WWSA's first bill for a suffrage referendum. In 1910, when Richland Center sent her father to the state senate, Ada sent him to Madison with a mission: to complete the "unfinished work my mother did," to sponsor another referendum bill—but this time, unmistakably, for full suffrage.

This time, the bill would not be submitted on behalf of the WWSA, although Ada James was vice president of the organization by 1910. In 1910, she represented the WWSA as Brown's proxy, and at her request, at a NAWSA convention in Washington, D.C. But the program on strategies and tactics only added to Ada James's awareness of suffrage "excitement" elsewhere. Frustrated with the WWSA's inactivity and Olympia Brown's absentee leadership, James plotted with her father on the bill to be submitted to the legislature in 1911. She also began planning statewide organization of a branch of the new, national Political Equality League. To conduct the campaign, she would look to the legions of women who had won suffrage—school suffrage—once before.[31]

The 1911–12 referendum campaign would be led by clubwomen, the same women who had won a series of reforms for the progressive movement, and even set its agenda. Of leaders of the WFWC, more than a third would actively work for the vote, according to an analysis by Janice Steinschneider. There were antisuffragists among them, but for every "anti" in the WFWC, five would be "drawn to the suffrage fight." As Steinschneider writes, although clubwomen were "nonvoters, they had learned that they might make a significant impact on the world by disseminating information and channeling public opinion."[32] They would provide the new leadership which the campaign long had lacked—none more than the woman who had led the suffrage campaign once before, Theodora Winton Youmans.

No matter how well-schooled clubwomen were in the strategies and tactics needed to win in politics and the "public sphere" in a new century, as significant as their experience and expertise was the characteristic they had yet to lose: political innocence. Clubwomen had come far in the "public sphere"; they were newly cynical and hardly naive. But neither they nor the most expert and experienced of suffragists were hardened sufficiently to anticipate further shocking revelations to come on the conduct of "official housekeeping" out of public view, in the backrooms of politics. The 1911–12 suffrage referendum campaign would be an education for women—and for Wisconsin.

7

Retreat from Progressivism
Suffrage Referendum, 1911–1912

I N March 1911, when Ada James's suffrage referendum bill was submitted to the legislature, she had the help of many women and men.
First was her father, David G. James, the state senator from Richland
Center who submitted the bill but was one of "many men known to
be friendly in the membership of the legislature," according to Theodora Winton Youmans of the *Waukesha Freeman*. Youmans' own connections by marriage included two members of the assembly; both would
vote for the bill. Another willing assemblyman cooperated with Senator
James to submit concurrently, on both sides of the Capitol, an identical
bill for a suffrage referendum.

However, passage hardly was assured; Ada James's bill still had to
hurdle more legislative hearings, where she enlisted the help of a cadre
of women — clubwomen — accustomed to packing the galleries. As Youmans described the occasion, "a number of well-known women were
about the legislature . . . in behalf of various measures concerning the
welfare of women and children. They interested themselves in the suffrage
situation" and "made a thorough canvass of the senate and assembly."
Then, at a joint hearing, clubwomen were among "a large group of prosuffrage speakers," thirteen in all, while others augmented "a crowd of
sympathizers" including an estimated six hundred women in the audience. "Facing this array of numbers and talent . . . was one lone antisuffragist," an unnamed assemblyman. So cynical had clubwomen
become that his address "called forth 'roars of laughter' and later hisses
from the unruly audience" in the hearing room.[1]

The scene in the Capitol was symbolic of the referendum campaign to come, as the last decade of the suffrage movement opened with a range of activity for reform like none Wisconsin ever had seen—and by women. Abandoning ladylike measures to win the ballot, they staged a startling display of publicity and press agentry, taking to street corners and even cornering legislators for the state's first referendum on full woman suffrage.

To an astonished press as well as politicians and the public, the manner in which women—especially once well-mannered clubwomen—conducted the 1911–12 suffrage referendum campaign seemed to come suddenly and from out of nowhere. However, women simply put to the test all the lessons learned in their long schooling in abolition and temperance, in women's crusades and the WCTU and, especially, in women's clubs. "Many women who continued active in suffrage work until success crowned the cause first enlisted in the movement in the campaign of 1912," wrote Youmans, who epitomized the new claimants to the cause. The most prominent of the recent recruits, Youmans was a leader in her own milieu but a latecomer to suffrage compared with the likes of Olympia Brown and Ada James. Yet, although Youmans belonged to neither the WWSA nor the Political Equality League until 1911, after the campaign she would emerge crowned—somewhat reluctantly—as the successor to both Brown and James.

Neither the legendary longtime leader of the Wisconsin Woman Suffrage Association nor the rebellious founder of the new Political Equality League would be unscathed by the schism in the state movement "on account of diverse opinions as to the manner in which the campaign should be conducted," according to the ever-diplomatic Youmans. As Brown wrote to James, the WWSA's strategy was to "flood the legislature with letters" from the first but wait until the last weeks of the campaign, just prior to the election, to present the idea to the voting public. It was the same strategy, the "still hunt" for suffrage, that Brown had counseled a quarter of a century before.

In the spring of 1911, the PEL already was under way under Ada James, the premier strategist of the campaign. But she was not alone in contradicting Brown's counsel. As a co-worker wrote to James at the time, a low political profile was not appealing to the "second generation" and not appropriate in the new century. "It's useless to try organizing quietly," she wrote. "Besides, publicity is absolutely necessary to success these days." However, whether the *Sentinel*'s coverage of a meeting in Milwaukee in March 1911 was welcomed by the women was not recorded, but can be surmised because they were dismissed as "dodder-ing old ladies."[2]

In the publicity-conscious new century, the presswise Theodora Win-ton Youmans of the *Freeman* would be the most visible advocate of suffrage in Wisconsin from 1911 until the Nineteenth Amendment was won. In 1911, upon submission of the referendum bill, Youmans was in the Capitol—although whether to cover the story or to lobby among the "well-known clubwomen about the legislature," or both, was not clear—and was recognized and recruited by Ada James to be "press cor-respondent" for the PEL. Youmans later recalled the moment of her conversion—her "first plunge into suffrage surf"—in typically breezy style. "Of course, I was always a suffragist," Youmans wrote, "but after a while, I became an active working one."[3]

Suffrage was in the news from 1911 on because Youmans was in the newsroom. She covered the work of the campaign weekly in a column first called "Votes for Women" in the *Freeman* that was disseminated—in effect, syndicated—statewide. Many a *Freeman* reader, familiar with Youmans' work from her first "Woman's World" column a quarter of a century before, recognized the endearing combination of suffrage items, editorial asides, and personal diary, dashed off on deadline in a delight-fully conversational style. The content of her column continued to come from a wide range of "exchanges" and correspondents. But her primary source became Ada James, who would use Youmans' column as a means of communication to women statewide in the same way that Lavinia Goodell had turned to Emma Brown's *Wisconsin Chief* as a channel of communication, almost three decades before.

Youmans' column captured the attention of the new converts to suffrage and their ebullience; the new momentum in the movement seemed to revive everywhere and to reach every woman. In the West, where one million women already voted in five states, suffragists con-ducted campaigns in Arizona, Kansas, and Oregon in 1912. In the Mid-west, women in Ohio and Michigan as well as in Wisconsin worked to bring full suffrage east of the Mississippi River for the first time.

The optimism of 1911 was premature; in the end, suffrage campaigns would fail not only in Wisconsin but everywhere east of the Mississippi River, and full suffrage would remain a phenomenon of the West. But in the beginning, because Wisconsin's referendum won approval first of any state, the campaign captured women's imagination countrywide. As national organizer Crystal Eastman Benedict wrote to NAWSA from Milwaukee, owing to the state's "great reputation as a pioneer among progressive states, suffragists everywhere felt that the campaign presented a tremendous national opportunity. . . . In answer to our appeals, the word went out and echoed back and forth throughout the country, 'Help Wisconsin!'"[4]

Wisconsin's reputation for progressivism aside, the state still was famed among women for resistance to woman's rights reforms from temperance to suffrage. As never before, funds and personnel poured across the borders because Wisconsin women would need all the help they could get.

In 1911, women's work in the Wisconsin legislature lasted late into the spring—later than they had hoped, because they did not get the help of the governor. The senate passed the bill by a vote of sixteen to four at the end of March, when it went to the assembly and went through by a two-to-one vote in April. But Governor Francis E. McGovern kept women waiting until June before signing the bill. As yet an undeclared antisuffragist, he only acted "on the ground that it was the sort of problem which should be solved by the common sense of all the voters," wrote Youmans.

Women, especially clubwomen, knew better than to count on the "common sense" of an electorate so adamantly against suffrage for so long in Wisconsin, and the new PEL lured away many a longtime member of the WWSA as well as the WFWC. Jessie Jack Hooper of Oshkosh's Twentieth Century Club was auditor of the WFWC and a leader in local school reform and statewide public health campaigns. Two other clubwomen prominent in the PEL also were well known among Wisconsin Germans: Sophie Gudden of Oshkosh, a leader in the Consumers' League as well as the WFWC; and Meta Schlichting Berger of Milwaukee, wife of Congressman Victor L. Berger and a leader among Wisconsin's Socialist women.

Whether in the WWSA or the PEL, clubwomen who came into the suffrage campaign were motivated by "expediency," by the collective experience of frustration in seeking reform without the ballot. But each also brought personal experience to the cause, as was evident in Youmans' interviews. Ada James, the daughter of an early WWSA officer, saw suffrage as the means to see "the mother instinct made a direct influence in our national housekeeping" because "concerted effort means victory and an end of the struggle for the tool which we need so badly, and which the women laboring outside of the home need even more." To Sophie Gudden, "becoming a good American citizen" meant being "a student of the economic conditions of working women and children"

"Concerted effort means victory and an end of the struggle for the tool which we need so badly, and which the women laboring outside of the home need even more"—Ada L. James of Richland Center, a vice president of the Wisconsin Woman Suffrage Association and a founder of the Political Equality League and the National Woman's Party in Wisconsin. Photo courtesy of the State Historical Society of Wisconsin.

and "believing that the ballot in the hands of women will be productive only of good for herself, for her child and for society." A similar rationale was offered by another Oshkosh municipal reformer, who described Jessie Jack Hooper as "tired of trying to dig a hole with a teaspoon" when a "steam shovel" was needed.[5]

Although Youmans never directly revealed her reasons, her hundreds of columns suggest that she and many women were motivated by the justice of the cause, although more for altruistic reasons than for themselves. The injustice of being denied the ballot was an affront to Youmans, but she was appalled by the suffering of less fortunate women for whom suffrage offered at least some recourse. Yet, ever a realist, Youmans realized that the ballot alone would not save women, or the world, as when she wrote that "to hear some people talk, one might think the millennium would put in a prompt appearance the day after she cast her first vote, and that crime and misery and vice would disappear forthwith and forever. Come, let us be sensible. Let us be reasonable. Women's votes do just what men's votes have done, make changes slowly."

Youmans, for one, also freely admitted that the suffrage campaign provided the self-fulfillment found in women's clubs writ large, as she wrote in a poignant column on the personal rewards.

> The first experience of the woman who becomes interested in woman suffrage is the sense of loosening the petty restrictions about her, and a very agreeable experience it is, too. She looks outside her little social clique, and finds to her surprise that there are numbers of "nice" people beyond the sacred pale. . . . This enlarging of her acquaintanceship is even more enlarging to her mental horizon. She begins to see how extremely narrow and restricting her outlook has been. Some dim realization comes to her that her "set" is not really the hub of the universe. . . . The great truth of the brotherhood of man, the sisterhood of woman, comes to her, not clearly or all at once, but even though it comes vaguely it is yet highly illuminating. She has seen the light.[6]

More succinctly, she wrote that "the greatest effect of woman suffrage is, in our opinion, its influence upon the woman, herself."

The most telling evidence that the cause was far different for the "second generation" was their determination to make suffrage only a secondary career. In contrast with Olympia Brown, who had made suffrage her life's work, younger women stayed active in club work and often held office in the WFWC—and many continued their other careers as well. For example, Youmans was "press correspondent" for the PEL while she remained associate editor of the *Freeman,* retained her political posts, and held offices in her local women's clubs. Officially, she worked three days a week at the *Freeman* and two days a week for suffrage; only later would Youmans admit that "suffrage work took most of my time."

Although most clubwomen already in the WWSA also enlisted in the PEL, some stayed at Olympia Brown's side. The most prominent WWSA loyalist and WFWC officer was Zona Gale of Portage, formerly a *Milwaukee Journal* reporter and later a Pulitzer Prize-winning novelist. But the most burdensome duty fell to Brown's daughter, Dr. Gwendolen Brown Willis of Milwaukee-Downer College, who chaired a committee to coordinate campaign work between the WWSA and PEL. Although similar infighting at the national level was the subject of a letter to a NAWSA officer from Olympia Brown in June 1911, the PEL undoubtedly was on her mind when she wrote that "shallow false talk of . . . harmony" was "so false that it makes me vomit."

Willis' task was made worse by an eastern suffragist, Mary Swain Wagner of New York, who apparently had instigated Ada James's revolt from the WWSA and helped to organize her PEL. Wagner lobbied in Madison for the referendum bill and lingered long enough to alienate Ada James's father and others in the legislature, and to conduct a duplicitous correspondence with Olympia Brown as well as the PEL that further complicated the already-strained relations between the suffrage organizations. Wagner stayed well past her welcome in Wisconsin to start another but "short-lived society" in Milwaukee, until she attempted to control the PEL and was ousted by Ada James.[7]

By September 1911, within six months of her defection from the WWSA to found the PEL, James attempted a reconciliation of the two organizations under new leadership, to no avail. Acknowledging that neither she nor Brown would be acceptable to both sides in the feud, James wrote to Youmans in a subtle appeal for assistance in finding the woman with suitable characteristics: "We *must* have women of broad experience . . . strong, influencial [*sic*] women," wrote James. But no one was willing and able to take the post; WFWC founder Lucy Smith Morris had promised her time to a hospital project in Berlin, while Lutie E. Stearns responded with disdain of the PEL's "soap-box pedestals campaign." In December, James offered the position outright to the one woman who had won a successful suffrage campaign in Wisconsin once before.

Youmans refused James's request, regretfully passing on an opportunity to make her mark on posterity. "You don't know how much I want to do what you want me to do. It's such a chance to help in a big thing, a thing that will affect all women who come after, making their lives as I believe a little easier, a little better," Youmans wrote. Her regret was increased by the knowledge that she was just the woman for the job, and one of the rare women who would enjoy it. "It's the kind of work I like to do. But I can't do it—there isn't any use pretending for a moment that I can. My life is already overcrowded, my strength appropriated to its last bit. With my newspaper work, my housekeeping, my normal school work [as a regent], my club work, and an astonishing number of incidentals—I have reached the limit."[8] James apparently had reached the end of her list of candidates, and the end of her hope for a united campaign. The referendum drive went forward with no known further attempts at reconciliation of the WWSA and PEL.

Well before negotiations fell through, women were at work. Upon passage of the referendum bill, national suffrage headquarters and other state associations sent their salaried organizers to set up headquarters in Milwaukee for both the WWSA and the PEL: NAWSA salaried WWSA organizer and "girl orator" Harriet Grim of Illinois and PEL campaign manager Crystal Eastman Benedict, a lawyer from New York who had recently moved to Milwaukee. Benedict accounted to NAWSA for salaries and traveling expenses for herself, a PEL stenographer, and at least five other "salaried suffrage workers in the field": Alice B. Curtis of Milwaukee, Sarah James of Oshkosh, Mabel Judd of Lancaster, Maud Leonard McCreery of Green Bay, and Meda Neubecker of Waukesha. Benedict reported that they "carefully and laboriously built up" at least fifty "active, solvent, dues paying locals" in Wisconsin, "often beginning in towns where there was not even one suffragist to entertain the organizer."

Women from other states paid their own way to come to Wisconsin, especially suffragists— and clubwomen—from Illinois. In the summer of 1911, they included NAWSA vice president and Hull House founder Jane Addams, her protegé and National Consumer League president Florence Kelley, Madison native and University of Wisconsin alumna Dr. Anna Blount who managed a "suffrage bookstore" for the Chicago PEL, as well as Chicago PEL president Grace Wilbur Trout and Chicago PEL founder Catharine Waugh McCulloch—who combined her six-week tour with a family vacation, her husband and "all their children trundling along." A lawyer and the first woman justice of the peace in Illinois, McCulloch offered expertise in politics and the press. Advising a two-tiered approach to publicity and press agentry, she suggested that little time be spent on smaller towns where press releases sufficed for weekly papers whose editors preferred photos to "fine speeches." Instead, she advised women to concentrate effort on mass-circulation city dailies and Sunday editions, although competition for column inches would require women to stage events from serious speakers to "stunts."

Although Illinois sent by far the greatest number of suffragists, the campaign drew dozens of women from NAWSA in the East and former Wisconsinites already enfranchised in the West. One of the latter was Emma Smith DeVoe, who had worked with the WWSA as early as the 1890s but then moved to Washington State, where she had led women to victory only a year before valiantly returning to Wisconsin. NAWSA president Dr. Anna Howard Shaw traversed Wisconsin several times on her endless tours of suffrage referendum states in 1912; in all, Shaw covered fourteen thousand miles in three months alone and spoke as often as three times a day—an itinerary which was "enough to kill most any man," Youmans wrote. Other speakers from the East included the Reverend Anna Garlin Spencer, "society suffragist" Alva Erskine Smith Vanderbilt Belmont of New York, and Inez Mulholland, the "beautiful Vassar graduate" whose suffrage speeches had caused a "sensation" in the New York press. Women more familiar to Wisconsin included Fola La Follette, the senator's stagestruck daughter, who came between curtain calls in Chicago. Belle Case La Follette rushed back from Washington, D.C., for thirty-one speeches in fourteen counties in one twelve-day tour, a tour de force of "writing, persuading, speaking almost continuously," Benedict wrote. "Many another splendid woman . . . put in a week or two weeks or six weeks, to help Wisconsin."[9]

The Wisconsin campaign even drew speakers from overseas, including Emmeline Pankhurst, a heroine of the British suffrage movement. In Milwaukee on a nationwide tour in the fall of 1911, she was introduced by Congressman Berger and Olympia Brown and spoke before a capacity crowd of four thousand, women and men, many in town for the state teachers convention. Pankhurst also was interviewed by Youmans for her first *Freeman* "suffrage department"—a stellar debut, but not as significant to the Wisconsin campaign as another item on the page: the election of Mary Davison Bradford as president of the Wisconsin Teachers Association and, not by coincidence, the organization's endorsement of full suffrage.

For her part, Pankhurst endorsed the PEL's strident tactics. Recently released from an English prison, she related her years of "working in quiet, ladylike fashion" through speeches, petitions, and "all the other routine" for which women "received promise after promise" from Parliament, until discovering "the art of deliberately created commotion." Their artwork was evident in America by 1912 when, according to historian Nancy F. Cott, "suffragists showed new imagination and urgency, making up or adapting from British examples . . . publicity-generating practices [that] were consciously modern stunts, relying on and taking advantage of the existence of mass media." As Youmans paraphrased Pankhurst, "public attention must be attracted to the cause if it were ever to win."[10]

In the 1911–12 campaign, Wisconsin women would not adopt the more confrontational tactics of their English counterparts, but they did adapt many an attention-getting tactic first attempted earlier and elsewhere. One was the "street meeting" characteristic of the British campaign but a departure from what a historian calls "NAWSA's tea-party style of organizing." Street meetings were imported by militant suffragists in New York City as early as 1908 and imitated by Massachusetts suffragists in 1909 — and embraced with enthusiasm in Wisconsin in 1911, although the women were "rather shy at first," as were their audiences. Soon, they and their onlookers alike came to enjoy the spectacle of women on soapboxes, speaking to passersby who would not otherwise "under any circumstances attend a suffrage meeting," Youmans wrote. Women "also held outdoor meetings at lunch time before the factories and wherever it seemed best." As Youmans wrote in a more poetic moment, "suffrage speeches were scattered over this long-suffering commonwealth as a brisk wind scatters dry leaves in autumn."

The most colorful "suffrage stunt" of the 1911–12 campaign was the "motor tour," a tactic introduced into Wisconsin a year earlier by Chicago suffragists tracking Illinois voters on vacation "up north." As reported to NAWSA, the Chicago PEL's Grace Wilbur Trout took a team of women "with mud bespattered 'Votes for Women' still flying" across the state line to Lake Geneva, "where meetings with women speaking from automobiles were held under the auspices" of a Gold Coast grande dame "who entertained the suffragists in her spacious summer house." The tour was publicized across two states because Trout had "visited the offices of the newspapers and secured their cooperation. . . . and the edition of the [Chicago] *Tribune* the day before [the tour] contained a full colored page of the women in the autos and nearly a half page more of reading material. . . . The paper sent two reporters on the trip,

"Sometimes I get simply heartsick and my courage is at twenty-eight below zero. But it never stays long at this temperature."—Sophie Gudden of Oshkosh, a publicist for the Political Equality League and the Wisconsin Woman Suffrage Association, pictured at the wheel of a "motor tour" in the 1911–12 referendum campaign with (in back, from left) Ruth Fitch, Bertha Pratt King, and Helen Mann. (The man is unidentified.) Photo courtesy of the State Historical Society of Wisconsin.

who rode in the car with the speakers. The *Examiner, Record Herald, Post* and *Journal* sent reporters by railroad and trolley, who joined the suffragists at their stopping places." As historian Steven M. Buechler suggests, women "combined public relations and modern technology" in a campaign which "reflected a new tactical sophistication among suffragists, and a new appreciation of the public relations aspect of politics in the modern world."

The Illinois tour won headlines as no "suffrage stunt" had before and was imitated later in 1910 in Washington State and in 1911 in California—and Wisconsin, where the sight of cars and women passengers alike festooned in "suffrage yellow," careening from town to town, drew many an onlooker; the state had only a few thousand cars, and far fewer miles of paved roads. Veterans of the Illinois campaign came north to initiate Wisconsin women in auto touring, and one Chicago suffragist was a certain crowd pleaser, according to Youmans, because she could "drive an auto and play a cornet," apparently at the same time. After her own "motor tour" debut—although without musical accompaniment—Youmans wrote of "bowling along gaily" as "the native Badger experienced the destructive shock of seeing a woman stand up in an automobile on a street corner and plead for her political freedom."

In Wisconsin, as elsewhere, suffragists seemed fascinated by new-fangled transportation, from motorboats to "flying machines," which carried the cause to every corner of the state. A "great air pilot, Lincoln Beachey, scattered suffrage flyers from the airship which he took up into the clouds at the State Fair," Youmans wrote, while "suffrage steamer tours" traversed the Fox River. "A 'Votes for Women' tour up the Wolf River was also a feature of the campaign. The little launch *Mary E,* carrying its burden of suffrage speakers and literature, made a trip of fifty miles up the picturesque Wolf, stopping at every available landing for such suffrage propaganda as seemed most fitting to the situation."

The campaign also featured more traditional forms of transportation; although funds for a hoped-for "suffrage train" never materialized, horse-power was still at hand. Buffalo Bill Cody carried a suffrage banner as he led his Wild West circus into Green Bay, and famous pacing horse Dan Patch paraded a yellow "Votes for Women" banner at the state fair, a stunt repeated later in Ohio.[11]

In Wisconsin and across the country, suffragists seized on a twentieth-century marvel: moving pictures. A two-reel "photo-play" from NAWSA headquarters, "Votes for Women," ran at vaudeville theaters in several cities in Wisconsin, and ten smaller towns were sent a storefront stereopticon show on working conditions of women and children, "accompanied by a typewritten explanation" to be read aloud. In Baraboo, suffragist Georgiana J. Koppke enlisted the aid of Al Ringling of the famed circus family who loaned his head artist, "known as the best theatrical artist in the United States," to create "a six-foot square canvas" depicting the progress of women, to be accompanied by her "harmonious and effectual suffrage talk." Suffragists also took to the stage with scripts provided by NAWSA, including "the amusing play, 'How the Vote Was Won,'" which was presented by Milwaukee schoolgirls at a "suffrage matinee" fundraiser, Youmans reported. In Oshkosh, after "a little farce, 'The Suffragette's Dream,'" the PEL's Sophie Gudden made a ten-minute speech and "a great hit with the audience."

"Suffrage stunts" could not be surpassed for creating awareness but could not substitute for a cohesive strategy, as women knew. Two campaigns in 1910, one won in Washington and one lost in Oregon, were covered in the *Woman's Journal* and had an impact on women nationwide. In Washington, suffragists conducted a meticulous campaign under trained organizers who sent speakers to "unions, grange meetings, state and county fairs, and the popular Chautauqua lecture series" in every corner of the state. Plays, billboards, and a monthly newsletter composed a multifaceted print media campaign which "conveyed the message" to male voters. On election day, even the most hard-hearted of men melted at the polls as "middle-aged women and white-haired grandmothers stood for hours handing out little reminders" in a soaking Washington State rain. At the same time, women lost in Oregon in 1910 owing to their leader's cautious insistence on a "quiet campaign."

Another victory in the West reinforced the lessons of Washington State, when California women won suffrage in 1911 with a campaign which "set a new standard for massive organization and flamboyant tactics," according to historian Sara M. Evans. Fortunately, Wisconsin women did not go so far as to entirely emulate Californians' literally "brilliant campaign"; the bucolic Wisconsin countryside was spared "electric signs" for suffrage.[12]

In Wisconsin, women had only to look into their own history. As Youmans wrote of "street meetings," "motor tours" and other attention-getting tactics, "that campaign was as lively as we — some trained, some untrained, in suffrage campaigns — could make it. In general we followed the suffrage styles of other states and imitated the stunts of those who had passed that way before." But "street meetings" were not new, and resembled the women's temperance crusade as much as British suffragettes' campaign. In training and in organization, suffragists drew from the WCTU. And clubwomen knew that a "quiet campaign" had been the correct strategy at the turn of the century, when lobbying the legislature was all that was required to write the suffrage law. However, they also knew that the law had been lost in 1888 because of Olympia Brown's insistence on a "still hunt" in a referendum campaign, when creating awareness was crucial.

Another significant change for Wisconsin suffragists was a less elitist campaign. The women's "work at the grass roots level" was "a dramatic shift in strategy" from "appealing only to the upper classes," according to Brown's biographer, Charlotte Cote. For the first time, the WWSA "addressed working women, housewives and farm women" in an attempt to reach "every city and village" in the state, which took Brown to at least twenty-three counties. As for the PEL, Ada James wrote that the women "could not possibly fill the demand for speakers made upon us if we had not secured some new recruits," especially in ethnic enclaves of Milwaukee where a rabbi and a city schoolteacher, Pauline Wies, lectured in the German language.

The PEL also breached the racial barrier in Milwaukee. But the "colored league," led by Carrie Horton, did not succeed. In part, the problem was lack of both a sufficient population base and a black press in Milwaukee. The city's "Bronzeville" section was home for fewer than a thousand African-Americans, and its last black paper had folded four years before. An offer of long-distance assistance came from the New York City office of the *Crisis,* the publication of the National Association for the Advancement of Colored People, but even the widely respected work of editor W. E. B. Du Bois could not substitute for a local press.

Recruiting women of color, even in "separate but equal" clubs, was a progressive and even radical strategy at the time. But the effort was tainted by the racism of the times, evident in correspondence among even the most enlightened suffragists—and many were not—that was condescending at best. "I am glad you are organizing your colored people," wrote Catharine Waugh McCulloch to Ada James in July 1911, boasting that "we have some brilliant colored people in Chicago who are suffragists" but naming only two women. Both were exceptional, and acceptable—Ida B. Wells-Barnett and Fannie Barrier Williams—and both had "lawyer husbands."[13]

With many a borrowed idea and a few of their own, Wisconsin suffragists developed a plan for a public opinion campaign as thorough as any at the time—and many since. For example, Youmans' column listed "some of the things" to be done when "barely three months" were left before the election. Writers were needed to "supply 88 periodicals published in Wisconsin, not including daily or weekly papers, with propaganda" and to "edit two daily papers some day during September." Women with organizational ability were sought to "find speakers for 75 county fairs during September and October," to "arrange booths at said 75 fairs," and to get "all ward and precinct organizations under way." Women with experience in public speaking "for the purpose of raising money" were needed to "give two benefits" or to "sell 500 washing machines and turn at least $1,000 into the treasury." Women with a yen for the stage were sought to "put on suffrage plays at some theatre."

The daunting "to do" list also included "the regular routine" of "answering of hundreds of letters daily, arranging meetings, sending out literature, [and] begging automobiles for use of speakers." Finally, in a refrain familiar to any campaign, Youmans pleaded for assistance in "keeping of accounts—for the most part paying bills from a long-suffering and depleted treasury."

But bills and correspondence that survive from the campaign suggest that suffragists' creditors also were "long-suffering," from the telephone company to the teamsters who hauled tables and chairs in and out of rented halls. The largest bills were from printers who often waited months for payment on "literature," like the Milwaukee printer who billed the WWSA a total of $24.50—for three "circulars" in quantities from one thousand to ten thousand—but apparently was not paid until Olympia Brown took out a personal loan for $100. It was not the last. Brown's frequent bank notes were interspersed among invoices and repeated requests for payment, and notes from frantic suffragists claiming "mistakes in counting" on their part—or fraud on the part of suppliers.

The WWSA never balanced its account books, but women became expert at the balancing act of keeping creditors at bay by spreading accounts among several suppliers. In some cases, the cause may have been the pressure of the campaign; at one point, women contracted with one Milwaukee printer for two thousand *Citizen* subscription forms, at $3.50; with another for five thousand WWSA membership forms, at $5; and with another for twenty thousand handbills, at $25. But switched accounts also resulted from refusals by previous suppliers, apparently the reason that the *Citizen* was printed by two or three different firms during the campaign, at the cost of graphic continuity and identity.

But no creditors suffered more, or were more patient, than suffragists themselves. Bills submitted by "the National" for literature or "suffrage novelties"—perhaps the ten thousand "shield-shaped suffrage bangle pins," priced at $50—were outnumbered by donations from NAWSA leaders. Dr. Anna Howard Shaw alone sent several personal checks for $100 each "for literature," often appending a note recommending NAWSA favorites like "Rainbow Flyers," the multilingual versions of the same call for suffrage that were color-coded for ease in distribution in ethnically diverse areas.

Many women in Wisconsin apparently waited months for reimbursement of bills submitted, from a brief note requesting "$2.50 for fair admission" to three- or four-page lists of expenses by full-time suffrage organizers. One posted a bill from the road for a total of $10.43, detailed down to "five-cent bus fares." Another sent a report of funds raised in five weeks of work in fifteen towns, for a total of $49.40. However, her account was accompanied by a request for reimbursement of expenses, also itemized and with receipts attached, that added up to $50.72. "Confound the women," wrote one fund-raiser after collecting $4 from an "attentive" but tightfisted audience. "They never have their pocketbooks with them"—or so, she wrote, the women claimed.

Despite difficulty in getting some women to open their pocketbooks, suffragists' account books indicate their increasing efficiency in the campaign. The WWSA actually dunned *Citizen* subscribers for payments due, at twenty-five cents a year, reversing the decades-long and less methodical practices of Olympia Brown. Unfortunately, the attempt apparently made little impact on WWSA coffers. Few women were as forthcoming, or forthright, as one in Wrightstown who sent full payment with the next post—and with an apology. Signing her note "yours for the cause," she vowed that "when I can vote, I will be more businesslike."

The most efficient contact with voters occurred at state and county fairs, an annual pilgrimage for thousands of Wisconsinites seeking oddities such as woman suffragists. At the 1911 state fair, the WWSA tent housed a platform for suffrage speeches and a counter with suffrage literature. Not to be outdone, the PEL distributed yellow balloons emblazoned "Votes for Women." Both organizations again sponsored popular booths at the 1912 state fair.[14]

Suffragists also covered seventy-five county fairs in 1912—more fairs than there were counties in Wisconsin. Belle Case La Follette spoke at seven fairs in ten days. In Chippewa Falls, women furnished a "model porch as a background" for serving tea and suffrage literature on state laws concerning women. At the Vernon County fair, managers gave Vandalia Varnum Thomas "a most hearty welcome," she reported to Youmans' readers. Although "competition with vaudeville stunts and big snakes and trick ponies and jumping deer and horse racing was something to be reckoned with," and the crowd was more interested in a "favorite pacer," Thomas stood beneath the familiar "yellow banner floating far and wide before the throng" and distributed literature, until "in no part of the grounds could a single leaflet be found loose."

The women were not made welcome by all fair managers. Of two who refused them, one was the unfortunate Robert Orton in Lafayette County. The Ortons were one of the leading local families; his father was a former Wisconsin Supreme Court justice and his sister was a physician in Darlington—and an officer of the local suffrage association. When the request for a fair booth was refused by her brother, she enlisted their father to get a permit for a tent to "take care of babies," and the women "did a thriving business in talking suffrage literature to every mother who came in," Youmans wrote. Slyly, suffragists also entered the fair's floral contest with a "huge bank of flowers, bearing in yellow suffrage colors the words 'Votes for Women,'" handed out scorecards backed by "suffrage arguments"—and won a ribbon. Lafayette County women, Youmans wrote, "now declare themselves grateful for the refusal. They did so much better than they would have done merely with a speaker."

In addition to speakers and "stunts," suffragists conducted a quieter campaign to reach the elite and the educated, in churches and libraries rather than in storefronts or at fairs. The PEL set a "Suffrage Sunday" and asked ministers "to preach on suffrage as it affects moral and social questions." The PEL also held a Christmas book bazaar and sold "suffrage novelties": stationery, buttons, paper napkins, and "Christmas cards and postals." In March 1912, at the state librarians' convention in Janesville, the PEL mounted a book exhibit and sought donations to put "literature touching on the progress of women . . . in the libraries of all the cities of the state." The PEL also conducted a "statistical survey" of state librarians which showed that, among book borrowers in 1912, suffrage was the most popular literary topic.

Even less visible were suffragists' fund-raising efforts, by design. Behind the scenes, the PEL's Benedict was meticulous in identifying potential donors, making personal calls, and compiling pledge cards, and raised more than $13,000 in thirteen months. NAWSA donated $200 per month and more in later months, and other states also sent sizable sums. Chicago suffragists sent $500 to be split between the WWSA and the PEL, and New York women sent Benedict back from one eastern tour with $2,700, after a special Wisconsin issue of the *Woman's Journal*—with which Olympia Brown and the WWSA refused to cooperate —was sold at a "great suffrage parade in New York City," setting a record for street sales. "But do not think we let you give all the money," Benedict said to other states' delegates at a NAWSA convention. One Milwaukee matron gave $3,000 to her state campaign, and another $1,000 to NAWSA, said Benedict. "Others—men and women—gave lesser sums, from $300 to five one-cent stamps."[15]

Suffragists' fund-raising efforts were ceaseless. A "society" theater benefit for suffrage in Milwaukee brought in $175, but many events broke even at best. Women collected coins at street corner speeches and fees for scheduled speakers. At one point, women even sold washing machines for $3.50 apiece. The project, conceived by a Chicago suffragist who came north to demonstrate the invention, was promoted by Youmans for the "double purpose of lightening the work of women and making money without begging for it."

Women's success in fund-raising became too visible for their opponents in high places. Although the WWSA spent only $5,000 at most in the campaign, PEL expenditures were as much as $1,000 per month for more than a year, not including county associations' local promotions. Suddenly, late in the campaign, the state attorney general ruled that suffrage organizations came under the corrupt practices law and limited each to $10,000 in expenditures, which would have—as he intended—ended the PEL's campaign.

Benedict turned the PEL's crisis into an opportunity, hiding the excess funds in a front group which would surprise women as a new area of support. Benedict recruited her brother, Max Eastman, editor of *The Masses,* who had served as secretary of a Men's League for Woman Suffrage in New York. Now, from afar, he lent his name for a similar organization which received the surplus funds in the East and funneled the money back to a Men's League officer in Milwaukee—his brother-in-law, and Benedict's husband.

Members of the Wisconsin Men's League for Woman Suffrage represented "the pulpit, the bar, the forum of public affairs, the mart of business," as Youmans wrote. Many provided quotes for a PEL leaflet, "Prominent Wisconsin Men Favor Woman Suffrage," including Senator La Follette and Congressman Berger; presidents of the state medical society and the University of Wisconsin; Chief Justice of the Wisconsin Supreme Court John B. Winslow, who had ruled for Olympia Brown in her school-suffrage suit thirty years before when he served on the bench in Racine; and Neal Dow Brown, a prominent Wausau businessman and lawyer, former legislator, and past president of the state bar, who was the son of the *Wisconsin Chief*'s Thurlow Weed Brown and a nephew of the redoubtable Emma.[16]

Far more important to the campaign, to answer the continued claim that women didn't want the vote, were membership drives. The PEL's recruitment effort revitalized support across the state, benefiting both suffrage organizations. Retracing her circuit of state campuses with Olympia Brown in 1908, NAWSA's Dr. Maud Wood Park now established College Equal Suffrage League chapters on thirteen state campuses in only fourteen days. Brown's WWSA, which came into the campaign with inactive county auxiliaries, counted sixty-one working branches by the end.[17] The PEL founded branches in more than half of Wisconsin counties in its first year alone, and boasted fifty-eight by the end of the eighteen-month campaign.

An even better measure of support than membership was a mainstay of reform from the first: petition drives. The number of dues-paying suffragists was dwarfed by the number of women, and men, willing to give no more than their names to the campaign. In only three years since a WWSA drive netted 18,000 names, suffrage support had soared in Wisconsin. Women took petitions door to door or to central locations—in Waukesha, petitions were available at the *Freeman* office—and secured 116,582 signatures on petitions presented in the House of Representatives by Congressman Berger on the Fourth of July.

Suffragists let up on legislators upon passage of the referendum bill, but lobbying of influential politicians continued by less direct means. Although NAWSA was to coordinate lobbying, Wisconsin women discovered that "the National" was in disarray and cultivated their congressmen on their own. Youmans used her column for editorial endorsements of politicians who endorsed woman suffrage in turn, and none was so favored so often as her mentor, Senator La Follette. As significant as his support was a list of his supporters, a major contribution to the campaign from Belle Case La Follette. As her husband's unofficial campaign manager, she shared her expertise on ward- and precinct-level organization, and offered the senator's office list for a last-minute direct-mail effort.[18]

Of all the tactics employed in the 1911–12 campaign, none was so crucial in creating awareness as publicity. Youmans won recognition from "the National" for her contribution of a unique publicity plan at NAWSA's sixteen-state Mississippi Valley Conference in Chicago in May 1912, a year into the campaign. The conference, or "suffrage school," was "in theory and in fact devoted to local problems and methods of work" such as press relations, Youmans reported. It also was the first formal training for many of the twenty Wisconsin women in attendance including Youmans, who was pleased when her PEL *Press Bulletin* won NAWSA leaders' praise. "No other state," she wrote with pride, "attacks the publicity side of the campaign in quite this way." Ada James called the *Bulletin* "the most important item" of the many activities undertaken by suffragists in the Wisconsin campaign.

Youmans' publicity plan exhibited admirable regularity and range. She duplicated her *Freeman* suffrage column as the *Press Bulletin*, a press kit which went weekly "to all the newspapers in the state, six hundred or more," and to papers in Illinois and Minnesota with Wisconsin circulations. As election day neared, Youmans' "press committee" also distributed releases daily to major papers. The *Bulletin* packaged suffrage news to serve editors by promoting the WWSA as well as the PEL and by inclusion of "straight news," features, editorials, and snappy "suffrage fillers." Youmans interviewed state, national, and international suffrage leaders but also looked for local angles, especially endorsements from Catholic cardinals, German Turners, and other "distinguished advocates" of suffrage—the equivalent of latter-day "celebrity spokesmen."

Letters to the *Bulletin* editor debated suffrage pro and con, a colorful correspondence. Readers also sent original compositions, poetry, and "suffrage songs," such as "The Women of 1912" by a "W.E.":

> Here's to the women of 1912 who are working for the ballot,
> Firm as a rock, they'll stand the knock of opposition's mallot.
> They've watched the game of politics and found it very rotten.
> When vote they may, they'll prove that they cannot be bribed or
> boughten.[19]

Unfortunately, the level of originality in the first verse was not sustained in the second and third, and "W.E." did not suggest a rousing tune to which "The Women of 1912" might be sung.

Youmans conducted opinion research, if rudimentary, to measure editors' support of suffrage and their use of the *Bulletin*. From Bloomer and Brillion to Viola and Wauzeka, her "post-card questionnaire" found "friendly papers" statewide. Regular "suffrage departments"—often quoting her *Bulletin*—ran in Chicago's *Herald* and *Tribune*, Madison's *State Journal*, and the *Racine Times*. Even a few foreign-language papers were won over by PEL "press committee" member Sophie Gudden, who supervised translation of releases into German, Polish and "Scandinavian." The prosuffrage *Kuryer Polski* was appreciative, but not all respondents to Youmans' survey were so "friendly." The reply from the *Two Rivers Chronicle* needed no translation: "Do not waste more of your ammunition on us."

Youmans also monitored press colleagues through "exchanges" and used her column and *Bulletin* to counter antisuffrage coverage. In a regular feature called "Browsing Among the Editors," Youmans' favorite target was the *Milwaukee Free Press*, "an intelligent newspaper . . . with the most astonishing if unintelligible streaks it is possible to imagine." She admonished *Free Press* editors to read "any suffrage literature except their own effusions." When editors reiterated that women didn't want the vote, she retorted that the "assertion . . . is becoming more difficult to make every day." When even the reform-minded *Whitewater Register* and *Racine Times* compromised the cause, subscribing to a popular proposal that women be given a onetime opportunity to prove that they wanted the vote, Youmans was caustic: "We have not heard of any such test being submitted for men. As a matter of fact, a very considerable percentage of men do not vote and yet we never hear of their being disenfranchised on that account." When she levied the lowest of journalistic blows by calling the compromise "an old story," editors rushed to recant. "Almost before the ink was dry on our paper," wrote an abashed colleague in Racine, "Mrs. H. M. Youmans, who conducts a 'Votes for Women' column in the *Freeman*, was on the trail of *The Times*." Youmans accepted his apology, in her column.

Youmans did not spare colleagues closer to home, even "the esteemed *Freeman*." Page two was hers alone, but the editorial page was the province of the publisher—her husband, Henry Mott Youmans—whose belief that the *Freeman* ought to serve as a public forum often provided insight into their private life. For example, when the editorial page mildly suggested that "suffrage states" were laggards rather than leaders in reform, page two rebutted with "statistical facts" which did not abate for weeks in print—and perhaps at home. Her "suffrage department" also took frequent aim at Theron W. Haight, the past publisher of the *Freeman*, her husband's brother-in-law and her own early mentor in the newsroom. He opposed the ballot for any but the educated elite, among whom he counted few women. In a particularly curmudgeonly piece after the sinking of the *Titanic*, he mused that the rule of the sea—"women and children first"—would be moot in the event of woman suffrage. Haight's onetime protegé penned a slashing reply. Acknowledging "in general a profound respect" for his "intellectual grasp" and her debt for his "kind training," she asserted that "great ability and learning does not prevent his having wrong ideas."

The most powerful press opposition to the suffrage campaign, predictably, came from Milwaukee. Of the city's dozens of weekly papers and nine dailies, almost all opposed suffrage. Courageous exceptions among daily papers included the *Leader*, published by Congressman Victor Berger, spouse of the PEL's Meta Schlichting Berger, and the Polish-language *Kuryer Polski*. Another notable exception was the weekly *American Turner*, which, like the *Leader*, was an English-language paper with a largely German audience. Most German-language papers followed the lead of the vituperative *Banner und Volksfreund* in opposing suffrage—as did most in the English-language press in Milwaukee, led by the largest-circulation papers in the state: the *News*, the *Free Press*, the *Evening Wisconsin*, the *Sentinel*, and the largest of all, the *Journal*. At a circulation of sixty-five thousand, the *Milwaukee Journal* reached more than ten times the readership of the largest-circulation paper in the state capital, Madison's prosuffrage *Wisconsin State Journal.*

An analysis of *Milwaukee Journal* coverage of the 1911–12 campaign suggests that, at best, the paper "displayed a puzzling attitude toward suffrage." According to historian Elizabeth Burt, most coverage predictably "poked fun at women in general and woman suffrage in particular," even before passage of the referendum bill. For example, in March 1911, the *Journal* opined that "out of 15,000,000 women it has been estimated that twenty-three are dying to vote and all the rest are dying for a new hat. Our legislators should appropriate accordingly." The paper did not deign to print an apology when, eleven days later, more than eight thousand women registered to vote in the city in response to a recent court ruling which extended school suffrage to school-related races in spring primaries. Upon legislators' approval of the bill, the *Journal* could comment only that "the man with a suffrage wife is going to have a disagreeable time of it in the next two years. The 'votes for women' bill with its referendum clause, has passed."

Still, aside from predictable editorial asides, the *Journal* supported suffrage until late in 1911, when the paper defied all predictions, and logic; as suffragists' publicity and press agentry increased, *Journal* coverage drastically decreased. The shift came suddenly, and almost immediately after the German-American Alliance came out against suffrage, speaking for a membership of six hundred thousand—almost ten times the circulation of the paper—just as the *Journal* debuted a new and profitable Sunday edition. By 1912, some suffragists abandoned the *Journal* altogether. Lutie Stearns refused to send a requested photograph of herself for press use, not only because she "objected to that sort of publicity" but also because of the objectionable *Journal*. Nor would she "write anything for that sheet, that is so determinedly unfair to us."[20]

Teutonic opposition to suffrage, too often a scapegoat in the movement nationwide, truly was significant in Wisconsin. In 1910, almost four-fifths of state residents were foreign-born or next-generation, mainly German, although other ethnic blocs also opposed suffrage. For example, Benedict wrote to NAWSA that "we overestimated the friendliness of the large Scandinavian vote, and when we came to campaign among them we found many . . . just as conservative about woman suffrage as the majority of the Germans." Dryly, she added that "I do not need to remind you of what made Milwaukee famous." Ida Husted Harper of NAWSA also toured the state and wrote that winning suffrage was "impossible" in Wisconsin because of economic dependence upon the state's most famed product by rural and urban areas alike: farmers who grew grain for beer, brewers who manufactured it, and Germans who consumed it.[21]

Youmans and other women native to Wisconsin were among the least nativist in the movement nationwide. Compared with newcomers like Benedict and others less comfortable with the state's ethnicity like Harper—and in contrast with the virulent nativism of Olympia Brown—the PEL's official spokesperson was moderate. Youmans' approach to what she called "old-country conservatism" may have resulted from her upbringing with Germans or from working with German women—or from her adherence to the progressive tenet of expediency, since alienating Germans was politically inexpedient in Wisconsin. Repeatedly cautioning "those who assert that the Germans are as a class opposed" to the cause, she countered with examples from Mathilde Fransziska Anneke to the PEL's Meta Schlichting Berger and Sophie Gudden, a member of Youmans' press committee and a "tireless worker in the cause."

Gudden rarely tired of her extraordinary workload in the campaign, despite severe physical disabilities, a serious illness in 1912, and an uphill battle among her generally antisuffrage German countrymen. Gudden gave more than 150 addresses around the state, and historian Eleanor Flexner calls her a "quiet hero" of the campaign. Even in the bitter cold of a Wisconsin winter, when the woman born to Bavarian nobility found "these ignorant, hardhearted Germans" especially inhospitable, Sophie Gudden was indefatigible. "Sometimes I get simply heartsick. Today my courage is at twenty-eight below zero," she wrote to Ada James. "But it never stays long at this temperature."[22]

A Polish suffragist exhibited especial insight and enterprise in persuading ethnic opinion leaders on her tour of the state. A. V. Jackowska-Peterson of Milwaukee "made it her business to first interview the resident priests of the Polish church," who were "quite amenable to reasonable argument," and "in the end, gave her valuable assistance," Youmans wrote. But reason was less effective with the men than emotional appeal, and "one experience she related quite took the fancy" of suffragists. "She found that foreign born men who would not for a moment listen to arguments in favor of suffrage as affecting their wives, were easily touched when these same arguments were presented as affecting their daughters."

But the German-American Alliance and Milwaukee's brewers almost eradicated any goodwill gained by the good works of Gudden and other foreign-born suffragists. By 1910, with the rebirth of suffrage sentiment and the concurrent prohibition campaign, brewers and distillers combined to mount a formidable antireform coalition. Only years later would a congressional investigation uncover the undercover activities of the United States Brewers Association in prohibition and suffrage campaigns across the country. Since its inception in Wisconsin as the Brewers Congress, the organization had grown to "vigilance committees" countrywide, lobbyists in Washington, D.C. and headquarters in New York City, with "literary managers" to oversee publicity and publications. The paramount focus was on the press to "first of all, reach and teach the teachers"—journalists—whom they reached by planting letters to the editor, buying news and editorial columns, even bribing editors—and, above all, by placing or withholding advertising.

The congressional investigation would confirm what women could only conjecture to be the source of antisuffrage propaganda and front groups which flooded the state. But they knew. As Benedict wrote in 1912, "of course, the brewers didn't fight us openly. They didn't need to. The important thing was that everybody who did business with them . . . knew how they stood," from farmers to "big city newspapers who sold them advertising space."[23]

Youmans described the campaign propaganda which confirmed for her "the determined hostility of the liquor interests" to suffrage.

> The magazine issued by the State Retail Liquor Dealers' Protective Association. . . . called *Progress* for weeks preceding the election was filled with argument and innuendo and abuse in prose and verse and picture, all designed to impress the reader with the absurdity and the danger of giving the vote to women. It appealed to the farmers and to every class of people connected in any way with the manufacture and sale of beer, saying in headlines: "Give the Ballot to Woman and Industry Goes to Smash," "It Means the Loss of Vast Sums to Manufacturer, Dealer and Workingmen," and this was kept up to the end.[24]

The "liquor interests" carefully targeted campaign literature, at times supporting ethnic custom and at other times attempting to disassociate dealers from the very "immigrant vote" upon which their custom counted. "DANGER! Woman's Suffrage Would Double the Irresponsible Vote," read one nativist flyer. "It is a MENACE to the Home, Men's Employment and to All Business."[25]

Youmans dealt with the dealers' countercampaign by using her wit and others' wisdom. Dismissing a 112-page hardbound book entitled *How to Make the Best of Life vs. Woman Suffrage* as "an extended dis-

quisition on the assumption that voting is not a 'womanly' occupation,"
she sniffed that "the editor of this column has not 112 pages in which
to answer Mr. Tibbles, and would not apply it to that purpose if she
had." However, Youmans did devote a full column to "copying a few
gems" by the unfortunate Tibbles, grammatical errors and all—and countered with better-written arguments from a better-known philosopher,
John Stuart Mill.

Youmans wrote most bitterly, yet still wittily, of brewers' most effective counteroffensive, the front groups of women who claimed that
women didn't want the vote. The organizations arose overnight in every
state with a suffrage campaign, and many clubwomen more conservative than their counterparts enlisted in the National Association Opposed to the Extension of Suffrage to Women. In Wisconsin in 1912,
"Ladies' Anti-Suffrage Leagues" encouraged what Youmans called a
"common old garden variety of conservatism." Editorializing against
the "relentless logic" of "that remarkable sisterhood" who traveled far
to reaffirm that women's place was in the home, Youmans defined "the
antis" as "ladies who go into politics to keep other ladies out of politics."

Women held their own in the press against the Brewers Association
but could not compete in the backrooms of politics, where corrupt
officials at state and local levels crippled the 1911–12 campaign in its
final weeks. The secretary of state's campaign instruction pamphlet
quoted incorrect information from a Madison chapter of the brewers'
national antisuffrage front group. Worse, the attorney general ruled that
the suffrage referendum would be on a separate ballot, and specified
that the suffrage ballot would be pink. Women attempted to turn the
unwelcome visibility to advantage, distributing flyers reminding prosuffrage voters to look for the "potent pink ballot." Brewers responded
by distributing reproductions of the suffrage ballot with illustrated instructions to "be sure and put your cross (X) in the square after the word
'no' as shown, and—be sure and vote this pink ballot."

Suffragists fought back as best they could in the waning weeks of the
campaign. Women distributed and mailed an estimated 125,000 pieces
of promotional literature, purchased from NAWSA headquarters or lo-
cally written and printed. Madison's *State Journal* and Berger's *Milwaukee Leader* turned over entire editions to suffrage, a tactic introduced
by clubwomen. Ads paid by an anonymous Dane County donor ran daily
in Madison papers, and the PEL increased its advertising placements
to twenty-four papers statewide.[26]

Then, almost on the eve of the election, Youmans scored a publicity coup by engineering a crucial endorsement from Wisconsin clubwomen to counter the brewers and their "antis." Although her access to the press and journalistic expertise already had proved significant in the suffrage campaign, equally valuable was her experience in clubwomen's public opinion campaigns. Poised on the podium and adept at parliamentary practice, she won Wisconsin clubwomen to suffrage in 1912, well ahead of most states—and then exploited her stunt to win headlines for suffrage across the state.

The official endorsement of the Wisconsin Federation of Women's Clubs was not easily won; although many members were prominent in the PEL and WWSA, some were leaders of "Ladies' Anti-Suffrage Leagues." A year earlier, at the 1911 convention, WFWC officer Jessie Jack Hooper introduced requests from both suffrage organizations, but the WWSA's pressure for immediate action met with initial resistance. When the PEL asked only that suffrage be a priority on the program of the 1912 convention, prior to the referendum, clubwomen approved the request and resolved to study the issue in the intervening year. Clubs in Berlin, Fond du Lac, Green Bay, Richland Center, Waukesha, and Wausau invited PEL and WWSA speakers, while others set suffrage as a discussion topic.

In 1912, prior to the WFWC convention, the national GFWC convention evaded the issue. The GFWC would not come to "the logical culmination of club ideology," in historian Karen J. Blair's phrase, until 1914.[27] In 1912, the Wisconsin campaign—and Youmans—could not wait that long. "Club women were headed for the ballot box from the beginning," she wrote, and began a one-woman campaign.

Youmans prepared carefully to win the Wisconsin federation's endorsement. Ever enamored of "statistical facts," she surveyed other federations and found seven which had endorsed suffrage, four in surrounding states: Michigan in 1910, Illinois and Iowa in 1911, and Minnesota in 1912. Youmans publicized her findings statewide and presented results to the WFWC policy committee, which she chaired. However, committee membership had been altered in previous months—perhaps purposefully—and not in suffragists' favor. The committee refused its own chair's report, and voted to recommend against her resolution at the convention. Then further discouraging news came from the federation's beloved founder. Youmans and her faction had counted on Lucy Smith Morris' support of suffrage to carry the state convention, but she could not attend.

In Milwaukee in October 1912, Youmans correctly read the mood of the convention. She also read a telegram from Morris urging club-women to endorse suffrage. But Youmans' reading of the rules of parliamentary procedure would win the endorsement. Demanding the floor for a minority report-of-one from her own committee, she spoke fervently for suffrage and offered a dissenting resolution. Ranking WFWC officers registered their opposition, but members approved Youmans' resolution, two to one. By similar majorities, the convention also endorsed legislation to protect rights of married women, widows, and deserted wives, and elected outspoken suffragist Sophie Strathearn of Kaukauna as president.

As the tumultuous 1912 convention concluded, Youmans wrote an exultant *Freeman* column which she exploited in her *Press Bulletin,* and won wide publicity for the event she had engineered.

> This action . . . was a most significant indication of the growth of suffrage sentiment among the people. . . . Club women, who are generally home-keeping wives and mothers, are among the most conservative people in the world. A few years ago they would have held up their hands in horror at the idea of endorsing equal suffrage. And yet by a vote so decisive that there can be no question of their sentiments . . . the club women of Wisconsin declared to the world that they were not afraid, that they were alert to the trend of the times, and were willing to stand openly and positively for what they believed to be right.[28]

Youmans kept her own story in the headlines for weeks by circuitous means, quoting comments from papers statewide which had quoted her column. Coyly claiming a fear of "losing her reputation for self-effacing modesty," she also ran congratulations. One letter from a LaCrosse reader—a male—hailed Youmans for her "manly fight."

But women fought a last barrage of publicity from brewers' front groups as election day neared, and wearily prepared for the worst in Wisconsin. In a last letter to readers, Youmans opened optimistically by reminding "Mr. Voter" of endorsements from press, politicians, clergy, labor, and ethnic associations, even Germans. To the rest of her readers —women—she was straightforward: "If we should be disappointed, we shall at least have the satisfaction of knowing that we have laid broad and deep the foundations of a public sentiment which will a little later ensure victory." A week later, on election day but before returns were in, Youmans already was reconciled to the inevitable result: "In other states it has, without exception, I believe, taken two campaigns to convince the voters of the desirability of woman suffrage. If it should require two campaigns in Wisconsin or three or ten, we are prepared."

Privately, writing to PEL co-workers while awaiting returns, Youmans betrayed more emotion but again underscored campaign gains: "We have known all the time deep down in our hearts that this and only this could be the result, this time. We know too, deep down in our hearts, what will be the result next time or the time after that. We have done much to hasten the happy day of its coming." She predicted that a federal amendment would not be won until 1925 — and did not suggest that Wisconsin would see suffrage any sooner.

On election day, November 4, women statewide went to the polls — providing transportation and working as poll watchers. Some also worked outside the polls, for the cause, as in Fox Lake where a suffragist reported to the WWSA that "our WCTU has done all the suffrage work in this town. . . . to get out on the streets on election day" when the women handed out literature, "cheerfully and effectually." But women could only watch helplessly as their referendum was lost, 227,024 votes to 135,545. "The papers have published it as a two-to-one defeat, but you see it wasn't nearly so bad as that," reported Benedict to NAWSA. But she was quibbling. Analyzing returns county by county, even ward by ward in Waukesha, Youmans reported that "of the 71 counties but 14 were carried for suffrage. Douglas county in the extreme northwest on Lake Superior had the best record, a majority of 1,000. Milwaukee county, including the city, gave 40,029 votes against and 20,443 for"— a two-to-one defeat. The result in Douglas County surprised some women in southern Wisconsin, but not its proud natives. As one wrote to the WWSA, the northland was "not so far behind the march of progress as has been intimated to us by the rest of the state" where "many people have talked about Superior as a howling wilderness, populated by half-breeds and lumberjacks."[29]

Other suffragists' only consolation was that their campaign had caused a high voter turnout, at least for their referendum. More than ninety percent of voters cast ballots — separate ballots — on the suffrage referendum, while three other referendum issues on the regular ballot each attracted little more than twenty percent of voters at best. Ballots cast on the amendment, for and against, exceeded by more than one hundred thousand the combined total for all three constitutional amendments decided that day, and the total for the victorious — and antisuffragist — incumbent governor. The "unprecedentedly large vote," as Youmans wrote, was "due partly, we flattered ourselves, to our efforts, and partly, we knew and did not flatter ourselves, to the efforts of our adversaries."

Reasons for failure of the referendum were many, and most far beyond women's ability to alter. Petty political switches occurred in suffrage strongholds such as Racine, where ballots were not the much-publicized "potent pink" but white. Elsewhere, the separate ballots arrived too late, too few—or not at all.

The "immigrant vote" and the "liquor lobby" did combine to defeat suffrage in many rural counties and in Milwaukee. Even in Milwaukee's Socialist wards, men gave a mandate to prosuffrage Congressman Victor Berger while voting down suffrage two to one. "The defeat was conceded to have been due," Youmans wrote, to "the large foreign population and the widespread belief that it would help largely to bring prohibition." However, hoped-for support from La Follette followers also had failed. As Benedict wrote in a caustic report to NAWSA, "I sometimes think the last thing a man becomes progressive about is the activities of his own wife."[30]

Youmans differed with Benedict and blamed the defeat on suffragists' schism and failure to resolve their feud in time to reach the voter, which she termed "an insufficiency of general education on woman suffrage, and of organization." Historians Lawrence L. Graves and Marilyn Grant concur that by competing, even feuding, the two organizations could only cause public confusion and costly internal duplication of effort, and women divided could not conquer better-organized—and far better-funded—opposition. However, the historians also agree that the campaign was a turning point for the movement in Wisconsin owing to two significant signs of progress: suffragists recruited new leadership, and created awareness of the cause—Youmans' contribution.[31]

Although never before in Wisconsin had tactics refined in earlier reform campaigns been combined so well, Youmans recognized the limitations of publicity and press agentry: "press work" and "stunts" were attention-getting, and only that. More than headlines were needed to make headway in a Wisconsin so resoundingly against suffrage; "Mr. Voter" had to want to hear the story, which required that suffragists have a strategy.

Other Wisconsin suffragists also recognized that the schism, and especially their feuding leadership, had hampered the campaign. "Their hostility had been more than half-friendly," Youmans later wrote of the WWSA and PEL—but not much more, and there was no hope for a

"The last thing a man becomes progressive about is the activities of his own wife." —Crystal Eastman Benedict, the campaign manager of the Political Equality League in Wisconsin, and a lobbyist for the National American Woman Suffrage Association and for the Congressional Union. Photo courtesy of the State Historical Society of Wisconsin.

reconciliation of Olympia Brown and Ada James. Although Youmans would claim in one later history for local consumption that women "easily forgot their differences and buried the hatchet," she was more forthright in admitting dissension in a report to NAWSA. National leaders already knew, all too well, of the Wisconsin feud. As NAWSA president Dr. Anna Howard Shaw had written to Ada James, months before, "Mrs.

Brown had been by bad temper and by constantly having a chip on her shoulder, a menace to the work." But NAWSA would not intervene then, or at the campaign's bitter end.

At no time, of course, had a hint of the feud surfaced in Youmans' *Freeman* column; even Olympia Brown relied on the PEL "press correspondent" to relay information to WWSA members, a reassuring sign to the casual reader. However, reliance on the press rather than the *Citizen* for internal communication in the WWSA as well as the PEL, which had no organ of its own, revealed the extent of disorganization in the WWSA and the lack of preparation in the PEL.

Now, negotiations for reunion resumed but were made more difficult by the acrimony of the campaign. Only three days after the defeat, PEL leaders again initiated the effort by posting to WWSA officers "a letter proposing a union of the two under a new name and on condition that the president of neither should be made president of the new one," Youmans recalled. The WWSA responded in favor of reunion, but "insisted that the old historic name . . . should be retained." The PEL conceded the point—fortunately, for continuity in the perceptions of the press and the public—but held to the condition that Brown be replaced.

The next concession came at the WWSA convention in November 1912, when women eased out Brown and elected an interim president "to serve until the union was effected": Lutie E. Stearns, the longtime clubwoman known statewide as the founder of the Wisconsin Free Library Commission. The women attempted to placate Brown with an honorary presidency, a post she agreed to accept. But the woman who had led the WWSA almost alone for almost thirty years was not the retiring sort, nor were loyalists who lobbied for her reelection. That their new president won by only one vote, of thirty-eight cast, did not bode well. By January, before "the union was effected," a "heart-sick" Lutie Stearns would resign. As a letter writer from as far as Land o' Lakes could see, "Mrs. B. goes right ahead just as tho [*sic*] there were no thot [*sic*] of union. What will we do?"

The union was stalled, as Youmans later recalled. Instead, "there were only ultimatums and counter-ultimatums," until both sides agreed upon "a call for a joint convention" to be held in Madison in January 1913. Ada James signed the call for the PEL, but the WWSA delayed until the deadlock was broken by Zona Gale, who unilaterally signed the call. The first vice president of the WWSA and Brown's second-in-command, Gale was a born mediator who deserves the most credit for the merger because she refrained from the feud—and remained capable of putting "the cause" foremost. As Gale wrote to James regarding the coming convention, "that meeting is going by the force of the great spirit that is back of the movement, if only we can get out of the way and let it."[32]

As the year's end neared, negotiations were still stalemated because the proposed union was predicated upon new leadership, but none was forthcoming—understandably. Suffragists sought a woman of stature with the expertise and experience of a leader, yet their agreement specifically excluded a list of the most logical candidates. WWSA loyalists could not abide Ada James, while the rebellious PEL would not work under Olympia Brown—nor was she willing to cede control. Worse, her successor would have to be willing to lead a lost cause, in Wisconsin.

The new WWSA awaited a woman acceptable to all, almost necessarily a latecomer to the cause who had alienated neither side in the suffrage feud. Several women were suggested for political reasons, including two state WCTU officers: Mary Scott Johnson, the spouse of a congressman from Superior whose support of suffrage had helped women win Douglas County in the campaign, and Edna Phillips Chynoweth of Madison, close to the Capitol to lobby for another referendum bill—the next item on Ada James's agenda. James already had appealed to Belle Case La Follette, but she was too often out of the state.

The name that surfaced most often among suffragists was that of Theodora Winton Youmans. As Rose C. Swart of the Oshkosh Normal School wrote, "she is an able, tactful, and fearless woman. She has the advantage of being married, and has a printing establishment at her command. She will do things." On the "advantage" of marital status, Swart later wrote that "it helps to down one argument—silly but common—of the opposition." Sophie Gudden was more succinct, and emphatic: "WE MUST PREVAIL ON MRS. YOUMANS TO ACCEPT THIS OFFICE."

But Youmans had refused the position before because of her other offices: at the paper, in politics, and in women's clubs. James again appealed to Youmans and again was refused, twice, although this time for personal reasons. Youmans' adored father died just days after the referendum defeat, she had taken her elderly mother into her home, and had taken on the care of another ailing relative. The usually ebullient Youmans wrote to James that "somehow burdens of all kinds seem to grow heavier and to multiply with each year."

By year's end, Youmans' byline and her "suffrage department" had disappeared from the *Freeman*. As she recalled, "we rested a bit after that campaign. We needed it. But the rest was short." The next president of the WWSA, and the last, would be "vastly surprised to find herself in that position"—a position that would continue to provide her readers, then and since, with a unique vantage point on the "inside story" of the suffrage campaign until the Nineteenth Amendment was won, and this time from the top.[33]

Women's Work
Suffrage Reorganization, 1913–1915

I N 1913, within weeks of assuming the presidency of the Wisconsin Woman Suffrage Association, Theodora Winton Youmans revived her "suffrage department" in the *Waukesha Freeman* as "a medium of expression on the suffrage proposition for all who have anything to say," a forum for suffrage news and editorials, even suffrage songs and poetry. However, her "Votes for Women" also invited antisuffragists to "smash her arguments"—in no more than five hundred words. In sum, the content of Youmans' column was much the same as in the 1911–12 campaign. But its author was not.

Youmans' accession to the WWSA presidency signaled a significant change not only in the movement's style but also in her own, as both became less ebullient and more businesslike. After the disappointment of the 1911–12 campaign, she rarely again wrote with the almost girlish naiveté of her first giddy experience as a suffragist. Instead, she later described her tenure at the top wearily, in managerial terms: "Looking back over the last seven years of the struggle there are some high lights; but mainly it is a sober record of doing the day's work as well as one could, educating and organizing, raising money and expending it, writing and exhorting, and never for one moment failing in faith as to the justice of our cause or its final outcome."[1]

As before, Youmans and her column did double duty. During the campaign, she had reprinted portions in the PEL *Press Bulletin,* a news release packet sent statewide. From 1913 forward, the column continued to serve as a publicity vehicle outside of the WWSA when picked up by papers statewide, to be disseminated to suffrage sympathizers and dissenters alike. With characteristic efficiency, Youmans also adapted excerpts from her *Freeman* column and publicity for her "president's letter" in the WWSA's monthly *Wisconsin Citizen,* the internal communiqué from management to membership founded a quarter of a century before by Olympia Brown.

In retrospect, that Brown had stepped down after nearly a thirty-year reign as WWSA president for a successor who was a "second-generation" suffragist seems logical. After all, Youmans offered savvy in politics and the press, and a proven record of success; she had led Wisconsin women to suffrage—school suffrage—once before, for good. That clubwomen, not the WWSA, had won back the "school ballot" marked a transition in the state suffrage movement which was only formalized in 1913.

But the transition was not obvious or easy for many "first-generation" suffragists, including Olympia Brown. They did not ease the way for the "second generation," which suggests to some historians that women went forward with disregard for those gone before. Brown's biographer blames Youmans and Ada L. James for the rift, writing that they "viewed her with suspicion, even antagonism. Few understood her." Brown was an enigma, even to many women and men in her own generation, but her endeavors were appreciated. Youmans, for example, acknowledged a debt to Brown as "the burning flame in the souls of a few women which lighted and led the way." Youmans also credited her predecessors with her own political career and with progress for all Wisconsin women. "We do what we do now," she wrote, "because of what they did then."

But "what they did then" in the nineteenth century no longer was appropriate, or perhaps even possible. The new era in politics and the press required organization on a massive scale—bureaucracy—and led to a reorganization in the WWSA. Youmans' attempt to establish efficiency in women's "lines of work" would be resisted, her tenure almost unbearably complicated by internal discord which seemed to arise from differences with—and interference by—Olympia Brown.

Ahead of her time and out of place in "women's place" in the nineteenth century, Brown was forever embittered by the injustice of the Fourteenth Amendment and denied justice by the courts. Another biographer calls Brown a "pioneer and individualist," traits which had served her well. But the same characteristics put her at odds with clubwomen, whom she called "uneducated, half-baked"—and whom she was unwilling to meet halfway. Brown never overcame her dislike for the press and still deemed politics "not worthy of a Christian," a comment not conducive to winning either the support of legislators or the confidence of clubwomen. Above all, Brown despised the "age of organization"—clubwomen's forte.[2]

By contrast, Youmans was the consummate clubwoman, always in the right time and place. Her "second generation" was schooled collectively in the colleges and clubs available to women in the latter nineteenth century, long after the Fourteenth Amendment became law. Many found the earlier ideological rigidity on the "justice" of suffrage almost incomprehensible. Clubwomen, ever the realists and rarely philosophical, argued for the "expediency" of the ballot, not as an end in itself but as a means to other ends.

Yet Youmans and Brown only epitomized a generational change occurring everywhere amid wider forces at work since before the turn of the century in the suffrage campaign—and, indeed, in all political campaigns. The influx of clubwomen legitimized "the struggle" to the public at large, but the once-radical cause of suffrage moved into the mainstream at the cost of struggle within, in every state. In few states would the internal struggle be so inevitable as in Wisconsin, or so personified. Brown and Youmans—one a suffrage philosopher, the other an enthusiast of the "club philosophy"—were destined for conflict from 1913 forward, but the difference in their ages only clouded deeper issues.

"Second-generation" suffragists were more diverse than was apparent at first and also differed in ideologies as well as strategies and tactics, which soon would cause a schism in the movement nationwide. In Wisconsin, although Youmans yielded to James's appeals to take the presidency, Youmans never would persuade James on strategy. The potential for dissension was evident even in Youmans' initial letter of refusal. Although she agreed that merger was preferable to "two old organizations, tied together not welded and each presumably struggling for supremacy," Youmans differed diplomatically with James on "beginning another campaign immediately. Don't you think it best for us to rest a bit and let our arguments of last year have time to sink in?"

The question foreshadowed significant differences between Youmans and James which would surface within months and never would be resolved. James was a bridge between generations; the earlier suffrage philosophy had been inculcated in her from childhood. Raised in a political family, she focused on the legislative process with relentless referenda until the opposition finally was worn down and suffrage was won. Youmans, a latecomer to suffrage, was less impatient and more attuned to the importance of a winning record—in a word, image. Rather than risk another failure, she preferred the painstaking process of building public support, because "the success of a movement like ours depends first upon education, and second upon legislation effected by this educated public opinion."[3]

Negotiations for the merger of Wisconsin's two suffrage organizations also suggest the fragile nature of the new WWSA in 1913, following the infighting of the 1911–12 campaign, when neither James nor Brown instilled faith among their followers. The merger allowed for some former officers in lesser posts: James, first vice president of the WWSA before her defection to found the PEL, became executive secretary in an apparent last-minute ploy, although actually the result of careful plotting with Crystal Eastman Benedict before her departure from the state. But women frustrated by the feud did not mind behind-the-scenes machinations. As Zona Gale wrote to Ada James of "the executive secretary arrangement," it "gave us both you and Mrs. Youmans." Gale, who had assumed the WWSA first vice presidency upon James's departure, stayed in the post. Brown remained honorary president of the new WWSA, a position which Youmans later ruled was "for life."

But some suffragists—especially James, and possibly Youmans herself—saw the new president as also holding an "honorary" post at most, and balancing the board of the new WWSA between the factions made some resistance to reorganization and even a stalemate over strategy and tactics almost certain. Worse, as the excitement and enthusiasm engendered by women's whirlwind 1911–12 campaign came to an end, so did support—moral and financial—from outside the state. Disheartened and destitute, Wisconsin suffragists faced a public opinion campaign of uncertain duration and without direction from the National American Woman Suffrage Association—although isolation from NAWSA also allowed Wisconsin women to work without the disadvantage of interference, until the national schism in the suffrage movement seeped down to the state level later in 1914.[4]

If autonomy initially was welcome in 1913, suffragists in Wisconsin may well have wished it away by 1915. Not until the next and last chapter of the suffrage story would "the National" again provide help—and hope—to a state considered a hopeless case for the cause by many women nationwide as well as in Wisconsin.

The first test of faith in the new WWSA merger came in Youmans' first months as president, in a power struggle with James over postreferendum strategy—the disagreement which had been raised, but not resolved, in their earlier correspondence on the wisdom of an immediate return to the polls. Youmans was right in resisting a new campaign too soon; as historian William H. O'Neill suggests, "the stunt era of suffrage had long since passed."[5]

Some women remained mesmerized by the referendum route, especially James and Belle Case La Follette, who lobbied within the WWSA for a new referendum bill against Youmans' wishes. She acquiesced only when her political mentor, Senator La Follette, took his wife's side. Both La Follettes may have been swayed by a concurrent report from a Senate subcommitte which endorsed a federal amendment for eight reasons, encompassing both the "justice" and the "expediency" of enfranchising women, and concluded that "woman suffrage could no longer be considered a novel or radical movement."

Olympia Brown testified before the Senate subcommittee, but not on behalf of the WWSA. Another of her affiliations, a Federal Woman's Suffrage Association, also opposed the state referendum route. At the same time, she refrained from endorsing her successor's attempt to stave off the La Follettes and Ada James. Still, it was the last time Brown and Youmans would be in agreement.

In Wisconsin, optimism on another referendum was misplaced because the opposition remained well organized and well funded, unlike the WWSA. The organization could not be effective because it was not yet fully "effected," owing to the disorganization of the previous WWSA. For months after the merger, Dr. Gwendolen Brown Willis retrieved membership lists, other records, and receipts from her mother ⹁nd others. She finally closed the account books—in the red by $5.60—and turned them over to Youmans to pay, in mid-May.

In addition to the WWSA's disarray, political conditions also argued against another campaign. The national Brewers Association's primary beneficiary was Milwaukee's German-American Alliance under Robert Wild. The only witness to testify in Madison against the bill for a new referendum, Wild did not act alone; Milwaukee's archbishop openly sided with the Alliance, stating from the pulpit that women's "natural gifts" made them unfit to vote. Youmans denounced both the Alliance and the "pronunciamento" by "his reverence," but dealt carefully with the state's powerful Catholic electorate. Noting that the church had not taken an official stand and that the archbishop "speaks as an individual," she publicized a list of prominent prosuffrage Catholic laity. No matter how many, they could not counteract the impact of the clergy.

Worse, the suffrage bill fell prey to political infighting among Wiscon-

sin men which rivaled any within the WWSA. In 1913, Senator La Follette's support proved somewhat unreliable because he was recovering
from a serious illness, apparently depression, while his behind-the-scenes
activity also was politically unwise and even suspect in his ongoing
feud with Wisconsin's governor. No governor appreciated a senator's
interference in his state, and Francis E. McGovern—no friend of suffrage—saw the bill as an opportunity to embarrass his foe. James bravely
lobbied the bill through the legislature only to see it vetoed by the vin-
dictive governor.[6]

As Youmans had foreseen, the referendum bill not only was futile but
also resulted in a further setback for suffrage. Still, she was gracious
in the face of others' defeat, especially a defensive Ada James. Although
their private correspondence suggests the relationship became increasingly strained during the ill-fated referendum bill campaign—James's
affectionate salutation of "Dear Pardner" yielded to "My Dear Mrs. Youmans"—the WWSA president publicly rallied to the side of James, the
woman who had overpowered her in the WWSA. Youmans railed instead at the ubiquitous brewers and the governor, whom she previously
had placated in print. Now, in the *Freeman,* she advised McGovern
to "read the papers these days," deemed him "hardly up-to-date," and
attributed his action to personal spite, party politics, and "doing the
work of the liquor interests."

As always, Youmans saved her worst invective for "the antis" in the
National Association Opposed to Woman Suffrage and especially enjoyed ridiculing their leader as the "Anti Rampant." Admittedly, the
"antis" were an easy target. Their publication, the *Woman's Protest,*
blamed suffragists for any sign of cultural decline in Western civilization, from "salacious magazines" and "degraded dancing" to "vulgar
conversation" and a "bacchanalia of fashion" in the "gossamer stock-
ing" and the "diaphanous skirt."

Youmans also declared, more stridently than ever before, that brewers
were the source of funding for antisuffragists from politicians to front
groups, a supposition which brought on press attacks—and brought out
gentlemanly defenders of the president of the Wisconsin Association
Opposed to Woman Suffrage, the wealthy, well-connected socialite wife
of the state attorney general, Mrs. Charles E. Estabrook. Although Youmans admitted that her charges were made not "factually" but from
"womanly intuition," she was vindicated—five years later. When a Senate investigation into unrelated activity by the Brewers Association unexpectedly revealed the existence of clandestine antisuffrage campaigns,

one report exhumed had been sent to headquarters by a Wisconsin organizer in 1913, probably Wild: "We have had the usual bills, like every other state," including "women's suffrage in about six different forms . . . which were all defeated," but "only by organization and by active work of the brewers being on the job all the time." Another report to a Milwaukee brewing company, marked "confidential," boasted that "we are . . . in a position to establish channels of communication with the leaders of the antisuffrage movement for our friends in any state where suffrage is an issue."[7]

At the time, the well-coordinated campaign by the opposition had the welcome effect of turning the WWSA from hope of a short-term solution—at least in the 1913–15 legislative biennium—to Youmans' long-range plan for internal reorganization. "The coming campaign in Wisconsin is to be carried on wholly for the purposes of education, so that when another election comes in this state, the voters will be ready for it," she wrote. The need was not for lobbying legislators but for persuading the public, which then would exert pressure upon elected representatives—or, as Youmans bluntly put it: "Progress is made before the legislator acts. He is called upon to register the popular will, to enact what we are pleased to call public opinion, and not to create it."

More realistic than a referendum campaign, Youmans' plan set suffrage as a goal to be achieved in stages. The 1911–12 campaign had produced awareness of the cause; the next stage was cultivating understanding of the issue, Youmans wrote. In a firm statement in the *Freeman* in the midsummer of 1913, echoed in the *Citizen,* she warned that the task which women faced was tedious, the tactics time-consuming, but it was the way to "educate" the target public. Among the most difficult tasks would be rebuilding the demoralized WWSA and, above all, fund-raising.

This is a call. It is a message. It is an appeal. The campaign for woman suffrage must go on in Wisconsin. The voters must know more about woman suffrage, its philosophy, its actual results in the states and countries where it prevails. Only by education are measures like this ever carried. A state-wide campaign is planned, to open now and to close only when the women of Wisconsin vote. The campaign which we plan is not to be noisy or sensational. It is to be quiet and educational. We shall open headquarters in Madison, we shall disseminate literature, we shall send speakers where they can do the most good—we do not propose to talk suffrage exclusively to each other any longer—we shall strive for more and better local organizations. *All this takes money.*[8]

The work would not resemble the referendum campaign. Attention-getting, headline-grabbing tactics were downplayed for the duration to "ready the voter." First, Youmans had to ready the WWSA.

With the priority of fund-raising to rebuild the penniless WWSA, Youmans set a goal of $5,000 to be raised by the WWSA's November convention, only four months away, and gave each county organization a quota. She also gave the WWSA examples of personal and organizational accountability. Youmans set the quota for her home chapter at $200, one of the highest for any county, and kicked off the fund drive herself by calling a "suffrage convention" in Waukesha where she presented carefully prepared "suffrage maps" of the county, state, and country and "several charts giving pertinent statistics." She also detailed WWSA expenditures, "so that every person present might know when she gave money, just what that money is to be used for." The preparation and her presentation worked; Waukesha women raised $175 that day alone and planned a benefit play at the local college. A pleased Youmans reported her "little experience in Waukesha" to instruct other county organizations.

Within three months, women across Wisconsin rallied to the call. By October, Youmans reported pledges totaling $3,000 from sixteen counties and the enterprising work of the WWSA's social education committee, whose projects raised funds as well as public consciousness. One project was *Social Forces,* a "how-to" manual for clubs and other community organizations that was primarily credited to Susan Miller Quackenbush of Portage and Lutie Stearns, the longtime clubwoman and onetime Milwaukee city librarian, and founder and head of the state's free traveling library service. The manual was almost one hundred pages long and included study guides, bibliographies, and a section entitled "Things to Do" toward resolution of a list of "seventy to eighty" issues from national industrial problems to local "morals and citizenship" curricula for the schools. The first printing of five thousand copies of *Social Forces,* sold at fifteen cents each, had "already paid for itself and brought into the treasury fifty dollars more" over costs of production and distribution, Youmans reported.

Although the WWSA board approved Youmans' reorganization plan, the women apparently did not acquiesce so readily to her simple requests for office staff—or even an office. "The first year of my presidency we had no office," she recalled, "and I took care of an extensive correspondence with my own pen." She also wrote her monthly president's letter to membership in the *Citizen* and her weekly, lengthier "suffrage department" in the *Freeman;* the latter was in effect syndicated around the state in English, German, and sometimes Polish through the "WWSA regular press service" to one hundred state papers which were "sufficiently hospitable to our cause to warrant expenditure for paper and stamps," as determined by monitoring of the media by the WWSA's press committee—which Youmans also chaired. At last, in October, Youmans told the board that she would not single-handedly lead the WWSA, as had her predecessor. In a word, she threatened to resign due to overwork. The announcement apparently was unexpected by most of the board members, but not by Ada James and Zona Gale. Both women apparently planned the ploy with Youmans, although the greater part of the task fell to the unfortunate Gale, whose ability as a mediator was relied upon again. "They are a peculiar lot," wrote James about the board. "Poor Miss Gale won't know how to deal with them, she is so pacific."

By forcing the issue, Youmans won several concessions from her board, but she also acceded to some compromises, if only for the sake of appearances. The board agreed to hire a stenographer but not an office staff, and to establish an office but not in Waukesha. That site apparently was Youmans' preference, but Ada James won the board's support for an office seventy miles to the west in Madison. However, Youmans reconsidered and never threatened resignation again. She did not need to.

Once concern for appearances was past, Youmans got her way and within weeks had well under way what she called her "general policy of concentration"—centralization—for the WWSA. She brought back former Milwaukee Normal School teacher Alice Curtis, whose new career as a salaried PEL recruiter in the 1911–12 campaign had led to a similar post in Illinois. An experienced organizer with the task of "making the headquarters what it ought to be—the center of information and inspiration for suffrage work in Wisconsin," Curtis was made "executive secretary" instead of stenographer, an adroit way of replacing Ada James. Youmans also delegated the WWSA press committee to Sophie Gudden of Oshkosh, despite Zona Gale's repeated pleas that the WWSA "*get a man* to head the press committee . . . for men *can* convince men better than women." Gale's preference was editor Richard Lloyd Jones of the *Wisconsin State Journal,* but Youmans wisely held firm for putting a woman in the post. And, within a year, Youmans moved WWSA headquarters from Madison to Waukesha—where she also found funds for a stenographer on her staff.[9]

Youmans' first presidential address, at the 1913 convention, reflected newfound confidence in her authority as the result of her first significant victory in reorganizing the WWSA. The address also focused on strategies and tactics, and afforded short shrift to suffrage philosophy. As Youmans said, "you who are here do not need exhortation of that kind. Your ideals are placed high. What you want, I take it, is practical means of reaching these ideals, which are the ladders by which we climb. . . . We reach our ends in this, as in other undertakings, by ceaseless personal effort, and in no other way." Promising "to drop hyperbole," Youmans used the podium less to preach to the converted, as had her predecessor, and more as a combination of prayer rally and pep talk.

In a rousing resumé of the new WWSA's first fund-raising drive, Youmans commended county organizations, which had almost met the goal of $5,000 by the fall convention. For other women still reluctant to solicit donations, she counseled that "it is not an overwhelmingly difficult thing to do" and became easier over time, once women "started a number of people in the excellent habit of giving money for the woman suffrage cause." She especially commended the WWSA education committee for raising a considerable sum toward the goal, mainly from brisk sales of its *Social Forces* following a favorable review in *La Follette's Magazine,* whose co-editor and co-publisher was WWSA member Belle Case La Follette. So well did the manual sell that the WWSA was planning a second printing, and the education committee projected more income from ticket sales for a scheduled tour of a "suffrage movie" across the state. Youmans called "selling tickets for the moving picture show . . . the stoutest and longest of the ladders to climb" but, given the interest in the new invention, a manageable goal.

Youmans also provided women who wanted instruction on "practical means" of suffrage work with a succinct list of professional techniques, from regular reading and monitoring of the press to raising money and writing to public officials. She also suggested a time-honored technique for avoiding what would come to be called professional "burnout," by setting ever-greater personal goals.

> Make the press work a regular part of your activities. Read *Social Forces,* woman suffrage literature, *The Wisconsin Citizen, The Woman's Journal.* Study the history and the philosophy of the basis of the woman suffrage movement. Raise your quota of money for the state work and don't be afraid of making that quota too large. It is for your soul's good as well as for the state treasury. Support with all your strength the proposed federal amendment conferring suffrage upon women. . . . To this end, write your congressmen individually and collectively. . . . Make it your duty to study political conditions.[10]

The 1913 WWSA convention in Madison sounded like a professional development seminar and looked the part, complete with an exhibits hall and merchandising giveaways—although items were more often for sale with proceeds toward the WWSA fund-raising goal.

Youmans promoted the work of the exhibits committee with a copy-writer's flair. Chaired by the Dane County chapter's Edna Phillips Chynoweth, the exhibit included "something of the literature of the movement, a vital literature, full of inspiration and illumination [by] many of the finest and strongest minds of the times, writing of woman and her upward struggle," Youmans wrote. The exhibit also included, "besides books, all kinds of suffrage novelties, post cards, napkins, calendars, stickers, and various other things which will make capital Christmas remembrances."

The WWSA's mercenary zeal may have met resistance from more conservative women, because Youmans addressed the concern at the convention. "We must keep the question constantly before the public mind—get the public used to the idea. . . . we must ring constant changes on basic principles, so as to make them new and alluring at each appearance." No promotional ploy was too plebeian, no matter how noble the cause, because "high ideals" would be won only by "all the hundred ways known to the ingenuity of woman."

Women's ingenuity, as Youmans saw it, was the modern subliminal science of mass persuasion, which she couched in the condescending metaphor of clubwomen who had come to see the world as but a classroom for their "educational" campaign.

> We must teach our class, the public, what is true democracy. . . . Fortunately, we are pedagogues of the new school, who believe that sparing the rod is sometimes saving the child. . . . We teach and the pupil does not know he is undergoing the agony of learning. He absorbs his lesson from the news in the morning paper, from the leaflets that fall upon him . . . fitting his condition, from the comments of the pulpit and the platform, from ordinary every-day discussion. . . . And lo—he is for woman suffrage without ever being conscious of having been converted.[11]

However, as the 1912 referendum had made clear, a mass conversion of men would be required. "We polled 135,000 votes. The opposition polled 90,000 more than we did, so that, at that time, we needed nearly 50,000 more votes. When our next election on woman suffrage rolls around, some of our friends will have passed away; possibly some will have had the bad taste to change their minds; the population of the state will have increased. We shall have to convert 60,000 or 70,000 more men in Wisconsin," Youmans said.

Reduced to simple arithmetic, the task of "turning men to a belief in our cause before we women of Wisconsin can win the ballot" was made manageable. Humor also helped; Youmans leavened her "statistical facts" by comparing suffragists in Wisconsin to missionaries "likewise going into a foreign land to convert the heathen."

In outlining her objectives for the next year, Youmans called on members to maintain fund-raising levels but added the next objective in her reorganization plan: recruitment and training of new members. To educate "60,000 or 70,000 men," the WWSA would need "as many or more women" selectively targeted according to the extent of their sympathy with suffrage. Youmans put priority on motivating latent publics before attempting to persuade those opposed to suffrage or, as she said, on "educating our friends first and later those who are not our friends now, but will be when they are educated. The education of our friends is most important." As a means of motivation, Youmans advised women to work "somewhat along financial lines" by enlisting sympathizers first as donors and then as active workers to protect their investment. Along those "lines," she enlisted University of Wisconsin professor Ford MacGregor, to speak on "Practical Politics for Women."

The WWSA's own traveling suffrage troupe also spoke on new strategies and tactics in use nationally and even internationally, from firsthand experience. Zona Gale gave her recollections of marching in 1911 with "the professional women" in New York City's "great suffrage parade." Maud Leonard McCreery of Green Bay had marched in another suffrage parade, in Pennsylvania, where she and Edna Wright of Milwaukee were paid organizers. Rachel Szold Jastrow of Madison spoke on a "great international gathering" in "Buda Pesth," Hungary, where she had served as one of only twelve United States delegates chosen from more than three hundred hopefuls and had met women from twenty-six countries and "many different classes of society, yet working shoulder to shoulder for a single end."

However, the high point of the convention was provided by speakers on strategies and tactics employed across the Wisconsin border in Illinois, the pride of the movement; only months before, the WWSA's border state to the south had become the first "suffrage state" outside of the West. Dr. Anna Blount, the graduate of the University of Wisconsin who managed a Chicago suffrage bookstore, spoke on the importance of "literature," and another co-worker in the 1911–12 campaign

was Catharine Waugh McCulloch. Another Illinois leader long familiar to Wisconsin women was Ruth Hanna McCormick, daughter of
the late Senator Mark Hanna and wife of Chicago press mogul Medill
McCormick.

The Illinois Equal Suffrage League also sent Antoinette Funk of the
"famous suffrage lobby" which had won limited "presidential suffrage"
by legislative enactment. "The Illinois strategy" of winning without a
referendum was certain to interest Wisconsin women in "how the miracle
was wrought," as Youmans wrote. The answer was methodical organization and meticulous research, as Youmans reported. In her address, Funk
"said that in making the preliminary arrangement for the assault upon
the legislature the lobby made a card catalogue of members. On each
card . . . was his age, his place of birth and residence, his lodge if he
had any, his social and business connections, the names of his confidential friends, main factors of his political career and any and all other
data covering as far as might be his character and predilections [and]
sufficiently comprehensive so as to form an excellent basis for work with
any individual member." In an analysis of the campaign, historian Steven M. Buechler suggests that Illinois women were notable not only for
adroit lobbying but also for a strategy of building coalitions across classes
and systematic, cohesive use of new tactics such as polling and telephone
solicitation, all coordinated by a full-time, salaried staff.[12]

However, Youmans again warned women that suffrage would not accomplish miracles—especially in Illinois, now more than ever a world
away from Wisconsin. "If that great and wicked city of Chicago does
not emerge from the first women's election as pure and clean as a wind-
swept prairie village, wiseacres will be sure—as indeed they are now—
that woman suffrage is a failure." The Illinois victory made their sisters
to the south the envy of Wisconsin suffragists, so close and yet so far,
and reinvigorated the movement nationwide. However, many a national
and state leader like Youmans would come to rue the aftermath of the
Illinois coup.

Nationwide, suffragists still faced the problem resolved in Wisconsin
earlier in 1913: the need for new leadership. Across the country, the
movement was emerging from "the doldrums," the era from 1896 to
1910, years when there had been no statewide victories for suffrage.
NAWSA's beloved but indecisive Dr. Anna Howard Shaw could no
longer contain the increasing internal disagreement over strategy and
tactics, and "the National" was nearing a schism similar to the earlier
rift between Brown and James in Wisconsin. In 1913, NAWSA Congres-

sional Committee lobbyist Alice Paul abandoned the traditional well-mannered and diplomatic courting of lawmakers and, instead, adapted a British tactic of working for the defeat of antisuffrage incumbent congressmen. Soon, Paul also abandoned NAWSA entirely and founded the Congressional Union.

Paul's tactics were new to NAWSA, but her strategy was not; the Congressional Union stayed loyal to the late Susan B. Anthony's plan to win full suffrage nationwide by a federal amendment. But allegiance to the "Anthony amendment" eroded elsewhere amid revived interest in the strategy of settling for limited suffrage, state by state, as in Illinois. State leaders struggled to hold the ranks in line while national leaders wavered at the whim of the movement.[13]

Wisconsin suffragists were aware of the rift in NAWSA at the time of the WWSA convention, by the end of 1913, but remained relatively aloof as the national convention neared. It was the first NAWSA convention for Youmans, who filled reports wired to the *Freeman* with names of national leaders whom she long had admired—notably, Carrie Chapman Catt. A Wisconsin native, a clubwoman and a journalist whose column had inspired a younger Youmans, Catt had risen to the NAWSA presidency as Susan B. Anthony's handpicked successor in 1900. However, Catt had stepped down in 1902 owing to her husband's fatal illness. She was succeeded by Dr. Anna Howard Shaw, a charismatic speaker "strong on inspiration" but "weak on organization," who lacked the "tact and managerial expertise" which the movement required, according to historian William H. O'Neill.

Now, in 1913, Catt again was in the forefront of the movement—and Youmans' coverage of the convention. Catt was a born manager and problem solver, a premier strategist who would find "ways to translate womanly enthusiasm into political pressure," writes O'Neill. But in 1913, as president of both the New York State and International Suffrage Associations, she was not yet ready to return to the presidency of NAWSA.[14]

Youman's coverage also highlighted new tactics discussed and demonstrated at the NAWSA convention. She enthused about the "contagion" of a rally where "women looked first among their own in fundraising" and pledged almost $14,000 toward a projected annual budget of $20,000. Less than half of the previous year's total, the estimate for 1914 did not include all "lines of work" because delegates voted to separately incorporate NAWSA's "literature department" as a self-sustaining publishing company with a separate budget of another

$20,000. Half of that amount immediately was raised by selling company stock to women at the convention—all practices put in place by the WCTU in the previous century.

"Anxious to learn of any new methods of work which might be available," Youmans learned many another tactic soon seen in Wisconsin. For example, changes in NAWSA's structure encouraged specialization and elevated the status of the emerging field of "press correspondents" or publicists. The importance of the press to the campaign led NAWSA to separate publications from publicity, the latter in a "national press bureau" which impressed Youmans with its sophistication in adapting from needs of traditional one- or two-person newsrooms, which ran copy as written, to those of larger papers newly staffed with reporters who preferred to compile and write the articles themselves. As Youmans described the new bureau, NAWSA now employed a trained researcher "solely for the use of the press," who did not "so much provide 'stories,' as this term is used by metropolitan newspapers, but furnished various facts and data" so that "reporters found whatever they might desire."

NAWSA's decision to better define the work of "press correspondents" in recognition of increased press demand for information was overdue but innovative. Similar "bureaus" in the corporate sector still made little distinction between the functions of publications, publicity, and advertising, despite conflicting needs of printers and the press and conflicts of interest between newspapers' news and business departments.[15]

NAWSA's priority on the press reflected the fact that the "suffrage beat" was heating up, especially in the host city of the national convention, the nation's capital. Senator W. S. Kenyon of Iowa came before the 1913 convention to enlist support for his campaign to eradicate "the red light district in Washington" and galvanized women to go home to organize a campaign of petitions, telegrams, and letters in support. Within two months, the Kenyon Bill became law. The next month, the "Anthony amendment" that had been buried for decades "suddenly" emerged from a congressional subcommittee. Although voted down, the bill's reemergence was "rightly regarded as a victory" for NAWSA, as Youmans wrote.

One lesson in tactics learned at the NAWSA convention which women implemented immediately in Wisconsin was a "suffrage school" to recruit and train more women in campaigning skills. The concept was new to membership, although Youmans and other WWSA officers had attended a NAWSA workshop as early as 1912 in Chicago. However, amid the hectic 1911–12 campaign, the women had not had a week to spare for education of membership—and had hoped that success would negate the need for further training in "suffrage skills."

Now a "suffrage school" not only was appropriate to the WWSA's objective of recruiting and training new members but also was desperately needed in the Wisconsin campaign, as Youmans wrote: "One of the reasons why we do not advance more rapidly toward our goal is in the fact that we have so few trained workers. It is one thing to believe in woman suffrage. It is quite another thing to be able to do effective work for woman suffrage. . . . The art of campaigning and of converting other people is not an art learned in a day, and not an art that comes to many people without learning."

Many a willing student enrolled in the WWSA "suffrage school," the most significant new program in 1914. The weeklong event, planned by experienced organizers Alice Curtis and Ada James, exceeded all expectations for attendance at both intensive training for volunteers and programs of public interest. In June 1914 in Madison, daytime and evening public lectures drew hundreds to hear a slate of speakers led by Chief Justice John B. Winslow of the Wisconsin Supreme Court—the high court which had overruled him when, as a district judge in 1886, he had upheld Olympia Brown and the state's first suffrage law.

The remarkable faculty of fifteen reunited Winslow and Brown and also included famed University of Wisconsin professors. Winslow taught a popular course on women's property rights, while Olympia Brown taught women's history, the subject she knew literally by heart. Other instructors included her daughter, Dr. Gwendolen Brown Willis, late of Milwaukee-Downer College and soon to join the faculty of Bryn Mawr College; University of Wisconsin sociologist E. A. Ross; and the Madison journalism school's Willard G. Bleyer, the spouse of WWSA board member Alice Haskell Bleyer.

As a recruiting tactic to reach a new public, "working girls," the WWSA offered scholarships to cover tuition of twenty-five cents for each session, or one dollar for all six. One "working girl" from Washington, D.C. was Margaret Wilson, the president's daughter, a summer intern on a Madison magazine. In all, sixty-six women enrolled in the "suffrage school," some from out of state, in coursework which distilled the lessons of a century into intensive but comprehensive study: "the organization of suffrage societies, the schedule of work, the number and character of committees, the management of indoor and outdoor meetings, the raising of money, the application of the art of public speaking to different audiences," as Youmans summarized the curriculum.

As Youmans taught her topic, the "gentle science of introducing suffrage news and propaganda into the daily and weekly press," women apparently needed more knowledge of psychology than of journalism. According to a participant, "she showed pupils how to conduct a suffrage column, the way to secure space in the papers [and] to choose attractive subjects, and how to turn in copy in such a way as to keep editor and office force in good humor and insure continued use of space." The aspiring reporter was Helen Haight of Waukesha, a relative of Youmans who learned her lessons well. She soon worked as the WWSA office manager, initially handling *Citizen* advertising and postal distribution, became the WWSA "press correspondent," and soon ran a new "press bureau."

Youmans was a student of "press work" as well, from a managerial perspective. In 1914, she applied the lessons of NAWSA's new bureaucratic structure at the state level but adapted to WWSA priorities by delegating publicity and putting emphasis on internal communication toward the goal of recruiting and training new members. To the previous four WWSA committees—finance, legislation, education, and "press work"—the board approved the addition of "literature" to separate publicity from publications.

Regarding publicity, the plan went forward well. Sophie Gudden of Oshkosh replaced Youmans as chair of the press committee, which swiftly redoubled research on "facts and data" for reporters seeking statistics on suffrage "sentiment." One release counted twenty-eight women serving on school boards in the state. Another released results of a survey at the University of Wisconsin which revealed that two-thirds of women students wanted the vote. Gudden also continued to oversee translation of "suffrage letters" for foreign-language papers, in at least German and Polish, in addition to regular releases to one hundred English-language press outlets. As Youmans wrote of Gudden, "such was her ability and standing that she was able to secure regular publication" from editors statewide.

Gudden's ability and efficiency were evident in her constant communications with the WWSA office, accompanied by clippings of her "velvetfooted articles" on votes for women. In a typical plea for faster turnaround of copy from her "country press chairs" of county committees, Gudden warned that "news two days en route and one day set in type [at] a country newspaper becomes stale." Gudden wrote fresh copy for papers from the *Sonntagspost* to Milwaukee's *Free Press,* "for which news must reach me Thursday or Friday morning," and needed news on Tuesdays for a "stingy one-fourth column" in the *Milwaukee Jour-*

nal. The *Journal's* "stinginess" extended to refusing to participate in "exchanges" with the *Citizen* or put Gudden on the "free list"—a common practice for unpaid contributors—but Youmans readily agreed that the WWSA would pay for the paper. Yet receipt of the *Journal* only enraged Gudden: the "publisher is apparently *not* a suffragist. He heads my contributions 'Suffragette Movement'"—the diminutive ending was incorrect, and seen by American women as demeaning—"regardless of enticing titles I used." But Gudden endured, and made inroads at the *Journal.* "Though the publisher is not friendly," she wrote, "the editor seems to be very friendly." Even more encouraging was the editorial advice from a secretly suffragist reporter at the paper with the memorable byline of Telza Babetta Hirsch, who helped Gudden get her allotted space in the *Journal* expanded to a full third of a column.[16]

Compared to Gudden's success with the press, Youmans did not do as well with the literature committee. That she chaired the new committee was an indication of the importance of improved internal communication. But, despite board approval of Youmans' plans to take over—and make over—the *Citizen,* implementation of the policy was immediately blocked by Olympia Brown.

Brown had yielded her presidency but not the publication that she had founded a quarter of a century before, although Brown long had proclaimed that the *Citizen* belonged to the WWSA. Youmans' plan for the paper was no departure, on paper; she wrote that the *Citizen* would "remain the defender of one faith, political equality." But Youmans also announced that the publication would be "redesigned," with its "character to be somewhat changed" to serve "principally as a medium of communication among the suffragists of the state." By contrast, according to Brown's biographer, her communiqués from the East to the *Citizen* editor were "almost royal in tone."

By 1914, Brown again regularly missed board meetings, not only because she wintered in the East but also because of her dislike for detail. "The dull routines of organizational meetings which many of the women seemed to enjoy" held no pleasure for her, and she heard of Youmans' plans for the *Citizen* only after board approval. Belatedly, Brown enlisted her daughter to write a stinging letter to Youmans, and vowed in her own five-page invective that she would vote against "any change in size and character" of the *Citizen.* She refused to yield the right to handpick the editor and printer—the former in Brodhead, the latter in Baraboo—which caused Youmans to despair of "close cooperation."

But the *Citizen* was only a symbol of Brown's increasing disaffection

from the WWSA and NAWSA, and signaled the end of Wisconsin suffragists' all-too-brief isolation from the schism rending the movement.
Until mid-1914, the WWSA carefully managed to remain neutral amid
mounting strife. For example, when Catt named Chicago's Ruth Hanna
McCormick to replace Alice Paul as chief lobbyist and chair of NAWSA's
Congressional Committee, Youmans managed to uphold "the National,"
praise McCormick, and applaud the "brilliant" and "amazing" Paul, all
in a single column.

Before the schism in NAWSA seeped down to the state level, the WWSA
had seemed to heal from its own rift, rebounding from the referendum
defeat as well as from Ada James and Belle Case La Follette's ill-advised
campaign for another referendum. Since 1913, the WWSA had established programs for fund-raising, membership recruitment, and training, had improved upon committee structure, and at least had attempted
to improve internal communications. The year had not been easy but
was idyllic in comparison with the months ahead. By the end of 1914,
the WWSA's apparent unity would prove all too tenuous.

In 1914, Youmans would be less complimentary of Alice Paul, who
allied with Brown and vied for the WWSA in the battle between NAWSA
and the new Congressional Union for control of state organizations.
In Brown's own battle for the *Citizen,* she first tried to rally support
within the WWSA by writing to board members, but they ignored her.
Then Brown turned to Paul, who had wooed her to join the Congressional Union a year before to little result. Now Brown asked Paul to
send copies of her *Suffragist* to *Citizen* subscribers since, as Brown wrote,
"their own paper is to be reduced to a mere bulletin." With Brown's op-
portune appeal as her entrée into the state, Paul dispatched a Congressional Union recruiter with connections in Wisconsin, Crystal Eastman
Benedict—who had served as campaign manager of the now-defunct
Political Equality League in opposition to Olympia Brown and the
WWSA.[17]

The dizzying machinations of Brown, Paul, and Benedict were deplored by some women in the WWSA. To Youmans, the discerning
Lutie Stearns wrote of her doubts that Brown sincerely sought to save
the *Citizen.* "It has always been a 'bulletin' and will alter little except
that Olympia Brown doesn't contribute to it. It never did cover the field
at large," Stearns wrote. "Olympia is evidently seeking other harvest
fields."[18]

Brown would sow only dissent in the WWSA, although Youmans appeared to have won her way. From June 1914 on, the *Citizen* was printed

at the *Freeman* under Youmans as editor. She cut the paper's eight pages to four and pared the mailing list of fourteen hundred to four hundred, primarily WWSA members and donors; others subscribed for twenty-five cents annually. Press releases replaced "exchanges" with the *Citizen,* which now was restricted to internal communication. In a joint promotion with the *Woman's Journal* that offered subscribers both publications for one dollar a year, Youmans reiterated the separate purposes of the national and state organs — although the plug, apparently meant to be complimentary, made neither sound compelling: "In a less pretentious way the *Citizen* is a capital paper too. Friends of suffrage should read both — one for general news and the other for state news."

In June 1914, more news of state and national interest came from Illinois, where the General Federation of Women's Clubs at its Chicago Biennial convention at last came to the side of suffrage. Women hailed the endorsement as a symbol of the movement's entry into the mainstream, which meant that the ballot could not be far behind. Wisconsin clubwoman and suffragist Lutie Stearns was given the honor of seconding the motion for endorsement, guaranteeing statewide coverage of Youmans' first-person report from the "wicked city." In her story wired to the *Freeman* from the convention, Youmans could not resist recalling the Wisconsin state federation's endorsement in 1912, which she had engineered. "Crown the editor of this column a prophet in her own country," Youmans crowed.

Another local angle for Wisconsin editors was the "star speaker" of the Chicago Biennial, Ripon-born Carrie Chapman Catt. According to Youmans, Catt's "splendid breadth of vision, fine oratorical powers, and dignified and noble appearance" helped to win the historic endorsement from the General Federation. On the same day, within hours of the crucial vote on the suffrage resolution, clubwomen erupted again in "grand jubilation" upon word from women stationed at the Illinois Supreme Court that justices had upheld the partial-suffrage law — although Illinois women would be forced to resort to the courts again when major parties refused to allow women to serve as delegates to national conventions.[19]

Still, the enviable success of Illinois suffragists started to attract some Wisconsin women to the Congressional Union as a way out of NAWSA's lethargy, although not out of NAWSA. Ada James was first to join and first to resign as WWSA chief lobbyist, although she continued to chair a WWSA committee. Zona Gale and Meta Schlichting Berger enlisted next, both also retaining their WWSA offices. Youmans also joined the

Congressional Union, apparently in a somewhat transparent attempt to placate WWSA dissidents, although also out of loyalty to the "Anthony amendment"; she publicly applauded Paul's "fearless defiance" of opposition to the federal amendment route. At the same time, in correspondence with James, Youmans worried privately whether the Union was "wholly wise."[20]

Neither the Congressional Union controversy nor other crucial issues were resolved at the next NAWSA convention, which, as Youmans correctly predicted, was not "wholly a love feast." She recalled her first NAWSA convention, only a year before, with nostalgia. Now, in November 1914, Youmans, Zona Gale, and Jessie Jack Hooper led the Wisconsin delegation to Nashville, Tennessee, with hope, but returned disheartened. Instead of new leadership at the top, delegates replaced six of nine national officers but not NAWSA president Dr. Anna Howard Shaw, because Carrie Chapman Catt declined to be a candidate owing to her commitment to an upcoming referendum campaign in New York State. Instead of resolving the Congressional Union controversy, delegates endorsed state-level campaigns for legislative enactment of limited suffrage—the "Illinois strategy"—and abandoned the federal amendment route first mapped by Susan B. Anthony, to Youmans' dismay; she was convinced of the need for a Constitutional amendment not only "on principle" but also because Wisconsin was an example of states where women had limited expectations for legislative enactment.

WWSA delegates also left the convention with another critical concern unresolved: women's position on the war in Europe, which already echoed in ethnic Wisconsin. In her advance, Youmans had hope of "consideration for, say, the condition of the country," a disarmingly casual reference which did not deceive her readers. However, NAWSA had avoided the issue. With little resolved, and that little not to her liking, Youmans' postconvention report was atypically reserved in comparison to her standard extensive coverage.

That women despaired of NAWSA at the close of 1914 also was evident in an advance on Youmans' year-end address to the WWSA, written within a week of her return from the national convention. She assessed fund-raising and recruitment, her priorities for the year past, as only "fairly effective," despite a balance of better than $6,000 and an increase in membership. "We still search for a magic which shall make organized groups stay organized, and for a vital spark which shall inspire those women who are comfortably certain that it [woman suffrage] is 'coming anyway,'" she wrote.

Youmans' address was unduly pessimistic. The same address credited women with accomplishments from the "suffrage school" to the "experiment of concentration," which put "under one roof"—at least within a few blocks in Waukesha—the president, the *Citizen,* and WWSA headquarters. In addition, a Self-Denial Day for Suffrage proposed by Harriet Bain of Kenosha was adopted nationwide.

Other projects new to the WWSA in 1914, if familiar to followers of *La Follette's Magazine* and progressive reform, continued to make lawmakers more accountable to constituents. As early as 1901, the La Follettes issued a *Voter's Hand-book* which listed legislators' records on reform issues. The project was repeated in the magazine, founded in 1909 and run by Belle Case La Follette as co-publisher and co-editor. In 1914, the project was adapted by Ada James's legislative committee as the WWSA's "Wisconsin Legislators and the Home." The "little yellow pamphlet" listed roll calls on fifty bills which "every intelligent woman, who has interests beyond her four walls, ought to know about," said Youmans. A document "valuable not only as history but as prophecy," it "demonstrated plainly that women are on guard."[21]

Another demonstration of women's continued interest in progressive reform was a massive direct-mail drive in which WWSA volunteers sent thirteen thousand "circular letters" in a single week for a proposed state amendment for initative and referendum. The amendment failed at the polls, but "we are entitled to believe that our letters counted," said Youmans, because the campaign met her criteria: "It won more votes than most other amendments, it was good propaganda and it did not cost our treasury one cent."

Despite the work of a few women for worthy causes, there was cause for concern. In 1914, most suffragists had reverted to "stunts" and street parades reminiscent of the 1911–12 campaign and reveled in socials, card parties, bake sales, suffrage fairs, and the ubiquitous booths at county fairs and the state fair. As Youmans later wrote, "an important feature of our work each autumn was at state and county fairs, where from a booth or tent emanated suffrage speeches, literature, and friendly argument with the hundreds who drifted in and out." Yet interpersonal tactics were increasingly ineffective in an era of mass communication— and that modern technology had its advantages over earlier methods was evident when the WWSA's state fair tent was vexed by problems from high winds to vandalism by "high-spirited" boys.

By contrast, Youmans sternly wrote, the WWSA convention would stress serious work rather than a "stereotypical socializing" event. "Little effort will be made toward mere entertainment and small thought wasted on cultural lines. The convention will be made as practicable as it can possibly be made, the whole aim being to help members to help with suffrage work," she wrote.

The 1914 WWSA convention was a "suffrage school" on a larger scale, with workshops on organization, legislation, finance, and the always-popular "press work." The session included *Citizen* bookkeeper Helen Haight on "The Business End of Our State Paper," Lucy E. Strong of the Kenosha *Evening News* — and also of the Haight clan — on placing publicity in the "City Press" and similar instruction by Youmans on use of the "Country Press." Modestly, she reported that Strong and Haight "made decided hits."

The 1914 WWSA convention was not all "serious work" and was a hit with the press in the host city of Milwaukee. A "movie play" called *Your Girl and Mine,* with a cast of three hundred, was "the best kind of propaganda on legal disadvantages of the married woman," Youmans wrote. Another highlight, a Pfister Hotel luncheon "noted by the Milwaukee papers as a brilliant affair," drew record attendance for speakers from Milwaukee-Downer College and the University of Wisconsin as well as a WWSA member with a comic bent who gave an "amusing characterization of an anti speech." Women also were regaled with "suffrage songs," most set to hymn tunes, in a standard feature of suffrage conventions that pained the WWSA's somewhat imperious president, ever worried about the women's image. "Personally, I don't care for music at business meetings," she had written. "But if the program committee feels strongly that it is wise to have music, I shall not in the least object."[22]

Yet even Youmans yielded to the frivolity, leading a songfest at the luncheon as the lyricist of another "hit" at the convention. "The Wisconsin Slogan," based on the state motto of "Forward," was set to the tune of "On, Wisconsin."

> On Wisconsin, On Wisconsin, Grand Old Badger State,
> We shall surely win the ballot, Be it soon or late.
> On Wisconsin, On Wisconsin, "Forward" be the cry,
> Slow but surely, late but coming, Bound for Victory.
>
> On Wisconsin, On Wisconsin, We thy daughters true,
> Bound to make a land of Freedom, We are, out of you.
> On Wisconsin, On Wisconsin, Cannot stop or stay
> 'Til thy children all are equal. Hail the mighty day![23]

Despite the deficiencies in rhyme and meter, the song became the WWSA's anthem as women closed every convention session with a rousing rendition of Youmans' irreverent version of her state's "hymn."

Even the convention's most "serious work" of fund-raising became a "budget-raising," where "the fun was fast and furious" and, in less than an hour, women pledged $4,327 toward the WWSA's projected budget of $5,400. Emulating the rally which had impressed Youmans at her first NAWSA convention, she took to the podium to take pledges in memory of mothers or children, in recognition of co-workers or in celebration of joyous events. The spouse of circus owner Al Ringling of Baraboo donated $5 in the name of a "newly arrived grandson," Sarah James pledged the same amount "for the honor of having Ada James for her cousin," and Youmans was "charmed" by another pledge in her own honor. Women pledged designated gifts for office rent and janitorial services, and one donated "one month of work at organizing, for her expenses only." Another popular fund-raiser was the "Melting Pot," kept at WWSA headquarters and brought to the convention where women contributed gold coins, "old silver spoons and a variety of ancient and honorable ornaments" to be melted down. Proceeds went to suffrage campaigns in other states which had sent funds for the 1911–12 campaign in Wisconsin, as Youmans reminded the women. Now, they had "a moral obligation . . . to repay a little portion of that amount."

Of several public events in conjunction with the convention, the most popular was the WWSA's evening "peace meeting." Two women on an international tour from war-torn countries, Emmeline Pethick Lawrence of England and Rosika Schwimmer of Hungary, spoke on "the two sides of the Pan-European contest." The audience of more than a thousand women and men unanimously adopted and sent to President Wilson a call for armistice overseas and neutrality at home.[24]

The "peace meeting" marked the last time that neutrality was possible in the last months before pacifism and patriotism became incompatible in a Wisconsin increasingly at war over the "European war." The 1914 convention camaraderie also was the last display of unity in the new WWSA, more than two years in the making.

With a new legislative biennium in 1915, some women immediately returned to internal warfare. The WWSA resurrected the familiar diversion of a referendum although Youmans again deemed an attempt unwise, especially without a veteran lobbyist; Ada James still served on the legislative committee but was by then on the national board of the Congressional Union. Pitted against the WWSA board, Youmans yielded again lest more leaders leave. The result was a lackluster campaign that also lacked strategic planning, with submission of three bills: municipal suffrage or full suffrage, both requiring referenda, or presidential suffrage needing only legislative action. "If one fails we may fall back on another and then on the third," Youmans wrote in a desultory tone.

The 1915 legislative campaign was significant as a learning experience for Jessie Jack Hooper, who replaced James as lobbyist and later would work Congress for NAWSA, because she learned legislative maneuvering at its worst. For long months, lawmakers stalled on the WWSA bills, but Hooper used the time to interview all 133 legislators "except two members of the assembly who refused point blank to see her." Those who did were too attentive at times. As Youmans wrote, Hooper "found it of strategic advantage to say occasionally, to a flirtatious legislator, what he found difficult to believe, that she was a grandmother."

At last, women earned a hearing where several WWSA members spoke, including Hooper and Maud Leonard McCreery, an expert on working conditions of women and children. Youmans prepared a fourteen-page brief which presented new research and traditional rhetoric. The WWSA education committee had conducted a nationwide survey of states with and without woman suffrage, a "comparison of the kind of laws made by men alone and those made by men and women together," which showed "suffrage states" well ahead — even of allegedly progressive Wisconsin — in laws on issues from child labor and joint custody to eight-hour workdays, arguing for the expediency of suffrage. Youmans also argued for the justice of the ballot for women because "if bad conditions and bad laws do not prove that it is wrong for men to vote, bad conditions and bad laws do not prove that it is wrong for women to vote."

When antisuffragists won the majority of Milwaukee press coverage, Youmans impugned the women with her worst accusation: that they did not write their own news releases but "signed their names to newspaper articles sent them from the East." She later attempted to dismiss the "two anti-suffrage societies . . . in Milwaukee and Madison," which "together formed a so-called state association," as "of slight importance." But the "so-called" Wisconsin Association Opposed to Woman Suffrage, still led by wives of prominent politicans, swayed the press.[25]

The lone witness against woman suffrage again was Robert Wild, as in 1913, but he and his German-American Alliance — funded by the Milwaukee brewers — grabbed the headlines above undeniably biased stories. Youmans castigated the *Sentinel* for making only brief mention of women's testimony and the *Free Press* for arguing, despite the testimony, that women didn't want the vote. Press reports also failed to point out that suffragists had succeeded in winning widespread support from organizations such as the WCTU, although one leader had asked members to "lay aside their white ribbons when speaking for suffrage," according to the WWSA's Susan Miller Quackenbush. "But no amount of additional yards of white ribbon could add anything to the already existing antagonism of the brewers," as she wrote. The *Free Press* applauded the "antis" for ladylike comportment in refraining from speaking publicly at the hearing, but did not mention their aggressive lobbying of legislators and distribution of literature, as Youmans did. Still, she wrote, "suffragists have no quarrel with frank antagonists, whom they knew where to find" by following the "trail of the liquor lobby" which funded the front groups.

Youmans reserved her fury until after the session for the lawmakers "seduced" by the "liquor interests," whose legislative maneuvers on the floor left the WWSA "rather dazed." Opponents slyly amended a bill by adding abolition of some "dower rights"—but not all. The remnant of common law relegated women to the status of property and disinterred other "dead letters" long buried in lawbooks, forcing suffragists to oppose their own bill. In retaliation, Youmans vowed that the WWSA would issue an updated version of *Social Forces,* the compilation of legislators' voting records on "various representative measures." Since publication in 1913, she warned, "at least one assemblyman with a bad record" blamed his defeat on the women's "little yellow pamphlet."

Youmans refrained from blaming the legislative debacle on NAWSA's endorsement of state-level campaigns, but actions by the WWSA board in 1915 indicated preference for the Congressional Union's strategy and lobbying tactics. The WWSA board approved a restructuring of legislative work, in stages, agreeing first to deputations of "callers" on every congressman because, although both Wisconsin senators supported a federal amendment, only two of the eleven members of the House of Representatives favored full suffrage. The board later reworked WWSA boundaries to correspond to congressional districts, each with a convention, chairperson, and press officer; the practice, used by the Congressional Union, had been introduced by the WCTU and adapted by clubwomen long before.

The personal strain of appeasing NAWSA and espousing its policies, while preferring the Congressional Union's strategy and many of its methods, was evident in Youmans' relief when NAWSA called a conference for discussion of long-deferred "differences with the Congressional Union to be thoroughly threshed out." Instead, she would receive a thrashing from NAWSA for her candor in public and with the press, which apparently was uncommon among suffragists—or, for that matter, in politics.

In Chicago in June 1915, the contretemps occurred at the first mention of the Congressional Union controversy, when Youmans put forward a proposal for an arbitration process which for some women went too far in airing the internal dissension. NAWSA's Dr. Anna Howard Shaw ruled Youmans out of order—incorrectly—and tabled the resolution, which resulted in the "end of any formal action so far as the conference was concerned," Youmans wrote. Infuriated, she denounced Shaw's "decidedly arbitrary" action in a "solemn protest" which appalled some women in the audience but was appreciated by a hard-hitting bigcity press looking for a story.

Far from her "country press" practice of journalism, Youmans was not far enough to escape headlines in Chicago which preceded her home. In response to a *State Journal* item headlined "She Can Run the Toot Toot, Too," Youmans denied that she had "shouted 'steam-roller' or 'gag-rule'" and denounced the "startling inaccuracy" of reporters. "Stories printed in the Chicago papers that I was likely to be expelled or that I left the conference in a rage had their source only in the picturesque imaginations of . . . the city press," wrote the aggrieved source. "If anyone in future criticizes the *Freeman* for mistakes, I shall recommend that they give an interview to the Chicago *Examiner* or *Post* and see how it comes out."

From the Chicago fracas, Youmans, Gudden, and others in the Wisconsin delegation also returned to face further inroads on the WWSA. In their absence, Alice Paul announced plans for her own conference on "congressional work" in Wisconsin, against the wishes and the work of the WWSA. Only a week before, Youmans had proposed that it was "not necessary for us to agree in every detail with an organization to be able to work harmoniously." Now she was forced to take a firmer stand, declaring herself "wholly out of sympathy with many of the methods of the Congressional Union." The WWSA board unanimously supported Youmans and countered with a proposal for a joint committee and conference, which Paul rejected.

While still fending off Alice Paul and internal problems, the WWSA was blindsided by state lawmakers who suddenly proposed a bill which withdrew one of Wisconsin women's few political rights. For the WWSA, Youmans waged and lost a summerlong press campaign against a bill to replace elective county boards of education with appointive commissions. In Waukesha County, the *Freeman* campaign did succeed in winning an appointment to the board of education for a woman who previously had won by election, but other incumbents in the state were "legislated out of existence," Youmans wrote.

By the summer of 1915, the dismal outlook in Wisconsin sent discouraged state suffragists scattering across the country to more promising campaigns. Harriet Grim, the superintendent of schools in Darlington, spent her summer vacation working for suffrage in Pennsylvania. Milwaukee schoolteacher Flora Gapen Charter left her job for the New Jersey campaign. Maud Leonard McCreery of Green Bay worked as a paid organizer in Minnesota for two months and went on to New York State. The WWSA staff—Alice Curtis, Helen Haight, and Youmans— also fled headquarters by fall for the New York State campaign. In their absence, Youmans appealed to members to run the WWSA office and annual convention. Although she avowed trust in the democracy and discipline of the organization, her tone indicated only a desperation to escape from Wisconsin.

The New York State campaign revitalized the movement because of the innovative tactics of "General Carrie Chapman Catt" and her "flying squadrons" of suffragists. A "telephone brigade" conducted what may have been the first phonathon, each woman calling at least five men for a combined fund-raiser and opinion survey which found three-fourths of respondents favorable to suffrage. Catt called a boycott by working women to show their worth by returning to the "domestic sphere" for a day. The threat was sufficient; as New Yorkers and their press pondered women's place in schools, offices, stores, and even elevators, Catt called off the boycott. "New York women also were able to utilize all the experience of other states," Youmans wrote. "Methods in suffrage campaigning have improved greatly since our campaign was waged in Wisconsin."

Youmans worked in upstate New York, managing the Rochester publicity office in a methodical manner and wiring reports on the campaign to co-workers through her *Freeman* column. "The work is not different from what I am used to at home but more thorough and complete. I sent a budget of suffrage news to the three afternoon papers every morning and another of different items to two morning papers every afternoon." Although all but one of the papers were "editorially opposed" to suffrage, she reported that all were "fairly liberal in printing our contributions" in news columns.

The New York campaign was an example for suffragists across the country, according to historians and to Youmans, who called the campaign "an education and an inspiration." New York women were neither "cast down nor discouraged" when the referendum lost, but redoubled efforts; two days after the defeat, women in Manhattan alone raised $100,000 for a new campaign. Whether the money would fund a state or national campaign awaited the outcome of the next NAWSA convention, anticipated by suffragists everywhere.[26]

The 1915 New York campaign was most significant to the suffrage movement in freeing Catt from her commitment to the state organization. In December 1915, the WWSA delegation went to the NAWSA convention in Washington, D.C., to cast Wisconsin's vote for Catt without Youmans, who had championed her candidacy for years. For Youmans, the dismal year ended with a double burden of "illness and bereavement" when her mother died.[27] At the end of 1915, the low point of Youmans' presidency, her *Freeman* "suffrage department" was silent for six weeks as suffragists elsewhere rejoiced in the return of Carrie Chapman Catt to the presidency of "the National."

If change at the end of 1915 was welcome to Wisconsin suffragists, the challenge of autonomy was gone. Although NAWSA had provided few solutions and only increasing problems, the WWSA had survived and even prospered after the demoralizing referendum defeat. That the WWSA sometimes strayed from coordinated effort or seized on inappropriate tactics resulted from widespread desperation without direction from NAWSA. Women elsewhere did the same, as suffragists everywhere sought any means to the ballot.

After 1915, although the advent of Carrie Chapman Catt and her approach to winning the ballot would be reminiscent of their earlier reorganization of the WWSA, Wisconsin suffragists remained a diverse collective of women united only for the cause. Some would find that working under national direction offered a new challenge: conformity.

9

Women at War
Suffrage and Ratification, 1916–1919

I N January 1916, as the National American Woman Suffrage Association underwent its first change in leadership since almost the turn
of the century, Theodora Winton Youmans secretly acceded to a strategy
which would win full suffrage, nationwide, at last—but at the sacrifice
of Wisconsin first. NAWSA president Carrie Chapman Catt proposed
her "Winning Plan," which resolved the longstanding debate in the movement over strategy, between state-level and federal campaigns, by encompassing both routes to victory. First, state-level campaigns would ac-
crue sufficient electoral college pressure to force Congress to pass a federal amendment. Then, when the Constitutional amendment was sent
back to the states, women would conduct ratification campaigns—if,
Catt warned, women in "suffrage states" would remain organized.

Although Catt returned NAWSA to the "Anthony strategy," which Alice
Paul's Congressional Union had never abandoned, the plan did not resolve internal dissension in the suffrage movement. As historian Sara M.
Evans writes, "their strategic disagreements ran deep." The organizations differed even more on tactics, a rift which would widen irreparably
before the year was out.

The crucial commitment to Catt's "Winning Plan" was within NAWSA,
from state presidents, of whom Youmans was the prototype. Catt wanted
no more national and state leaders who were selected out of "sentiment
or gratitude." Instead, according to historian Eleanor Flexner, Catt sought
"a *working* board" of women with ability, independent means, and con-

nections to power—in other words, women like herself. Catt and Youmans were remarkably alike in many ways; both were Wisconsin natives, woman journalists, and early leaders in women's clubs. The two were even more alike in management style. As Evans writes, "the day for the amateur reformer had given way to the professional organizer."

Youmans' approval of the "Winning Plan" was a foregone conclusion when Catt called her "professional organizers" to the secret meeting in NAWSA headquarters in Washington, D.C., in January 1916. National board members and state presidents signed pledges to submit to national direction, to concentrate effort on a federal amendment, and to forestall further "hopeless campaigns." In few states were suffragists less hopeful than in Wisconsin.[1]

In Wisconsin, Youmans resumed her column in the *Waukesha Freeman* with new resolve in 1916, but she did not divulge the "Winning Plan" or her pledge for months, until Catt could come to the state. Instead, Youmans wrote only that women were "started on the last lap of our painful journey" with "the goal in sight" and personally vowed to "continue as long as it may be necessary."

Women could not know that suffrage would become a political necessity for a president and would be won by the end of the decade, the last decade in the "century of struggle." Historians suggest that in 1916, when Catt proposed her "Winning Plan" and women became a political priority, their suffrage seemed a certainty. However, women's accounts suggest otherwise. In 1913, Youmans had predicted that suffrage would not come until 1925; since, nothing had occurred to make her more sanguine. As late as 1916, even Catt predicted that success was six years away.[2]

That victory would come sooner was the result of women's new managerial approach to the business—a big business, by 1916—of winning suffrage. For the same reason, the "last lap" would be long and painful as women worked even harder to maintain the movement but a few years more. At the end, they would be remarkable less for their enterprise, as in earlier eras, than for their endurance.

In 1916, after a year in which the WWSA struggled to retain its hard-won stability against attempts to again split the state movement, some Wisconsin suffragists—especially Youmans—welcomed an end to the years of autonomy with relief. But not all. Her uncharacteristic delay in announcing the new strategy and her acquiescence to Catt's plan, as well as the NAWSA president's personal appearance, suggest that they anticipated displeasure in the WWSA when women would discover that Wisconsin clearly fell in the category of states where further referenda were deemed futile.

At last, weeks after the secret meeting in Washington, Youmans announced that Catt would come to the state to personally win Wisconsin women to her "Winning Plan." At a two-day conference in Milwaukee in March, Catt and suffragists from other states met with delegates from at least twenty Wisconsin towns. After hearing the speakers, women in the WWSA also heard out each other when Youmans concluded the conference with a "question box" to share "experiences and difficulties." Apparently, there were many.

Their difficulty in accepting Wisconsin's relegation to secondary status is understandable because, by 1916, suffrage was on the rise elsewhere. While the WWSA was to lobby only for legislative enactment of limited suffrage, Illinois women were preparing for their first presidential election since breaking the Mississippi River barrier. Western states now formed almost a solid "suffrage column," as women well knew. From California, the WWSA's Zona Gale and Harriet Bain sent best wishes to Catt and co-workers at the conference. "Greetings," they telegrammed, "from two political slaves in a land of free women."[3]

As women foresaw a WWSA which would be less entrepreneurial, indeed almost inseparable from "the National," new reasons for a rift arose. They now would implement national policy, not decide their own direction, and women who had resisted reorganization under Youmans were even more reluctant to follow Catt's plan. Even the WWSA board would not endorse the plan for months, and some women in the ranks simply awaited the next legislative biennium to rebel.

In 1916, in the second year of a legislative biennium, there was little for most members to do. Even leaders' attention to state lawmakers was minimal and the women's work essentially was accomplished by midyear. Instead, in a presidential election year, women targeted delegates to upcoming conventions of national parties to press for suffrage planks in their platforms. In May, Wisconsin Democrats invited the women to meet with delegates for the first time. At the time, Youmans was in Minneapolis to address a NAWSA conference but curtailed plans to stump Minnesota and sped back to represent the WWSA. Youmans found the men attentive, a few even sympathetic, and all polite—although state Democrats did not endorse suffrage. State Republicans did not issue a similar invitation to meet with delegates. But they would hear from the women anyway, because NAWSA called a parade for the national Republican party convention in Chicago in June to impress delegates with women's determination.

Upon Catt's call to come to Chicago, Youmans seized on the parade to serve another purpose in the WWSA: maintaining morale of impatient members. Promoting a turnout with the most elaborate preparations yet seen in the state movement, she commissioned an artist to design colorful "suffrage regalia"—yellow tunics emblazoned with "On Wisconsin" and coordinated hats, available at $3.10 "including expense of round-trip ticket" in a Milwaukee department store—and WWSA office manager Helen Haight made a matching banner.

On the day of the parade, most women met in Milwaukee at the public library and marched east more than a mile and a half down Grand Avenue to the Chicago and Northwestern depot, to the beat of a Grand Army of the Republic drum corps which accompanied them onto a waiting train. "Special suffrage cars" also came from Madison and Waukesha, where women also had marched in step to the station with "drums beating and banners flying," Youmans reported. Banners, drums, and all, the "suffrage train" headed south, adding another car of women in Kenosha en route to Chicago.[4]

In Chicago, NAWSA arranged for parade elephants to bear a symbolic "suffrage plank"—literally, a board—missing from the GOP platform, but a sudden prairie storm stole the show, soaking the festive garb of ten thousand "weary, bedraggled women," who would not stop their "two-mile tramp" in gale-force winds. "The suffrage hosts marching down Michigan Avenue in a downpour of rain and gale of wind testified to their heartfelt desire for the ballot, in the presence of the delegates to the national Republican convention there looking on—at least we ardently desired them to be looking on," Youmans wrote. They were looked upon with awe by unruly male onlookers, who ridiculed the marchers at first but fell silent in admiration as women stayed in the ranks despite a driving torrent.

Another scene-stealer in the parade was Olympia Brown, past WWSA president and past eighty years old. Amid the Wisconsin contingent's regimented line of march and colorful regalia, she wore her usual dark dress and left the line to march with her niece in the Kansas unit. Despite Brown's defection, Youmans counted Wisconsin's "imposing" showing as a success; the state had the second-largest contingent, surpassed only by that of Illinois.[5]

Through the summer of 1916, Youmans continued to encourage parades and other diversionary tactics for the WWSA. She called on local suffrage associations to bring out women for Independence Day festivities on the Fourth of July. Racine women built a suffrage float and Berlin suffragists rode in cars draped in yellow roses. In Waukesha, Youmans carried the "On Wisconsin" banner as she led a contingent of women costumed in Chicago parade regalia down Main Street. Weeks later, she won a vague "declaration of loyalty" to Catt's "Winning Plan" from the WWSA board, at last.

At the same emergency meeting, called by Youmans in July in response to an invitation to participate in a "preparedness parade" in Milwaukee, the WWSA board also made clear that, no matter how much suffragists loved a parade, the women would not be lured into marching to war. Youmans' public explanation of the unanimous board action was revealing; the suffrage banner no longer was symbolic of a broad moral crusade for a better world. Instead, the WWSA was a special-interest group prey to shifts in politics and public opinion. As she wrote, many members were "ardent advocates of peace," but the WWSA "stands for only the one thing, woman suffrage, thus uniting in its membership people of the most widely differing opinions on other subjects."

Neutrality pleased few papers in Milwaukee, in the German- or English-language press, and many escalated editorial attacks on suffragists by mid-1916. To her critics, Youmans replied "that this preparedness propaganda . . . has grave elements of danger. It is idle to assert that we are preparing only 'for defense.' All countries arm nowadays, 'for defense' only."

But as late as 1916, the WWSA's morale was endangered less by impending war than by inactivity. In the summer and into the fall, most WWSA funds and many members went to more promising states in Catt's "Winning Plan." Maud Leonard McCreery of Green Bay contracted to give a suffrage speaking tour in South Dakota. Two Iowa natives, WWSA vice president Jessie Jack Hooper and executive secretary Alice Curtis, who took a leave from her post, returned to their childhood home to help in the state's referendum campaign and were supported by $500 from the WWSA.

For another former Iowan, NAWSA's Carrie Chapman Catt, the referendum was more than one of three crucial campaigns for the first year of her strategic plan; it also was a matter of pride. Catt returned four times, including one monthlong marathon, to the state where she first led campaigns almost three decades before. But suffrage was lost by ten thousand votes, mainly in "wet" counties where the WCTU found almost as many fraudulent ballots. As Catt wrote, "some dead men vote,

"Some dead men vote, as do some who have never been born, and yet the women are not let in . . . with the boys."—Carrie Chapman Catt, a Ripon native, the last president of the National American Woman Suffrage Association and the founder and first president of the National League of Women Voters. Photo courtesy of the State Historical Society of Wisconsin.

as do some who have never been born, and yet the women are not let in . . . with the boys."[6]

Youmans and her shorthanded staff stayed in place in 1916. Helen Haight temporarily took on organizing duties ordinarily conducted by Curtis and spoke at several small-town fairs. Haight also helped Youmans at a weeklong membership-training session held at Tower Hill in Iowa County, a "colony" for "suffrage pilgrims." In the office, Youmans and Haight also modernized the WWSA's publicity operations as the Wisconsin Woman Suffrage Press Service. Youmans restricted use of multipurpose organizational stationery to correspondence; for news releases, it was replaced by a special letterhead listing Haight as on-site contact for reporters' queries — a practice as yet uncommon in the corporate sector.[7]

WWSA publicity held up Wisconsin as a holdout against suffrage. For example, one featured a letter from a former Waukesha woman who wrote of her shame for her homeland. At a faculty gathering at her out-of-state college, women from Illinois, Colorado, California, and Washington — some "who could not remember when their mothers didn't vote"—were amazed that Wisconsin still withheld suffrage. "I was made to feel very backwoodsy indeed, to be so desperately behind the trend of things," she wrote Youmans. "It's the first time I ever had to be ashamed of Wisconsin."

The WWSA news service also publicized NAWSA research. Releases noted that in the West and the steadily growing number of limited-suffrage states, an estimated four million women were eligible to vote for president; that in full-suffrage Montana, former NAWSA worker Jeanette Rankin was running for Congress; that railroads asked for office space in national party headquarters to assist women from suffrage states, working in Washington, to return home to vote — a standard practice for men in the nation's capital.

As the 1916 election neared, publicity by NAWSA and the new National Woman's Party exerted pressure on the primary holdout against suffrage, President Woodrow Wilson. The Woman's Party was founded in the West, where women already voted, by Alice Paul, the founder of the Congressional Union who had defected from NAWSA to lobby more stridently for suffrage. Paul and co-worker Lucy Burns then brought their new organization to the East and almost to the president's door, where they placed responsibility for the Democratic party's failure to achieve suffrage despite control of the White House and both houses of Congress. The two women raised over $25,000 for headquarters in

Washington, D.C., to defeat Democratic candidates, whether for or against suffrage.

Publicity on the diametrically opposed tactics of NAWSA and the Woman's Party served the suffrage movement well. "Together they succeeded more rapidly than either could have alone," writes Sara M. Evans. A rare example of cooperative effort had been a massive parade on the day of President Wilson's first inaugural. When he arrived, "his greeters had already left to see the suffrage parade," where "five thousand women stole the scene as they pressed their way through a hostile crowd down Pennsylvania Avenue."

More often, the Woman's Party practiced more militant tactics that contrasted with NAWSA's constraint—but their differences also served the movement. The "aggressive lobbying and publicity campaign" conducted by Alice Paul "provided a radical voice within the movement redefining the parameters of the debate" and "made the disciplined and effective work of NAWSA seem moderate and reasonable by comparison," writes Evans, echoing William H. O'Neill's point that the militancy of the Woman's Party only "emphasized the reasonableness of NAWSA's position."

Once radical, now moderate, NAWSA's positioning attracted women and Wilson by 1916 when, if the time for suffrage had not come, for the first time a president came to a suffrage convention—the largest convention in suffrage history. Not so subtly, Catt moved up the national convention months earlier than usual, to precede the presidential election in 1916. By then, NAWSA membership had more than doubled in a decade to more than one hundred thousand women, as Wilson knew when he came before their delegates in Atlantic City.[8]

Youmans covered the 1916 national convention for the WWSA news service as well as the *Freeman* and gave Wisconsin editors an eyewitness account of a major story. With the First Lady at his side, President Wilson addressed the women last on the program, as he had asked. But Wilson did not have the last word. As Youmans reported, he first commended the women on "the force behind you," four million voters strong, and then infuriated them: "'I have not come to ask you to be patient, because you have been, but . . . you can afford a little while to wait,' the president said. When he closed, the audience made another lively demonstration, but perhaps the real climax of the evening came when Dr. Shaw," the beloved past president of NAWSA, "was asked to say a closing word, looked straight at the president and said: 'We have waited long enough to get the vote. We want it now.'"

Catt called the moment a turning point in the campaign for the president's support, but the response of women to Wilson and to Shaw is a point of debate. According to historian Eleanor Flexner, when Shaw stood down the president, the audience of women rose spontaneously and silently to stand with her. According to Youmans' eyewitness account, "the audience shouted with delight at Dr. Shaw's appeal," while "Mr. Wilson smiled with some self-consciousness." The more moving anecdote has entered the history of the movement but may be mythology—although the creation of suffrage mythology, of perception over reality, itself suggests how expert women had become in the tactics of a political campaign.[9]

To suffragists, the president's appearance before the convention was evidence of their comeback in less than a year under Catt. To the managerial Youmans, ever mindful of the bottom line, the convention demonstrated that women wielded economic power as well as electoral pressure; at one session, they "could afford" to raise $800,000 in a single hour. To Youmans and her readers, the convention also indicated Catt's regard for the WWSA contingent of Jessie Jack Hooper, Meta Schlichting Berger, and Dr. Ellen Sabin, president of Milwaukee-Downer College, as well as Youmans. Hooper had served in a "women's honor guard" to receive Wilson, while Youmans was made a member of NAWSA's platform committee. As she summed up the story in the *Freeman,* "the whole convention" had "a strong political flavor, very suggestive of our advanced position."

The WWSA increased press coverage and political pressure as election day neared, not only initiating news releases but also staging news events, which served the secondary purpose of occupying idle state suffragists. In Waukesha, women presented a "Voiceless Speech," miming messages on banners in a "gaily decorated store window all in suffrage yellow," Youmans wrote. The stunt was part of a nationwide NAWSA promotion, "Federal Amendment Days," held late in October "to impress the people in general and candidates for congress in particular" on the eve of the election. The WWSA news service tied reports of stunts to nationwide research, a NAWSA "suffrage survey" of candidates' stands on the issue. Almost half of Wisconsin candidates replied to Youmans' questionnaires, a return rate which suggests suffragists' success. Survey results also seemed promising; a WWSA release reported, in both tabular and interpretive forms, that sixteen of eighteen respondents favored a federal amendment. However, only three represented major parties.

Nationwide, the 1916 election results encouraged suffragists—especially the election of one of their own to Congress, Jeanette Rankin of Montana. Trained by "the National," Rankin used "the knowledge she acquired of human nature in the suffrage campaign" to win her race for the House of Representatives, wrote Youmans. Rankin gave her "maiden speech" not in the House but from the porch of NAWSA headquarters, to the rejoicing of "women who gave her a proud and happy escort to the Capitol." There, Youmans wrote—with apparently unintentional irony—"the House rose as one man upon her entrance."

Regarding President Wilson's reelection, reaction among suffragists was split. NAWSA publicity claimed that women in the West reelected Wilson as the candidate most likely to "loosen his position" on suffrage. But Alice Paul claimed that the National Woman's Party had almost cost Wilson the election, while her earliest recruit in the WWSA, Olympia Brown, wrote to Youmans that the Woman's Party held the only hope of success. Imperturbable, Youmans reported all claims in the *Freeman* and in the *Citizen,* and concluded that "indications are, on the whole, promising."[10]

In Wisconsin, the WWSA was especially pleased by results of state congressional and legislative races—to the displeasure of some in the press. Antisuffrage Democratic candidates for Congress were defeated, and all three incumbents won reelection as "open and recorded suffragists, good friends and supporters," Youmans wrote. She predicted that results in legislative races also would give women a "fair chance" for presidential suffrage in the state. The relatively mild editorial aside drew an enraged response from a longtime foe, the *Milwaukee Free Press.* Youmans countered with a lengthy and feisty "open letter" to the editor, reminiscent of her press debates in the 1911–12 campaign, with carefully researched and referenced "statistical data" from the *Wisconsin Blue Book* and the *Milwaukee Sentinel.* Youmans also disseminated her defense to other papers and published it in her column because she "doubted the letter's appearance in the paper to which it was sent"— and was gleeful when the *Free Press* "feared to print" the letter, as the *Freeman* reported in a self-righteous stand for free speech. Her attention to local "press surveys" included praise as well; she singled out Kenosha *Evening News* reporter Lucy E. Strong for "regular support" amid a "generally antisuffrage" state press.

The election results clearly revived Youmans and the WWSA to a level of energy and cooperative effort not seen since mid-1914. Although many in the WWSA still were resistant to NAWSA strategy, Youmans eased her relentless internal campaign to win their pledge to Catt's "Winning

Plan." Although she reiterated the long-term purpose of amassing electoral pressure for a federal amendment, Youmans publicly and endear-
ingly admitted a personal distaste for piecemeal, state-by-state suffrage.
"It is not fair to force women to seek enfranchisement in this difficult
and humiliating way," she wrote. Youmans' candor apparently moved
her co-workers. The WWSA board, whose support had been vague at
best, at last endorsed a legislative campaign for presidential suffrage
only. Pleased, Youmans promised women that "legislative as well as congressional work will be our main lines of activity during the coming
year."

Yet, once again, Youmans turned the WWSA to national directives
as NAWSA's more immediate priority—money—intervened. With a
nationwide campaign becoming ever more costly, Catt launched a "Dollar
Friends" drive which relied heavily on "hopeless" states like Wisconsin
to support more promising campaigns elsewhere. Youmans set a statewide goal of $25,000 and promoted the fund drive weekly in print and
almost daily in person, in more than one hundred Wisconsin cities and
towns. In a single week, she spoke in Milwaukee and Kenosha on Friday, on Saturday in Stevens Point, and twice on Monday in Oshkosh,
where she declined a third opportunity. The next week, in Waukesha,
Youmans held the equivalent of a modern "phonathon" from the *Freeman* and secured $100, dollar by dollar.

For the good of the national cause, Youmans also stripped the WWSA's
operation to essentials. To reduce salary expenditures she did not replace Alice Curtis, the WWSA executive secretary who had taken leave
for the Iowa campaign and since had resigned to work as an organizer
in West Virginia. WWSA office manager Helen Haight, who had filled
Curtis' position unofficially, now expanded her job description to include the duties of state organizer, while Youmans handled her own
secretarial work. She also saved rent and overhead by closing WWSA
headquarters in Waukesha and moving into the Milwaukee local office.
Uncomplaining, Youmans took the train almost daily, although a too-
distant office and onerous secretarial duties had led her to threaten
resignation three years before. In 1916, the suffrage momentum made
the personal sacrifice worthwhile.

Youmans also suspended the *Wisconsin Citizen,* the state "suffrage
banner" first published by Olympia Brown almost thirty years before,
and substituted a monthly leaflet to local societies. The move may
not have been entirely to Youmans' credit—or blame, in the minds of
some in the WWSA—because, at the same time, Catt was streamlining

NAWSA publications. Youmans later praised the "long-expected con-solidation" of the three largest suffrage periodicals in the country: the *Woman's Journal* founded in 1870 by Lucy Stone and Henry B. Black-well; the *Woman Voter,* founded in 1910 as the monthly organ of New York City suffragists; and the *National Suffrage News,* the monthly or-gan of NAWSA. The new *Woman Citizen,* a weekly "staffed by women for women" that eventually reached a circulation of two million mem-bers, was made possible by the promise of a million-dollar bequest to Catt from Miriam Florence Follin. Also known as the Baroness de Bazus, she had been better known to women as "Frank Leslie," publisher of *Leslie's Magazine.*[11]

Catt also laid plans for a far more massive and costly publicity cam-paign to be undertaken upon receipt of the Leslie legacy, a shift in em-phasis from internal to external publics of which Youmans approved. "The amount expended for press, literature, etc. is much too little," she wrote. "We cannot change public opinion without this most effective aid, liberally employed."

Then Catt upped the stakes, apparently causing internal upheaval in the WWSA. Catt called a nationwide "Million Dollar Drive" to replace the ongoing "Dollar Friends" campaign and set Wisconsin's goal at $25,000. That the amount was uncannily the same as the goal already set by Youmans for the WWSA's donation to the earlier drive was coinci-dental, she claimed. The continued emphasis on national rather than state needs — and the similarity in fund drive goals — apparently rankled the WWSA ranks, and finally turned Youmans testy. Suffragists' "fun-damental finance problem," she wrote, was that asking for money was "rather a bugaboo to some women," beyond her understanding. "They have not approached the matter from a properly scientific standpoint. Raising money is a question of applied psychology of the most absorb-ing kind."

For 1917, Youmans outlined a "most systematic line of work" which anticipated modern management techniques. First, in the prescribed form of the later "management by objectives" format, she set broadly stated goals at state, county, and local levels, defined specific objectives to meet the goals, and assigned dollar amounts and deadlines. Youmans' plan for 1917 also predated by half a century several models of modern "two-way" public relations that stress monitoring publics over disseminating information.[12]

The first objective of county suffrage committees was "to keep us in-formed of local conditions." Only secondarily were committees "to carry out requests from headquarters" and "to bring pressure to bear from all parts of Wisconsin on our national and state representatives" in "every congressional district, eleven in all," all to complement the work of organizer Helen Haight. As Youmans wrote, "What can one woman do to organize women all over the state of Wisconsin?" Lobbyist Jessie Jack Hooper's work to organize men was going well, Youmans wrote. She now counted seven prosuffrage members of the state's delegation in the House of Representatives, up from two only two years before, while Wisconsin's senators both still favored a federal amendment.

But state legislators needed to see legions of suffragists. Youmans' plan included a line-item budget which corresponded to goals and objectives by emphasizing expansion of the base of suffrage support. She listed expenses for organization at $2,400, almost equal to overhead itemized down to postage and utilities. Sums of $1,000 each were allotted to "press work," to "literature," and to costs of all WWSA standing committees including "legislative work." With a tithe to NAWSA of ten cents from every hard-earned local dollar, the WWSA budget for the coming year totaled $7,496.

As 1917 opened, the WWSA attempted to conduct suffrage business as usual at its convention in Madison in January, delayed from its usual fall date owing to the rescheduling of the NAWSA convention. Youmans delivered her best presidential address yet, a balance of anecdotes and data, logic and persuasion, biblical passages and personal reminiscence. Recalling her New York State campaign stint in the "cultured East," she provided an optimistic perspective on Wisconsin's situation; the proud descendant of Pilgrim stock had not enjoyed her encounter with "Plymouth rock-ribbed conservatism." In the East, she said, "there are actually people there who take the antis seriously." Suffragists also faced the intransigent "political boss," a corrupt institution which rivaled the scourge of Wisconsin, the Brewers Association.

Attendance appeared to support Youmans' optimism, as turnout almost lived up to the convention slogan of "Every County There." A record number of women came from across Wisconsin with "the ability, the initiative, the energy and the inclination to become active in suffrage work," Youmans wrote. "The average reader cannot imagine what this means to those who are carrying the heat and burden of the suffrage campaign." The average reader also was told only that the convention had approved Youmans' plan for the coming legislative biennium, a campaign limited to presidential suffrage. Above all, in her convention address and postconvention coverage, Youmans minimized dissent and emphasized unity, although the approval of a limited-ballot campaign came only after long debate, and some suffragists were notable by their absence. Ada James now served on the national council of the Congressional Union, and Olympia Brown refused all invitations to WWSA events. However, neither had made her defection widely known, which suggests that Youmans was not alone in concern for an appearance of unity.[13]

More notable by its absence from Youmans' presidential address in 1917 was any mention of the conflict overseas, or within the WWSA. Women may have feared that exposure of their internal dissension would result in a repeat of the 1912 debacle, when their feud had contributed to defeat. The feud still was fresh in the collective memory of the movement and the press, as Youmans noted. Summing up 1916, she stressed the strides which the WWSA had made since the referendum in "getting out from under the shadow of that catastrophe for the cause." The loss "is still quoted against us," she said, although "conditions have changed so radically since that vote was taken that it can no longer be quoted *fairly* against us."

The reference to the futility of the referendum route also may have been a warning. Continued resentment by Wisconsin women of their state's relegation to secondary status soon would erupt, eroding their carefully constructed semblance of unity—even before Catt amended her "Winning Plan" to take women to war.

For suffragists elsewhere, the war did not come so close to home until February 1917. For example, as the year opened, Catt wrote from Washington headquarters with eastern condescension—and incomprehension—to Youmans and other state presidents "who lived in the interior" where "the war may seem a long way off." Clearly, Catt had been away too long from her native Wisconsin, long war-torn by nativist debate.

Within weeks, the possibility of war precipitated a crisis for the suffrage cause as well as the country. The Woman's Party continued to protest the president's lack of support for suffrage by adopting picketing, a tactic employed earlier in England and a "public act even more spectacular than parades and demonstrations," according to historian Aileen S. Kraditor. In January 1917, when the Woman's Party began picketing the White House daily, the ploy earned few headlines, until antiwar protesters picketed the White House as well. The press and public confused the issues and deemed not only the Woman's Party but all suffragists to be disloyal.

Unfortunately for the WWSA, the 1917 convention coincided with the escalation in the East of more militant women's tactical war on Wilson. The story even had a local angle for the state press when Olympia Brown, at eighty-two years old, came from her daughter's home in Baltimore to join the Woman's Party's picket line at the White House. In Wisconsin, editors combined stories on suffragists meeting sedately in the state Capitol with coverage of women picketing at the White House. To Youmans' dismay, the press made no attempt to distinguish between the WWSA and the Woman's Party or between antiwar protesters and anti-Wilson pickets.[14]

The WWSA also earned a storm of press disapproval during the 1917 convention for sponsorship of a speech by an antiwar Socialist. Max Eastman, editor of *The Masses,* had longstanding ties to Wisconsin suffragists; his sister, Crystal Eastman, had been PEL campaign manager in 1912 when he had served as the titular head of a men's suffrage league in the state. In Madison on business during the WWSA convention, Eastman offered to give a benefit address. The assembly chamber "was packed to the ceiling, in the high balconies, and packed to the doors, with scores of people standing the whole evening" for Eastman, who "kept the audience in a chuckle of merriment and a ripple of applause" and brought in $70 for the suffrage cause, Youmans wrote.

The applause died in the days after the WWSA convention when "some Milwaukee papers" questioned suffragists' patriotism, despite Youmans' endless reiterations that Eastman's address had been only on suffrage. She attempted to defend the WWSA and even the Woman's Party until at last, exasperated with the press, she wrote that "whatever plan is adopted by suffragists is bound to be the wrong thing in the eyes of critics." Unfortunately for the WWSA, Youmans' prediction proved to be all too correct.

Two weeks after the 1917 WWSA convention, Youmans reported with relief that Catt had called NAWSA's national executive council to an emergency meeting on suffragists' role in the event of the country's entry into the war. In print, Youmans worried about "the certainty that war, real war, war that is bloody and brutal beyond words is coming to this country." But she also fretted for the suffrage cause, wondering "What will happen to the woman suffrage movement in case the worst happens and this country goes to war? What is best to do with the suffrage organizations, which cannot, it may be presumed, go on effectively with their regular work?"

But, as before, Youmans did not reveal the new directive from "General Catt." At the meeting in NAWSA headquarters in Washington, D.C.,

in February 1917, well before the president called on Congress to declare war, Catt called on NAWSA's national board and state presidents
to support Wilson—whichever way he went.[15]

Youmans returned from Washington to restlessness in her ranks with
the new legislative biennium in 1917, as unhappiness with Catt's plan
for the state surfaced again, for good reason; increasingly, Wisconsin
was an outpost of antisuffragism. After the 1916 election, the number
of eligible women voters nationwide doubled to more than eight million
as suffrage won in eight states—even in Ohio, to the astonishment of
Youmans, since the state was "almost as much a center of the brewery
interest as Milwaukee."

The parallel with Wisconsin proved all too true as Youmans and her
readers followed the saga of suffrage in Ohio. "The liquor interests" won
repeal of Ohio's legislative enactment of suffrage. Ohio women then won
a bill for a referendum on full suffrage, and won again at the polls—
only to lose on a recount when antisuffrage ballots were suddenly "discovered." Ohio women had made suffrage history by winning and losing the ballot twice in a single year, as Youmans wrote. On her own
state's intransigence, she added with rare sarcasm that "Wisconsin's pro-
gressiveness has weak spots."

The WWSA's own "weak spots" were spotlighted in 1917 when impatient members refused to abide by the convention's recent endorsement of a campaign for legislative enactment of limited suffrage. Instead, they submitted a bill for a full-suffrage referendum.[16] Reaction
was immediate; Catt censured the WWSA, and Jessie Jack Hooper resigned as lobbyist. Youmans waited. When chagrined sponsors backed
down on their own bill, which failed, she issued a stern public rebuke
and suggested that "suffragists will endeavor to keep it in mind in future
political contests."

By the time that Youmans quelled the Wisconsin revolt against the
"Winning Plan," resentment turned to open rebellion with the entry of
the United States into war—a war which nowhere was more divisive
than in Wisconsin. As early as 1914, upon the outbreak of the "European War," Youmans had called for suffragists and clubwomen to "declare for peace," and a WWSA-sponsored public "peace meeting" had
passed a resolution sent to President Wilson in favor of neutrality. However, in 1915, fear of public censure had led the WWSA to reject the
same resolution. In 1916, when the WWSA refused to march in Milwaukee's "preparedness parade," the press was fanning prowar and anti-
German sentiment so ardently that the *Journal* would win a Pulitzer

Prize for its "loyalty crusade."[17] Still, Youmans and the WWSA had stood firm for neutrality, if not outright pacifism — although both stances were equally prone to editorial denunciation as treason in the *Milwaukee Journal.*

In April 1917, when Wilson called for war, the WWSA was the first woman's group in the state to enlist on the homefront. When Youmans offered the WWSA's services to the Wisconsin Council for Defense, her action was not unusual. In the war hysteria, many in her field did the same; historian J. A. Thompson suggests that "progressive publicists" found an "opportunity to revive the evangelical idealism which was the essence of progressivism," with its "heightened social spirit, cooperativeness and self-sacrifice." Women also enlisted nationwide, a newly "organized and aroused womanhood" with whom "the war turned out to be enormously popular" and "made it possible for women who were not feminists to work for the common good" in "the Great Crusade," according to J. Stanley Lemons. In Wisconsin alone, a Woman's Committee soon organized eighty thousand women in twenty-five hundred branches.[18]

Yet Youmans, the premier spokesperson for suffragists, had been an impassioned pacifist in print. As early as 1914, she wrote that "women have always hated war. They see the blood and the loss and the pain, rather than the emptiness of military glory. The opinion of women counts more today than it ever has before . . . to abolish this unspeakable infamy." As late as April 1917, upon the declaration of war, Youmans defended the first woman in Congress when she cast her first vote in Congress against Wilson's call. Press accounts implying that Representative Jeanette Rankin could not handle the pressure incurred Youmans' wrath. A source in the House had personally assured her that, although Rankin "was profoundly agitated at the time," she "did not weep and did not faint. That was a picturesque detail added by the reporters."[19]

Now the press was equally critical of Youmans for her support of war. Pressed to explain her sudden switch, "illogical but true," logic failed her. Youmans could not bring herself to criticize Rankin but repudiated antiwar suffragists closer to home, Congressman Berger and Senator La Follette. In Youmans' apologia for putting patriotism over pacifism, her distress is evident in her atypical resort to the rhetorical device of writing in the third person, apparently an attempt to distance herself from words penned with pain: "The editor of this column is a pacifist. BUT — She believes that this is not the time to push the peace propaganda, and that those who insist upon doing so are in fact using their influence against peace. . . . intelligent people who appear to believe that it is a proper thing to chant the glories of peace even when the enemy is at your doors. I insist that my pacifism is just as genuine as theirs—and far more practical."

Previously, in each instance of internal differences, single-minded dedication to the cause of suffrage had triumphed in the Wisconsin suffrage movement, but this time, when Catt's calculated patriotism became public knowledge, WWSA leadership split openly and irreparably. Many women were forced to choose between the ballot and their German heritage or their Socialist or progressive politics. Some undeniably saw suffragism as secondary to a higher principle, pacifism. However, although some opted for principle over Catt's calculated patriotism, other defections from the WWSA clearly were overdue because they paralleled battle lines long drawn over differing strategies and tactics.

This time, WWSA defectors had an alternative in the neutral National Woman's Party. Sophie Gudden, born to nobility in Bavaria, apparently left her post as chair of the press committee first. She was followed by Zona Gale, an avowed pacifist, in June 1917. Her successor as first vice president served only a few months; Meta Schlichting Berger, the Socialist women's leader and wife of the congressman who was censured by the House of Representatives for his antiwar stance, soon resigned to work for the Woman's Party.

While Catt and her cohort placated the president, the continued picketing of the White House by the Woman's Party resulted in a confrontation which roused women across the country—including Olympia Brown. In June 1917, on Wilson's orders, White House pickets were arrested, imprisoned illegally, and treated brutally. As their plight became public, women from around the country came to Washington to take the pickets' place, including Olympia Brown. Her rage increased when Catt, who was in a position to protest to the president, disassociated NAWSA from the pickets.

The matriarch of the Wisconsin movement retained tenuous ties with the WWSA for a few months more. But within a year, Brown would exchange a bitter correspondence with Youmans. Youmans rejected an offer from Brown to campaign in Wisconsin because "their methods of work were different," singling out the wartime protest by the Woman's Party as "particularly objectionable." Brown responded with a considerable rewriting of history, claiming to have founded the WWSA and to have stepped down from the presidency "contrary to the wishes of all members," while denying any role in repeated rifts. "I have never sought to thrust myself into the enterprise of the society or to interpose my own idea or personal opinions," wrote Brown, who embarked on a campaign across Wisconsin anyway.[20]

Of the leaders from 1913 who had formed the new WWSA, the last to leave was Ada James, whose mother had helped to found the first WWSA almost forty years before. Well before 1917, James had resigned her committee posts in the WWSA to serve on the national council of the Congressional Union and then of the Woman's Party. However, she remained a member throughout the controversies over Catt's "Winning Plan" and wartime stance, until the fall of 1917.

Although the exodus of many WWSA leaders in 1917 may have been inevitable, the loss of Ada James was avoidable had Youmans handled a minor misunderstanding with her usual tact. In fall 1917, James and Berger received a request to represent suffragists at the state teachers' convention and accepted, apparently unaware that the invitation was intended for the WWSA. Convention planners apparently were unaware of the women's new affiliation—their attempt to minimize public exposure of internal schism succeeded, too well—until Youmans openly denounced both women and the Woman's Party. The conflict was smoothed over, publicly; the Woman's Party and the WWSA were represented at the convention and won state teachers' endorsement of a federal amendment—although the presence of Congresswoman Jeanette Rankin also helped immeasurably in securing the endorsement. Privately, Youmans apologized and James reciprocated, but she still quit the WWSA.[21]

Youmans' sensitivity to criticism was uncharacteristic but understandable in 1917 when, within days of the first arrests of women in Washington, D.C., she became embittered by a tragedy closer to home. In Waukesha in 1917, a scandalous "love triangle" ended in the murder of a leading townswoman by her husband's lover, and began a yearlong ordeal for Youmans. Not only was the victim a friend, but both murderer and victim also were past presidents of the Suffrage Club and prominent clubwomen. When a "free love" book reviewed by the murderer at a club meeting became part of her defense, the story lured reporters to Waukesha from as far as New York, and suffrage became a scapegoat in the courtroom and a laughingstock in the sensationalist press.

Although women at the White House committed no violence, the jailings in Washington and Waukesha commingled in Youmans' mind as she fell prey to the same unfair confusion of which she had often accused her colleagues in the press. Now, she sent out a WWSA news release that called the Woman's Party "that party of picketing and bonfires and fails," and penned a scathing but perceptive analysis of Alice Paul's "psychologically foolish" and "bad tactics." The Woman's Party, she wrote, "lives on publicity, and is press agented as no other organization in this country ever was press agented. It started out to put woman suffrage on the front page and it has succeeded in doing so. Waukesha people have had a demonstration just lately that first-page publicity is not always to be desired."[22]

But publicity was exactly what NAWSA needed, and Catt used the war as a catalyst for suffrage to prove women's patriotic worth. From "the National," the WWSA news service disseminated a dizzying mix of information, instructions, and appeals, from Liberty Bond drives to fund-raisers for the Red Cross and Navy League, from "new food knowledge" on planting "victory gardens" to old-fashioned patterns for knitting soldiers' socks and layettes for Belgian babies. Soon, NAWSA membership soared to two million women.[23]

NAWSA also conducted nationwide petition drives which addressed new and serious concerns of women in wartime. For men off to war, NAWSA funded a hospital on the front in France and campaigned against liquor sales and prostitution in Army training camps, which won "safety zones" for soldiers. For women taking men's place in the workforce, NAWSA's "equal pay for equal work" campaigns won major concessions from railroads. For women in the military, antidiscrimination campaigns relieved women doctors of demeaning nursing duty. In her column, Youmans took an even more courageous stand by promoting wider use of women in the military, citing the role of Russian women on the front lines of the 1917 revolution, as reported by American war correspondent Rheta Childe Dorr, who was "personally known to the writer."

NAWSA also endorsed temperance on the homefront but not the Anti-Saloon League's campaign for a Prohibition amendment, which competed for attention with suffrage.[24] In Wisconsin, where the campaign was especially controversial, the WWSA officially did nothing, no doubt fearing further attacks from the Brewers Association. Youmans personally endorsed Prohibition and acknowledged that the WWSA was a direct descendant of the state temperance movement. But Youmans carefully kept her position distinct from that of NAWSA and the WWSA, although she did serve on the state Council of Defense and its committee for promotion of Liberty Bonds.

Still, women's war for suffrage seemed endless until several significant events in 1917. One was a windfall of diamonds, pearls, emeralds, rubies, cash, and bonds delivered to NAWSA headquarters, only the first payment from the million-dollar bequest left by the publisher of *Leslie's Magazine*. The incredible infusion of funds enabled Catt to enact her long-awaited "nationwide campaign of agitation, education, organization and publicity" with the national Leslie Press Bureau of Suffrage Education under Ida Husted Harper, a national publicity council with departments in each state, and four campaign directors and two hundred organizers for monthly "propaganda demonstrations" simultaneously across the country as well as suffrage schools, speakers' bureaus, a campaign for "non-English speaking" publics, and other "innumerable activities."[25]

Also in 1917, a crucial victory in New York which suddenly swelled the "suffrage column" and electoral college count was a turning point in women's morale nationwide. "In spite of the great war with all its sorrow and apprehension," Youmans wrote, "the great triumph in New York was felt as a personal triumph by every woman . . . and as an earnest of still greater things to come." From correspondence with former WWSA members who had worked in the campaign and "made New York seem very close to Wisconsin," Youmans detailed work "of so amazing a character as to stagger the imagination": a petition which secured one million women's signatures "against that perennial objection that women do not want suffrage"; organization "on political lines down to the precinct level"; advertisements in every paper in the state, "drawn by the best advertising talent that could be secured"; the support of "the governor of New York State, the mayor of New York City [and] many other men in high position who were persuaded with all the ingenuity and mother-wit that could be imagined, not only to favor the suffrage amendment but to come out in its favor"; and "the patriotic work of New York women," from running army camp coffee houses to funding ambulance units to fund-raising for Liberty Bonds to conducting the military census statewide, door to door. "I doubt if a campaign of such extraordinary efficiency has ever been waged on the face of the earth before, either by men or women," she wrote.[26]

A veteran of the 1915 New York State campaign, Youmans felt "absolutely vindicated" by the victory which "practically settled keenly contested points in suffrage policy" such as Catt's "Winning Plan" for the WWSA. More mischievously, she envisioned the effect of the victorious campaign on New York politicians, "every one of whom, I venture to assert, is now assuring his new constituents that he always really believed in woman suffrage in his heart but felt obliged, under the circumstances, etc., etc."

Youmans' revived spirits and return to wry humor did not signify that the WWSA's worries were over; NAWSA's orders to remain organized for ratification campaigns became increasingly difficult to carry out after 1917. In Wisconsin, after the abortive attempt at a referendum in the 1916–17 biennium, there was little to do but lobbying. The task was handled by new first vice president Jessie Jack Hooper, who called in Youmans to cultivate congressmen and party platform committees and also cooperated with James, Berger, and other former WWSA members who lobbied for the Woman's Party.

Most women in the WWSA had nothing to do but wait, a new concern for leaders as docile members no longer fought conformity to the "Winning Plan." Instead, as Catt had feared, with the probability of success came the possibility of complacency.

To maintain morale, Youmans took on the task of rallying a WWSA less divided and more receptive to her weekly missives to do "double duty" for war as well as suffrage. For 1917, she called a "loyalty convention" in Milwaukee in November to be "devoted to patriotism and patriotic worth and permeated by patriotic fervor," she wrote, with a redundancy which suggested her own lack of fervor for endless exhortation. Creativity relieved the tedium of the convention program as Youmans called on each local organization to "tell briefly in a sort of 'feature story'" about war efforts and was rewarded with anecdotes from Kenosha women who raised funds with a "white elephant" sale, Oshkosh and Milwaukee women who held "jonquil markets" and sold Liberty Bonds, and Sheboygan women who sponsored a "Soldiers Supper." Speakers' topics included women in the workforce, food conservation, Americanization, "The First Line of Defense—Our Boys," and "The Last Line of Defense—Our Women."

In marked contrast to the WWSA convention of a year before, Youmans' 1917 presidential address was uninspiring and her coverage innocuous. Only alluding to the losses of the year, and only at the end of her speech, she noted that the WWSA had "been entangled with certain pacifist, obstructionist difficulties now squarely cut through." Months later, she reported the passage of resolutions which "emphatically" repudiated the tactics of the Woman's Party.

In 1917, the loss of WWSA leaders made little difference to the state movement. There was little work in Wisconsin for the Woman's Party, which was strong only in states where women voted. From 1917 on,

Ada James and other former WWSA leaders, who constituted almost the entirety of the organization's presence in the state, primarily continued to cultivate legislators.[27] Their lobbying expertise was not lost to the cause and would prove crucial in the last days of the suffrage campaign in Wisconsin.

The news in 1917 was at the national level, as suffragists across the country awaited the NAWSA convention in the nation's capital to measure the effect of their war effort. In an advance, Youmans assured readers of a "final effort" for the federal amendment because "war service of women has become . . . more and more conspicuous," while NAWSA's "large staff of sanguine workers" knew that "not many more conventions of this association will be necessary." Indeed, the convention went so smoothly that Youmans had nothing substantive to add to the advance. Instead, she filed a revealing report on the convention's "social features," from a reception by cabinet wives to a luncheon by one of the city's "best ladies." Washington, D.C., now saw suffragists as acceptable, even fashionable, Youmans reported. The previous year's coup—the president's appearance—now made suffragists, for so long "outré, freaks and dowds," suddenly sought after and "distinctly 'in it.'"

At the same time, women still worried that their wartime tactics were not working, with reason. By November 1917, the House had created a subcommittee on the "Anthony amendment," but in hearings women heard only new objections to suffrage. NAWSA's Dr. Anna Howard Shaw, head of the women's committee of the National Council for Defense, attempted to reassure congressmen who were concerned that women's "largely developed sympathy for human suffering would tend to weaken prosecution of the war and lead to a speedy and ill-advised peace," wrote Youmans in near despair.

In Wisconsin, amid calls that organizations "cease activity during continuance of the war," Youmans feared for the cause. "The dropping of suffrage work now would mean . . . the disintegration of headquarters, the cessation of suffrage argument. It would mean the practical loss of all the tremendous amount of labor . . . needed to bring the suffrage situation up to the point at which it now is. The war may last several years." Women who had upheld their end of the wartime bargain with Wilson could not know that the war actually would accelerate suffrage. The president still had not come out publicly for the ballot by the end of 1917.

In 1918, owing only in part to Wilson's influence, the House at last passed the "Anthony amendment" first introduced forty years before. Women across the country rallied to NAWSA's call for pressure on members of the House. In Wisconsin, a "frightfully tired" Jessie Jack Hooper recounted to Youmans her frantic, last-minute work in key congressional districts, in correspondence cited as a classic account of suffrage lobbying: "I traveled over a good deal of districts not making public speeches but seeing men who were politically prominent. Some days I got up at 5:30, took an electric train, and did not get home until midnight, talking the question out with from six to eight men and going from office to office all during the day." Overcoming snowstorms and small-town streetcar service, Hooper "worked up until the last moment, until I knew nothing more could reach Washington, and then I gave it up." Although apologetic for her "nervous and physical exhaustion," she was "not complaining," wrote Hooper. "I would do it all over again to get the result even if I were in bed for six months."[28]

The House vote encouraged Hooper. She was "sure of six votes and hoped for seven" of eleven Representatives, Youmans wrote, but snared a surprising eighth toward the total of 274 yeas to 135 nays. Congressmen were no less surprised when women watching from the House galleries responded to the historic vote with an eerie hymn-sing of "Old Hundredth." In Wisconsin, Youmans responded instead with a wartime metaphor: "We have won. We are over the top. We have captured one of the three most important trenches on the way to complete enfranchisement." However, women still needed Wilson's outright support to carry Congress across the second "trench": Senate passage.

In Wisconsin, the WWSA reenlisted with new enthusiasm in "Woman Suffrage and Women's War Work," the new name which Youmans adopted for her *Freeman* "suffrage department," long under the logo of "Votes for Women." Women's causes of suffrage and war became so intertwined in the column that NAWSA fund-raising appeals ran next to promotions of Liberty Bonds and Americanization campaigns, calls for "Potato Patriots" and student nurses, recipes for meat and wheat substitutes, and items on a "patriotic essay" contest run by Ada James. Youmans even interviewed a Red Cross worker for knitting tips on turning out a respectable toe, in an unwittingly hilarious column that revealed how little of the homebody she had in her.

Youmans also toured the state incessantly to rally her troops to suffrage and war work. In a week, she spoke in Racine one day, Rhinelander the next, and Manitowoc two days later. Reviewing a speech in Racine, the *Times-Call* praised Youmans as "'seething and boiling' with

"Some days I got up at 5:30 . . . and did not get home until midnight, talking the question out with from six to eight men. . . . I worked up until the last moment, until I knew nothing more could reach Washington, and then I gave it up. . . . I would do it all over again to get the result."—Jessie Jack Hooper of Oshkosh, a lobbyist for the Wisconsin Woman Suffrage Association and the National American Woman Suffrage Association, and the first president of the Wisconsin League of Women Voters. Photo courtesy of the State Historical Society of Wisconsin.

patriotism." Bemused, she expressed her appreciation for "a compliment which takes time to assimilate."

In June 1918, Wilson cautiously tested press reaction when he wrote to Catt with his first public endorsement of suffrage. In Wisconsin, Youmans gleefully reported an onslaught of state editors clambering aboard the suffrage bandwagon, including the *Evening Wisconsin* and *Sentinel* in Milwaukee, the *Oshkosh Northwestern,* the *Watertown Times,* and the *Superior Telegram.* However, the *Milwaukee Free Press*—her nemesis—remained recalcitrant, and Youmans remained watchful even of prosuffrage papers. For example, one "friendly paper" invited her ire for its play of a straight news story, an article on women in overalls replacing men in uniform, which ran with the lighthearted headline, "Who'll Wear the Pants?" Dashing off a personal endorsement of the "practicality" of the apparel, she archly informed her offending colleague that "the editor of this column finds the heading extremely objectionable. What have 'pants' to do with a great question of democratic principle?"

Through 1918, suffrage publicity pointed out the hypocrisy of advancing democratic principles overseas while denying women the ballot at home. A NAWSA news release timed for play on Independence Day counted more than forty million women now enfranchised in other countries including England, Canada, and Russia. At last, with the war almost behind him but a battle ahead for public support of his peace, the president capitulated. In October 1918, Wilson personally appeared before the Senate to plead women's cause, to no avail. "Not a vote was changed," a despondent Youmans wrote.

Despite the setback in the Senate, suffragists in Wisconsin halted their statewide activity only for the postwar influenza epidemic. In the fall of 1918, restrictions on public events to reduce the chance of contagion canceled the WWSA convention. Relieved of the need to repeat the unrelenting patriotism of the previous year's convention, Youmans relied on the WWSA's newsletter and news service to publicize her annual presidential address, committee reports, and suffrage fund appeals.

On election day in fall 1918, state after state yielded to displays of women's patriotic worth. The addition of three more "suffrage states" raised to eleven million the number of women able to vote nationwide, reported Youmans, and antisuffrage congressmen were forcibly "retired" by voters even in Wisconsin. At the same time, she was troubled by the impact of the coming peace on the suffrage campaign in Congress, where NAWSA lobbyists were told to wait again, wrote Youmans bitterly, because "the Senate is terribly crowded with important legislation these days."

In February 1919, while watching Washington, women greeted Wisconsin's belated enactment of limited, presidential suffrage with the restraint the bill deserved. The new biennium reunited Youmans, James, and others for their routine pilgrimage to Madison, where legislators passed the bill with surprising speed but little enthusiasm; the men apparently had resigned themselves to the inevitable. Youmans also credited the easy victory to crude lobbying methods employed by a "fairly active" antisuffrage association, whose "letters of protest enraged legislators." Nationwide, lawmakers were subjected to an increasingly "shrill" campaign, as "the antis" degenerated to "slander and vilification," exemplified by renaming their publication, previously *The Remonstrance,* as the *Woman Patriot,* according to historian William H. O'Neill. According to Catt, "the antis" also expanded their "extensive press bureau," which caused her worst "nerve stress" of the entire campaign.[29]

Youmans' lackluster reporting of the long-sought legislative enactment in Wisconsin is understandable, since women saw the law for limited suffrage—and that not to take effect until 1920—as, literally, the least that lawmakers could do. Signing the bill into law also was more than Governor Emanuel L. Philipp wanted to do, and it stayed on his desk for days. As Youmans wrote when the bill finally was signed, "he 'yolled' some about doing it but it is now a law."

Wisconsin legislators' action was especially anticlimactic because, at the same time that Wisconsin legislators acted, the federal amendment again came up in Congress and would have made the state's limited suffrage moot, had it passed. But a lame-duck Democratic Senate defeated the amendment by only one vote before the end of the session — the end of some senators' political careers. When Congress next convened and numbers of newly elected lawmakers took their seats, swift passage of the federal amendment seemed assured.

In 1919, at NAWSA's fiftieth "Jubilee Convention," a mood more businesslike than jubilant reigned. From St. Louis in March, Youmans reiterated Catt's exhortations to suffragists to remain organized, "so that when the federal amendment reaches Wisconsin it will be ratified at once." But her missives became more forced in the face of maintaining the WWSA through months of inactivity, and her column became little more than a scorecard of the "suffrage column," which now accounted for 339 of 531 electoral votes. From four million women voters in fall 1916, fifteen million held presidential or full suffrage in thirty-two states and the Alaska territory, with referenda pending elsewhere, in May 1919.[30]

In May 1919, the "Winning Plan" worked and Wilson capitulated. When he called Congress back to Washington for a special session, Catt called NAWSA forces back to the Capitol as well, including Youmans and Hooper. In Washington, Youmans wired back to Wisconsin that NAWSA was optimistic, although women knew better than to rely on promises of politicians. "Suffragists have counted up as carefully as is possible," she wrote, but could not count on Congress because "experience has taught them that a measure is much safer after it has actually passed than before."

Late in May 1919, Youmans and Hooper watched from the House galleries in seats reserved for "Mrs. Catt's ladies," aptly placed between the press section and a section set aside for the National Woman's Party. The same bill passed a year before, the "Anthony amendment," was passed and sent to the Senate again by a vote of 304 to 89. This time, Youmans wrote, women held their hallelujahs. "There was no excitement, no jubilee on our side. We knew the outcome beforehand. . . . The fight had been so long and the victory had come so gradually that it was difficult to grasp. We filed out smiling quietly at each other and that was all."

Two weeks later, on June 4, 1919, when the Senate passed the Nineteenth Amendment by a vote of 56 to 25, women did celebrate, Hooper among them. However, Youmans already was back in Wisconsin and back to work, because her state legislature still was in session.

That Wisconsin, for so long the despair of suffragists, would become the envy of the movement resulted in part from luck but primarily came from careful planning. A yen for glory also was a factor for legislators and suffragists alike, as Youmans wrote: "We of Wisconsin have been extremely ambitious to secure for our state the honor of being the first state to ratify, but other states have similar ambitions," and "half a dozen states have their legislatures now in session." She slyly singled out Illinois as having "set her heart on being first"—fighting words to awaken the competitive spirit in any Wisconsinite.

Legislators were still in session in Illinois as well as Wisconsin, while Michigan men swiftly went into special session, as lawmakers rushed to ratify suffrage only six days after the Senate vote. Illinois legislators actually acted first but erred; they had to recall and redo their document eight days later. In Wisconsin, wrote Youmans, "our lobby got settled to its task," as women anticipated every detail down to legal language of ratification and a recommendation to the governor of a courier to carry the document to Washington: David G. James, seventy-six years old and retired from the legislature where he had sponsored the 1912 referendum bill but in Madison for the day.

In Wisconsin, women divided by differences over strategies and tactics worked together again to win the ratification race: with Youmans in the Capitol was Ada James, whose "traveling bag" was "commandeered" by her father. By train, by car, and on foot, he went to Washington, D.C. There, women had alerted Wisconsin Senator Irvine L. Lenroot, a longtime suffragist who awaited James's arrival and expedited the document to the State Department — and then telegraphed confirmation to Youmans.[31]

For weeks women waited for further word from Washington, until the secretary of state sent Youmans official verification: on June 10, 1919, Wisconsin at last had earned its place in suffrage history.

The race to ratify the Nineteenth Amendment suggests that the honor was easily won. However, few suffrage campaigns were as hard-fought as in Wisconsin. Seven years earlier, full suffrage went down to defeat in a referendum, two to one. Even limited suffrage, withheld from women for so long and lost once before, came so late as to make Wisconsin among the last, reluctant states in the "suffrage column" only months before ratification and only by legislative enactment. Indeed, on the day of ratification, legislators still were debating a bill for a referendum — which, based on women's history in Wisconsin, might well not have won.

Neither by a referendum of the voters nor by enactment in the legislature did Wisconsin ever grant full woman suffrage before Congress amended the Constitution. As Youmans wrote, full suffrage was won in the state only when, "at length, it was taken out of the hands of the male voters of Wisconsin by the federal government."

Ironically, Wisconsin women won in the end because, from the beginning, they faced the best-organized opposition and were still in place to win the race to ratification, while women elsewhere had disbanded after securing suffrage. "To exasperated suffragists, it seemed as if those states where women had the vote longest were the slowest," writes Eleanor Flexner. In her classic history of the suffrage campaign, she credits the Wisconsin victory to Youmans' determination, despite her "grueling years" in the presidency, to abide by Catt's orders to remain organized for ratification.[32]

In one of her histories of the Wisconsin campaign, Youmans reiter-

"We of Wisconsin have been extremely ambitious to secure for our state the honor of being the first state to ratify."—Theodora Winton Youmans, the last president of the Wisconsin Woman Suffrage Association and founder of the Wisconsin League of Women Voters, speaking for suffragists in the 1919 legislative campaign including Ada L. James (fifth from left) and David G. James (center), holding the historic document of ratification of the Nineteenth Amendment prior to his race to Washington, D.C. Photo courtesy of the State Historical Society of Wisconsin.

ated that victory was hardly inevitable and that winning suffrage was hard work, "the result of ceaseless, unremitting toil." And women's work was not done with Wisconsin's ratification won, as Youmans reminded the women in calling the 1919 WWSA convention. "Until the federal suffrage amendment is ratified by thirty-six states, the work is not completed," she wrote. Even then, "legislation has done for us all it could do."[33]

Suffragists knew that there was much work yet to be done to disprove the perennial cliché that women didn't really want the vote. At the 1919 convention in Milwaukee, "six lectures on various phases of citizenship" convinced women to adopt "a plan of education" that would "secure a trained woman on salary to travel around the state," to set up "suffrage schools" in every county and even at the precinct level, and to publish a voting manual for women across Wisconsin. Setting a goal of $6,000, "a good sum of money to pay off obligations to the National and to begin the new work," women raised $2,800 in a single session with a "flood of bills and silver to add to the coffers," from one pledge of $1,000 down to gifts of $2 apiece "from women who could little spare it."

The costs of the suffrage campaign were incalculable, although Catt made an attempt. In 1920, Catt counted at least nine hundred separate campaigns for suffrage over the century, at state and national levels. From 1916 to 1920 alone, the cost of the national suffrage campaign was estimated in the millions of dollars[34]—and did not include the "opportunity cost" to a country which had lost an incredible expenditure of energies by thousands of women.

There were other costs, to women. As Youmans wrote, they regretted the loss of "sisterhood" in the perpetual schisms over strategy and tactics, but winning suffrage required forsaking personal sentiment for the sake of "public sentiment." Youmans' willingness to yield state-level autonomy and follow Catt's national directives, from sacrificing suffrage at the state level to surrendering her pacifism, won Wisconsin a historic victory. Still, the costs of parting company for Ada James, Sophie Gudden, Meta Schlichting Berger, Zona Gale, and Olympia Brown, as well as Youmans and other women, were painful—and the most incalculable.

The costs of schism could be seen in Wisconsin, in the end. Suffrage leaders united in 1913 were the most politicized and politically experienced women in the state. Yet only Theodora Winton Youmans and Jessie Jack Hooper remained to carry the Wisconsin Woman Suffrage Association forward in its post-1920 form.

10

Women in League
Epilogue, 1920 Forward

T H E woman suffrage campaign was not over in 1920, nationwide or in Wisconsin. The last NAWSA convention opened on February 15, the centenary of the birth of Susan B. Anthony, with an impromptu celebration befitting any political convention. Upon the first appearance of Wisconsin native and NAWSA president Carrie Chapman Catt, "hundreds of delegates raised their voices and their horns [and] state standards and banners, and went marching around the room tooting and shouting and singing," wrote Theodora Winton Youmans. Among them were dozens of women "chanting 'On Wisconsin'" and "waving our handsome yellow satin banner wildly in the marching line. . . . It was a great and joyous occasion and a good noisy one, just as it should have been."

More accolades, noisy or not, awaited Wisconsin women at the convention in Chicago. In a program of addresses on each decade of the "century of struggle," Youmans was selected to speak on the 1870s. Another program on women in the professions featured an address by the Reverend Olympia Brown on women's progress in the field of theology. Brown again was singled out at a fete for pioneering suffragists, a last "love-feast" where the veterans spent the afternoon "rejoicing over the final victory after their long years of toil and sacrifice such as the younger ones had never known." The women were led in "songs, reminiscences and clever speeches" by Olympia Brown, according to the official record of the convention. At eighty-four years old, she was — as ever

294

—in "excellent voice not equalled" by any in the "second generation."[1]

However, Wisconsin was denied a final triumph. At the convention banquet, each state was honored "in their order of ratification," as Youmans wrote—an order legally determined by the date of filing documentation with the secretary of state, who had ruled, in response to Youmans' inquiry, that Wisconsin had done so first. However, NAWSA ruled otherwise, deciding that the initial, invalid bill passed by the Illinois legislature "was in no wise the fault of that state," long the favorite of the movement as the first to win suffrage east of the Mississippi. Illinois women held "moral claim" to the honor and in the order of march, according to NAWSA, which placed Wisconsin women behind their sisters to the south. Youmans accepted defeat gracefully, walked "with head held high"—and immediately wired her dissent from the decision to the *Freeman* and the WWSA news service. "It was a bit painful that Illinois came first," admitted Youmans, and reminded readers that their state remained "first in the [official] registration."

Far more significant than the first ratification of the Nineteenth Amendment was securing the last state, as women knew. As late as the last NAWSA convention, five states still were needed for "the fateful thirty-six," Youmans wrote, although their lack "did not interfere with the hilarity of the occasion." Wisconsin women remained confident of full enfranchisement by election day in spring 1920. Once again, they would be bitterly disappointed.

Within women's power was another and equally significant step taken in 1920, in Wisconsin and at the national level. At the convention, Catt officially changed NAWSA's name to the League of Women Voters. In Wisconsin, a similar reorganization already had been approved at the 1919 WWSA convention and was effected less than a week after the 1920 NAWSA convention, at a special meeting in the Milwaukee Public Library. "With a sense of sadness and yet also with great rejoicing," Youmans presided as the WWSA was "dissolved, and succeeded by the Wisconsin League of Women Voters."

The woman suffrage campaign continued without pause, and with little change in leadership. In Wisconsin, Youmans yielded the gavel to WWSA first vice president Jessie Jack Hooper, although the women simply swapped titles, not tasks. As president, Hooper led the league's lobbying effort, as before. Youmans served as first vice president and managed the league's new public opinion campaign, "Good Citizenship for Women"—a slogan which also became the new name of her weekly *Freeman* "suffrage department"—and led the new league's recruitment campaign toward an enrollment goal of ten thousand members, at dues of only a dollar.

At the national level, too, Carrie Chapman Catt continued to lead the new league and to wage the ratification campaign, as did Alice Paul and the National Woman's Party. Antisuffragists stood fast in several holdout states, threatening failure of the Nineteenth Amendment until the last. More than a year after the historic first ratification in Wisconsin, women secured the last state, Tennessee. On August 26, 1920, woman suffrage became the law of the land.

With the League of Women Voters, women anticipated and achieved the last, requisite step in a modern public opinion campaign: to maintain support, once won. Winning suffrage was only the first step toward the league's avowed goal of "good citizenship" by women well versed in reform. Now, the task was to educate women not on how to win the ballot, but in how to exercise it wisely—lest it be lost again.

That NAWSA took its new name even before the Nineteenth Amendment became law was not overconfidence on women's part but the logical result of the latter strategy of "the struggle." Once written out of the Constitution, women never again could claim enfranchisement as a "right" or a "principle"; instead, the ballot became a "privilege." With their initial argument of "justice," suffragists had demanded the vote, to no avail. With the argument of "expediency," suffragists vowed to deserve the vote. Victory meant only that the ballot had become a privilege subject to "public sentiment," to be won from men—and sustained by women. Of course, few women were so philosophical as to identify or even analyze their ideological shift. As the usually eloquent Catt said of suffrage, inelegantly, "whatever it is, the women want it."

Whatever it took to win suffrage, women did it—and well. In the end, following Frances E. Willard's similarly straightforward slogan for the WCTU, they had to "Do Everything" with a public opinion campaign of proportions unseen, with every known strategy and tactic of opinion formation and a few which women invented. They fulfilled the promise made upon passage of the Fourteenth Amendment, when Elizabeth Cady Stanton and Susan B. Anthony vowed no "season of silence" until women rewrote the Constitution, again. Or, as Catt again aptly said, women learned how to end their silence in the "public sphere," to "keep so much 'suffrage noise' going all over the country that neither the enemy nor friends . . . discover[ed] where the real battle is."[2]

In the end, a significant lesson women learned was that the long battle within the movement for unity—whether they spoke with one voice or many—mattered little, at least not to the success of the suffrage campaign. Although neither Catt nor Youmans could reconcile women divided over strategies and tactics, the militancy of other suffragists actually worked to make the work of NAWSA and the WWSA seem moderate. In the end, women did not need to be united to win suffrage; they needed only to be organized to barter for the ballot with a president who had other battles to fight.

In the end, the "real battle" was with the real enemy to reform, as always: apathy. Many a battle was yet to be waged in courts of law and in the "court of public opinion," for far more than suffrage and with far less support from organized women.

The wisdom of women's reorganization as the League of Women Voters is also attested by the histories of other reform movements, from abolition forward, which did not similarly sustain support. Abolitionists won an end to slavery, if bloodily, and founded the American Equal Rights Association, which won the Fourteenth and Fifteenth Amendments for freedmen's citizenship and suffrage, but then disbanded.[3] They did not remain organized to achieve for African-Americans their full civil rights—a movement which would not again reach a similar level of organization or success for a century.

The temperance movement provides the best comparison to measure suffragists' success, because Prohibitionists won the Eighteenth Amendment at the same time, but their campaign was lost to repeal. According to historian K. Austin Kerr, while suffragists "formed the League of Women Voters . . . for new tasks once the Nineteenth Amendment was in place," the Anti-Saloon League failed to "maintain or enlarge its base of support" owing to organizational rigidity and clung to an outmoded self-image as "the keeper of a reform, rather than its advocate." The men did not "modify or adapt to new national political conditions" and redefined neither their goals nor their role. The result for the Anti-Saloon League "as an organization, was disastrous." At the same time, suffragists defeated a campaign to repeal the Nineteenth Amendment in the courts, and in the "court of public opinion." Kerr argues that conditions differed between Prohibitionists and suffragists because "once woman suffrage became part of the Constitution there was no apparent need for maintaining vigilance."[4]

Women saw their situation otherwise, as did their organized opposition. "The antis" were "always entertaining, but particularly so" after passage of the Nineteenth Amendment, wrote Youmans, when antisuffragists in Wisconsin "announced that they did not intend to discontinue their efforts to prevent women having the vote." Although they did not prevail in Wisconsin, "the antis" distracted suffragists from their new work and did delay suffrage elsewhere.

In the fall of 1920, nine months after the League of Women Voters' founding, women voted for president in most states—but not all. In Alabama and Georgia, legislators refused to enact required statutes, and women were refused at the polls. Legal challenges to the Nineteenth Amendment's constitutionality arose across the country, and two cases rose to the United States Supreme Court. The last, at considerable legal cost to Catt and to the League of Women Voters' coffers, was not decided until February 1922.[5]

Even then, when "the struggle" was won in every state, the woman suffrage movement was not over. As Youmans wrote, "the woman suffrage movement, in its truest meaning, now commenced."

In the post-1920 period, nationwide, women not only voted but also entered politics, or tried. Initially, the League of Women Voters attempted to work as a single-interest power bloc on the order of the Woman's Party, especially for the cause of women candidates, with little success. In 1920, before the Nineteenth Amendment became law, Youmans counted two women in state senates and twenty-two assembly-women in eleven states. By 1924, even Wisconsin had three women in the assembly, and more than four hundred held municipal office. But their numbers would alter little. By the mid-1920s, the league abandoned the direct political approach and became a nonpartisan organization.

The Woman's Party held true to its purpose, working for women in politics and for passage of equal rights amendments at the federal and state levels, which led to another historic victory in Wisconsin—or, again, so it seemed. In 1921, the Woman's Party led a lobbying effort which persuaded Wisconsin legislators to pass the first state equal rights bill granting women the same rights and privileges as men, with the exception of "special protection and privileges which they now enjoy for the general welfare."

The problem of protective exemptions became apparent by 1923, when the Wisconsin attorney general refused to allow employment of women in the legislature as prohibited in a 1905 law that restricted women and children to an eight-hour workday. He asserted that legislative employment required "very long and often unreasonable hours"—

a comfort to many taxpayers, no doubt, but not to those who were banned from some of the better jobs in the state Capitol.

In 1923 in the nation's Capitol, the Woman's Party submitted to Congress the first Equal Rights Amendment to the Constitution, which women had drafted that fall at Seneca Falls, at a conference commemorating the seventy-fifth anniversary of Elizabeth Cady Stanton's Declaration of Sentiments. Fifty years later, when the Equal Rights Amendment would pass Congress and be submitted to the states, Wisconsin would refuse to ratify.[6]

In Wisconsin in the 1920s, the experience of several women who tried and failed for a place in politics was similarly discouraging. In May 1920, even before the Nineteenth Amendment became law, Youmans announced that she and fifteen other women would go with the state delegation to the national Republican party convention in Chicago as "Real Party Members Now," or so read her headline. However, women went as alternates and never cast a vote; as Youmans wrote in a *Freeman* report headlined "The Elephant Hunt—At Close Range," men were "chained to their seats." While waiting for men to become unchained from their seats and give them a chance, women did not neglect nonvoting activities. "Women attended every session, conscientiously trying to learn everything they could about doing the new work for which they had volunteered while the attendance of men at the sessions dwindled," Youmans wrote. But she was "not accusing men delegates of shirking. They have not the same task ahead of them that we have and no doubt they were doing other important work of quite a different kind."

Other women also were doing work of quite a different kind at the convention. Youmans wrote again with amusement of "the antis" who came from across the country to the Republican convention to explain why woman's place was in the home. The Woman's Party also was represented but remained outside the hall, picketing in protest of the stalled suffrage ratification campaign. Among the picketers were Wisconsin women, including octogenarian Olympia Brown. Youmans disagreed with Brown's tactics, again, but could only applaud Brown's "vigor and strength and lasting enthusiasm."

But the women never would know quite what different work was done in the backrooms of politics. Youmans' hope of an opportunity to "express women's desires" rose again when she was the only woman among three Wisconsin appointees to the Republican party's platform committee, of nineteen women appointed nationwide among the approximately one hundred members. When the committee essentially approved planks already drafted, Youmans was disappointed again.

In the 1920s, in a regression to antebellum reform, women again were relegated to auxiliary status. Youmans served first as state chair of a women's division of the Republican party, and then as first vice president of a subsequent women's state auxiliary. In 1922, she ran for the state senate, but lost for lack of party support. Jessie Jack Hooper also ran for office in 1922, as a Democrat for Robert M. La Follette's Senate seat, but also lost without promised party support and never again attempted political or party office. Another likely candidate was Ada L. James, who did hold office in the state Republican party, but briefly; owing to increasing deafness, she became homebound in Richland Center.[7]

Women discovered that winning the ballot did not mean "the millennium," as Youmans had warned, and increasingly returned to women-only organizations. The lure of a nonpartisan, civic-oriented organization—much like a women's club—had been evident well before 1920, in a farewell exchange of correspondence between Youmans and James upon the latter's departure from the WWSA for the Woman's Party. Although James's rival organization to the WWSA had contributed to defeat in 1912, which had caused her to put merger paramount—the same merger which had made Youmans president—she had reverted in 1917, writing that "it is as deadly to suffrage to have one organization as it would be to politics to have but one political party." Youmans did not argue. "We may work along different channels for a while," she wrote, "but I fancy that we shall all be working together for certain civic ends when the Federal Amendment is finally passed and endorsed."[8]

Now, after the Nineteenth Amendment, Wisconsin's suffrage leaders—Youmans, James, Hooper, and even Olympia Brown—worked together again in the League of Women Voters, the legacy left by Elizabeth Cady Stanton, Susan B. Anthony, Lucy Stone, and other founders of the first woman suffrage organizations founded in 1869. League activities reflected its legacy of reform: fund-raising and membership drives, lobbying and petitioning, the press agentry of parades and fairs, and "citizenship schools." Nationally and at the state level, the league published legislative and congressional voting records, which recalled an earlier WWSA project, "Wisconsin Legislators and the Home," the "little yellow pamphlet" adopted, in turn, from the La Follettes' *Voter's Hand-book* first begun in 1901. Women also initiated new projects, such as the candidate debates by which the league would become best identified for decades to come.

In addition to their work in the league, "second-generation" suffragists continued working politically but outside of elective politics. James continued crusading for causes by correspondence, especially for underprivileged children. Hooper rose to leadership in the Women's International League for Peace and Freedom. Meta Schlichting Berger continued to serve on the Milwaukee school board and in the Socialist party until the 1930s, when the "independent and politically confident widow" turned to communism and toured the Soviet Union. Zona Gale won a Pulitzer Prize for fiction, served on the Board of Regents of the University of Wisconsin, and stayed a steadfast supporter of Senator La Follette. Upon his death, Belle Case La Follette declined to fill out her husband's term in the Senate; instead, she wrote his biography, continued to publish their magazine, renamed *The Progressive,* and continued active in both the Peace League and League of Women Voters. Youmans and her husband retired from the *Freeman* in 1920, but she continued to write for the paper and for the League of Women Voters' publication, *Forward.*[9]

All "second-generation" suffragists also remained active in women's clubs. Youmans served again as president of the Waukesha Women's Club, twice, and also held office in other clubs and civic organizations. Hooper also remained active in her Twentieth Century Club in Oshkosh and other civic organizations. In the 1920s, both Hooper and Youmans held office in the Wisconsin Federation of Women's Clubs, which still annually bestows the Theodora W. Youmans Award upon a Wisconsin woman who, whether through her clubs or career, significantly contributes to her community.

The Reverend Olympia Brown, the amazing "first-generation" holdover who won and lost the vote in Wisconsin long before the Nineteenth Amendment, lived to vote again — and again. In 1920 and again in 1924, Brown campaigned for La Follette. Until her death in 1926, Brown also was a charter member of the American Civil Liberties Union and worked for the women's international peace movement, the League of Nations, and the League of Women Voters. But, to the end, Brown continued scornful of what she called the "age of organization" under the likes of Catt and Youmans.[10]

Especially discouraging in the post-1920 period for suffragists was the apparent lack of interest by women with the vote. Lack of support from men and major parties hardly was surprising. However, on the eve of suffrage, Youmans had been hopeful. "Women voters will I believe bring more independent thought to their choice of policies and candidates and it may be hoped that the resultant conditions will also stimulate more independence on the part of men voters, too," she had declared. By 1924, in the league *Forward,* she decried a "disgracefully small turnout" of women and men in the presidential election.[11]

So close to the cause for so long, Youmans and other suffragists could not or would not see what was evident to most voters, women or men: by 1920, the ballot no longer meant what it had when the "century of struggle" began. And, even then, suffrage had been only one of many rights sought by women at Seneca Falls.

Many historians also have misunderstood the post-1920 period in the woman's rights movement, and some even succumb to the age-old argument that women didn't really want the vote. William H. O'Neill's obituary on the suffrage movement suggests that women's own overly "romantic" expectations, after the "exhilarating victories or heart-wrenching defeats" of the campaign, caused the "fall of feminism." Another study even blames women for an "all-time low" in voter turnout in the 1920s by men as well, based upon evidence drawn primarily from Chicago, including data on elections before 1920, when Illinois women held only presidential suffrage. William Henry Chafe suggests that women reneged on their promised agenda because they "responded to public affairs as individuals" rather than as a single-interest bloc capable of wresting reform from politicians.[12] In other words, because women refused to vote on the basis of gender alone or voted independently after being rejected by parties—because they voted on the same basis as did many men—women were to blame, once again, for the withholding of women's reforms by the men of the political parties.

Other historians assert that voter turnout was on the wane among men even before woman suffrage was won. J. Stanley Lemons suggests that "ordinary women exerted as little influence as ordinary men." J. A. Thompson finds a loss of "popular support for progressivism generally," accelerated by the "shock" of the Great War. Paul Kleppner suggests that voter participation declined as the result of a de facto one-party system, of "Republican hegemony" in the North and Democratic dominance in the South. His "costs-to-benefits analysis" of using the ballot concludes that "for newly or recently enfranchised women, their costs of participation were higher—they had to overcome standing and internalized norms that defined their sex roles as apolitical. For most women, in the face of visibly diminishing benefits, the cost was exorbitant."[13]

Still, many women—more women than men—were willing to pay the dues of citizenship. Allen J. Lichtman finds that men's rate of participation at the polls declined while women's turnout at the polls actually increased in the presidential elections of 1924 and 1928, a period when "politics lacked its earlier intensity." William E. Gienapp's studies of the genesis of the Republican party suggest that suffrage meant far more to men and women alike a century before, when the woman's rights movement was born.[14]

However, even historians who admit that the ballot was but a symbol of political equality by 1920 may misunderstand the post-1920 period if they do not see that suffrage never had been more than a single plank in the wide-ranging platform of woman's rights in the Declaration of Sentiments at Seneca Falls, to which women now returned.

After 1920, women made strides in access to education, to the workforce, and to the professions, from the traditional fields of law, medicine, and the ministry to journalism — and the "new," post-1920 career fields once the province of "professional organizers and agitators" of "public sentiment." Although women in Wisconsin and elsewhere were expert in the strategies and tactics of managing public opinion campaigns by 1920, their resumés in reform were not easily parlayed into related careers. In Washington, D.C., there was the example of three former NAWSA publicists, "looking around for new worlds to conquer" after 1920, who founded the first all-female public relations firm in the nation's capital. In Wisconsin, there was Lutie E. Stearns. Her historic speech to the General Federation of Women's Clubs in Chicago in 1914, when clubwomen nationwide endorsed suffrage, had "made a great hit," and "consequent invitations poured in upon her," according to Youmans. Stearns resigned from the traveling department of the Wisconsin Free Library, after more than twenty years, and became a public speaker and "suffrage missionary, with a roving commission." For nearly the next two decades, Stearns toured the lecture circuit to promote education, literacy, and literature, and eventually covered thirty-eight states.

In 1920, in a progress report on educational opportunities for women in one of Theodora Winton Youmans' last columns in the *Freeman,* she noted that women students outnumbered men in only one field at the University of Wisconsin: the department of journalism, founded only fifteen years before. Still, women were "segregated in the penthouse" at the *Milwaukee Journal,* where Lutie E. Stearns later wrote a women's column and Kenosha suffragist Lucy E. Strong was hired after 1920.[15] For decades, few women would be in news management despite their increasing numbers. The "new" fields of advertising and public relations also became known as a "velvet ghetto" where women outnumbered men — except in management.

Few similar examples of former suffragists in the "literary" professions can be found in the post-1920 period in Wisconsin, for a simple reason: "the struggle" had taken so long that many of its leaders did not outlive it. The state's "first generation" of woman journalists survived only in newspaper archives — the nameless correspondents to the *American Freeman,* Mathilde Fransziska Anneke of the *Deutsche Frauen-Zeitung,* Emma Brown of the *Wisconsin Chief,* Lavinia Goodell of *The Principia, Harper's Magazine,* and the *Janesville Gazette* as well as the *Chief,* the *Woman's Journal,* and more. Only Olympia Brown lived into the 1920s, long after she had sold her *Racine Times-Call* and lost her *Wisconsin Citizen.* Even the survivors, the "second-generation" leaders like Theodora Winton Youmans of the *Waukesha Freeman,* gave their working lives to their "suffrage careers."

However, Youmans continued to make women's history, as a historian. A member of the board of the State Historical Society of Wisconsin and a founder of the Waukesha County Historical Society, she had begun her oral histories with Olympia Brown, Alura Collins Hollister, and others well before suffrage was won. Youmans wrote the first of her histories of the state suffrage movement for her last address to the WWSA, and also published it in the *Freeman.* After 1920, she revised her work for a wider audience, in the *Wisconsin Magazine of History* and in the *History of Woman Suffrage,* begun by Stanton and Anthony half a century before.

In her histories, Youmans addressed the next generation of women in the hope that they would learn from their history. The world, she knew, would not. "The careless world will probably continue to think that woman suffrage just happened, that it was 'in the air,'" wrote Youmans, pensively, "but we know that the changes in the opinions of society which made it possible are the result of ceaseless, unremitting toil."

In her best history of the movement, "How Wisconsin Women Won the Ballot," Youmans detailed the work of conducting a public opinion campaign, from the challenge of devising and revising strategies and tactics to the chore of repetitive tasks — primarily, repeatedly, organizing women. "We do not minimize the importance of what has been done," she warned. "The enfranchisement of women, in the face of the prejudice against it, a prejudice woven into the very web of human nature, is a marvelous achievement."

That women finally achieved numbers sufficient to win suffrage — if not to overcome prejudice — was a significant factor, Youmans wrote. However, more crucial were the few "in the fight" from the first: "The political equality of women came because a little group of women had profound conviction that the enfranchisement of women was so fundamentally right and so absolutely necessary that it must be brought about. It was the burning flame in the souls of a few women which lighted and led the way."

Yet, as Youmans feared, a generation of women would forget the legacy of suffrage, their heritage of reform in lessons so carefully preserved and handed down through the decades by the first few "in the fight" to enlighten their "daughter's daughters." Youmans' histories, and the monumental *History of Woman Suffrage,* would not be rediscovered until the rise of the modern feminist movement, when women again would relearn the strategies and tactics of Elizabeth Cady Stanton and Susan B. Anthony who had "solemnly vowed," a century before, "that there should never be another season of silence until woman had the same rights everywhere on this green earth, as man."[16] And women again would work for change in their political, social, and economic status — which required far more than suffrage then, or since.

However, if women in the post-1920 period were quieted, they were not quelled. The Nineteenth Amendment was not followed by a "fall of feminism," a dark ages in women's history between a revolution and a renaissance of woman's rights. In a movement ever cyclical, the post-1920 period was only a "season of silence" come too soon. New generations would find, in the first woman's rights campaigns, a source of pride in their past — a usable past, a resource for the strategies and tactics with which women had struggled to change a Constitution and a country, and won, more than once before.

Notes

Selected References

Index

NOTES

Works and archives frequently cited have been identified by the following abbreviations:

FAHS   Fort Atkinson Historical Society, Fort Atkinson, Wisconsin.
HWS   The *History of Woman Suffrage,* published in six volumes. Volumes 1, 2, and 3 were edited by Elizabeth Cady Stanton, Susan B. Anthony, and Matilda Joslyn Gage and published in 1881, 1882, and 1886 in Rochester, New York. Volume 4 was edited by Susan B. Anthony and Ida Husted Harper and published in 1902 in Rochester. Volumes 5 and 6 were edited by Ida Husted Harper and published in 1922 in New York.
MCHS   Milwaukee County Historical Society, Milwaukee, Wisconsin.
SHSW   State Historical Society of Wisconsin, Madison, Wisconsin.
WCHS   Waukesha County Historical Society, Waukesha, Wisconsin.
WMH   *Wisconsin Magazine of History,* published by the State Historical Society of Wisconsin, Madison, Wisconsin.

Preface

1. Theodora W. Youmans, "How Wisconsin Women Won the Ballot," *WMH* 5 (1922), 24.
2. Crystal Eastman, "Political Equality League (Report on the Wisconsin Suffrage Campaign)," in Blanche Wiesen Cook, ed., *Crystal Eastman on Women and Revolution* (New York: Oxford University Press, 1978), 67.
3. Anne Firor Scott, *Natural Allies: Women's Associations in American History* (Urbana: University of Illinois Press, 1991), 138.
4. Carrie Chapman Catt and Nettie Rogers Shuler, *Woman Suffrage and Politics: The Inner Story of the Suffrage Movement* (New York: Charles Scribner's Sons, 1923), 462.

Chapter 1. *Women's Place, Men's Press:*
Moral Reform, Abolition, and Temperance, to 1866

The primary sources for this chapter are the *American Freeman,* later the
Free Democrat, from 1844 to 1860, and the *Cayuga Chief,* later the *Wisconsin*
Chief, from 1853 to 1866; specific citations of these sources are given only for
exceptions to the time period or for quotations of length.

1. Alice E. Smith, *The History of Wisconsin,* Vol. 1: *From Exploration*
to Statehood (Madison: SHSW, 1973), 655–72; Leslie H. Fishel, Jr., "Wisconsin and Negro Suffrage," *WMH* 46 (Spring 1963), 180–96; [Louise Phelps]
Kellogg to Theodora W. Youmans, "Question Box: Negro Suffrage and Woman's
Rights in the Convention of 1846," *WMH* 3 (1919), 227–30; Catherine B.
Cleary, "Married Women's Property Rights in the Wisconsin Constitution of
1846," MS.

2. *HWS* 1:67–74; Margaret Hope Bacon, *Valiant Friend: The Life of Lucretia Mott* (New York: Walker, 1980), 140–43.

3. Edward Mathews, "An Abolitionist in Territorial Wisconsin: The Journal of Reverend Edward Mathews, Part I," *WMH* 52 (Autumn 1968), 3–18;
Louis Saxton Gerteis, "Antislavery Agitation in Wisconsin, 1836–1848," M.A.
thesis, University of Wisconsin–Madison, 1966, 5–7; Peter E. Weisensel, "The
Wisconsin Temperance Crusade to 1919," M.A. thesis, University of Wisconsin–Madison, 1965, 1–3; on other early societies, see also Salmon Stebbins,
"Journal of Salmon Stebbins, 1837–1838," *WMH* 9 (December 1925), 188–212.

4. Ruth Rosen, *The Lost Sisterhood: Prostitution in America, 1900–1918*
(Baltimore: Johns Hopkins University Press, 1982), 7–9; Sara M. Evans, *Born*
for Liberty: A History of Women in America (New York: Free Press, 1989),
74–75; Eleanor Flexner, *Century of Struggle: The Woman's Rights Movement*
in the United States, rev. ed. (Cambridge: Belknap Press, 1975), 41–43; Theodora Penny Martin, *The Sound of Our Own Voices: Women's Study Clubs,*
1860–1910 (Boston: Beacon Press, 1987), 6; Carroll Smith-Rosenberg, *Disorderly*
Conduct: Visions of Gender in Victorian America (New York: Oxford University Press, 1985), 114.

5. "Constitution of the Female Moral Reform Society of Prairie Village,"
Female Moral Reform Society File, WCHS; *Waukesha Freeman,* July 3, 1890
and March 2 and May 18, 1899.

6. Paul L. Rempe, "Government and Politics in Waukesha County: The Last
150 Years," in Ellen D. Langill and Jean Penn Loerke, eds., *From Farmland to*
Freeways: A History of Waukesha County, Wisconsin (Waukesha: WCHS, 1984,
87–137, and Mary Ella Milham, "Waukesha County Origins: From Plymouth
to the China Sea," ibid., 137–74; Theron W. Haight, *The History of Waukesha*
County, Wisconsin (Chicago: Western Historical Company, 1880), 563; *Waukesha Freeman,* Feb. 24, 1887.

7. *Waukesha Freeman,* March 2 and May 18, 1899.

8. Mathews, "An Abolitionist, Part I," 17; Carolyn Stewart Dyer, "Political

Patronage of the Wisconsin Press, 1849–1860," *Journalism Monographs* 109 (February 1989), 3; Kate Everest Levi, "The Wisconsin Press and Slavery," *WMH* 9 (July 1926), 424; William J. Maher, "The Antislavery Movement in Milwaukee and Vicinity, 1842–1860," M.A. thesis, Marquette University, 1954, 14–15; Frank L. Byrne, "Cold-Water Crusade: The Ante-Bellum Wisconsin Temperance Movement," M.A. thesis, University of Wisconsin–Madison, 1951, 12–13; see also Alfred L. Lorenz, Jr., "Harrison Reed: An Editor's Trials on the Wisconsin Frontier," *Journalism Quarterly* 61 (Winter 1984), 417–22, 462.

9. Weisensel, "Wisconsin Temperance Crusade," 1–4; Byrne, "Cold-Water Crusade," 1–12, 37–53, 71–90; Robert C. Nesbit, *Wisconsin: A History*, 2d ed. (Madison: University of Wisconsin Press, 1989), 237; Jed R. Dannenbaum, *Drink and Disorder: Temperance Reform in Cincinnati from the Washingtonian Revival to the WCTU* (Urbana: University of Illinois Press, 1984), 28; Joseph R. Gusfield, *Symbolic Crusade: Status Politics and the American Temperance Movement*, 2d ed. (Urbana: University of Illinois Press, 1986), 48–49; Jack S. Blocker, Jr. *"Give to the Winds Thy Fears": The Women's Temperance Crusade, 1873–1874* (Westport, Conn.: Greenwood Press, 1985), 34.

10. Maher, "Antislavery Movement," 16–18, 23–24; Levi, "Wisconsin Press and Slavery," 425; *Dictionary of Wisconsin Biography* (Madison: SHSW, 1960), 80; Edward Mathews, "An Abolitionist in Territorial Wisconsin: The Journal of Reverend Edward Mathews, Part III," *WMH* (Spring 1969), 249–56; H. S. Durand (to Maj. Elisha A. Cowles), "A Letter from Racine in 1843," *WMH* 5 (March 1922), 323. The document of purchase was discovered decades later in the office of Liberty party leader and Prairieville lawyer Vernon Tichenor; see *Waukesha Freeman*, Feb. 24, 1887.

11. Evans, *Born for Liberty*, 75.

12. Dorothy Sterling, *Ahead of Her Time: Abby Kelley and the Politics of Antislavery* (New York: W. W. Norton, 1991), 124–25; "Diary of Edward A. Holton," Holton Papers, MCHS; Mukwonago Anti-Slavery Society Papers, SHSW.

13. Youmans, "How Wisconsin Women," 5.

14. Carol Kaplan Harris, "Sherman Miller Booth and Crystallization of Anti-Slavery Sentiment in Wisconsin," M.A. thesis, University of Wisconsin–Madison, 1973, 8–13, 45.

15. Byrne, "Cold-Water Crusade," 75–90; Gusfield, *Symbolic Crusade*, 50; Joseph Schafer, "Prohibition in Early Wisconsin," *WMH* 8 (March 1925), 282–92; "P. W. of Sheboygan" to *Michigan Christian Herald*, July 7, 1847, in Sidney Glazier, ed., "Wisconsin as Depicted in the Michigan Press," *WMH* 27 (September 1943), 93.

16. Laura Ross Wolcott, "Wisconsin," in *HWS* 3:639; William F. Whyte, "Chronicles of Early Watertown," *WMH* 4 (1920–21), 288.

17. Margo Anderson Conk and Renny Harrigan, "Recovering Our Past: Mathilde Fransziska Anneke (1817–1884)," *Feminist Collections* 7 (Spring 1986), 3–6; Steven M. Buechler, *The Transformation of the Woman Suffrage Move-*

ment: The Case of Illinois, 1850–1920 (New Brunswick, N.J.: Rutgers University Press, 1986), 60–61.

18. *HWS* 2:381–98.

19. *HWS* 2:381–98; Janet Wilson James and Edward T. James, *Notable American Women,* Vol. 1 (Cambridge: Harvard University Press, 1971), 51; Richard N. Current, *The History of Wisconsin,* Vol. 2: *The Civil War Era, 1848–1873* (Madison: SHSW, 1976), 123; Youmans, "How Wisconsin Women," 11–12; see also Nancy Madison Lewis, "A Century of Wisconsin Woman Journalists," M.A. thesis, University of Wisconsin–Madison, 1947, 1–7, and Ann Russo and Cheris Kramarae, eds., *The Radical Women's Press of the 1850s* (New York: Routledge, 1991), 110–12.

20. Byrne, "Cold-Water Crusade," 90–95, 115–16, 130–32, 143–47; Frank L. Byrne, "Maine Law Versus Lager Beer: A Dilemma of Wisconsin's Young Republican Party," *WMH* 42 (Winter 1958–59), 115–20; Kathleen Barry, *Susan B. Anthony: A Biography of a Singular Feminist* (New York: Ballantine, 1988), 75–77; Antoinette Brown to *The Una,* Sept. 16, 1853, in Russo and Kramarae, *Radical Women's Press,* 55–58; Youmans, "How Wisconsin Women," 5.

21. Harris, "Sherman Miller Booth," 71–84, 87–88, 99–100, 111–20; Levi, "Wisconsin Press and Slavery," 423–34; Joseph Schafer, "Stormy Days in Court — The Booth Case," *WMH* 20 (1936), 89–110; Joseph Carman Cover, "Memoirs of a Pioneer Country Editor," *WMH* 11 (March 1928), 249.

22. Youmans, "How Wisconsin Women," 5–7; *HWS* 1:632; Wolcott, "Wisconsin," *HWS* 3:639; Louise Phelps Kellogg to Theodora W. Youmans, *Waukesha Freeman,* Oct. 30, 1919.

23. Blocker, "*Give to the Winds*," 34; *Wisconsin Chief,* Sept. 17, 1878, Feb. 28, 1880, June 13, 1884, and Jan. 28, 1887; see also *The History of Jefferson County, Wisconsin* (Chicago: Western Historical Company, 1879), 493–94, 501, 511, 515, 548; *Modern Agitators, or Portraits of Living American Reformers* (Auburn, N.Y.: Miller, Orton & Mulligan, 1856); Thurlow Weed Brown, *Temperance Tales and Hearthstone Reveries* (Auburn, N.Y.: Derby & Miller, 1853) and *Minnie Hermon, or the Night and Its Morning* (Auburn, N.Y.: Derby & Miller, 1855), SHSW.

24. Alexis Crane Hart, "An Autobiography of Alexis Crane Hart," Alexis Crane Hart Papers, SHSW.

25. Byrne, "Cold-Water Crusade," 169.

26. H. A. Reid, [*Dodge* (County) *Citizen*], "Memorial Address," presented to the Wisconsin Editors Association at Janesville, June 20–21, 1866, in the *Chief,* July 16, 1866; see also *Minutes of the Wisconsin Editors Association,* inscribed to Emma Brown, FAHS.

27. Ruth Bordin, *Frances Willard: A Biography* (Chapel Hill: University of North Carolina Press, 1986), 150; see also Evans, *Born for Liberty,* 114.

28. Current, *History of Wisconsin,* 370; *Waukesha Freeman,* May 30, 1895 and May 14, 1896; Patricia G. Harrsch, "'This Noble Monument': The Story of the Soldiers' Orphans' Home," *WMH* 76 (Winter 1992–93), 82–120; Leslie

Miljat, *Admissions Applications 1867–1872: National Home for Disabled Volunteer Soldiers* (Milwaukee, 1992). The Madison facility housed war orphans until 1877, and was razed in 1895. The Milwaukee facility is now named the Clement J. Zablocki Veterans Administration Center.

29. *HWS* 2:57–66, 78–80, 885–86, emphasis in the original; Sterling, *Ahead of Her Time*, 337–38; Scott, *Natural Allies*, 72; Evans, *Born for Liberty*, 117. Anthony's Madison correspondents were Ladies' Union League president Mrs. W. A. P. Morris and secretary Mrs. E. S. Carr.

30. Nesbit, *Wisconsin*, 257–58; Ellen D. Langill, *Carroll College, The First Century: 1846–1946* (Waukesha, Wis.: Carroll College Press, 1980), 47–48; Olympia Brown, "Wisconsin," in *HWS* 4:985; Current, *History of Wisconsin*, 387–89, 400–401.

31. Louisa T. Whittier to *The Sibyl*, January 1863, in Russo and Kramarae, *Radical Women's Press*, 204–5.

32. *Chief*, Jan. 17 and Feb. 28, 1867, and April 29, 1880.

33. *Dictionary of Wisconsin Biography*, 80; Mathews, "An Abolitionist, Part I," 3; Harris, "Sherman Miller Booth," 124–26, citing *Chicago Chronicle*, Nov. 1, 1896, and *Wisconsin*, March 12, 1897.

34. Evans, *Born for Liberty*, 118.

Chapter 2. Women's Crusade, Press Crusaders: Temperance and Suffrage, 1866–1874

The primary source for this chapter is the *Wisconsin Chief* from 1866 to 1874; specific citations of this source are given only for exceptions to the time period or for quotations of length.

1. *Chief*, Jan. 28, 1887; Current, *History of Wisconsin*, 387–401; Evans, *Born for Liberty*, 114–15; Barry, *Susan B. Anthony*, 214.

2. Flexner, *Century of Struggle*, 116; Sterling, *Ahead of Her Time*, 39, 126; Smith-Rosenberg, *Disorderly Conduct*, 114; Catherine B. Cleary, "Lavinia Goodell, First Woman Lawyer in Wisconsin," *WMH* 74 (Summer 1991), 242–71; Gail E. Mason, "Justice for the 'Weaker Vessels': William Goodell Fathers the *Female Advocate*," presented to Association for Education in Journalism and Mass Communication, Montreal, 1992.

3. Russo and Kramarae, *Radical Women's Press*, 11–16; E. Claire Jerry, "The Role of Newspapers in the Nineteenth-Century Woman's Movement," in Martha M. Solomon, ed., *A Voice of Their Own: The Woman Suffrage Press, 1840–1910* (Tuscaloosa: University of Alabama Press, 1991), 17–29, and Edward A. Hinck, "*The Lily*, 1849–1856: From Temperance to Woman's Rights," ibid., 30–47; Louise R. Noun, *Strong-Minded Women: The Emergence of the Woman-Suffrage Movement in Iowa* (Ames: Iowa State University Press, 1969), 12–13.

4. Evans, *Born for Liberty*, 122–23; Barry, *Susan B. Anthony*, 169–71; *HWS*

2:267–68; Lynne Masel-Walters, "'To Hustle With the Rowdies': The Organization and Functions of the American Suffrage Press," *Journal of American Culture* 3 (Spring 1980), 167–83, and "Their Rights and Nothing More: A History of *The Revolution, 1868–1870*," *Journalism Quarterly* 53 (Summer 1976), 242–51; Bonnie J. Dow, *"The Revolution, 1868–1870*: Expanding the Woman Suffrage Agenda," in *A Voice of Their Own*, 71–86, and Susan Schultz Huxman, "The *Woman's Journal, 1870–1890*: The Torchbearer for Suffrage," ibid., 87–109; *HWS* 2:267, 309–12; Charlotte Cote, *Olympia Brown: The Battle for Equality* (Racine, Wis.: Mother Courage Press, 1988), 70, emphasis in the original. See also Dana Greene, ed., *Suffrage and Religious Principles: The Speeches and Writings of Olympia Brown* (Metuchen, N.J.: Scarecrow Press, 1983).

5. See Gerald J. Baldasty, *The Commercialization of News in the Nineteenth Century* (Madison: University of Wisconsin Press, 1992); Hazel Dicken-Garcia, *Journalistic Standards in the Nineteenth Century* (Madison: University of Wisconsin Press, 1989); and Michael Schudson, *Discovering the News: A Social History of American Newspapers* (New York: Basic Books, 1978).

6. See Karen J. Blair, *The Clubwoman as Feminist: True Womanhood Redefined, 1868–1914* (New York: Holmes & Meier, 1980).

7. Wolcott, "Wisconsin," *HWS* 3:640–41; J. T. Dow to the *Wisconsin State Journal*, March 7, 1868; *HWS* 2:923.

8. Youmans, "How Wisconsin Women," 9–11; Current, *History of Wisconsin*, 530–31; Brown, "Wisconsin," *HWS* 4:985; *HWS* 2:374. Brown states that Peckham was "a bright young lawyer," but Stanton apparently was correct in calling her a law student; see Cleary, "Lavinia Goodell," 251. In deference to Brown, Youmans dates the WWSA to 1882 but recognizes it as a revival of the earlier organization, variously named the Wisconsin Women's Suffrage Association, the Wisconsin Woman's Suffrage Association, and the Wisconsin Woman Suffrage Association until approximately 1884, after which the last title was used; see Lawrence L. Graves, "The Wisconsin Woman's Movement, 1846–1920," Ph.D. thesis, University of Wisconsin–Madison, 1954.

9. Wolcott, "Wisconsin," *HWS* 3:640–41; Youmans, "How Wisconsin Women," 9–11. On conflicting dates, Youmans' account is preferred.

10. *HWS* 2:373–75.

11. *HWS* 2:374.

12. *HWS* 2:373–75; Cleary, "Lavinia Goodell," 271.

13. Wolcott, "Wisconsin," *HWS* 3:642–43.

14. Brown, "Wisconsin," *HWS* 4:993; Wolcott, "Wisconsin," *HWS* 3:643; on Colby, see also Edward T. James, *Notable American Women, 1607–1950* (Cambridge: Harvard University Press, 1973), 355–56, and Olympia Brown, *Democratic Ideals: A Memorial Sketch of Clara B. Colby* (Milwaukee: Federal Suffrage Association, 1917); on Mortimer, see Diane Long Hoeveler, *Milwaukee Women Yesterday* (Milwaukee: Milwaukee Humanities Program, 1979), 23–24.

15. Youmans, "How Wisconsin Women," 9–11; Wolcott, "Wisconsin," *HWS* 3:643; Noun, *Strong-Minded Women*, 12–13, 142–47.

16. *HWS* 2:392–94; Barry, *Susan B. Anthony*, 194; Paula Giddings, *When and Where I Enter: The Impact of Black Women on Race and Sex in America* (New York: William Morrow, 1984), 65–67; Buechler, *Transformation of the Woman Suffrage Movement*, 61.

17. Wolcott, "Wisconsin," *HWS* 3:642.

18. Byrne, "Cold-Water Crusade," 145–46; Twylah Kepler, "The Cradle of the Woman's Suffrage Movement in Richland Center," MS, 5; *Chief*, April 15, 1857; Dannenbaum, *Drink and Disorder*, 199–203; Blocker, *"Give to the Winds,"* 1–24; Current, *History of Wisconsin*, 457–60, 479–80.

19. Cleary, "Lavinia Goodell," 243–49; Lavinia Goodell to Maria Goodell Frost, Feb. 24, June 27, July 2[?] and Nov. 18, 1873, Goodell Family Papers, Berea College, Kentucky. Lavinia's sister Maria was the mother of William Goodell Frost, president of Berea College, 1892–1921; see Catherine C. Mitchell and C. Joan Schnyder, "Public Relations for Appalachia: Berea's *Mountain Life and Work*," *Journalism Quarterly* 66 (Winter 1989), 974–78, 1049.

20. *Chief*, Aug. 15, 1860; Current, *History of Wisconsin*, 289–93, 587–88; Herman J. Deutsch, "Yankee-Teuton Rivalry in Wisconsin Politics of the Seventies: Temperance," *WMH* 14 (1930–31), 267–75.

21. Current, *History of Wisconsin*, 268–71.

22. William Goodell to E. Brown, Aug. 7, 1873, in the *Chief*, Aug. 27, 1873, citing *Janesville Gazette*, July 16 and 23, 1873.

23. Goodell to Frost, July 2[?], 1873.

24. Lavinia Goodell to the *Woman's Journal*, Aug. 16, 1873.

25. Blocker, *"Give to the Winds,"* 12–15, 23–25, 33–39, 226, 245; Ruth Bordin, *Woman and Temperance: The Quest for Power and Liberty, 1873–1900* (Philadelphia: Temple University Press, 1981), 20–26, 39.

Blocker, Bordin, and other historians credit the crusade not to women but to a male temperance lecturer, touring Ohio and upstate New York. However, according to an account by a crusader of the talk at a Templars meeting, "it was not [he] that so moved that audience; he was just as much surprised as any one." Instead, she attributed the uprising to lack of enforcement of an 1870 law similar to Wisconsin's Graham Law; see Mrs. E. McNeil to Eliza Daniel Stewart, citing the *Fredonia Censor*, Dec. 17, 1873, in E. D. Stewart, *Memories of the Crusade: A Thrilling Account of the Great Uprising of the Women in Ohio in 1873, Against the Liquor Crime* (1893; rpt. New York: Arno Press, 1972), 85–86.

Blocker provides the best estimate of participation in the crusade because it is based on contemporary accounts, but for the same reason even his estimate may be an undercount because it is based on accounts only in large daily papers, and only from December 1873 on. For example, in Wisconsin, his study relies only on the *Milwaukee News*—which was admittedly opposed to the women's crusade—and only in 1874, which excludes earlier crusades in Janesville and elsewhere in Wisconsin, and the *Wisconsin Chief.*

26. Stewart, *Memories of the Crusade*, 126; Blocker, "*Give to the Winds*," 17, 245.

27. Blocker, "*Give to the Winds*," 12–15, 37; Nesbit, *Wisconsin*, 357.

28. *Chief*, May 15, 1874.

29. Cleary, "Lavinia Goodell," 245; Goodell to Frost, July 2[?], 1873; Goodell to the *Woman's Journal*, Aug. 16, 1873.

30. Mrs. E. [B.] Wolcott to the *Woman's Journal*, May 16, 1874; Susan J. Steele, "Wisconsin," in Annie Wittenmyer, *History of the Woman's Temperance Crusade* (Philadelphia: Christian Woman, 1877), 657–66.

31. Cleary, "Lavinia Goodell," 252, emphasis in the original; William Fiske Brown, *Rock County, Wisconsin* (Chicago: C. F. Cooper, 1908), 787; *Milwaukee Sentinel*, June 19, 1874; Lavinia Goodell to Maria Goodell Frost, Aug. 6, 1874, emphasis in the original.

32. Goodell to Frost, Aug. 6, 1874; Cleary, "Lavinia Goodell," 252–54.

33. Bordin, *Woman and Temperance*, 48; Stewart, *Memories of the Crusade*, 91, 528, emphasis in the original.

Chapter 3. Women's Alliances, Press Allies: Temperance and Suffrage, 1874–1882

The primary source for this chapter is the *Wisconsin Chief* from 1874 to 1882; specific citations of this source are given only for exceptions to the time period or for quotations of length.

1. Blocker, "*Give to the Winds*," 25; see also Barbara Leslie Epstein, *The Politics of Domesticity: Women, Evangelism, and Temperance in Nineteenth Century America* (Middletown, Conn.: Wesleyan University Press, 1981), 115.

2. Deutsch, "Yankee-Teuton Rivalry," 281.

3. Current, *History of Wisconsin*, 268–71.

4. Weisensel, "Wisconsin Temperance Crusade," 10; Deutsch, "Yankee-Teuton Rivalry," 281–82; David Paul Thelen, *The Early Life of Robert M. La Follette, 1855–1884* (Chicago: Loyola University Press, 1966), 89.

5. Byrne, "Cold-Water Crusade," 90–95.

6. Weisensel, "Wisconsin Temperance Crusade," 6; Current, *History of Wisconsin*, 146, 561.

7. *Chief*, March 24 and May 15, 1885, Nov. 27, 1886, April 27 and June 24, 1887, and Oct. 1, Nov. 2, and Dec. 1, 1888.

8. *Waukesha Freeman*, hereafter *Freeman*, July 20 and Aug. 3, 1882.

9. *Chief*, Oct. 27, 1883 and June 13 and Aug. 2, 1884; see Nesbit, *Wisconsin*, 357–61. Kanouse later led the Dakota Territory Templars.

10. *Freeman*, Jan. 31, 1901.

11. Cleary, "Lavinia Goodell," 254; Wittenmyer, *History of the Woman's*

Temperance Crusade, 666; Frances E. Willard, *Woman and Temperance, or the Work and Workers of the Woman's Christian Temperance Union,* 6th ed. (Chicago: Woman's Temperance Publishing Association, 1897), 121–27.

12. Epstein, *Politics of Domesticity,* 115–17; Glenda Riley, *Frontierswomen: The Iowa Experience* (Ames: Iowa State University Press, 1981), 129–34; Noun, *Strong-Minded Women,* 27–31; Bordin, *Woman and Temperance,* 37, 39–42.

13. Willard, *Woman and Temperance,* 20–21, 618–19; Frances E. Willard, *Glimpses of Fifty Years: The Autobiography of an American Woman* (Chicago: Woman's Temperance Publication Association, 1889), 94–98, 198–205; Bordin, *Frances Willard,* 3–23, 50, 95; *Freeman,* Nov. 24, 1887, citing a Willard address in the *Chicago Inter-Ocean.*

14. See Doug Newsom, Alan Scott, and Judy Van Slyke Turk, *This Is PR: The Realities of Public Relations,* 4th ed. (Belmont, Calif.: Wadsworth, 1989), 97. Willard dated her first temperance speech Sept. 14, 1874; see *Glimpses of Fifty Years,* 13.

15. *Chief,* July 13, 1875.

16. Cleary, "Lavinia Goodell," 254–55.

17. Willard, *Woman and Temperance,* 643; Epstein, *Politics of Domesticity,* 117; Blocker, *"Give to the Winds,"* 17, 245.

18. Willard, *Woman and Temperance,* 121–27; Bordin, *Woman and Temperance,* 136.

19. Aileen S. Kraditor, *The Ideas of the Woman Suffrage Movement, 1890–1920* (1965; rpt. New York: W. W. Norton, 1981), 4; Robert C. Nesbit, *The History of Wisconsin,* Vol. 3: *Urbanization and Industrialization, 1873–1893* (Madison: SHSW, 1985), 464–65.

20. Riley, *Frontierswomen,* 150; Cleary, "Lavinia Goodell," 262–63; Buechler, *Transformation of the Woman Suffrage Movement,* 62–64.

21. Cleary, "Lavinia Goodell," 255–65; see also *Christian Union,* Dec. 1 and 15, 1875; *Providence* (Rhode Island) *Journal,* Oct. 19, 1876; *Woman's Journal* 8, Nov. 10, 1877, and L. Goodell to the *Woman's Journal,* reprinted in the *Sentinel,* Jan. 31, 1879. On John Bascom, see Thelen, *Early Life,* 91–96, and J. David Hoeveler, Jr., "The University and the Social Gospel: The Intellectual Origins of the 'Wisconsin Idea,'" in *The Quest for Social Justice* (Madison: University of Wisconsin Press, 1983), 185–207.

22. Cleary, "Lavinia Goodell," 263–65; Barry, *Susan B. Anthony,* 270–71.

23. Wolcott, "Wisconsin," *HWS* 3:643, Youmans, "How Wisconsin Women," 12–13; *HWS* 3:57–59, 75.

24. Smith-Rosenberg, *Disorderly Conduct,* 259–60.

25. Cleary, "Lavinia Goodell," 265–67; Youmans, "How Wisconsin Women," 13.

26. Bordin, *Woman and Temperance,* 26, 72, 90–98; Epstein, *Politics of Domesticity,* 119.

27. K. Austin Kerr, *Organized for Prohibition: A New History of the Anti-Saloon League* (New Haven: Yale University Press, 1985), 27, 175.

28. *Sentinel,* Oct. 1, 1882; Blocker, "*Give to the Winds,*" 221–22; Current, *History of Wisconsin,* 457–60, 479–80.

29. Cleary, "Lavinia Goodell," 270–71; *Sentinel,* March 27, 1880.

30. Youmans, "How Wisconsin Women," 12–13; Wolcott, "Wisconsin," *HWS* 3:644; *Sentinel,* Feb. 28, 1882.

31. Nesbit, *Wisconsin,* 356–57.

Chapter 4. Women in the Newsroom, Women in the News: Temperance and Suffrage, 1882–1890

The primary sources for this chapter are the *Wisconsin Chief* and the *Waukesha Freeman* from 1882 to 1890; specific citations of these sources are given only for exceptions to the time period or quotations of length.

1. Youmans, "How Wisconsin Women," 11, 14–15; Graves, "Wisconsin Woman's Movement," 47, 52; Janice Steinschneider, "'Not a New Woman, But an Improved Woman': The Wisconsin Federation of Women's Clubs, 1895–1920," M.A. thesis, University of Wisconsin-Madison, 1983, 142–43; Kepler, "Cradle of the Woman's Suffrage Movement," 1–9; *State Journal,* June 9, 1882.

2. Cote, *Olympia Brown,* 48–51, 94–96, 104–13, 117–24; *HWS* II, 95–97; Youmans, "How Wisconsin Women," 13. Willis' paper later merged with the *Racine Journal-Times,* which is still in operation.

3. Cote, *Olympia Brown,* 109–10, 127–29.

4. Youmans, "How Wisconsin Women," 15; Kepler, "Cradle of the Woman's Suffrage Movement," 6.

5. Evans, *Born for Liberty,* 127; Thelen, *Early Life,* 89; Bordin, *Woman and Temperance,* 26, 89–90.

6. Bordin, *Woman and Temperance,* 58–59; Kraditor, *Ideas of the Woman Suffrage Movement,* 4–6; Evans, *Born for Liberty,* 128; Merle Curti, "The Changing Concept of 'Human Nature' in the Literature of Advertising," *Business History Review* 41 (Winter 1967), 335–57.

7. Flexner, *Century of Struggle,* 188; Epstein, *Politics of Domesticity,* 123, 136; Bordin, *Woman and Temperance,* 94; Nesbit, *History of Wisconsin,* 467n; Sarah A. Powers to Laura Briggs James, March 14, 1884, Ada L. James Papers, SHSW; Youmans, "How Wisconsin Women," 15; Thelen, *Early Life,* 91–96, Wolcott, "Wisconsin," *HWS* 3:647.

8. Wolcott, "Wisconsin," *HWS* 3:645; Brown, "Wisconsin," *HWS* 4:985; Kepler, "Cradle of the Woman's Suffrage Movement," 15; anonymous to Mrs. James, n.d., Laura Briggs James Papers, SHSW; Theodora W. Youmans, "Wisconsin," in *HWS* 6:701; Youmans, "How Wisconsin Women," 4–9, 15. Wolcott's account lists Griswold as elected in 1885, apparently a typographical error; here, Youmans' account and contemporary reports in the *Chief* are preferred.

9. Brown, "Wisconsin," *HWS* 4:988–89; Alura Collins to Laura James, 1887,

Laura Briggs James Papers, SHSW; Youmans, "How Wisconsin Women," 15; Olympia Brown to T. W. Youmans, *Freeman*, Jan. 29, 1920; Alura Collins Hollister to Theodora W. Youmans, *Freeman*, May 18, 1919; *Sentinel*, March 27 and 30, 1885.

10. Alura Collins to Theodora Winton, *Freeman*, March 22, 1888.

11. Collins to Winton, *Freeman*, March 22, 1888; Brown to Youmans, *Freeman*, Jan. 29, 1920; Hollister to Youmans, *Freeman*, May 18, 1919. The James quote varies slightly in other reminiscences by Brown; see Cote, *Olympia Brown*, 124–25.

12. Brown, "Wisconsin," *HWS* 4:988; E. Claire Jerry, "Clara Bewick Colby and the *Woman's Tribune*, 1883–1909: The Free Lance Editor as Movement Leader," in *A Voice of Their Own*, 110–28.

13. Brown, "Wisconsin," *HWS* 4:985; Youmans, "How Wisconsin Women," 16; Cote, *Olympia Brown*, 126; Hollister to Youmans, *Freeman*, May 18, 1919.

14. Brown, "Wisconsin," *HWS* 4:986–89; Brown to Youmans, *Freeman*, Jan. 29, 1920; Nesbit, *History of Wisconsin*, 463.

15. Hollister to Youmans, *Freeman*, May 18, 1919; Brown to Youmans, *Freeman*, Jan. 29, 1920; Cote, *Olympia Brown*, 109–10, 127–29.

16. Youmans, "How Wisconsin Women," 16–17; Brown, "Wisconsin," *HWS* 4:990; Brown to Youmans, *Freeman*, Jan. 29, 1920.

17. Pioneer Scrapbooks, FAHS; Weisensel, "Wisconsin Temperance Crusade," 187.

18. Cote, *Olympia Brown*, 128; Brown to Youmans, *Freeman*, Jan. 29, 1920; Brown, "Wisconsin," *HWS* 4:990–91; Nesbit, *History of Wisconsin*, 250–51, 464–65, 468.

19. Nesbit, *Wisconsin*, 377–78, 395; Kraditor, *Ideas of the Woman Suffrage Movement*, 4–5; Brown to Youmans, *Freeman*, Jan. 29, 1920; Cote, *Olympia Brown*, 128–30; Brown, "Wisconsin," *HWS* 4:990–92; Bordin, *Woman and Temperance*, 90–96, 135–44; Kepler, "Cradle of the Woman's Suffrage Movement," 18.

20. *Freeman*, Jan. 25, 1912.

Chapter 5. Ladies of the Clubs: Municipal Reform, 1890–1898

The primary source for this chapter is the *Waukesha Freeman* from 1890 to 1898; specific citations of this source are given only for exceptions to the time period or for quotations of length.

1. Evans, *Born for Liberty*, 153; Blair, *Clubwoman as Feminist*, 1–4; Bordin, *Francis Willard*, 41; Nesbit, *History of Wisconsin*, 460; Kerr, *Organized for Prohibition*, 147, 242.

2. *Freeman*, Oct. 3, 1912; Nancy F. Cott, *The Grounding of Modern Feminism* (New Haven: Yale University Press, 1987), 87; Anne M. Boylan, "Women

in Groups: An Analysis of Women's Benevolent Organizations in New York and Boston, 1797–1840," *Journal of American History* 71 (December 1984), 502, 514.

3. Martin, *Sound of Our Own Voices,* 52–54; Flexner, *Century of Struggle,* 11–13; Evans, *Born for Liberty,* 67–92; Henry Ladd Smith, "The Beauteous Jennie June: Pioneer Woman Journalist," *Journalism Quarterly* 40 (Spring 1963), 160–74; Jane C. Croly, *The History of the Woman's Club Movement in America* (New York: H. G. Allen, 1898), 1158–59; *Chief,* Sept. 3, 1868.

4. Ladies' Art and Science Class of Milwaukee College, Papers, 1874–1886, Milwaukee Area Research Center, Golda Meir Library, University of Wisconsin–Milwaukee.

5. Mary A. Mariner, "Woman's Club of Wisconsin, 1876–1923," 7–12, in the author's possession; Hoeveler, *Milwaukee Women Yesterday,* 23; Martin, *Sound of Our Own Voices,* 1, 181, emphasis in the original.

6. Steinschneider, "'Not a New Woman,'" 6–7, 133; Marlin Johnson, "Natural Features and Land Use," in *From Farmland to Freeways,* 15, and Philip Runkel, "Culture and Recreation," ibid., 435–39.

7. *Freeman,* Nov. 11, 1886 and Sept. 1, 15, and 22, 1887. The existence of daily editions is construed from promotions in the paper, although only weekly editions are available on microfilm.

8. Winton Family, New Berlin File, Pioneer Notebooks, WCHS; Theodora W. Youmans, "In Memory of My Father," *Freeman,* Dec. 26, 1912, "An Old-Time Merchant's Account Book," *Freeman,* Sept. 20, 1917, and "A Pioneer Church at Prospect," *WMH* 9 (1925), 321–32; interview, Libbie Nolan, Curator of the New Berlin Historical Society, Waukesha, Wis., May 22, 1989. Theodore Sumner Winton and Emily Tillson Winton were distant cousins—his mother was Sarah Tillson Winton—born in Butternut, Otsego County, New York. He came to Wisconsin in the early 1840s, as a child, and his wife first came to visit the Winton family in the 1850s, returned as his bride, and bore four children. The Winton homestead and store now house the museum and offices of the New Berlin Historical Society.

9. "Dora E. Winton of Prospect," *1880 Carroll College Catalogue,* Carroll College Archives, Waukesha, Wis. Some sources suggest that Youmans was a college graduate. However, from 1860 until almost the turn of the century, Carroll was reduced to academy status while retaining its college charter, and although Carroll first admitted women at the academy level in 1863, the first college degree awarded to a woman was in the 1890s; see Langill, *Carroll College,* 44, 111.

10. Steinschneider, "'Not a New Woman,'" 124–25. In religious affiliation, Youmans also was typical of suffragists and clubwomen who primarily were Protestant, although more than half of Wisconsin women were Catholic. Youmans' marital status also was typical of Wisconsin clubwomen, although suffrage leaders more often were single. However, Youmans was atypical of clubwomen but typical of suffrage leaders in remaining childless, in that her stepchildren al-

ready were grown upon her marriage; on demographical data on suffragists, see Kraditor, *Ideas of the Woman Suffrage Movement,* 265–82.

11. Theron W. Haight Papers, SHSW; Robert W. Wells, *The Milwaukee Journal: An Informal Chronicle of Its First 100 Years* (Milwaukee: Milwaukee Journal, 1881), 1–2; Will C. Conrad, Kathleen Wilson, and Dale Wilson, *The Milwaukee Journal: The First Eighty Years* (Madison: University of Wisconsin Press, 1964), 5–6. On Anne Eliza Youmans, "well known as a writer on botany and kindred subjects in a style suitable to children's study" and a "close associate in the studies and works" of her brother, Edward, and on Edward L. Youmans, author of widely published books and the chief editor of *Popular Science Monthly* from its founding in 1872 until 1887, see *Freeman,* Jan. 27, 1887. On the early *Freeman,* which had no connection to the earlier *American Freeman* in Waukesha, then called Prairieville, see Gilbert H. Koenig, *Once Upon a Prairie: Waukesha's Yesteryears* (Waukesha, Wis.: Waukesha Freeman, 1985), 88, and Henry M. Youmans, "Fifty Years," *Freeman,* Oct. 7, 1920.

12. Youmans, "How Wisconsin Women," 13; Alura Collins Hollister to Theron W. Haight, undated, in the Haight Papers, SHSW; Theodora W. Youmans, "A Woman's Life at the *Freeman,*" *Waukesha County Centennial and 75th Anniversary Edition of the Waukesha Daily Freeman* (Waukesha, Wis.: Waukesha Freeman, 1934).

13. Noun, *Strong-Minded Women,* 228–30.

14. See also Nesbit, *History of Wisconsin,* 250–51, 464–65, 468.

15. *Freeman,* Nov. 22, 1888, citing the *American Newspaper Annual of 1888.* Wisconsin ranked fifth nationally for the number of newspapers per state.

16. Koenig, *Once Upon a Prairie,* 88.

17. Youmans, "Women as Journalists," *Sentinel,* March 15, 1891; "Youmans Dies," *Freeman,* Aug. 18, 1932; Nesbit, *History of Wisconsin,* 470; Conrad et al., *Milwaukee Journal,* 44–46; Wells, *Milwaukee Journal,* 32–34. Male colleagues' acceptance may not have come until later in Youmans' career; as late as 1900, when her husband went on tour with the Wisconsin Editors' Association, she took separate vacations. Their annual travelogues, wired to Waukesha from points apart, apparently caused considerable comment; see, for example, *Freeman,* April 5, 1900.

18. James S. Bradshaw, "Mrs. Rayne's School of Journalism," *Journalism Quarterly* 60 (Fall 1988), 513, citing U.S. Census Office, *Compendium of the Eleventh Census,* part 3 (Washington, D.C.: U.S. Government Printing Office, 1897), 516; Maurine Beasley and Sheila Silver, *Women in Media: A Documentary Source Book* (Washington, D.C.: Anaconda Press, 1977), 1–3; Marion Marzolf, *Women in American Journalism: A Preliminary Bibliography* (University of Michigan Department of Journalism, 1971), 1. The census first included a category for journalists in 1870; then and later, the figure is undoubtedly low, although proportions of men and women in the profession are probably more accurate. By 1920 the census listed 5,730 newswomen, 16.7 percent of all journalists.

19. Nesbit, *History of Wisconsin,* 245–51, 451–54.

20. Mariner, "Woman's Club of Wisconsin," 14–16; Hoeveler, *Milwaukee Women Yesterday,* 30; Grace Norton Kieckhefer, *The History of Milwaukee–Downer College, 1851–1951* (Milwaukee: Milwaukee–Downer College, 1950), 38; Steinschneider, "'Not a New Woman,'" 137. The Athenaeum still houses the Woman's Club of Wisconsin and the College Endowment Association. Milwaukee–Downer College closed in the 1960s and transferred its endowment to the Downer Music Conservatory at Lawrence University, Appleton. The Downer College buildings were purchased by the state and now are part of the University of Wisconsin–Milwaukee campus.

21. Beacon Lights File and Ideals Club File, Organizations Papers, WCHS; *Freeman,* Feb. 13, 1902; on officers of the WWSA, see Graves, "Wisconsin Woman's Movement," 373.

22. Evans, *Born for Liberty,* 150; Buechler, *Transformation of the Woman Suffrage Movement,* 157.

23. Wolcott, "Wisconsin," *HWS* 3:641; Brown, "Wisconsin," *HWS* 4:993; *Freeman,* June 8, 1882; Estelle B. Freedman, *Their Sisters' Keepers: Women's Prison Reform in America, 1830–1930* (Ann Arbor: University of Michigan Press, 1984), 59, emphasis in the original.

24. On vocational education campaigns, see Steinschneider, "'Not a New Woman,'" 86–87; on Milwaukee clubwomen's campaigns, see David Paul Nord, "The Paradox of Municipal Reform in the Late Nineteenth Century," *Journalism Quarterly* 48 (Winter 1982–83), 128–42.

25. Ann Colbert, "Notes on Women's Editions: Introducing the Truly 'Exceptional,'" presented to the Commission on Status of Women, Association for Education in Journalism and Mass Communication, Boston, August 1991; Conrad et al., *Milwaukee Journal,* 51–53; Wells, *Milwaukee Journal,* 45–47. According to Colbert, the *Boston Globe* in 1884 sponsored the first "women's edition," which later was emulated by women in San Francisco, Chicago, Memphis, Atlanta, Omaha, Philadelphia, Washington, D.C., and Elmira, N.Y., the last edited by the Reverend Annis Ford Eastman, mother of journalists and suffragists Max Eastman and Crystal Eastman Benedict.

26. Steinschneider, "'Not a New Woman,'" 11, 37–38, 140; Hoeveler, *Milwaukee Women Yesterday,* 27; Lutie Stearns, "My Seventy-Five Years: Part I, 1866–1914," *WMH* 42 (Spring 1959), 211–18; David P. Thelen, *The New Citizenship: Origins of Progressivism in Wisconsin, 1885–1900* (Columbia: University of Missouri Press, 1972), 86–93.

27. Blair, *Clubwoman as Feminist,* 1–5.

28. See Nesbit, *History of Wisconsin,* 467, 469.

29. Steinschneider, "'Not a New Woman,'" 37–38, 55, 60–61, 86–87, 132, 140; on Henrotin, see Buechler, *Transformation of the Woman Suffrage Movement,* 164–65.

30. Jerry Bower, "Social Housekeeping in Richland Center: The Federation of Women's Clubs, 1898–1925," *MS,* 3–15, emphasis in the original; Kepler,

"Cradle of the Woman's Suffrage Movement," 7; Elsie McFarlane, MS dated 1945, Practical Club File, Organizations Papers, WCHS.

31. Kraditor, *Ideas of the Woman Suffrage Movement*, 4–7; Jerry, "Clara Bewick Colby," 120.

32. Brown, "Wisconsin," *HWS* 4:987, 991; "Proceedings, 1890," WWSA Papers, SHSW.

33. Bordin, *Frances Willard*, 1–3; Bordin, *Woman and Temperance*, 90–96, 135–44; Nesbit, *Wisconsin*, 377–78; Gusfield, *Symbolic Crusade*, 86; *Janesville Gazette,* Jan. 3, 1898; Anna A. Gordon, *The Beautiful Life of Frances E. Willard: A Memorial Volume* (Chicago: Woman's Temperance Publishing Association, 1899), 281; Weisensel, "Wisconsin Temperance Crusade," 10–12.

34. Steinschneider, "'Not a New Woman,'" 56, 63; Lucy Freeman, Sherry La Follette, and George A. Zabriskie, *Belle: The Biography of Belle Case La Follette* (New York: Beaufort, 1985), 48–49.

35. *Freeman,* Jan. 29, 1914; Steinschneider, "'Not a New Woman,'" 73, 131; see also Blair, *Clubwoman as Feminist,* 41; Martin, *Sound of Our Own Voices,* 1; Boylan, "Women in Groups," 502; Daniel Walker Howe, "The Evangelical Movement and Political Culture in the North during the Second Party System," *Journal of American History* 77 (March 1991), 1216–39.

Chapter 6. Schooling for Suffrage: Progressive Reform, 1898–1910

The primary source for this chapter is the *Waukesha Freeman* from 1898 to 1910; specific citations from this source are given only for exceptions to the time period and for quotations of length.

1. William Chafe, *The American Woman: Her Changing Social, Economic and Political Roles, 1920–1970* (London: Oxford University Press, 1972), 36.

2. Brown, "Wisconsin," *HWS* 4:993.

3. Steinschneider, "'Not a New Woman,'" 90–91.

4. Gerda Lerner, *The Majority Finds Its Past: Placing Women in History* (Oxford: Oxford University Press, 1979), 104, 108.

5. *Freeman,* July 27, 1899.

6. See Giddings, *When and Where I Enter,* 102–7.

7. Charles Harris Wesley, *The History of the National Association of Colored Women's Clubs: A Legacy of Service* (Washington, D.C.: National Association of Colored Women's Clubs, 1984), 48–50; on other African-American women's clubs in Wisconsin, including the Cream City Social and Literary Society, circa 1880s, the Silver Leaf Charity Club, circa 1890s, and several post-1900 clubs, see Joe William Trotter, Jr., *Black Milwaukee: The Making of an Industrial Proletariat, 1915–1945* (Urbana: University of Illinois Press, 1985), 32–33.

8. Lerner, *Majority Finds Its Past,* 108; Giddings, *When and Where I Enter,* 102–7; Wesley, *History of the NACWC,* 48–50; Penelope L. Bullock, *The Negro*

Periodical Press in the United States, 1838–1909 (Ann Arbor, Mich.: University Microfilms, 1974), 252; Pauline Hopkins, "Josephine St. Pierre Ruffin at Milwaukee, 1900," *Colored American Magazine,* July 1902, 210–13, and "Some Famous Women," ibid., August 1902, 273–77. Some sources state that Ruffin was a member of the New England Press Association, which did not admit women, and that she was on the board of the General Federation, rather than the state federation. All sources cited vary on which "mixed clubs" selected Ruffin as their representative to the Biennial.

9. Wesley, *History of the NACWC,* 49.

10. Wesley, *History of the NACWC,* 48–50; Giddings, *When and Where I Enter,* 105; Lerner, *Majority Finds Its Past,* 108.

11. *Evening Wisconsin,* June 4, 1900; *Wisconsin Weekly Advocate,* June 7, 1900; Wesley, *History of the NACWC,* 49–50; Lerner, *Majority Finds Its Past,* 108; Trotter, *Black Milwaukee,* 30–33; Giddings, *When and Where I Enter,* 105; see also Genevieve G. McBride, "The African-American Press in Wisconsin," in H. Lewis Suggs, ed., *The Black Press of the Middlewest* (Westport, Conn.: Greenwood Press, 1994).

12. Ann J. Lane, *To Herland and Beyond: The Life and Work of Charlotte Perkins Gilman* (New York: Meridian Books, 1991), 228; Steinschneider, "'Not a New Woman,'" 58.

13. Steinschneider, "'Not a New Woman,'" 42, 81.

14. Freeman et al., *Belle,* 15–17, 54–55, 60–61, 67–68, 127.

15. Brown, "Wisconsin," *HWS* 4:993; Steinschneider, "'Not a New Woman,'" 42–43.

16. Youmans, "How Wisconsin Women," 17–19.

17. Steinschneider, "'Not a New Woman,'" 45; on Jones, see Hoeveler, *Milwaukee Women Yesterday,* 59.

18. Estelle B. Freedman, "Separatism as Strategy: Female Institution Building and American Feminism, 1870–1930," *Feminist Studies* 5 (Fall 1979), 512–28; Steinschneider, "'Not a New Woman,'" 41, 67.

19. "Address," n.d., Laura Briggs James Papers, SHSW; Youmans, "How Wisconsin Women," 17.

20. Steinschneider, "'Not a New Woman,'" 63.

21. Youmans, "How Wisconsin Women," 18, 31–32; Youmans, "Wisconsin," *HWS* 6:700; Steinschneider, "'Not a New Woman,'" 44, 53, 64.

22. *Freeman,* Nov. 7, 1901.

23. Steinschneider, "'Not a New Woman,'" 64, 144–45, 177, 180; on Gudden, see William H. O'Neill, *Everyone Was Brave: The Rise and Fall of Feminism in America* (Chicago: Quadrangle, 1969), 95–97; on Hooper, see Lawrence L. Graves, "Two Noteworthy Wisconsin Women: Mrs. Ben Hooper and Ada James," *Wisconsin Magazine of History* 41 (Spring 1958), 174–80.

24. Ideal Club File, Women's Club File, and McFarlane MS, Practical Club File, Organizations Papers, WCHS; Koenig, *Once Upon a Prairie,* 124–26;

Ellen D. Langill, "The History of Education in Waukesha County," in *From Farmlands to Freeways,* 298–301; *Freeman,* Oct. 25, 1918; see also Genevieve G. (McBride) Caspari, "One Hundred Years of Women Who Made Waukesha: Clubwomen Led Vote Fight," *Freeman,* Aug. 26, 1985, and "Youmans Took Suffrage 'to the World,'" *Freeman,* Sept. 3, 1985.

25. *Freeman,* Aug. 18, 1932; Steinschneider, "'Not a New Woman,'" 44, 47, 53, 69–73, 90–91, 141; Freeman et al., *Belle,* 92–98.

26. Steinschneider, "'Not a New Woman,'" 93–100, 111, 138–39, 176.

27. Cote, *Olympia Brown,* 65–66, 68–92, 120, 133–40.

28. Cote, *Olympia Brown,* 137–45; Youmans, "Wisconsin," *HWS* 6:699–700; Wolcott, "Wisconsin," *HWS* 3:639.

29. Cote, *Olympia Brown,* 65–66, 68–92, 120, 133–40; Brown, "Wisconsin," *HWS* 4:988. Brown's son, Dr. Parker Willis, was a professor of economics at Washington and Lee University until 1901, when he became a reporter for the *New York Evening Post.*

30. Kraditor, *Ideas of the Woman Suffrage Movement,* 7; Steinschneider, "'Not a New Woman,'" 11, 39.

31. *Freeman,* Jan. 18 and 25, 1912; Graves, "Wisconsin Woman's Movement," 111; Graves, "Two Noteworthy Wisconsin Women," 179; 1909 Political Equality Club program and Olympia Brown to Ada James, February 1910 and April 25, 1910, Ada L. James Papers, SHSW; Blair, *Clubwoman as Feminist,* 1–5.

32. Steinschneider, "'Not a New Woman,'" 100–101, 128.

Chapter 7. Retreat from Progressivism:
Suffrage Referendum, 1911–1912

The primary source for this chapter is the *Waukesha Freeman* in 1911 and 1912; specific citations from this source are given only for exceptions to this time period or for quotations of length.

1. Youmans, "How Wisconsin Women," 20.

2. Olympia Brown to Ada James, May 1911, Josephine Kudzick to Ada James, April 1, 1911, and Mary Swain Wagner to Ada James, April 11, 1911, Ada L. James Papers, SHSW.

3. *Freeman,* Nov. 6, 1919; Youmans, "A Woman's Life," 16; Theodora W. Youmans to Ada James, July 15, 1911, Ada L. James Papers, SHSW.

4. Flexner, *Century of Struggle,* 258; Crystal Eastman, "Political Equality League (Report on the Wisconsin Suffrage Campaign)," in Blanche Wiesen Cook, ed., *Crystal Eastman on Women and Revolution* (New York: Oxford University Press, 1978), 67. Crystal Eastman Benedict divorced soon after the 1912 referendum, and resumed her maiden name after leaving Milwaukee.

5. Steinschneider, "'Not a New Woman,'" 175–92; Youmans, "How Wisconsin Women," 20–21; Jessie Jack Hooper MS, Hooper Papers, SHSW; Mari Jo

Buhle, *Women and American Socialism, 1870–1920* (Urbana: University of Illinois Press, 1983), 129–31.

6. *Freeman*, Feb. 26, 1914.

7. Graves, "Two Noteworthy Wisconsin Women," 177–79; Cott, *Grounding of Modern Feminism*, 28–29; Youmans, "How Wisconsin Women," 20–21. For correspondence to, from, and about Mary Swain Wagner, January–April 1911, see the Ada L. James Papers, SHSW.

8. Lucy E. Morris to Sophie Gudden, n.d., Lutie Stearns to Ada James, n.d., Ada L. James to Theodora W. Youmans, Sept. 21, 1911, Theodora W. Youmans to Ada L. James, Dec.[?], 1911, Ada L. James Papers, SHSW.

9. Youmans, "Wisconsin," *HWS* 6:701; Eastman, "Political Equality League," 67; Graves, "Wisconsin Woman's Movement," 132, 144; Buechler, *Transformation of the Woman Suffrage Movement*, 164, 225–27; Freeman et al., *Belle*, 126.

10. Cott, *Grounding of Modern Feminism*, 28.

11. Youmans, "How Wisconsin Women," 21; Youmans, "Wisconsin," *HWS* 6:702–3; Koenig, *Once Upon a Prairie*, 60; Kenneth W. Duckett, "Suffragettes on the Stump: Letter from the Political Equality League of Wisconsin, 1912," *WMH* 38 (Autumn 1954), 32; Meredith Tax, *The Rising of the Women: Feminist Solidarity and Class Conflict, 1880–1917* (New York: Monthly Review Press, 1980), 170; Sharon Hartman Strom, "Leadership and Tactics in the American Woman Suffrage Movement: A New Perspective from Massachusetts," *Journal of American History* 62 (September 1975), 381–82; *HWS* 6:148–56; Flexner, *Century of Struggle*, 263–64; Buechler, *Transformation of the Woman Suffrage Movement*, 174.

12. Evans, *Born for Liberty*, 165; Lauren Kessler, "The Ideas of Woman Suffragists and the Portland *Oregonian*," *Journalism Quarterly* 57 (Winter 1980), 597–605; O'Neill, *Everyone Was Brave*, 166.

13. Cote, *Olympia Brown*, 149; Youmans, "How Wisconsin Women," 20–21; Youmans, "Wisconsin," *HWS* 6:703; Trotter, *Black Milwaukee*, 8, 131–32; Catharine Waugh McCulloch to Ada James, July 5, 1911, and Mabel M. Judd to Ada L. James, July 11, 1911, Ada L. James Papers, SHSW; see also McBride, "African-American Press in Wisconsin."

14. Youmans, "Wisconsin," *HWS* 6:702; Grace A. King to Gwendolen Willis, Sept. 30, 1912, J. M. Knowles to G. Willis, Oct. 1, 1912, and miscellaneous correspondence, WWSA Papers, SHSW.

15. Eastman, "Political Equality League," 67.

16. Graves, "Wisconsin Woman's Movement," 157–62; on Neal Dow Brown, see *Dictionary of Wisconsin Biography;* on the New York Men's League, see O'Neill, *Everyone Was Brave*, 68.

17. Graves, "Wisconsin Woman's Movement," 144–46.

18. Flexner, *Century of Struggle*, 270–72; Graves, "Wisconsin Woman's Movement," 210; Freeman et al., *Belle*, 126; Belle La Follette to Gwendolen Willis, Oct. 23, 1912, WWSA Papers, SHSW.

19. *Freeman,* Sept. 26, 1912.

20. Elizabeth Burt, "Mixed Messages in a Progressive Newspaper: The *Milwaukee Journal* and Woman Suffrage, 1911–12," presented to the Association for Education in Journalism and Mass Communication, Montreal, August 1992; Conrad et al., *Milwaukee Journal,* 78; Lutie Stearns to Ada James, July 1912, Ada L. James Papers, SHSW.

21. Eastman, "Political Equality League," 69; Graves, "Wisconsin Woman's Movement," 213.

22. Flexner, *Century of Struggle,* Sophie Gudden to Ada James, Jan. 29 and Dec. 17, 1912, Ada L. James Papers, SHSW.

23. Kerr, *Organized for Prohibition,* 27, 175; Elizabeth Burt, "Woman Suffrage, the Liquor Industry and the Press: Wisconsin, 1911–1912," presented to the Midwest Regional History Conference, Association for Education in Journalism and Mass Communication, Iowa City, Iowa, April 1991; Eastman, "Political Equality League," 69.

24. Youmans, "Wisconsin," *HWS* 6:703.

25. Youmans, "How Wisconsin Women," 22.

26. O'Neill, *Everyone Was Brave,* 57; Graves, "Wisconsin Woman's Movement," 137–38, 211–12, 223; Flexner, *Century of Struggle,* 279; Youmans, "How Wisconsin Women," 22.

27. Steinschneider, "'Not a New Woman,'" 13, 65, 147–48; Blair, *Clubwoman as Feminist,* 5.

28. *Freeman,* Oct. 3, 1912.

29. Youmans to PEL Workers, Nov. 6, 1912, Ada L. James Papers, SHSW; Mary F. Somerville to Gwendolen Willis, Nov. 15, 1912, WWSA Papers, SHSW.

30. Youmans, "Wisconsin," *HWS* 6:703; Youmans, "How Wisconsin Women," 23; Catt and Shuler, *Woman Suffrage and Politics,* 187–88; Alice Lindsay to Alice Curtis, Dec. 19, 1913, WWSA Papers, SHSW; Eastman, "Political Equality League," 67–69.

31. Youmans, "Wisconsin," *HWS* 6:703; Graves, "Wisconsin Woman's Movement," 213–14, 223; Marilyn Grant, "1912 Suffrage Referendum: An Exercise in Political Action," *WMH* 64 (Winter 1980–81), 116.

32. Youmans, "How Wisconsin Women," 23–24; Youmans, "Wisconsin," *HWS* 6:703–4; Anna Howard Shaw to Ada James, March 30, 1912, Lutie E. Stearns to Ada James, Jan. 14, 1913, Mrs. L. A. Doolittle to Ada L. James, January 1913, and Zona Gale to Ada James, Jan. 23, 1913, Ada L. James Papers, SHSW.

33. Graves, "Wisconsin Woman's Movement," 137–38, 223; Belle La Follette to Ada James, Nov. 26, 1912, Rose C. Swart to Ada L. James, Dec. 17, 1912, Sophie Gudden to Ada James, Dec. 17, 1912, Theodora W. Youmans to Ada L. James, n.d., and Theodora W. Youmans to Ada L. James, Jan. 13, 1913, in the Ada L. James Papers, SHSW; Youmans, "How Wisconsin Women," 23–24.

Chapter 8. *Women's Work: Suffrage Reorganization, 1913–1915*

The primary source for this chapter is the *Waukesha Freeman* from 1913 through 1915; specific citations from this source are given only for exceptions to the time period or for quotations of length.

1. Youmans, "How Wisconsin Women," 24.

2. Cote, *Olympia Brown,* 151; *Freeman,* May 18, 1919; Charles E. Neu, "Olympia Brown and the Woman's Suffrage Movement," *WMH* 43 (Summer 1960), 280–84.

3. Youmans to James, Jan. 13, 1913, Ada L. James Papers, SHSW; Youmans, "How Wisconsin Women," 30.

4. Ada L. James to Crystal E. Benedict, Jan. 7, 1913, and Zona Gale to Ada L. James, Jan. 23, 1913, Ada L. James Papers, SHSW; Flexner, *Century of Struggle,* 266–79.

5. O'Neill, *Everyone Was Brave,* 203.

6. See Cote, *Olympia Brown,* 162; Graves, "Wisconsin Woman's Movement," 230–34; Freeman et al., *Belle,* 137–40.

7. Flexner, *Century of Struggle,* 307; see also Kerr, *Organized for Prohibition,* 176.

8. *Freeman,* July 31, 1913, emphasis in the original.

9. Youmans, "How Wisconsin Women," 24; Graves, "Wisconsin Woman's Movement," 242, 246–47; Ada James to "Dear Pardner," Oct. 13, 1913, and Zona Gale to Theodora W. Youmans, December 1913, WWSA Papers, SHSW, emphasis in the original.

10. *Freeman,* Nov. 20, 1913.

11. *Freeman,* Nov. 20, 1913.

12. Buechler, *Transformation of the Woman Suffrage Movement,* 174–78; on the McCormicks, who also later served in Congress, see J. Stanley Lemons, *The Woman Citizen: Social Feminism in the 1920s* (Urbana: University of Illinois Press, 1973), 104–5.

13. Flexner, *Century of Struggle,* 266–79; Kraditor, *Ideas of the Woman Suffrage Movement,* 231–34.

14. O'Neill, *Everyone Was Brave,* 167, 186, 192.

15. See Alan R. Raucher, *Public Relations and Business, 1900–1929* (Baltimore: Johns Hopkins University Press, 1968), 6; see also Susan M. Caudill, "The Newspaper Industry's Campaign against Spacegrabbers, 1917–1921," *Journalism History,* forthcoming.

16. Sophie Gudden to Alice Curtis, Dec. 19, 1913, and Sophie Gudden to Theodora W. Youmans, Dec. 28, 1913, WWSA Papers, SHSW. On Haight, see Youmans, "Wisconsin," *HWS* 6:704; on Gudden, see Youmans, "How Wisconsin Women," 25.

17. Cote, *Olympia Brown,* 150–51; Gwendolen Willis to Theodora W. Youmans, Jan. 12, 1914, and Olympia Brown to Theodora W. Youmans, Jan. 14, 1914, WWSA Papers, SHSW.

18. Graves, "Wisconsin Woman's Movement," 242, 246–47; Lutie Stearns to Theodora W. Youmans, Aug. 15, 1914, WWSA Papers, SHSW; on Eastman, see O'Neill, *Everyone Was Brave*, 172, 176, 183, 286–88.

19. See Blair, *Clubwoman as Feminist*, 1–5; O'Neill, *Everyone Was Brave*, 167.

20. Graves, "Wisconsin Woman's Movement," 263, 267–68.

21. See Freeman et al., *Belle*, 57, 66, which suggests the *Voter's Hand-Book* was not imitated until 1933 and by the *New York Times*.

22. Youmans, "How Wisconsin Women," 25; Theodora W. Youmans to Alice Curtis, [1914?], WWSA Papers, SHSW.

23. *Freeman*, Dec. 10, 1914.

24. On Pethick Lawrence and Schwimmer's tour, see O'Neill, *Everyone Was Brave*, 171–72.

25. Youmans, "Wisconsin," *HWS* 6:705.

26. See Flexner, *Century of Struggle*, 277–81; O'Neill, *Everyone Was Brave*, 123–24.

27. Winton File, Pioneer Notebooks, WCHS.

Chapter 9. Women at War: Suffrage and Ratification, 1916–1919

The primary source for this chapter is the *Waukesha Freeman* from 1916 through 1919; specific citations from this source are given only for exceptions to the time period or for quotations of length.

1. Evans, *Born for Liberty*, 167; see also Flexner, *Century of Struggle*, 281–283, 291–92.

2. O'Neill, *Everyone Was Brave*, 167; see also Kraditor, *Ideas of the Woman Suffrage Movement*, 7; Flexner, *Century of Struggle*, 289.

3. Kraditor, *Ideas of the Woman Suffrage Movement*, 6–10; Zona Gale and Harriet Bain to Theodora W. Youmans, March 23, 1916, WWSA Papers, SHSW.

4. The train depot, since demolished, was on the lakefront at Grand Avenue, now called Wisconsin Avenue.

5. Youmans, "How Wisconsin Women," 25; Flexner, *Century of Struggle*, 287–88; Evans, *Born for Liberty*, 169; Cote, *Olympia Brown*, 170.

6. Noun, *Strong-Minded Women*, 227–57.

7. Although the news service may have been formalized earlier, the first mention in Youmans' column is concurrent with the first example extant of the letterhead stationery; see WWSA Papers, SHSW.

8. Evans, *Born for Liberty*, 166–67; O'Neill, *Everyone Was Brave*, 185, 190; see also Flexner, *Century of Struggle*, 297–300; Kraditor, *Ideas of the Woman Suffrage Movement*, 8–10, 231–48.

9. Flexner, *Century of Struggle*, 289.

10. See Cote, *Olympia Brown*, 153–54.

11. The Leslie legacy, left to Catt in 1914, was disputed by heirs until settle-

ment in 1917; Nancy Baker Jones, "Ida Husted Harper and the Leslie Bureau of Suffrage Education," presented to the History Division of the Association for Education in Journalism and Mass Communication, Memphis, Tenn., August 1985.

12. Newsom, Scott, and Turk, *This Is PR,* 41.

13. Cote, *Olympia Brown,* 154; Graves, "Wisconsin Woman's Movement," 285–90.

14. Kraditor, *Ideas of the Woman Suffrage Movement,* 8–9, 237–38; Cote, *Olympia Brown,* 152, 156–57.

15. Flexner, *Century of Struggle,* 294.

16. Graves, "Wisconsin Woman's Movement," 277–78.

17. Conrad et al., *Milwaukee Journal,* 100.

18. J. A. Thompson, "American Progressive Publicists and the First World War, 1914–1917," *Journal of American History* 58 (September 1971), 380, 382; Lemons, *Woman Citizen,* 5–10; Karen Falk, "Public Opinion in Wisconsin During World War I," *WMH* 25 (June 1942), 399.

19. Rankin would be the only member of congress, man or woman, who would vote against both world wars. Rankin lost her Senate seat in 1918 and left Congress, only to return in 1940 in time for the next declaration of war; see Lemons, *Woman Citizen,* 103.

20. Graves, "Wisconsin Woman's Movement," 285–90; Cote, *Olympia Brown,* 158–64; Kraditor, *Ideas of the Woman Suffrage Movement,* 239–40.

21. See Graves, "Wisconsin Woman's Movement," 288; see also Meta Berger to Ada James, Jan. 4, 1917, Ada L. James Papers, SHSW; Ada L. James to Theodora W. Youmans, Nov. 10, 1917, and Theodora W. Youmans to Ada L. James, Nov. 22, 1917, WWSA Papers, SHSW.

22. On Waukesha, see Koenig, *Once Upon a Prairie,* 142–54; on the Woman's Party, see Kraditor, *Ideas of the Woman Suffrage Movement,* 239–40.

23. Kraditor, *Ideas of the Woman Suffrage Movement,* 7.

24. Kerr, *Organized for Prohibition,* 41.

25. Jones, "Ida Husted Harper," 2–22.

26. See also Evans, *Born for Liberty,* 170.

27. Kraditor, *Ideas of the Woman Suffrage Movement,* 9; Graves, "Wisconsin Woman's Movement," 285–90.

28. Jessie J. Hooper to Theodora W. Youmans, June 31, 1918, WWSA Papers, SHSW; see also Flexner, *Century of Struggle,* 302–3.

29. On antisuffragism, see O'Neill, *Everyone Was Brave,* 228; on Catt, see Flexner, *Century of Struggle,* 300.

30. Flexner, *Century of Struggle,* 326–28.

31. Inez Hayes Irwin, *The Story of the Woman's Party* (1921; rpt. New York: Harcourt, Brace, 1971), 420.

32. Flexner, *Century of Struggle,* 329.

33. Youmans, "How Wisconsin Women," 24.

34. Kraditor, *Ideas of the Woman Suffrage Movement,* 5; Flexner, *Century of Struggle,* 324.

Chapter 10. Women in League: Epilogue, 1920 Forward

The primary source for this chapter is the *Waukesha Freeman* in 1920; specific citations from this source are not given.

1. *HWS* 5:615–17.

2. Kraditor, *Ideas of the Woman Suffrage Movement,* 45; Bordin, *Frances Willard,* 11; *HWS* 2:267; Evans, *Born for Liberty,* 170.

3. Sterling, *Ahead of Her Time,* 355.

4. Kerr, *Organized for Prohibition,* 10, 208–13, 241–43, 281.

5. Flexner, *Century of Struggle,* 329–37.

6. Cott, *Grounding of Modern Feminism,* 121–25; see also Lemons, *Woman Citizen,* 89–100; Mary Frances Berry, *Why ERA Failed: Politics, Women's Rights and the Amending Process of the Constitution* (Bloomington: Indiana University Press, 1986).

7. *Freeman,* Aug. 18, 1932; Graves, "Two Noteworthy Wisconsin Women," 177–79.

8. James to Youmans, Nov. 10, 1917, and Youmans to James, Nov. 22, 1917, WWSA Papers, SHSW.

9. Graves, "Two Noteworthy Wisconsin Women," 177–79; Buhle, *Women and American Socialism,* 319; Conrad et al., *Milwaukee Journal,* 78; Freeman et al. *Belle,* 186, 229–34; *Freeman,* Aug. 18, 1932. In 1920, Augustus H. Youmans became publisher and editor of the *Freeman,* which merged with two other Waukesha papers, the *Daily Herald* and the *Dispatch,* and became a daily; see H. M. Youmans, "Fifty Years," *Freeman,* Oct. 7, 1920. The *Freeman* remained under Youmans family ownership into the 1980s and still is in publication. *The Progressive* also is still in publication.

10. Graves, "Two Noteworthy Wisconsin Women," 177–79; *Freeman,* Aug. 18, 1932; Neu, "Olympia Brown," 282, 284.

11. See Theodora W. Youmans, "What Ails Wisconsin," *Forward* 3 (October 1924), 6–7.

12. O'Neill, *Everyone Was Brave,* 268–69; Kristi Andersen, *The Creation of a Democratic Majority, 1928–1936* (Chicago: University of Chicago Press, 1979), 40; Chafe, *American Woman,* 25–37.

13. Lemons, *Woman Citizen,* 106, 110–12; Thompson, "American Progressive Publicists," 381; Paul Kleppner, "Were Women to Blame? Female Suffrage and Voter Turnout," *Journal of Interdisciplinary History* 12 (Spring 1982), 621, 642–43.

14. Allan J. Lichtman, *Prejudice and the Old Politics: The Presidential Election of 1928* (Chapel Hill: University of North Carolina Press, 1979), 159–65; William E. Gienapp, *The Origins of the Republican Party, 1852–1856* (New York: Oxford University Press, 1990), 443, and "'Politics Seem to Enter Into Everything': Political Culture in the North, 1840–1860," in Stephen E. Maizlish and John J. Kushma, eds., *Essays on American Antebellum Politics, 1840–1860* (College Station: Texas A&M University Press, 1982), 15–17.

15. Maurine Beasley, "Women's National Press Club: Case Study of Professional Aspirations," *Journalism History* 15 (Winter 1988), 121; on Stearns, see Hoeveler, *Milwaukee Women Yesterday,* 27–28, and *Freeman,* Sept. 10, 1914; on Strong, see Wells, *Milwaukee Journal,* 145.

16. Youmans, "How Wisconsin Women," 31; *HWS* 2:267–68.

SELECTED REFERENCES

Newspapers

American Freeman, March 6, 1844–Aug. 4, 1848
Wisconsin Free Democrat, Aug. 11, 1848–Nov. 28, 1860
Cayuga Chief, Jan. 4, 1853–June 17, 1857
Wisconsin Chief, June 24, 1857–Jan. 4, 1889
Waukesha Freeman, June 8, 1882–Oct. 28, 1920

Collections

State Historical Society of Wisconsin, Madison, Wisconsin
    Sherman Miller Booth Papers
    Theron W. Haight Papers
    Jessie Jack Hooper Papers
    Laura Briggs James Papers
    Ada L. James Papers
    Wisconsin Woman's Christian Temperance Union Papers
    Wisconsin Woman Suffrage Association Papers
Milwaukee County Historical Society Research Center, Milwaukee, Wisconsin
    Sherman Miller Booth Papers
    Edward A. Holton Papers
Waukesha County Historical Society Research Center, Waukesha, Wisconsin
    Pioneer Notebooks
    Waukesha County Churches Papers
    Waukesha County Organizations Papers
    Henry Mott Youmans and Theodora Winton Youmans Papers
Milwaukee Area Research Center, Golda Meir Library, University of Wisconsin–Milwaukee, Milwaukee, Wisconsin
    Ladies' Art and Science Class of Milwaukee College Papers
Fort Atkinson Historical Society Research Center, Fort Atkinson, Wisconsin
    Pioneer Scrapbooks

Books

Anthony, Susan B. and Ida Husted Harper, eds. *History of Woman Suffrage.* Vol. 4. Rochester, N.Y.: Susan B. Anthony, 1902.

Bacon, Margaret Hope. *Valiant Friend: The Life of Lucretia Mott.* New York: Walter, 1980.

Barry, Kathleen. *Susan B. Anthony: A Biography of a Singular Feminist.* New York: Ballantine, 1988.

Beasley, Maurine, and Sheila Silver, *Women in Media: A Documentary Source Book.* Washington, D.C.: Anaconda Press, 1977.

Berry, Mary Frances. *Why ERA Failed: Politics, Women's Rights, and the Amending Process of the Constitution.* Bloomington: Indiana University Press, 1986.

Blair, Karen J. *The Clubwoman as Feminist: True Womanhood Redefined, 1868–1914.* New York: Holmes & Meier, 1980.

Blocker, Jack S., Jr. *"Give to the Winds Thy Fears": The Women's Temperance Crusade, 1873–1874.* Westport, Conn.: Greenwood Press, 1985.

Bordin, Ruth. *Woman and Temperance: The Quest for Power and Liberty, 1873–1900.* Philadelphia: Temple University Press, 1981.

Bordin, Ruth. *Frances Willard: A Biography.* Chapel Hill: University of North Carolina Press, 1986.

Buechler, Steven M. *The Transformation of the Woman Suffrage Movement: The Case of Illinois, 1850–1920.* New Brunswick, N.J.: Rutgers University Press, 1986.

Buechler, Steven M. *Women's Movements in the United States: Woman Suffrage, Equal Rights and Beyond.* New Brunswick, N.J.: Rutgers University Press, 1990.

Buhle, Mari Jo. *Women and American Socialism, 1870–1920.* Urbana: University of Illinois Press, 1983.

Catt, Carrie Chapman, and Nettie Rogers Shuler. *Woman Suffrage and Politics: The Inner Story of the Suffrage Movement.* New York: Charles Scribner's Sons, 1923.

Chafe, William Henry. *The American Woman: Her Changing Social, Economic and Political Roles, 1920–1970.* New York: Oxford University Press, 1972.

Clark, Norman H. *Deliver Us from Evil: An Interpretation of American Prohibition.* New York: W. W. Norton, 1976.

Conrad, Will C., Kathleen Wilson, and Dale Wilson. *The Milwaukee Journal: The First Eighty Years.* Madison: University of Wisconsin Press, 1964.

Conzen, Kathleen Neils. *Immigrant Milwaukee, 1836–1860: Accommodation and Community in a Frontier City.* Cambridge: Harvard University Press, 1976.

Cook, Blanche Wiesen, ed. *Crystal Eastman on Women and Revolution.* New York: Oxford University Press, 1978.

Cote, Charlotte. *Olympia Brown: The Battle for Equality.* Racine, Wis.: Mother Courage Press, 1988.

Cott, Nancy F. *The Grounding of Modern Feminism.* New Haven: Yale University Press, 1987.

Croly, Jane C. *The History of the Woman's Club Movement in America.* New York: H. G. Allen, 1898.

Current, Richard N. *The History of Wisconsin,* Vol. 2: *The Civil War Era, 1848–1873.* Madison: State Historical Society of Wisconsin, 1976.

Dannenbaum, Jed. *Drink and Disorder: Temperance Reform in Cincinnati from the Washingtonian Revival to the WCTU.* Urbana: University of Illinois Press, 1984.

Epstein, Barbara Leslie. *The Politics of Domesticity: Women, Evangelism, and Temperance in Nineteenth Century America.* Middletown, Conn.: Wesleyan University Press, 1981.

Evans, Sara M. *Born for Liberty: A History of Women in America.* New York: Free Press, 1989.

Flexner, Eleanor. *Century of Struggle: The Woman's Rights Movement in the United States.* Rev. ed. Cambridge: Belknap Press, 1975.

Freedman, Estelle B. *Their Sisters' Keepers: Women's Prison Reform in America, 1830–1930.* Ann Arbor: University of Michigan Press, 1984.

Freeman, Lucy, Sherry La Follette, and George A. Zabriskie. *Belle: The Biography of Belle Case La Follette.* New York: Beaufort, 1985.

Giddings, Paula. *When and Where I Enter: The Impact of Black Women on Race and Sex in America.* New York: William Morrow, 1984.

Gusfield, Joseph R. *Symbolic Crusade: Status Politics and the American Temperance Movement.* 2d ed. Urbana: University of Illinois Press, 1986.

Harper, Ida Husted, ed. *History of Woman Suffrage.* Vol. 5. New York: National American Woman Suffrage Association, 1922.

Harper, Ida Husted, ed. *History of Woman Suffrage,* vol. 6. New York: National American Woman Suffrage Association, 1922.

Kerr, K. Austin. *Organized for Prohibition: A New History of the Anti-Saloon League.* New Haven: Yale University Press, 1985.

Koenig, Gilbert H. *Once Upon a Prairie: Waukesha's Yesteryears.* Waukesha, Wis.: Waukesha Freeman, 1985.

Kohler, Ruth DeYoung. *The Story of Wisconsin Women.* Kohler, Wis.: The Committee on Wisconsin Women for the 1948 Wisconsin Centennial, 1948.

Kraditor, Aileen S. *The Ideas of the Woman Suffrage Movement, 1890–1920.* 1965; New York: W. W. Norton, 1981.

Langill, Ellen D., and Jean Penn Loerke, eds. *From Farmland to Freeways: A History of Waukesha County, Wisconsin.* Waukesha: County Historical Society, 1984.

Lemons, J. Stanley. *The Woman Citizen: Social Feminism in the 1920s.* Urbana: University of Illinois Press, 1973.

Lerner, Gerda. *The Majority Finds Its Past: Placing Women in History.* Oxford: Oxford University Press, 1979.

Martin, Theodora Penny. *The Sound of Our Own Voices: Women's Study Clubs, 1860–1910.* Boston: Beacon Press, 1987.

Marzolf, Marion. *Up from the Footnote: A History of Women Journalists.* New York: Hastings House, 1977.

Nesbit, Robert C. *The History of Wisconsin,* Vol. 3: *Urbanization and Industrialization, 1873–1893.* Madison: State Historical Society of Wisconsin, 1985.

Nesbit, Robert C. *Wisconsin: A History.* 2d ed. Madison: University of Wisconsin Press, 1989.

Noun, Louise R. *Strong-Minded Women: The Emergence of the Woman-Suffrage Movement in Iowa.* Ames: Iowa State University Press, 1969.

O'Neill, William H. *Everyone Was Brave: The Rise and Fall of Feminism in America.* Chicago: Quadrangle, 1969.

Riley, Glenda. *Frontierswomen: The Iowa Experience.* Ames: Iowa State University Press, 1981.

Rosen, Ruth. *The Lost Sisterhood: Prostitution in America, 1900–1918.* Baltimore: Johns Hopkins University Press, 1982.

Russo, Ann, and Cheris Kramarae, eds. *The Radical Women's Press of the 1850s.* New York: Routledge, Chapman, and Hall, 1991.

Scott, Anne Firor. *The Southern Lady: From Pedestal to Politics, 1830–1930.* Chicago: University of Chicago Press, 1970.

Scott, Anne Firor. *Natural Allies: Women's Associations in American History.* Urbana: University of Illinois Press, 1991.

Scott, Anne Firor, and Andrew McKay Scott. *One Half the People: The Fight for Woman Suffrage.* 1975; Urbana: University of Illinois Press, 1982.

Smith, Alice E. *The History of Wisconsin,* Vol. 1: *From Exploration to Statehood.* Madison: State Historical Society of Wisconsin, 1973.

Smith-Rosenberg, Carroll. *Disorderly Conduct: Visions of Gender in Victorian America.* New York: Oxford University Press, 1985.

Solomon, Martha M., ed. *A Voice of Their Own: The Woman Suffrage Press, 1840–1910.* Tuscaloosa: University of Alabama Press, 1991.

Stanton, Elizabeth Cady, Susan B. Anthony, and Matilda Joslyn Gage, eds. *History of Woman Suffrage.* Vol. 1. Rochester, N.Y.: Susan B. Anthony, 1881.

Stanton, Elizabeth Cady, Susan B. Anthony, and Matilda Joslyn Gage, eds. *History of Woman Suffrage.* Vol. 2. Rochester, N.Y.: Susan B. Anthony, 1882.

Stanton, Elizabeth Cady, and Susan B. Anthony, eds. *History of Woman Suffrage.* Vol. 3. Rochester, N.Y.: Susan B. Anthony, 1886.

Stewart, E. D. *Memories of the Crusade: A Thrilling Account of the Great Uprising of the Women in Ohio in 1873.* 1893; New York: Arno Press, 1972.

Still, Bayrd W. *Milwaukee: The History of a City.* Madison: State Historical Society of Wisconsin, 1948.

Tax, Meredith. *The Rising of the Women: Feminist Solidarity and Class Conflict, 1880–1917.* New York: Monthly Review Press, 1980.

Thelen, David P. *The Early Life of Robert M. La Follette, 1855–1884.* Chicago: Loyola University Press, 1966.

Thelen, David P. *The New Citizenship: Origins of Progressivism in Wisconsin, 1885–1900.* Columbia: University of Missouri Press, 1972.

Wells, Robert W. *The Milwaukee Journal: An Informal Chronicle of Its First 100 Years.* Milwaukee: Milwaukee Journal, 1981.

Wesley, Charles Harris. *The History of the National Association of Colored Women's Clubs: A Legacy of Service.* Washington, D.C.: National Association of Colored Women's Clubs, 1984.

Willard, Frances E. *Glimpses of Fifty Years: The Autobiography of an American Woman.* Chicago: Woman's Temperance Publishing Association, 1889.

Willard, Frances E. *Woman and Temperance: or the Work and Workers of the Woman's Christian Temperance Union.* 6th ed. Chicago, Ill.: Woman's Temperance Publishing Association, 1897.

Wittenmyer, Annie. *History of the Woman's Temperance Crusade.* Philadelphia: Christian Woman, 1877.

Women's Auxiliary of the Wisconsin State Historical Society. *Famous Wisconsin Women.* Madison, Wis.: State Historical Society of Wisconsin, 1976.

INDEX

Abolition: 1834–39, 7–8, 10, 12; 1840–49, 9–14; 1850–59, 19. *See also* Amendments (federal), Thirteenth
Acadia, Wis., 122
Addams, Jane, 166, 175, 179, 208
African-Americans, 6, 8, 19, 40, 51, 89, 173–79, 214
Age of protection, 131–32
Ainsworth, Roderick, 194–96
Alabama, 174, 298
Alaska, 145, 290
Allison, the Rev., 46
Amendments (federal): Thirteenth (abolition of slavery), 6, 32; Fourteenth (African-American male citizenship), 6, 40, 44, 46, 51, 136, 236, 296–97; Fifteenth (African-American male suffrage), 6, 51, 297; Eighteenth (prohibition), 6, 71, 135, 282, 297; Nineteenth (woman suffrage), 6, 89–90, 103, 108, 131, 228, 247–48, 254, 263–64, 285–92, 295–301, 305; Equal Rights Amendment (ERA), 299
American Association of University Women, 194
American Brewers Congress: in Wisconsin, 78, 96; in U.S., 224. *See also* United States Brewers Association; Wisconsin Association for the Protection of Personal Liberty
American Civic Association, 194
American Civil Liberties Union, 301
American Equal Rights Association, 39, 51, 297. *See also* Equal Rights Association, in Wisconsin
American Library Association, 190
American Red Cross, 161, 194, 282
American Woman Suffrage Association, 40, 100, 135. *See also* National

American Woman Suffrage Association
Andrews, Morilla, 163
Anneke, Mathilde Fransziska, 15–16, 19–20, 46, 51, 89, 114; mentioned, 37, 132, 140, 223, 304
Anthony, Susan B.: on Anneke, 16; in East, 30–32, 39–40, 51, 89, 137, 163, 197; in Wisconsin, 41, 46–47, 89, 98, 100, 120–22; death of, 198; mentioned, 21, 52, 94, 100, 103, 113, 125, 157, 186, 247, 254, 294, 300, 304–5
"Anthony amendment." *See* Amendments (federal), Nineteenth
Anti-German activity, 123, 132, 278–79
Anti-lobby bill, 171
Anti-Saloon League, 135, 282
Antislavery. *See* Abolition
Antisuffragism, organized. *See* American Brewers Congress; National Association Opposed to Woman Suffrage; State Retail Liquor Dealers' Protective Association; United States Brewers Association; Wisconsin Association for the Protection of Personal Liberty; Wisconsin Association Opposed to Woman Suffrage
Anti-tight lacing bill, 171
Anti-treat bill, 99
Appleton, Wis., 58, 64, 80, 87, 93, 195
Arizona, 203
Ashippun, Wis., 141

Bain, Harriet, 255, 265
Baker, Delphia P., 21
Baraboo, Wis., 30–31, 52, 212, 257
Barber, A. H., 12
Barlow, John M., 79
Barnum, Phineas T., 26
Barry, A. Constantine, 15, 18